DECISION MAKING
APPROACHES AND ANALYSIS

This reader is one part of an Open University integrated teaching system and the selection is therefore related to other material available to students. It is designed to evoke the critical understanding of students. Opinions expressed in it are not necessarily those of the course team or of the University.

DECISION MAKING
APPROACHES AND ANALYSIS

A reader edited by
Anthony G. McGrew *and* M. J. Wilson
at the Open University

Manchester University Press
in association with the Open University

Published by
Manchester University Press
Oxford Road
Manchester M13 9PL

British Library cataloguing in publication data

Decision making
   1. Decision-making
   I. McGrew, Anthony G.   II. Wilson, M.J.
   160   BF611

ISBN 0 7190 0890 5
ISBN 0 7190 0891 3 Pbk

Typeset by Williams Typesetting, Silverdale, Abergele, North Wales
Printed and bound in Great Britain by
Biddles Ltd, Guildford and King's Lynn

CONTENTS

Preface   *page*   vii
Introduction   1

Section 1   **Understanding decision making**   13

1.1   Choice and decision   *W.J. MacKenzie (1975)*   16
1.2   When is a decision not a decision?
      G. Parry and P. Morriss (1974)   19
1.3   Essence of decision   *G. Allison (1971)*   36
1.4   Approaching the problem   *P. Hall (1981)*   41

Section 2   **Rational decision making**   49

2.1   Individual decision making   *J. Jabes (1978)*   53
2.2   Analytic rationality   *M. Carley (1981)*   60
2.3   Problems of economic organization
      P. Samuelson (1976)   67
2.4   From substantive to procedural rationality
      H.A. Simon (1976)   87
2.5   The decision to vote   *B. Barry (1970)*   97
2.6   Policy-making models
      J.J. Richardson and A.G. Jordan (1979)   111
2.7   The artificial debate between rationalist and
      incrementalist models of decision making
      G. Smith and D. May (1980)   116
2.8   Still muddling, not yet through   *C. Lindblom (1979)*   125

Section 3   **The process of organizational decision making** 139

3.1   Cognitive dimensions of organizational phenomena
      J.D. Steinbruner (1974)   144
3.2   Survival inside bureaucracy   *G. Benveniste (1974)*   154
3.3   The economic theory of bureaucracy
      M. Perlman (1976)   167

3.4   Organizations, decisions and courts
       L.B. Mohr (1976)   175
3.5   Policy making and the State apparatus
       B. Salter and T. Tapper (1981)   190
3.6   Some constraints on defence policy makers
       J.C. Garnett (1976)   205
3.7   Transgovernmental politics and international
       organizations   *R. Keohane and J. Nye (1974)*   216

Section 4   The politics of decision making   227

4.1   Pluralism   *B. Smith (1977)*   231
4.2   The theory of pluralist democracy
       K. Newton (1976)   233
4.3   The political elite   *P. Saunders (1979)*   246
4.4   Educational planning: past, present and future
       G. Williams (1979)   255
4.5   Insiders and outsiders: the politics of pressure group
       influence on bureaucracy   *B. Guy Peters (1977)*   261
4.6   The policy process
       J.J. Richardson and A.G. Jordan (1979)   275
4.7   Tripartism: reality or myth?
       D. Marsh and W. Grant (1977)   291
4.8   Decision making in the EEC   *C. Webb (1977)*   303

Section 5   A critical perspective   315

5.1   The case of non-decisions   *W.I. Jenkins (1978)*   318
5.2   A police authority — the denial of conflict
       M. Brogden (1977)   327
5.3   Pluralism, corporatism and the role of the State
       A. Cawson (1978)   341
5.4   Foreign policies in modernized societies
       E.L. Morse (1976)   352

       References   366
       Index   388

PREFACE

This reader has been compiled as a component of the Open University course *D208 Decision Making in Britain*. Our courses are designed and written under the doctrine (and practice) of collective responsibility, and we are glad to acknowledge the assistance of the D208 course team in our work. The final responsibility for the selection of articles and for the commentaries must, however, be ours.

We should particularly like to thank Rosalind Levacic, Jeremy Mitchell, David Murray, and Victor Jupp for advice and guidance on articles; Ann Hunt, Yvonne Honeywell, and Mary Dicker for the typing of manuscripts; and Hilary Robertson for her valuable help with editorial and bibliographical tasks. Our personal thanks go to Christine and Francesca McGrew and to Glen McDougall and Aillinn Wilson for their support and forbearance during the labours of completing the manuscript of this book.

A note to the reader

We have abridged all the articles reprinted in this reader. Our editing has been sometimes drastic and sometimes cosmetic, frequently something of both. The lack of space has dictated our editing in the main, but we should add that we have often excised passages which appear to us to contribute little or nothing to the author's main argument, and which, occasionally, even impeded it.

Interpolations by the editors have been of two forms: some brief and explanatory notes for terms which the general reader might not be familiar with, and the occasional change of word or phrase or paragraph in order to make the author's intentions clearer. This has proved regrettably necessary where the dead hand of American Gothic vocabulary and phrasing has half-throttled the argument which the author apparently intended to make.

Excisions are shown by dots in the text, so ..., all editorial additions and interpolations are in square brackets. Those readers who wish to consult the full and untouched texts are invited to use the bibliography which is appended at the end of this book.

A.G. McGrew   M.J. Wilson

Faculty of Social Sciences   The Open University   28 January 1982

INTRODUCTION

Introduction

There are two reasons which justify a book of readings on decision-making and the makers of decisions. The concept of decision and the study of decision-making is at the centre of several intellectual disciplines: economics, politics, systems analysis and psychology to cite the main ones. All are concerned with choice between alternatives in a complex world; in economics, for example, millions of choices are made each day on prices, jobs, outputs, buying and selling. If social science has any claim to inform us systematically of how the world can be understood as an intelligible entity then these millions of choices by individuals and by organizations must be ordered from their particular and concrete individuality and reduced to comprehensible patterns, or *explained*.

My decision to place a bet on a horse, to change my job or to vote for this political party rather than that are the results of my perceptions of what I want and how I can achieve it. So also are your choices the results of similar processes, and we should look for a common language in which to express our choices and to move towards explanations of why there are regularities in our behaviour.

Apart from the need to explain and make intelligible a social world in which decisions are the stuff of everyday life, modern, complex society is increasingly reflective about decisions and decision-making. This is partly for the praiseworthy reasons that better ways of deciding important choices of policy should benefit us all, but partly also because the growth of the modern State has taken many decisions from the individual and the family and placed them in formal State-run organizations. The allocation of hitherto personal decisions to official agencies has itself prompted the intellectual curiosity which lies behind the attempts from many disciplines in the social sciences to regain, through scientific tools, the understanding we have lost because so many decisions which are important to us as individuals have become remote and apparently impenetrable.

Each organized attempt to grasp the logic of decision-making represents the distinctive contribution by a social science discipline. Rather than fragment our knowledge by treating separately each discipline's approach we have, in this reader (like the Open University course for which it was compiled) chosen to put forward an interdisciplinary treatment of the main issues in studying decisions. There is, we believe, a number of shared approaches to defining the problem which cuts across the disciplines and in which a great deal can be learnt by pooling concepts and forms of analysis. One fundamental (and early) approach to decision-making is the *rational actor model*, which is found in economics, sociology, and politics. The specific features in the model which each discipline stresses will vary somewhat, but by taking an interdisciplinary view we can cross-fertilize both the different concepts and, above all, the different criticisms which analysts have made when they have attempted to use an abstract model to grasp real cases.

The concept of 'model' plays an important role in this book and therefore requires explanation for readers unfamiliar with its use in the social sciences. A 'model' is a simplification and abstraction of some aspect of the real world. It is impossible to select those aspects of decisions which are significant without concepts which define for us what we should observe. Even thinking about what school to send our daughters to requires (if it is to be called thinking) that we first conceive of 'education' and what we value in it. We must, even at a rough and ready level, then find some working definition of how schools should be judged one against the other: examination performance? social atmosphere? proximity? Having defined what we select as significant about schools generally (and what we will ignore as not relevant) we must order our objectives in such a way that we can come to a decision to prefer this school to all others which are available to us. This is the sort of modelling process, simplifying and abstracting from reality in order to decide, which we all make every day of our lives either in trivial ways (take the bus today or walk) or in ways which fundamentally alter our lives (choosing a school or a job, for example).

Models, then, are essential to even a non-scientific analysis of the world. Much of the literature on decision-making is precisely the study of how real individuals at home or at work actually take decisions, that is, what models they use to structure and interpret their world. That is one general theme of the readings extracted here. The second theme is what models we should use as detached social scientists in order to explain the world; these models are necessarily different from those which actors use in their everyday lives. They must be different because science is a collective enterprise in which knowledge and findings are shared and sharing is only possible if scientists agree on a common approach to defining a problem such as decisions and decision-making. Our approach as social scientists is organized around three basic models of decisions which are first elaborated below and then further illustrated and elaborated in the five sections into which this book is divided.

Each model first tells us what to select; this is description of some aspects of the social world, since one cannot describe without knowing what to observe. Secondly, the model explains the phenomena we observe, it tells us why the decision was to choose this school rather than that one. To do this the model directs us to find out certain information on the individual's preferences and how he performs his calculations. If we can successfully show by use of the model how the given preferences and the given calculations (which may be very simple indeed) inevitably led to this decision then we have explained it, and explanation is the goal of social science.

Models are said to be heuristic, that is we judge them as good, better or worse, by how useful they are in our explanations. If a model predicted that individuals selected schools only with one end in mind — the best examination results within a half-hour travelling distance — and this model successfully explained most of the decisions on schooling which we examined in a large sample of parents then we should judge the model heuristically effective.

Another way of looking at models, both from the private viewpoint and from the scientific stance, is in terms of 'decision-space', a concept which occurs in several readings in this book. No decision is made without some pre-conceived ideas of what to aim for, what possible means there are for attaining it, and the costs to be incurred in choosing one means rather than another. The idea of an endless search for the ideal solution to a problem, roaming through every means available is so obviously costly, and so obviously what we do not do (if we want to be known as decisive!), that the idea of decision-space, where the decider forecloses nearly all options and goals and proceeds directly to a rapid evaluation of only a limited range of possibilities, seems a very convincing description of what happens in practice. The direct study of decision-space is one way of capturing how particular organizations show such continuity over time in the sorts of decisions they make; new members learn first how to categorize the issues and cases they meet (for an example, see Mohr (3.4) on the workings of the Courts). Decision-space is also a way of showing up the conceptual blinkers which the analyst wears when he looks at decision making; we too are selective in our approach to phenomena. We have used three broad decision-spaces to order the material in this book: the three models first set out below.

Two points before turning to the three models we use: the fact that these are offered as non-competitive alternatives for use simultaneously rather than exclusively, represents the philosophical truth that no one model has a claim to exhaust the meaning of phenomena. One model might be better than another for explaining behaviour in one particular context, but not another. Looking across the contexts, all the models and yet newer ones might be brought into play, each adding a partial explanation. Truth, then, is only temporarily established; better ways of analysis may be discovered tomorrow, and a model should not be thought of as 'true', only as 'useful' to a greater or lesser extent.

A special feature of the social sciences is that models may be both explanatory and prescriptive. They may seek to explain how decisions are actually made and they may also suggest how decisions *should* be made, for improved effectiveness. This duality of what *is* and what *ought* to be requires care in the reader (both of this book and in the social sciences generally) because the distinction is frequently not made explicitly; for example, analyses of rational decision making which show that many organisational decisions are grossly irrational from one point of view or another, also implicitly value rationality as the desideratum of *good* decisions and thus blur the line between analysis and prescription. A line which many social scientists have maintained is not a true distinction anyway.

What is a decision?

Decision making appears such a common activity that rarely is any thought devoted to discovering what a decision is. For most of us a decision implies an act of choice between alternatives. But the act itself is not as static as the everyday conception of decision implies. In fact a decision is the end state of a much more dynamic process which is labelled 'decision making'. It is conceived of a process since it consists of a series of linked stages of activity, not simply a discrete action. Thus when Mr David Howell announced in the House of Commons in December 1979 that the government had made the decision to expand Britain's civil nuclear programme, in order to ensure national electricity needs were met well into the future, the word 'decision' carried with it a wealth of implied notions about the extensive activity which culminated in this particular announcement. But what precisely is understood by the concept of decision?

Whether we are referring to individual or organizational decisions, the concept of decision retains a certain fixed meaning. This is most simply reduced to the notion of a final definitive solution in a problem-solving process. So in announcing a decision had been made, in our example above, the Minister was implicitly suggesting that the problem of electricity needs in the future had been dealt with. But in announcing the decision there is a further implicit level of argument involved, in that it is also assumed that behind the decision is an element of procedure. Thus the decision maker identifies the problem, clarifies the particular goals which are desired, examines the various possibilities for achieving the determined goals, and completes or terminates the process by a definitive choice of action.

The decision-making process is thus something tidy and which has its own internal logic. Yet the most important element in real decision making is that of uncertainty. If the decision maker operated in a totally certain world where the costs of employing any means and the benefits of every goal could be known completely then problems could be programmed. Once the programme relating goals and means was written (still a creative act because 'certain' relationships might still be complex) the decision maker would become merely a technician; the best solution to any problem would be simply a matter of calculation. In a world of certain relationships between ends and means there would be no real choices to be made, except in terms of pure values – guns or butter, war or peace. If the decision maker also faced negligible constraints in resources to deal with a problem, his function would become even more marginal, since everything would be possible if desired. But the real world is not certain, and there are always constraints of resources. So the distinguishing characteristics of a decision, and decision making, are that it involves choice under conditions of uncertainty, ranging from the marginal to the complete, and environmental constraints from the limits upon effective resources of all kinds. To clarify this in relation to our example, what made the government's decision distinct from a simple choice amongst alternatives was that it involved great uncertainty, not only over how best to solve the future electricity-supply problem, but also uncertainty as to whether this was the real problem in the first place, and whether the nuclear technology was safe, or even desirable on a whole range of other grounds. Such massive uncertainty was compounded by a complex of resource constraints, from economic and technological to industrial and scientific, within which any decision had to be feasible.

It is under these two general conditions that this particular choice was made. If there had been no such uncertainties or constraints then the problem would not have involved such a lengthy and disputed process. It is thus the elements of uncertainty and constrained choice which give the problem of decision and decision making its particular nature.

One further dimension to add to this clarification of the concept of decision lies in the identification of when a decision *is* a decision. Although it is possible to refine our conception of decision making to choices involving uncertainties and constraints, it is also possible to identify when a decision has been made? This at first glance may seem rather unimportant, yet it is crucial if one desires to provide some useful analysis of decision making. For dependent upon the locus of a decision there is the further question of the demarcation of the constituencies and participants in the decision-making process. Thus in our example, was the decision made in the Cabinet, a Cabinet committee, within the Department of Energy, the Central Electricity Generating Board etc? Contingent on the answer to this would be not only the boundaries to the relevant decision-making community but also which elements of that community were regarded as dominant in the decision-making process.

Such a question can only be answered by distinguishing between the formal rules and procedures, whether it be in government or any other organization, by which a decision is legitimized, and the underlying informal structures and relations which are complementary to these. Thus, were we to confine our identification of a decision, in the example, to the formal procedure, then it would restrict the boundary of the decision-making community to only the 'official' bodies and their official relations. However, by examining the informal relationships underlying this formal identification, a very different picture emerges of the decision-making community, including within it the various pressure groups such as Friends of the Earth, the British Nuclear Forum, the various trade unions, as well as the web of relations between the government agencies involved. Depending upon the rule we use to determine the identification of a decision is the scope we set for any enquiry into the decision-making process.

All of this is bound up with a much deeper analytical problem, which surfaces at various points in the following contributions, relating to the further distinction between decision and non-decision. At this point we may as well include negative decisions and indecision in this definitional review. Even granted that it is possible not only to define what a decision is, and identify it according to an explicit rule, a further analytical debate revolves around whether the focus of study should even be decisions rather than non-decisions. It is the belief of some theorists such as Bachrach and Baratz, Crenson and Lukes, that a focus upon decision making is less analytically sound than a concentration on the decisional agenda.[1] Whilst their argument is mainly concerned with how to elucidate 'who has the power to make decisions', it is of importance here. Their argument put simply is that the agenda of decision making always contains an inherent bias towards the dominant interests in society, and in consequence more can be garnered about decision making if one has a concern for why certain issues never arrive on the public agenda. Thus the focus of study should be upon non-decisions: the issues which are eliminated from the public agenda of decision. Such non-decisions are therefore quite distinct from decisions, which are 'real choices' amongst alternative courses of action, and indecision, which refers to the inability to actually arrive at a decision, and also negative decisions, which are those involving a 'real choice' not to make a formal decision. Whilst such a classification of 'decisions' may retain a certain validity, it can also be confusing, and in consequence we will confine discussion to decision and non-decision.

The major analytical difficulty with the concept of non-decision is precisely, as Parry and Morriss demonstrate, its lack of definitional clarity. It is a concept which can be 'stretched' to include a number of conceptual ideas. However, the notion behind non-decisions is none the less valid and no study of the decision-making process can afford to neglect the question of what issues are avoided in that process. Thus, in our example, a further picture of the process only emerges if consideration is given as to why, in the face of great uncertainty and economic constraints, a decision to reduce electrical energy demand had not been officially scrutinized. The answer may well reveal the inherent biases in the decisional system and it is important to recognize these if any fruitful enquiry into the process of decision making is to be generated. How non-decisions are actually defined and located will remain a problematic factor but this should not prevent a continued sensitivity to the drift of the argument.

Models of decision making

Whether our immediate concern is to explain decisions or non-decisions, the starting point must, as the earlier section demonstrated, be some form of conceptual framework or model. For the majority of analysts such frameworks always remain an implicit structural feature of their explanations of decision-making. This is a point which Allison makes, partly as a critique of much of the literature in the field. By underlining the requirement to make explicit what remained generally implicit in most studies, Allison has inspired a further intellectual controversy upon the nature and value of different analytical models for explaining decision making. This has generally been resolved into an argument about the relative merits and limitations of the three conceptual frameworks outlined in his *Essence of Decision*. However, it is generally accepted that whatever the limitations of Allison's models they provide a logical/analytical base from which to explore the universe of decision making, and can penetrate the processes of decision making with a revealing eye. For such reasons it was deemed appropriate to utilize an adapted form of Allison's models as the structuring principle for this reader. Like many others, we are indebted to Allison's intellectual clarity. What follows is a summary account of the three basic perspectives which structure the contributions in this volume.

In explaining the process of decision making all analysts make use of implicit models, or assumptions about behaviour, which condition the nature of their explanation. What is striking, however, is the degree of convergence between various writers and analysts in the models they do utilize. Here we will be solely concerned to elucidate three of the dominant perspectives upon decision making – the rational, organizational processes, and political bargaining models.

Rational decision-making model

To explain a decision as the result of a rational process is to make certain key assumptions about what the unit of analysis is, and what guides behaviour. For a decision to be rational implies that it can be both explained and justified by relating it to the objective of the decision maker.

In this sense then, decisions must have a purpose in so far as they only exist to further a particular objective or goal of the decision maker.

At the simplest level the decision maker is an individual. Thus, faced with a given problem the individual rational decision maker will attempt to rank his/her objectives or goals in some kind of relative order. By doing so the decision maker is then in a position to examine all the alternative means to achieve the desired goals and thus to choose that action which either maximizes the desired objectives or minimizes the costs of any possible failure to attain them. The explanation of a decision, therefore, is concerned with outlining the reason for which a decision was taken: what was to be attained and how was it to be done? Whilst this has been simplified (it disregards, for example, the problem of constraints) how does it apply at the collective level of decision making?

At the collective level, whether group, organization, or government, the unit is simply redefined as if it were a coherent and monolithic entity with an individual consciousness. Thus government becomes an undifferentiated 'black box' which seeks to achieve its goals in much the same way as any rational individual, except that it operates as the decisional mechanism of society as a whole. In consequence government decisions tend to be explained as a conscious choice to attain a calculated objective. A decision is thus explained as government, faced with a given problem, commencing by establishing its objectives and ordering them according to collective desirability, searching all the alternative possibilities for achieving its objectives, and finally settling upon that which maximizes its objectives or minimizes the costs of possible failure. Explaining governmental decisions in this context is thereby commensurate with discerning the objectives underlying its behaviour. Returning to our previous example, a rational explanation would focus upon the possible objectives of government in this case: security of future electricity supply; maintaining a nuclear industry; safeguarding the environment; and limiting expenditure. Thus, the explanation of why a decision to expand nuclear capacity was taken would suggest it to be a result of maximizing the communal benefits and limiting the communal costs in relation to these objectives. This is a plausible explanation. Are the remaining models as kind to such decisions as this model appears to be?

Organizational processes model

This is a model of decision making which deals with the problem that there is a real difference between an individual decision maker and an organization. An organization should not be considered as some sort of 'super-individual' behaving as a true individual but with greater information-handling and calculation capacities. An organization does not have, in practice, a single set of goals with an agreed order of preference amongst them, nor does it carry out a similar search process amongst its means, as an individual might. For once the decision process is fragmented or disjointed amongst many individuals, distinctive processes come into play and lead, other things being equal, to a different decision than would have happened if we imagine an individual capable of handling the same amount of work as the organization and having the same set of goals and constraints in his brief as did the organization. Although an individual could not possibly handle at the same level of detail the processes which went into a review of the Concorde project, for example, the analytical point of comparing the individual against the organization for the same task is still useful because it tells us something about how organizations behave. Since most important decisions in modern societies are taken by organizations this distinction is vital if we are to model the decision-making process.

The subunits or departments of an organization can never be assumed to have the same rankings of objectives or the same valuation of means for reaching those objectives as do other departments in the organization; above all, they cannot be assumed to 'set up' the problem according to the organization's initial definition of the problem to be solved or the decision to be taken. In this reader, Perlman, Garnett, Salter and Tapper, Keohane and Nye, Garnett and Benveniste amongst others point out that organizational officers place a value on such incidental goals as personal security, professional identity and professional links, and personal risk-avoidance which the organization does not even officially recognize, although its members privately realize that such things make as a big an input to the decision-making process as does the official brief. The capacity of individuals in an organization to control, manage, suppress, or otherwise distort the information on which decisions are based means that as the disjointed inputs are brought together in the decision-making process the end result may be one that so biasses the 'decision-space' or definition of the feasible solutions on the agenda, that the final decision taken at the summit of the organization may negate, directly or indirectly, the objectives of the initial problem-to-be-solved. If this sort of irrationality or miscalculation (see Garnett for some striking examples in the defence field) is possible with major or non-routine decisions it is even more evident with the large number of routine decisions which all large organizations deal with. The power of the lower cadres to define their own 'decision-spaces', favourable to themselves or to their departments, is greater where they are taking decisions of the structural form (Garnett), or the 'how to do it' sort of decisions, which are legitimated by the major decisions on strategy. (See Parry and Morris for the argument which shows the connection between routine decisions and so-called non-decisions.)

As Perlman notes, one need not think that bureaucrats are particularly wicked to explain the way in which decisions 'drift away' from the control of the organization's masters; it is simply that the very nature of organizations and fragmented decision making conduces to an output of irrational decisions from the point of view of the dispassionate observer who asks, for example, why the Manpower Services Commission in 1975 created more jobs within its own organization than it did outside. And in relation to our nuclear power example, one could similarly question why nuclear capacity is to be expanded in the face of strong, independent evidence of a stabilization in long-term electricity requirements. Organizational process, then, is an essential model for understanding decisions in modern society.

Political bargaining model

One of the requirements of a sufficient explanation of decision making must be its ability to resolve the difficult problem of collective choice. In the case of the rational model, the solution is to impose an individual identity on the collectivity and thus to fuse individual and collective rationality. The organizational processes model emphasises the centrality of routines and procedures in reducing the effects of uncertainty, and also emphasises the management of information to protect individual and departmental interests in the organization. Both approaches neglect the possibility that underlying any collective decision is a process of bargaining, with its own (usually) implicit rules, in which outcomes are determined by the relative resources devoted by each participant to the achievement of some satisfactory solution (see Richardson and Jordan, 4.6). Although each participant in the decision may define his position according to rational calculation, or by organizational criteria, the final collective outcome is completely dependent on the interplay of participants and on what is acceptable as a politically viable solution. Quite clearly, this form of explanation is altogether distinct from its more 'orderly' counterparts.

Underlying the political bargaining model is the view that individuals, groups, organizations, and even nations have self-defined interests to protect (see Smith, 4.1). When faced with a decision problem, participants focus upon those aspects of the problem which they perceive as affecting their parochial interests. In consequence, rather than a single strategic problem requiring solution, a myriad of intricately linked issues compete for the decision maker's attention. The decision-space is thus complicated by competing problems and competing preferred solutions in an attempt by each participant to ensure that any final decision is not damaging to their interests. We may ask, then, what structures the outcome of this process?

Clearly, any outcome is a product of a number of separate factors, amongst which the underlying informal structure of power is important (see Newton, 4.2), as are the resources which the participants are willing to devote to a solution, and the negotiating skills which each possesses.

Contingent upon these factors is the identification of the 'key' problems and the most effective solutions to them. By a general process of bargaining and trade-offs between participants a final outcome is arrived at which has general support and in which the interests of all are seen to be accommodated. Thus, any decision is, at root, one based upon a consensus, which limits the possibility of a serious disaffection of the participants from the final agreed outcome. In this sense, a decision arrived at by political bargaining is neither rational as a calculation of the most effective means to reach a preferred objective, nor does it follow established routines.

To explain decision making using this model poses very different questions for the analyst than does either the rational actor model or the organizational processes model. To return to our example, the government's decision to expand the civil nuclear-power programme may be seen not as the solution to a single strategic energy-resource problem but rather as the outcome of a complex set of formal and informal discussions between the Department of Energy and interests which range from the Central Electricity Generating Board, the National Nuclear Corporation, Atomic Energy Authority, industrial corporations, the Nuclear Installations Inspectorate, and Friends of the Earth, on a range of issues; and yet further negotiation and discussion within Government, at various levels from Departmental to Cabinet, between interested bodies such as the Treasury, the Department of Industry, the Department of the Environment, and the Central Policy Review Staff. The final decision is thus an outcome of such negotiation and bargaining rather than a specific solution to a specific problem.

The reader is divided into five sections; Section 1 defines the basic terms for a systematic study of decisions and decision-making; Sections 2 to 4 are based on each of the Allison models, except that later readings in each section are chosen to show the interaction between the models in the study of real cases; Section 5 reflects the debate on the issue of whether the study of decisions is a useful approach to take in examining the political process, where 'political' means 'power political'. Cawson mainly, but also Jenkins, engage with the view that the outcome of decisions is epiphenomenal and produced by underlying structures of power in society. A study of such structures, it is held, could explain both the form of resolution of strategic decisions (touching on issues of central concern to a society) and non-decisions or the failure of certain fundamental issues to appear on the decisional agenda. We take the view that the study of 'underlying structures' raises very serious questions of epistemology[2] and we believe that the systematic study of decisions is a field worthy of further development in its own right.

Notes

1   See Bachrach and Baratz (1971), Crenson (1971) and Lukes (1974).
2   The theory of the method or grounds of knowledge.

SECTION 1

UNDERSTANDING DECISION MAKING

What is decision making? How is decision making to be analysed? These are two basic questions which necessarily preface any serious study of the subject. As you will come to appreciate, the answers are more complex then generally assumed. However, within the bounds of this section, it is to be hoped, lucidity will overtake complexity and the 'answers' become more concise.

In the literature, decisions frequently become synonymous with choices, but, as MacKenzie (1.1) reminds us, there is an important distinction to be drawn between the two. For MacKenzie a decision is a 'real choice', by which he means a choice about ends, as well as a choice about means to arrive at those ends, whether at the individual or collective levels. Thus, the conception of decision which MacKenzie offers is one of a process: a cumulative sequence of stages of choice. But towards the conclusion he hints at the issues of power and non-decision and these are the central elements of Parry and Morriss's explication of decision making.

Within the social sciences a debate of lengthy pedigree lingers on over the 'correct' approach to the study of decision making. This debate is itself contingent on the broader arguments of 'who' has the power to make decisions in society. The core of this argument is the conflict between 'pluralist theory' and 'elite theory'. Pluralist theory suggests that power is dispersed between many groups in society, and in consequence societal decisions are the result of group conflict in which the role of government is one of arbitration amongst group interests. 'Elite theory' stresses the underlying concentration of power within a self-conscious minority which tends to shape decisions to meet its own interests.

In order to validate the respective arguments different methodological approaches are utilized: the 'pluralist' focuses upon case studies of decision making on key issues, since this displays observable conflicts of interests which require resolution; on the other hand 'elite theorists' focus upon the nature of the decisional agenda, the politics of the agenda setting, and thus on non-decisions. This they justify quite simply in terms of the fact that the power of an elite resides in its ability to control the agenda of decision thereby suppressing conflicts of interests and real choices. Non-decisions are thus the issues which elites are able to keep off the decision-making agenda. But although Parry and Morriss (1.2) recognize the deep method-ological conflicts between these two schools they conclude that the concept of non-decision has little conceptual clarity compared with the concept of decision. Thus for Parry and Morriss non-decisions are essentially what organizational theorists would regard as routine or programmed decisions. As all such routinized decisions contain an inherent bias in favour of the status quo, in consequence certain interests are favoured by the exclusion of issues from the agenda. By discarding the concept of non-decision Parry and Morriss also make the task of the analyst that much more manageable, although they necessarily engender a pre-occupation with how the process of decision making is to be explained.

Within this context Allison's contribution (1.3) is amongst the seminal works in the field, a classic, as Hall later refers to it, which has spawned an industry out of what had been previously regarded as 'Dullsville'. In fact, Allison's major objective was to demolish the implicit assumptions which guided the majority of studies in this field, but in particular in the area of foreign policy analysis. These assumptions he grouped under the label of the rational actor model. The characteristic of this model was its expla-nation of public decisions, those emanating from government, as com-parable with the explanation of the purposive acts of individuals.

In developing his critique of this model of explanation Allison intro-duced two further models of decision making behaviour, the organizational process and government politics models, both of which explained the process of decision making in entirely distinctive ways and according to different criteria. Thus in relation to his own case study of decision making in the Cuban missile crisis, decisions were not merely explained as the purposive acts of monolithic entities called governments, but as the programmed or standard outputs of organizations, or the outcome of bargaining and accommodation between powerful actors within and out-side government. Yet Allison's analysis can not be purely limited to this single historic episode but can be generalized in its application to the whole study of decision making. It is this which gives Allison's work its pre-eminence.

Allison also provoked a sensitivity to the intellectual 'trap' within which studies of decision making can easily become ensnared: that explanation becomes dominated by an entirely implicit conceptual framework which structures the whole process of enquiry. In exposing us to alternative and explicit explanatory frameworks, Allison demonstrated the possibility of escape. However, the exposition of three distinct frameworks of expla-nation creates an analytical dilemma in that it is not self evident which is a more valid explanation, nor whether each is a complementary or discrete explanation. These are the difficult epistemological questions which Allison's analysis induces, and there are no certain answers. Nor will there be any significant attempt here to assess these arguments, for epistemology has been regarded as the 'black hole' of social science — once entered, the process of enquiry collapses in upon itself, cumulatively regressing into a myriad of philosophical analysis.

However to some extent Hall (1.4) sidesteps this latter difficulty quite effectively. Although Hall's contribution is reliant upon Allison, its value lies in his development of Allison's ideas. Firstly, Hall expands upon the intellectual heritage of Allison's models. Then he utilizes this to take a further bold step to demonstrate how together these models can establish the basis of an eclectic theory of decision making, although the criteria for validating the explanatory value of this eclectic theory are not made explicit. But it is the substance of this theoretical enterprise which makes Hall's contribution both so interesting and so unique.

The academic study of decision making, since the publication of Allison's classic *Essence of decision*, has quite firmly shifted its analytical focus away from 'who makes decisions', to 'how are decisions made'. And it is to this latter question which the remainder of this reader devotes its considerable co-opted intellectual energy.

1.1   W.J.M. MacKenzie

CHOICE AND DECISION

From *Power, Violence, Decision* (Peregrine Books, 1975) pp. 176–9. Copyright © W.J.M. MacKenzie, 1975. Reprinted by permission of Penguin Books Ltd.

Difficulties of exposition increase when one comes to the concept of decision.

A problem at the outset has been whether to accept the word 'choice' as synonym for 'decision'. Sometimes I have found it natural to do so, without much thought; yet the words do not quite coincide in modern usage. One could perhaps express the shade of difference by saying that it is hard to say 'choice' without postulating a chooser, not so hard to say 'decision' without postulating a decider. Certainly there have been two strong examples of the latter in recent academic discourse; the emergence of 'decision theory' as a branch of mathematical logic, yielding algorithms for decision by computer; the reference to politics as a 'decision-making process',[1] a flow of outputs explicable in terms of inputs and system structure.

What is it to 'choose'? The question once put, one realizes that there is a constellation of words in this context, and that they are difficult words: what is it to act, to be a person, to will or wish, to contemplate ends and means? It has already been noted that for some time now there has been a convergence towards theories of action, theories which attribute importance and reality to this constellation of images and concepts. Gouldner (1970, p. 190) notes that the whole drift of Parsons'[2] thought is to the effect that human will, purpose, choice will have real effects, but not those anticipated by the chooser; whereas Lenin's extension of Marxism insisted that the chooser (or band of choosers) might choose and win, might indeed shape the future ...

The postulates of choice

What then are the requirements of 'real choice'? This not in the sense of free will versus determinism, but in terms of consensus about the use of language.

First, there is the problem of polarity between ends and means. If one has indeed chosen, one should be accountable, in the sense of being able to give an account of one's choice. 'Why did you do A?' The 'explanation' is that one did it as a step towards B. 'Why did you do B?' And so on, till regress is stopped: 'X is what I wanted to get'. But other chains of explanation may lead to Y and Z, other ends or purposes which are not means to one another, and are therefore commensurable only by the process of 'knowing one's own mind'.

'To know one's own mind' is not necessarily a fluke, an accident. It may be referred logically to a settled view of the world and man's place in it; non-rationally, to a settled cast of mind, a tradition of behaviour.

But (secondly) there is the problem of passing from individual preference to public choice, which can in principle be solved either by the operation of a free market or by a stipulated procedure. The problem is not quite as bad as it seems, in that the distinction of 'I' and 'we' is never absolute; we are all (or almost all) participants in some instances of the first person plural. To repeat what was said about choice of ends, choice of identities is a matter of 'knowing one's own mind'; and that may be based either on a settled view of the world or on a settled cast of mind, or on both.

Nevertheless, the problem of amalgamation of preferences is as difficult as that of assessing ends.

Thirdly, there is choice between different means to an agreed end. This is our common experience and most of the time we do it without thinking. If 'we stop to think', then things become harder: but if the end is settled then it is not hard to agree on a framework of thought for a choice of means.

But (fourthly) the choice of means is in any real situation restricted by lack of information and lack of power. The problem is to do the best we can with what we have; the algebras of maximization and probability exist, and can be used to place us as near to the peak as we can get by rational combination.

And (fifthly) the computation can tell us when it would be rational to spin a coin and take a fifty-fifty chance rather than to expend time and resources in trying to gain better information and better resources. Temperamentally, you may prefer to withdraw rather than to stake all on the spin of a coin. That in turn is an intelligible statement about your choice of ends.

Finally, there are problems of indecision, non-decision and decision by default.[3] We know these as individuals, but it is simpler to build a formal model of them in terms of the control of business in a committee, an assembly or any large-scale use of voting. In the last resort, decision is defined by voting procedure: and that will affect the tactics of the leaders. But there are two other keys to power; the power (whether violent or legalistic) to bring matters to an issue at a chosen moment, or to let them sleep, so that failure to decide becomes by lapse of time decision by default; the power to control the agenda, so that among many courses of action, many candidates, public choice is restricted to a few.

Notes

1   The Open University uses this approach (with ingenuity and caution) in the first two 'levels' of its Politics course. See for instance Murray and others (1972).
2   Talcott Parsons, a prominent American sociologist (eds).
3   A debate begun by Bachrach and Baratz (1962, pp. 947–52) and continued in Bachrach and Baratz (1970).

1.2   G. Parry and P. Morriss

WHEN IS A DECISION NOT A DECISION?

From *British Political Sociology Yearbook*, volume 1, 1974. Published by Croom Helm Ltd.

Perhaps the major contribution to political science made by the many studies of community power has not been the portrayal of local communities so much as the extra refinement they have brought to the analysis of political power in general. In this the work of Floyd Hunter and of Robert A. Dahl must take pride of place not merely for the quality of their own analyses but for the informative debate which their rival conclusions and methodologies aroused ... But of equal significance have been two short, theoretical articles which have come to play a major part in controversies not merely about the analysis of power but also about American society and its malaise. They were written by Peter Bachrach and Morton Baratz and appeared in the *American Political Science Review* in 1962 and 1963 ... [and reprinted in *'Power and Poverty: Theory and Practice'*].[1]

To this linked debate on community power and American policy these seminal articles contributed the notion of a 'non-decision'. The significance of what is, as we shall see, an unfortunate term lies in the fact that what has been called the 'decisional approach' had come to dominate the analysis of political power amongst American political scientists. In turn this approach was associated with what was also termed a 'pluralist' analysis of American power relations. The method was to isolate within any given community certain key 'decisions' which were thought likely to illustrate the power relations which prevailed. These key decisions were chosen from a range of different issue areas. The object was of course to test whether the same groups took the 'key decisions' in all or many of these different issues. If they did the community could be said to be ruled by an elite. If they did not, but instead different persons made decisions in each issue area, the community was said to be 'pluralist' in its decision-making process. The conclusions of research conducted along these lines were almost invariably that the communities were pluralist and this invited the hypothesis that America too was pluralist or, as Dahl termed it, 'polyarchal'.

This approach and its different attendant conclusions threatened to become an orthodoxy amongst political scientists ... The pluralist position came under attack quite early particularly from avowedly

- - -

radical writers[2] but it was perhaps the twin explosions of the urban riots and Vietnam which brought pluralist orthodoxy most into question. For a prime conclusion of the pluralist analysis had been the 'permeability' of American democratic institutions. The study of decision-making showed that any group with a grievance could make itself heard by conducting itself in conformity with the established decision-making procedures. A lack of protest indicated satisfaction. Yet the cities were in turmoil, apparently overnight and inexplicably if one were to accept the pluralist conclusions and the pluralist methodology.

It was almost certainly this crisis which gave the Bachrach and Baratz articles such currency after they had caused little impact on their first appearance. The authors suggested that the decisional approach was inadequate because it had failed by its very methodology to identify and describe 'non-decisions'. These 'non-decisions' occur when issues are prevented — for various reasons which will be examined later — from ever reaching the 'agenda' of a community. It then follows that a study of 'decisions' will not identify matters upon which there have never been any decisions. And equally clearly it seemed a plausible hypothesis to suggest that the 'crisis of the cities was the outcome of 'non-decisions' which had therefore been overlooked by the pluralists. It was also a hypothesis which was in line with what so many critics had long alleged about American urban policy, that it was a policy of neglect of public functions — that it formed part of a general picture of private affluence and public squalor. The concept of a non-decision was then an intuitively plausible idea which fitted in with what seemed to be frightening empirical confirmations of the most pessimistic critical analyses of American society. And indeed the 'non-decision' threatened itself to become a part of a new critical orthodoxy applied to any policy outcome with which the critic disagreed. But despite this success — or perhaps because of it — the idea of non-decisions is extremely difficult to pin down. A critical examination of the idea was due and indeed has been forthcoming in a recent article by Raymond Wolfinger — one of Dahl's original associates on the New Haven project — and in a reply to Wolfinger by Frederick W. Frey who attempts to mediate between the sides.[3] But, for reasons which we shall indicate, the restatement of the pluralist decisional approach is unsatisfactory. Accordingly, whilst pointing out some of the difficulty of the original account of non-decisions, we wish to suggest another way in which the problems raised by non-decisional analysis might be tackled. In particular, we want to argue that although primacy should be given to a 'decisional' approach to the study of power, not all exercise of power in society can be explained in terms of an actor 'A' *causing* another actor 'B' to act in a manner which he did not originally intend. Very often 'A' gains advantages and 'B' is disadvantaged by the performance of social 'routines' which go largely unquestioned. In this way 'A' acquires 'consequential' power although he may not have brought the routine into being and although he may be in no direct causal relationship with 'B'.

But before we go on to examine problems in detail, it might be useful to place the study of power and decisions in a wider context of the study of politics.

If the idea of a 'non-decision' seems intuitively plausible so does the study of politics by the study of political decisions. For is not this what politics is about? Political power is a matter of making key decisions. Let us then study these key decisions and see how they are taken – either proceeding as a historian does or as Dahl's team were fortunate enough to do by watching the decision-making process as it happened. What makes this approach the more understandable is that politics is widely thought of as concerned with the resolution of conflict. This is a view taken by political sociologists and traditional political philosophers. Compare two remarkably similar utterances. First Robert A. Dahl:

If everyone were perfectly agreed on ends and means, no one would ever need to change the way anyone else behaved. Hence no relations of influence or power would arise. Hence no political system would exist.[4]

And secondly Sir Isaiah Berlin opening his celebrated Inaugural Lecture on 'Two Concepts of Liberty':

If men never disagreed about the ends of life, if our ancestors had remained undisturbed in the Garden of Eden, the studies to which the Chichele Chair of Social and Political Theory is dedicated could scarcely have been conceived. For these studies spring from, and thrive on, discord.[5]

Such descriptions of politics would gain a wide measure of acceptance amongst political scientists even if some would wish to make some modifications, in particular to specify more particularly what kind of conflict counted as political.[6] Political conflicts are resolved by political decisions – the exercise of choice between conflicting policies, groups or persons. The 'key' decisions relate to the 'key' conflicts – those which have the greatest significance to the political unit, its members and its leaders.

Given this picture of politics as problem-solving then the study of decision-making will seem the correct path to an accurate description and explanation. This is probably in line with the popular image of politics as the sphere of action where individuals and groups conflict and where decisions are taken. It also permits the researcher to present his study in a narrative form, telling the story of the victories and reversals of the rival protagonists, and though this is not a major consideration in scholarly investigation it adds interest and conviction to the results.

It is not, of course, to be denied that much politics is of this sort. Decisions are taken, significant conflicts do occur. Politics includes the activity of authoritative community integration and this is why politics is of such importance, whether its importance lies in its being the supreme activity of man or in its being a necessary evil. The sense of being involved in the 'centre of things' constitutes the 'charm of politics' and its vocation for participants and theorists from Machiavelli to Weber or R.H.S. Crossman.

But there is another way of looking at politics which lays far less stress on conflict and its resolution through decisive action. Politics is also 'ruling'. 'Ruling' does of course imply the attempted resolution of conflicts but it implies, even more, regulation. A great deal of ruling consists in the performance of routines. Now, as Sharkansky has pointed out in one of the rare attempts to study this neglected yet essential part of politics, routines may be procedures leading up to decisions or may be decisions themselves.[7] The routine may indicate the criteria to consider, as in Sharkansky's example of the percentage increment from one year's budget to the next. Or the routine may lay down exact formal procedures for certain types of decision or the decision may itself be specified as when there is a routine answer to certain kinds of claim.

So politics is the application of fairly standard procedures to recurrent problems rather than the settlement of 'world-historical' conflicts. The regular meetings of government consultative committees involving unions, business and government are as much a part of ruling as the confrontation of unions and government over new industrial legislation. Indeed the consultative committees are far more numerous and frequent and are indubitably indicative of power relations in the society. More broadly, government routinely works within the prevailing mode of economic production and exchange. This is not to say that government cannot change this predominant mode, nor is it to say that governments never do fundamentally challenge it. Governments can and, on occasion, do. It is to make the more modest claim that governments ordinarily spend more time in administering an on-going political system than in making fundamental changes in it.

This is the sense in which Oakeshott is right in describing politics as '*attending* to the arrangements' of a community rather than as *making* the arrangements. The bulk of the 'arrangements' are there before the advent of any particular government and are still there after its departure. This is true of the basic institutions – parliament, the courts. It is true of the economic institutions, whether the planning system of socialist countries or the banking system of capitalist countries. It is also true of the ordinary legislation. A striking feature of democracies is the continuity of legislation and treaties from one government to the next. This is a basic fact of political life and a major presupposition of legal theory and of political obligation.

Politics conceived of as ruling has thus an inbuilt conservatism. As Sharkansky says 'routines are conservative mechanisms'.[8] The routines

Sharkansky studies involve incremental changes from previous standards and keep change under considerable control. The recognition of the conservative nature of 'ruling' need not commit one to the more prescriptive mood of some of Oakeshott's utterances[9] ...

Despite Oakeshott, for many people existing arrangements are matters for endurance rather than enjoyment but it remains true that 'the new is an insignificant proportion of the whole'. And that this understanding of politics may be viewed in a quite different light may be recognised by the analysis of 'non-decisions' by many of the more radical critics. They acknowledge the significance of routines and, like the conservatives, hold that the study of decision making, isolated from the wider cultural, ideological and economic contexts, is inadequate. But their emphasis is on what they hold to be the disproportionate power in the hands of the few — power which is best indicated by the routine, unquestioned and unspectacular activities of governments and of economic leaders. The implication is that the routinely powerful is the truly powerful.

To understand this process they employ two related concepts — 'non-decisions' and 'mobilisation of bias', the latter term being adapted from Schattschneider's study *The Semi-Sovereign People*. Despite its growing popularity the term 'non-decision' is by no means clearly defined. In their original articles Bachrach and Baratz did not offer a formal definition but their usage indicates what they had in mind. Non-decisions are acts which help support the 'mobilisation of bias' which in turn gives legitimacy to the non-decisions. Mobilisation of bias is defined in *Power and Poverty*. It is 'a set of predominant values, beliefs, rituals, and institutional procedures ("rules of the game") that operate systematically and consistently to the benefit of certain persons and groups at the expense of others'.[10] Consequently

when the dominant values, the accepted rules of the game, the existing power relations among groups, and the instruments of force, singly or in combination, effectively prevent certain grievances from developing into full-fledged issues which call for decisions, it can be said that a none-decision-making situation exists.[11]

These usages indicate a process by which opposition is thwarted before it reaches the formal stage of authoritative decision-making. The opposition's proposals do not reach the 'agenda'. But in *Power and Poverty* Bachrach and Baratz add an explicit definition which, while including these situations, goes still further and renders the concept too all-embracing to be useful. It is

A decision that results in the suppressing or thwarting of a latent or manifest challenge to the values or interests of the decision-maker. To be more nearly explicit, none-decision-making is a means by which demands for change in the existing allocation of benefits and privileges in the community can be suffocated before they are even voiced; or kept covert; or killed before they gain access to the relevant decision-making arena; or, failing all these things, maimed or destroyed in the decision-implementing stage of the policy process.[12]

Wolfinger being dismissive of the whole notion of non-decisions does not offer any definition but Frey in his more mediatory article does:

A non-decision occurs when a choice among alternatives by one actor is either not perceived by him or, if perceived, is not made, and always, in either case, because of some exercise of power by another actor.[13]

The general upshot is that non-decision-making procedures ensure that only those issues which are 'safe' in the sense of posing no fundamental threat to the existing decision-making elite are permitted to reach the community's agenda.

From these definitions and from the list of activities characterised as non-decisions it is clear that the term itself is by no means satisfactory and is misleading even if one acknowledges that the procedures described to require analysis.

One apparent meaning of 'non-decision' is any political activity which is not a 'decision' — i.e. that 'non-decision' stands to 'decision' as *non-p* to *p*. The wider the term non-decision is made the more it approaches this clearly useless notion. This is not, however, an insignificant quibble. One refrain of pluralist responses to non-decision analysis is to say, as Nelson Polsby does, 'For every event ... that occurs there must be an infinity of alternatives. Then which non-events are to be regarded as significant?'[14] And the reply this receives from Matthew Crenson:[15]

From the infinity of non-events available, why should we pick those related to air pollution instead of those related to the prevention of elephant stampedes or the persecution of witches?

begs the question of how to construct criteria of significance for distinguishing within a range of *possible* alternatives.

Nor can non-decision be regarded satisfactorily as the contradictory of decision. A decision is best seen as, to adapt Hobbes, an act of will which ends deliberation. It is a choice between alternative courses of action. There is therefore in principle a point of choice or of decision. There is a 'performative utterance'[16] such as 'I decide' or 'it is hereby decided' which indicates at least the formal decision and there are criteria embodied in the 'speech act' whereby one can discern who has the authority to make these utterances. This may be very difficult to study but it does seem to be what is involved in principle in the concept of a 'decision'.

To say that a 'non-decision' is the opposite of such a decision would imply that no point of choice had been reached, no performative utterance or 'illocutionary act'. There would be a continuing process of deliberation without formal termination. This may come close to one of the situations described by Bachrach and Baratz — the condition of 'drift' of the 'decisionless decision' as they call it. Yet even this situation where 'history is made behind men's backs,' as Wright Mills so perceptively put it, is not adequately portrayed as the contradictory of a 'decision'. What happens is a series of lesser decisions or choices each of which forecloses other courses of action and commits the actor or others, superiors and inferiors, to directions they might not have taken if starting *de novo*. But this is not to say that there has been no 'decision' since there have been many produced by 'big causes' — a view which many a historian would share. So, to accept Bachrach and Baratz's example, the Bay of Pigs may not have been the consequence of one major decision but it was the outcome of many lesser ones and even in this case someone with authority has to give the final go-ahead even if this is a mere *imprimatur*.

What we wish to argue is that in many cases non-decisions *are* decisions. They are not, however, necessarily the sorts of 'key decisions' studied by the 'decisional approach' associated with the work of Dahl and his associates. Many are lesser decisions which are component parts of a routine and the power which a routine reflects may be of a different kind to that discovered by the analysis of decisions. Bachrach and Baratz's own language gives support to this version of a 'decisional approach' to non-decisions. The definition of a non-decision cited above begins by saying that it is a decision. Unless non-decisions are approached in this way there will be the continuing danger that the notion will be devalued by the inclusion of what are very different political techniques. It is a danger present in Bachrach and Baratz's own study.[17] Both action and inaction are described as non-decisions. Some non-decisions appear to involve conscious choices, others to be the outcome of the unconscious acceptance of community values. Still others are identifiable only by their social and political consequences. To understand the power and the penetrability of any community it is better to replace blanket terms like 'non-decision' with a more precise analysis of the many different patterns decision-making can take.

Firstly one must try to sort out the 'chinese box' of decisions. We have suggested that a decision is a performative utterance discernible according to certain rules. This can be a highly formal definition of decision — the signature of the President or the announcement by a board of directors. This is *the* decision. But clearly this may be a mere *imprimatur*. The decision is thus the large 'box' which contains the lesser decision 'boxes'. What is being said here, and also in some of the non-decisional literature, is that there is a distinction between the formal structure of power and informal power relations. Clearly the more the 'decisional' approach confines itself to formal decisions the more it overlooks the informal. But it is also the case that the more the 'non-decisional' approach confines the term 'decision' to the formal procedures the more it will attribute power to 'non-decision'-making, to the greater confusion of all.

Moreover it is difficult to lay down a sensible universal definition of 'formality'. If one selected the moment of presidential or monarchical signature it would, absurdly, exclude the 'decisional' activities of legislators. If instead one chose to define the legislative process as 'the decision' and all else as non-decision stages this would have almost equally absurd consequences for the study of, say, British policy-making. It would place the relations between pressure groups and civil service, which is so crucial to British government, in the 'non-decision' category. Certainly these discussions do much to decide what is on the agenda for cabinet and parliamentary consideration but it would clearly be wrong to designate so regular a part of the governmental process as semi-legitimate. 'Non-decision' is not, then, just a temporal term, but an evaluative one as well.

When we in fact look at examples of so-called 'non-decision-making' we see how important it is to distinguish between them. Bachrach and Baratz distinguish four different forms of 'non-decisions'[18] and a couple of cognate types. Firstly there is the use of force. They list harassment, imprisonment, beatings and murder. Now, even if they have the same purpose of preventing an issue being raised, this is a rather mixed list which includes both criminal acts such as murder and constitutional acts such as imprisonment. However cynical one may be about some of the legal procedures of courts in the southern states of the USA – the example discussed in these pages – it is essential to take due note of the differences involved. Imprisonment does imply a formal decision procedure.

Secondly they cite the threat of sanctions against the reformer. Their list of sanctions again ranges widely from threats of dismissal to co-optation in a participatory democracy. Once more we would prefer to regard these as 'decisions' and decisions, moreover, which involve very different procedures, different degrees of legitimacy and different consequences for both agent and patient. The process of co-optation has, of course, been a long-standing technique of limiting opposition – almost a tradition in Britain – but it does involve costs for the elite who have at least to surrender exclusivity and usually have to make some concessions on policy. In the same category one should perhaps include the technique of the pre-emptive strike of 'stealing the Whigs' clothing'. This step, when taken by the Mayor of Baltimore in his dealings with CORE organisers, is termed by Bachnach and Baratz a 'direct case of none-decision-making'.[19] Yet, if ever there was one, here was a *decision*, taken by the authoritative political leader in a constitutional manner. He acted in a way he would not otherwise have done and in a direction which would benefit the poorer sections of the society. Certainly this also had the effect of keeping the initiative in his own hands rather than those of the CORE organisers but this consequence is scarcely enough to designate it a non-decision, any more than it would have been if an established party had been beaten to the gun. In politics someone gains and someone else loses but everyone has to bear some costs.

Bachrach and Baratz's third category of non-decision is the invocation of procedures to thwart or redirect innovation. The example given is the frequent practice of referring demands to committees of enquiry. The final category is strengthening and reshaping the 'mobilisation of bias'. Two instances are offered. One involves the introduction of new procedural barriers to change. The other involves calling on the norms of the society to limit demands or even render them illegitimate by regarding the control of business as outside the realm of politics and as part of the free-enter-prise system. Once again these cases are different and some involve clear decisions. Shelving a policy may be a ploy but it is also a decision, as is the introduction of new procedural barriers.

The final instance of the effect of social norms in thwarting demands is rather different and raises many problems precisely because this is less obviously an assignable decision. It belongs with a cluster of problems associated with routines, ideologies and what Banfield once termed 'steady state' situations.

Political routines and 'decisionless decisions'[20] are perhaps the easiest to deal with. The latter are situations of drift where a series of smaller decisions commits each actor towards a bigger decision which he would not have independently contemplated. Routines tend to display a type of decision-making termed 'disjointed incrementalism'. This is far nearer a conscious political style.[21] The decision-maker follows a pattern of chang-ing policy only at the margins. He does not think out every policy *de novo*. This would be an impossible undertaking. He operates instead within a framework of reference – not of his own making – which is largely com-posed of the precedents for his present decision and for comparable decisions[22] and by the minor amendments which most claimants press for. This description, undoubtedly accurate for most forms of ruling, has been upheld by some pluralists[23] as illustrative of the fallacies of the non-decision analysis. Since decision-makers cannot consider all conceivable policies they cannot be condemned for thwarting some conceivable reformist policies. But this assumes that this is a conscious decision where-as, in fact, the concept of the mobilisation of bias admits of a more subtle interpretation fully in accordance with Lindblom's and Sharkansky's analyses of routines. The decision-maker excludes possible options because he works within an established framework of ideas and procedures which may eventually rub off on the clients. They may then either only put in claims which are in line with established practices or may abandon their pressure since they are convinced it does not fit in with established precedent and is likely to be rejected as a consequence. Such anticipated reaction or 'renunciation' as Wolfinger calls it is, rather curiously and inconsistently, not treated by the authors of *Power and Poverty* as an example of non-decision-making — whether it is the mass anticipating the elite or the elite anticipating the mass. It is curious in that such anticipations are of the stuff of politics. Once again we should wish to treat them as decisions — though in this case it is the patient and not the agent whose performatives are at issue. The difficulty consists in knowing if they happened where no evidence is available of a kite being flown or of a minute which is not proceeded with or of a proposal hastily withdrawn.

Even graver difficulties of observability and identification face that familiar yet still problematic notion of 'false consciousness'. When faced with non-participation, why, asks Wolfinger, do neo-elitists attribute this to satisfaction and complacency when it is the elite which does not participate and to false consciousness when it is the poor or the masses who abstain?[24] The reply is that it is the elite which reaps the benefits from inaction and the poor which stands to gain by reform. But this, whilst plausible at first glance, raises difficulties which have been very readily pointed out by the critics of the Bachrach and Baratz approach. To suppose that the poor are subtly but deliberately prevented from participating ignores too hastily the possibility that such social consequences may not be intended even by those who benefit. More importantly it is alleged that the reply involves the insertion by the political scientist of his own bias. The failure by a group to conform to the commentators' independently premediated expectations is attributed to a 'non-decision' by some other group or else to 'false consciousness'.

The problem may be examined by turning our attention to the other side of the non-decision coin — the 'non-issue'. The alleged effect of a so-called none-decision is to prevent an issue being formally decided by nipping it in the bud before it becomes an issue. As with (non)-decisions so with (non)-issues it is necessary to differentiate between cases. Much seems to turn on what counts as a fully fledged issue. An 'issue' is a matter which is to be decided. But this supposes that someone recognises that it is to be decided and for this there are several candidates — authorised legislatures, pressure groups, ordinary citizens or outside observers.

Clearly there is no problem where all these groups recognise that a matter is to be decided. This is an issue and is likely to reach the authoritative decision-making stage. The problems arise when the situation falls short of this. Firstly it could happen that all parties recognise that a matter must be decided sooner or later but the political elite (assuming its existence for purposes of argument) would prefer to defer decision since it involves awkward commitments which could cost support. That part of the political elite currently in a position to deal with the matter would sooner see someone else burn his fingers. Such a situation should be observable by interviews, access to records and so on. It seems proper to call this an issue just as we suggested it was proper to describe the attempt to shelve the matter as a decision. Secondly it is possible for some groups to recognise something as an issue while others do not. Agger and his associate describe such situations in one of the cities in the southern USA which they studied.[25] Once again there is public evidence of both concern and lack of concern and, usually, of some efforts to make the other side show concern. Here once more we would wish to say that the issues had been raised even though one might wish to add that the 'issue had not been joined'. Whilst it is tempting to think, as Frey notes,[26] that an 'issue' implies controversy this is not so as is suggested by the qualifying phrases 'at issue', 'join issue' or 'take issue'.

All these examples are overt and can perfectly well be described in terms of 'decisions' and 'issues'.

The next examples raise more difficulties. Firstly the elite may seek to prevent an issue being raised by techniques ranging from rewards to legitimate and illegitimate sanctions. We have already noted that these techniques are themselves very different. They do moreover assume that the elite can recognise an issue on the horizon and to the extent that the evidence for this is fairly public it fits, in all its variations, into the overt issue category. It is when the stifling procedure is covert that the difficulties arise. There is little, short of a 'lead', that can uncover the discreet telephone call and without it the investigator is left with nothing but surmise. One would wish to say that there was an issue but it was suppressed before it received a public airing.

As ever the more one approaches the 'anticipated reactions' and 'false consciousness' end of the continuum the greater the problems of observability. Some anticipated reactions can be traced and can be described in terms of decisions. Some evidence in other cases may be available if, say, grievances can be elicited by means of interview and then these grievances contrasted with the apparent inaction of the aggrieved. If the contrast is put to the subject one may well receive answers couched in terms of 'rational apathy' which would do credit to Downs's voter.[27] Why bother to participate if the chances that one will fail are so high?[28] Antipathy and apathy must not be confused. It is true of course that one must take care with such evidence that it is not itself coloured by either later events or by the investigation itself ...

Nevertheless it is when the grievances cannot be readily elicited that the most vigorous opposition to 'non-decision' analysis arises and it must be acknowledged straight away that some of the doubts of the critics are justified. The opportunity to interpret the situation in the light of what the commentator would expect to find does exist. But there are still some steps one can take to investigate the reason for apparent satisfaction with what others might think unsatisfactory conditions. It is acknowledged even by Wolfinger that there are cases where such satisfaction is *prima facie* surprising – the Negroes in the southern USA are always safely cited.

Firstly it might be that a person's expressed satisfaction with his society and its social and economic relationships was inconsistent with his continued but frustrated attempts to marginally improve his situation by, say, wage demands.[29] Once made conscious of the limits of his 'trade unionism' he might in the classic Leninist manner turn his attention to the overall political system and be aroused from his inertia. This might give retrospective evidence of the state of 'false consciousness' which previously existed (though one must again beware of retrospective reanalysis).

Secondly if we adopt Brian Barry's view that a policy is in a person's interests if it increases his opportunities to get what he wants[30] then we can justify our saying what we frequently do say, namely that X has mistaken his interests. Wealth and power are evidently in a person's interests and his failure to put forward demands which would promote such interests is at least a phenomenon that demands explication. The comparative silence of the American ghettoes in the 1950s in the face of inadequate housing and jobs can thus be seen as a portent of disaster rather than as broad satisfaction with the social and political system. That said, it must immediately be acknowledged that such assertions cannot be so readily made where one is, as is so often the case, trying to explain the failure of one issue to appear rather than others, all of which would fit the criteria for being in the interests of, say, the ghetto poor. Why does education surface as an issue in some cities and not in others, or urban renewal or air pollution? The non-decisional answer is that only the 'safe' issues are permitted to become full issues. But this can be dangerously close to self-confirming when the definition of a 'safe issue' is also one which has been allowed to surface.

More promising are the attempts of Crenson to examine comparable communities in order to explain their varying performances on one issue — in this instance the issue was pollution. Failure in one community to deal with an issue becomes all the more striking and in need of explication if several other comparable communities face up to it. Another approach is to examine policy outputs in comparable communities. No doubt this is easier said than done. It is difficult to ensure comparability. It is fallacious to argue directly from outputs to intended use of power even if one can say something about the 'consequential' distribution of resources.[31]

One of the major difficulties in research into power is how one can identify the power agent — the 'A' in the examples of A getting B to do what he does not wish to do. There can be argument as to whether A acted or even, when dealing with the 'mobilisation of bias' or with certain kinds of routine, as to whether A exists as an identifiable person or group. But in these situations it may be possible to recognise the patient — the B who is doing something he does not want to do or who is getting considerably less than he wishes and much less than others in the system. One might then begin at the 'bottom' — with grievances — and study the decisions

(performative utterances or illocutionary acts) of B. Primacy should be
given to the causal approach which attempts to trace some identifiable
person or group acting to alter the balance of choices and advantages open
to others. But often this causal chain will arrive back at a routine and the
analysis of routine raises different problems of analysis.

The pluralist model of power is a causal one. It requires that one
shows that A is able to make B do something he would not otherwise do —
which has to be illustrated by some actual decision. In the case of 'non-
decisions' A must be shown preventing B raising an issue. If this is not
shown then A does not possess power over this issue at least. Several
community-power studies have examined the exercise of power in this
way. There are cases of A getting his way constitutionally, by force of
reputation and by covert, illegitimate threats. And there have been studies
such as Dahl's which have failed to reveal any such success — or even
attempts — at stifling threats to established interests.

But power need not be seen in this causal manner. Power can also be
understood as resources which may then be used to acquire the power-
holder's 'future apparent good'. Discovering the 'decision-makers' in a
routine does not necessarily indicate the 'men of power' if by this one
means either the persons who ultimately determine another person's
range of choices or those who gain in resources as a consequence of the
routine. The routine decision may be taken by an official who has not
himself laid down the procedure he follows and who does not gain in any
significant way from the decisions taken. Routines may however routinely
grant resources or powers to some and deny them to others. They routinely
ignore certain inputs and they routinely distribute the outputs.[32] As
Parenti points out, rules in politics are seldom neutral but are 'the embodi-
ment of past political victories'.[33] It can thus be difficult for certain
demands to penetrate the system and be fully recognised as issues. But
this does not necessarily mean that the powerful have to be, or can be seen
to be, consciously acting to thwart such demands. They may be the unconscious beneficiaries of the bias which does not have to be consciously
mobilised by the system. Nor do the various elite groups have to act
conspiratorially. One of the consequences of elite consensus is to confirm
elite position without the necessity of any power display in a causal sense.
This is what Crenson means when he suggests that 'a polity that is pluralistic in its decision-making can be united in its none-decision-making'[34] —
though this, as has been seen, is not the terminology favoured here. It
would also be misleading to describe those who support and maintain
the routines — administrators, judges, police — as the 'agents' of the
powerful. This implies more conscious direction than is always the case in
social affairs.

What the existence of routines suggests is that there are at least three
kinds of power to consider. Firstly there is the power to initiate the

routine. Secondly there is the power by which the routine is maintained. Thirdly there is the distribution of power which is consequential upon the performance of the routine. These should not be confused and it does not follow that the same persons possess all three forms of power. The initiatory power is of course causal in nature. It is analysable in principle as a decision whether it is overt or covert. The power to maintain the routine is similarly analysable in terms of decisions but not, this time, 'key decisions'. Rather these are the lesser decisions, limited by precedent and custom, which have been analysed in the work of Lindblom and of Sharkansky. Their analysis involves a study of incremental procedures, of the range of options considered by those involved in ruling, the impact these procedures in turn have upon the inputs. But this approach will rarely trace the resultant distribution of power resources to a specific command of a 'ruling elite'. The third type of power is not causal but 'consequential'. Though different in its nature it does not seem unreasonable to accept the ordinary usage by which those who benefit are termed 'powerful' even if they have not acted directly to secure such benefits. Indeed if two types of power were comparable one might be tempted to say that those who could rely on established routines to get what they wanted were more powerful than their ancestors who had to fight to establish such routines. But the real point is that these powers are not the same. And nothing in the analysis of the routines of ruling commits one to the belief that the 'elite' who benefit from a routine will be able to resist a challenge to the routine. They have what Mosca termed the advantages of *positions déjà prises* but these are not insurmountable. Some routines are democratically established and in principle subject to democratic control. The beneficiaries are therefore themselves dependent. One difficulty with such control is that routines by their nature tend to be conservative, that they have their own momentum. Their overthrow is hence more difficult. An extreme instance would be the difficulty of democratically altering the routines and expectations resulting from political boundaries. Both majoritarian and pluralist democratic theory have difficulties in dealing with secessionist movements.[35] The existence of routines may thus indicate the degree of 'openness' or 'permeability' of the polity.

The case of Ireland may illustrate in rough and ready fashion the distinctions we have in mind. We might then say, for sake of argument, that those who drew up the present borders between the North and Eire had the power to establish the various governmental and constitutional routines. They are not the same persons as those who now maintain these routines. Nor are they the beneficiaries of the routines (though some of their descendants may be). But as a consequence of the routines some groups in the North, notably the Orange Order, have gained in power, and others, notably the Catholics, have been relatively powerless.

This distribution of resources may be seen as by now embedded in the routines of Northern Ireland politics and society rather than as directly attributable to the 'key decision-makers' of fifty years ago.

In conclusion, we suggest that a sensible procedure in the analysis of political and social power would be to treat it in the first place as the taking of decisions. We propose to discard the notion of 'non-decision'. Most – though not all – so-called 'non-decisions' can be seen to fit into the category of decisions. Such as are not explicable as decisions are primarily examples of 'false consciousness' which remains a problem to be elucidated. The 'decisions' are those of both agent and patient – both A and B – since the performative utterances of both 'sides' are some indication of the conduct or the anticipated conduct of the other. The next task would be to distinguish between the very many types of decision from the 'key decision' of the pluralist analysis to the 'routine decision' and to the 'decisionless decision'. One would then be in a position to distinguish the types of power in each case – whether initiatory, routine or, for want of a better term, 'consequential'.

Primacy is then given to the 'decisional' approach since this is in principle the most economical explanation couched in historical terms. But it is not regarded as the only possible explanation of a given distribution of social resources. Politics is a matter of speaking and acting, of decisions and choices. But it is also a matter of customs and regulations, of traditions and of ruling. If politics is so 'pluralist' in its methods it perhaps ought to admit of a certain eclective 'pluralism' in its analysis. Different styles of governing demand different styles of explanation. Put together they may also help explain how 'non-issues' may become issues, how today's new demands are transformed into tomorrow's routines and what forms effective participation must take if today's routines are to be challenged by tomorrow's decisions.

Notes

1 Oxford University Press, New York, 1970.
2 E.g. Todd Gitlin. 'Local Pluralism as Theory and Ideology'. *Studies on the Left*, vol. 5, no. 3. Sunner 1965, pp. 21–45 and reprinted in A. McCoy and Playford. *Apolitical Politics,* Crowell, New York, 1967, a collection of much of this critical literature.
3 R. Wolfinger, 'Nondecisions and the Study of Local Politics', and F. Frey, 'Comment: On Issues and Nonissues in the Study of Power', both in *American Political Science Review*, vol. 65, no. 4, December 1971, pp. 1063–80 and 1081–1101 and a 'Rejoinder' by Wolfinger, pp. 1102–4.
4 *Modern Political Analysis*, Prentice-Hall, Englewood Cliffs, 1st edition, 1963, p. 72.
5 *Four Essays on Liberty,* Oxford University Press, Oxford, 1969, p. 118.

6 e.g. Bernard Crick, *In Defence of Politics*, Weidenfeld & Nicolson,
   London, 1962 and D. D. Raphael, *Problems of Political Philosophy*,
   Pall Mall and Macmillan, London, 1970.

7 Ira Sharkansky, *The Routines of Politics*, Van Nostrand Reinhold,
   New York, 1970, Ch. II and *passim*.

8 *The Routines of Politics*, p. 9.

9 'Political Education' in *Rationalism in Politics*, Methuen, London,
   1962, pp. 112–13.

10 *Power and Poverty*, p. 43.

11 'Decisions and Nondecisions: An Analytical Framework'. *American
   Political Science Review*, vol. 57, no. 3, September 1963, p. 641.
   This passage is not reprinted in *Power and Poverty*.

12 *Power and Poverty*, p. 44. See Wolfinger's comment on this passage,
   loc. cit., fn. 22, pp. 1065–6.

13 Frey, loc. cit., p. 1092.

14 *Community Power and Political Theory*, Yale University Press, New
   Haven, 1963, p. 97.

15 Matthew A. Crenson, *The Un-Politics of Air Pollution: A Study of
   None-Decision-making in the Cities*, Johns Hopkins University Press,
   Baltimore, 1971, p. 26.

16 See J. L. Austin, 'Performative Utterances'. *Philosophical Papers*,
   Oxford University Press, Oxford, 1961, pp. 220–39, and *How to Do
   Things with Words*, Oxford University Press, Oxford, 1962. See also
   W. J. M. Mackenzie, 'Models of Collective Decision-Making', *Social
   Sciences: Problems and Orientations*, Mouton for UNESCO, The
   Hague, 1968, pp. 356–70.

17 See the examples cited in *Power and Poverty*, pp. 70–3.

18 *Power and Poverty*, pp. 43–6.

19 *Power and Poverty*, p. 71.

20 See also above, p. 24.

21 On such styles see A. F. Davies, 'The Concept of Administrative Style',
   Australian Journal of Politics and History, Vol. 12, no. 1, 1966.

22 See Charles Lindblom, 'The Science of "Muddling Through" '. *Public
   Administration Review*, vol. XIX, no. 2, Spring 1959, pp. 79–88.

23 E.g. Wolfinger, *loc. cit.*, pp. 1066–70.

24 Wolfinger, *loc. cit.*, pp. 1070–7.

25 *The Rulers and the Ruled*, p. 307.

26 Frey, *loc. cit.*, p. 1087.

27 Downs argued in *An Economic Theory of Democracy*, Harper &
   Bros., New York, 1957, that in an election with a large electorate
   it is rational for an individual not to vote, since the chances of his
   vote swaying the result is very small, and does not outweigh the costs
   involved.

28 Some of Parenti's subjects fall into this category. See 'Power and
   Pluralism: A View from the Bottom', in M. Surkin and A. Wolfe,
   An End to Political Science, Basic Books, New York, 1970, pp.
   129–31.

29 Steven Lukes drew our attention in discussion to this possibility.

30 *Political Argument*, Routledge, London, 1965, p. 176.

31   See later, p. 000.
32   See Sharkansky, *The Routines of Politics*, p. 9.
33   Parenti, *loc. cit.*, p. 135.
34   Crenson, *The Un-Politics of Air Pollution*, p. 179.
35   See, e.g. John Locke, *Second Treatise*, section 117, and R. A. Dahl,
     A Preface to Democratic Theory, University of Chicago Press, Chicago,
     1963, Phoenix Books edition, pp. 96–7.

1.3 G. Allison

ESSENCE OF DECISION

The general argument

When we are puzzled by a happening in foreign affairs, the source of our puzzlement is typically a particular *outcome*: the Soviet emplacement of missiles in Cuba, the movement of U.S. troops across the narrow neck of the Korean peninsula, the Japanese attack on Pearl Harbor.[1] These occurrences raise obvious questions: *Why* did the Soviet Union place missiles in Cuba? *Why* did U.S. troops fail to stop at the narrow neck in their march up Korea? *Why* did Japan attack the American fleet at Pearl Harbor? In pursuing the answers to these questions, the serious analyst seeks to discover why one specific state of the world came about — rather than some other.

In searching for an explanation, one typically puts himself in the place of the nation, or national government, confronting a problem of foreign affairs, and tries to figure out why he might have chosen the action in question. Thus, analysts have explained the Soviet missiles in Cuba as a probe of American intentions. U.S. troops marched across the narrow neck in Korea because American objectives had escalated as a consequence of easy victories in the South. The attack on Pearl Harbor is explained as Japan's solution to the strategic problem posed by U.S. pressure in the Far East.

In offering (or accepting) these explanations, we are assuming governmental behavior can be most satisfactorily understood by analogy with the purposive acts of individuals. In many cases this is a fruitful assumption. Treating national governments as if they were centrally coordinated, purposive individuals provides a useful shorthand for understanding problems of policy. But this simplification — like all simplifications — obscures as well as reveals. In particular, it obscures the persistently neglected fact of bureaucracy: the "maker" of government policy is not one calculating decisionmaker but is rather a conglomerate of large organizations and political actors. What this fact implies for analysts of events like the Cuban missile crisis is no simple matter: its implications concern the basic categories and assumptions with which we approach events.

More rigorously, the *argument* developed in the body of this study can be summarized in three propositions:

1. *Professional analysts of foreign affairs (as well as ordinary laymen) think about problems of foreign and military policy in terms of largely implicit conceptual models that have significant consequences for the content of their thought.*

In thinking about problems of foreign affairs, professional analysts as well as ordinary laymen proceed in a straightforward, informal, nontheoretical fashion. Careful examination of explanations of events like the Soviet installation of missiles in Cuba, however, reveals a more complex theoretical substructure. Explanations by particular analysts show regular and predictable characteristics, which reflect unrecognized assumptions about the character of puzzles, the categories in which problems should be considered, the types of evidence that are relevant, and the determinants of occurrences. The first proposition is that bundles of such related assumptions constitute basic frames of reference or conceptual models in terms of which analysts and ordinary laymen ask and answer the questions: What happened? Why did it happen? What will happen? Assumptions like these are central to the activities of explanation and prediction. In attempting to explain a particular event, the analyst cannot simply describe the full scale of the world leading up to that event. The logic of explanation requires that he single out the relevant, important determinants of the occurrence. Moreover, as the logic of prediction underscores, he must summarize the various factors as they bear on the occurrence. Conceptual models not only fix the mesh of the nets that the analyst drags through the material in order to explain a particular action; they also direct him to cast his nets in select ponds, at certain depths, in order to catch the fish he is after.

2. *Most analysts explain (and predict) the behavior of national governments in terms of one basic conceptual model, here entitled Rational Actor Model.*

In spite of significant differences in interest and focus, most analysts and ordinary laymen attempt to understand happenings in foreign affairs as the more or less purposive acts of unified national governments. Laymen personify rational actors and speak of their aims and choices. Theorists of international relations focus on problems between nations in accounting for the choices of unitary rational actors. Strategic analysts concentrate on the logic of action in the absence of an actor. For each of these groups, the point of an explanation is to show how the nation or government could have chosen to act as it did, given the strategic problems it faced. For example, in confronting the problem posed by the Soviet installation of strategic missiles in Cuba the Rational Actor Model analyst frames the puzzle: Why did the Soviet Union decide to install missiles in Cuba? He then fixes the unit of analysis: governmental choice. Next, he focuses attention on certain concepts: goals and objectives of the nation or government. And finally, he invokes certain patterns of inference: if the nation performed an action of this sort, it must have had a goal of this type. The analyst has 'explained' this event when he can show how placing missiles in Cuba was a reasonable action, given Soviet strategic objectives. Predictions about what a nation will do or would have done are generated by calculating the rational thing to do in a certain situation, given specified objectives.

3. Two alternative conceptual models, here labeled an Organization Process Model and a Governmental Politics Model, provide a base for improved explanations and predictions.

Although the Rational Actor Model has proved useful for many purposes, there is powerful evidence that it must be supplemented, if not supplanted, by frames of reference that focus on the governmental machine — the organizations and political actors involved in the policy process. The Rational Actor Model's implication that important events have important causes, i.e., that monoliths perform large actions for large reasons, must be balanced by the appreciation that (1) monoliths are black boxes covering various gears and levers in a highly differentiated decisionmaking structure and (2) large acts result from innumerable and often conflicting smaller actions by individuals at various levels of bureaucratic organizations in the service of a variety of only partially compatible conceptions of national goals, organizational goals, and political objectives. The Rational Actor Model's grasp of national purposes and of the pressures created by problems in *international* relations must confront the *intra*-national mechanisms from which governmental actions emerge.

Recent developments in organization theory provide the foundation for the second model, which emphasizes the processes and procedures of the large organizations that constitute a government. According to this Organizational Process Model, what the Rational Actor Model characterizes as 'acts' and 'choices' are thought of instead as *outputs* of large organizations functioning according to regular patterns of behavior. Faced with the problem of Soviet missiles in Cuba, a analyst using the Organizational Process Model frames the puzzle: From what organizational context and pressures did this decision emerge? He then fixes the unit of analysis: organizational output. Next, he focuses attention on certain concepts: the strength, standard operating procedures, and repertoires of organizations. And finally, he invokes certain patterns of inference: if organizations produced an output of this kind today, that behavior resulted from existing organizational features, procedures, and repertoires. Thus the analyst has 'explained' the event when he has identified the relevant Soviet organizations and displayed the patterns of organizational behavior from which the action emerged. Predictions identify trends that reflect established organizations and their fixed procedures and programs.

The third model focuses on the politics of a government. Events in foreign affairs are understood, according to this model, neither as choices nor as outputs. Rather, what happens is characterized as a *resultant* of various bargaining games among players in the national government. In confronting the problem posed by Soviet missiles in Cuba, a analyst using the Government Politics Model frames the puzzle: Which results of what kinds of bargaining among which players yielded the critical decisions and actions? He then fixes the unit of analysis: political resultant. Next, he focuses attention on certain concepts: the perceptions, motivations, positions, power, and maneuvers of the players. And finally, he invokes certain patterns of inference: if a government performed an action, that action was the resultant of bargaining among players in games. Thus the analyst has 'explained' this event when he has discovered who did what to whom that yielded the action in question. Predictions are generated by identifying the game in which an issue will arise, the relevant players, and their relative power and skill.

A central metaphor illuminates the differences among these models. Foreign policy has often been compared to moves and sequences of moves in the game of chess. Imagine a chess game in which the observer could see only a screen upon which moves in the game were projected, with no information about how the pieces came to be moved. Initially, most observers would assume — as the Rational Actor Model does — that an individual chess player was moving the pieces with reference to plans and tactics toward the goal of winning the game. But a pattern of moves can be imagined that would lead some observers, after watching several games, to consider an Organizational Process assumption: the chess player might not be a single individual but rather a loose alliance of semi-independent organizations, each of which moved its set of pieces according to standard operating procedures. For example, movement of separate sets of pieces might proceed in turn, each according to a routine, the king's rook, bishop, and their pawns repeatedly attacking the opponent according to a fixed plan. It is conceivable, furthermore, that the pattern of play might suggest to an observer a Government Politics assumption: a number of distinct players, with distinct objectives but shared power over the pieces, could be determining the moves as the resultant of collegial bargaining. For example, the black rook's move might contribute to the loss of a black knight with no comparable gains for the black team, but with the black rook becoming the principal guardian of the palace on that side of the board.

Some reservations

This bald summary conveys none of my reservations about the persuasiveness of the argument in its present form. To make these points fully convincing would require greater length than seems reasonable here, and more success than I have had in coming to grips with several hard problems. First, the argument that most analysts tend to rely on a single conceptual model sounds crudely reductionist. In spite of my recognition and description of several variants of the Rational Actor Model, my insistence on their logical similarity may, none the less, seem procrustean. Second, because explanation and prediction of international events are not developed theoretical enterprises, few analysts proceed exclusively and single-mindedly within a pure conceptual model. Instead, they think predominantly in terms of one model, occasionally shifting from one variant of it to another and sometimes appropriating material that lies entirely outside the boundaries of the model. These first two problems give rise to a third. When examining uses of the Rational Actor Model, and especially when considering to what extent one has been relying upon some variant of this model, one can always find that it does not really capture *all* of his analytical activity. Fourth, the richness of variations on the classical theme makes a clearly specified account of the model seem little more than a caricature or a strawman. Fifth, the alternative models are not fully developed. Finally, since the body of literature applying these alternative models to problems of foreign affairs is quite small, my applications of them are simply initial, tentative efforts.

In spite of my limited success in dealing with these difficult problems, many readers have found the general argument a suggestive contribution not only to discussion of the Cuban missile crisis but also to general thought about governmental behavior, especially in foreign and military affairs.

Note

1   The term *outcome* is introduced here as a technical concept meaning a selectively delimited state of the real world importantly affected by the action of a government. The assertion is that in thinking about problems of foreign affairs, what most participants and analysts are really interested in are outcomes and the specific actions governments take that affect outcomes.

APPROACHING THE PROBLEM

From *Great Planning Disasters* by P. Hall, published by Weidenfeld & Nicholson, 1980.

Positive and normative analysis

An obvious way of starting ... is by distinguishing *positive* statements from *normative* statements: statements about what *is* from statements about what *ought to be*.[1] If we do this, we find that most normative statements predicate some ideally rational mode of policy-making or decision-making that may or may not be followed in this imperfect present world. Most start from economics and from the philosophical basis of that science, which is nineteenth-century utilitarianism ... Such an approach proceeds in a series of logical steps. The present environment is scanned to isolate main problems. A hierarchy of goals and objectives is set up, and is edited to manageable proportions. An inventory of available resources is established. Alternative ways of meeting the objectives are hypothesized and then evaluated in terms of some common metric of costs and benefits, generally associated with the achievements of the objectives. Usually, some calculation is made of probabilities of different courses of action; the preferred course is the one that maximizes the net expectation ... The choice is translated into managerial action and implemented. The implementation is constantly monitored and, if unexpected outcomes are discovered, appropriate modifications are introduced.[2]

Positive analyses, too, may start from a rational viewpoint. In other words, they may assume that actors in a decision all work according to normatively rational rules, to the best of their abilities. Classical and neoclassical economic theory, which is simultaneously positive and normative, is a good example of rationally based analysis — and so are its latter-day derivatives, such as systems theory. The problem is that, very soon, it will become obvious that some behaviour of actors cannot be explained in this way. First, the rational model requires perfect information, which is often lacking. It is generally impossible, for instance, to assess objective probabilities for outcomes; the best that can be done is to ask decision-makers for their subjective assessments.[3] Secondly, it assumes that all the actors hold the same values — which, in a complex decision, is highly unlikely. As will soon be clear, values and consequent preferences are very often in conflict. Thirdly, and stemming from this last, actors may well perceive that a gain to one group may mean a loss to their own group; the greatest good of the greatest number, in these circumstances, may prove an unhelpful guide. Fourthly, while some objectives are readily quantifiable, others are not. Arising from this, fifthly, there is no common agreement on an objective function which can be valued on a single scale, such as money values.[4] Sixthly, the rational model parameters of the decision remain fixed during the decision period, yet fluidity is a central feature of the real world. In practice, actors have different perceptions of and prejudices about the world they see. They have very different values, depending in part on their individual histories but also on their group or class affiliations including their loyalties to the institutions that employ them. And they must grapple with a changing environment where the factors in their decisions never stay still long enough to keep the decision stable.[5]

In consequence, rational positive analysts have developed alternative models to explain observed facts. The *incremental model*, set out by Dahl and Lindblom, assumes that decision-makers consider only incremental alternatives at any one time, together with a limited number of alternative means. Solutions will be considered only if they are realistic, or in other words appropriate to the available means. There is no clearly defined problem, no one decision; problems are never 'solved'. Such 'wicked problems' which lack definitive formulations or tests or one-shot solutions are special to planning.[6] But it can be argued that this, too, is oversimplistic: it ignores the fact that social change and innovation comes about through incorporation of new social values. Consequently, it has been claimed, the right mode of analysis is a kind of *mixed scanning*, which distinguishes fundamental *contextual* decisions from *individual item* decisions. Contextual decisions are made through a fundamental exploration of the main alternatives in the light of goals and objectives of the individual actor; at this stage, details are properly omitted. Then, piecemeal incremental decisions are made within the context of the fundamental ones.[7] Etzioni (1968, p. 284) concludes:

Democracies must accept a relatively high degree of incrementalism (though not as high as that of developing nations) because of their greater need to gain support for new decisions from many and conflicting subsocieties, a need that reduces their capacity to follow a long-run plan ... Democracies tend first to build a consensus and then to proceed, often accomplishing less than was necessary later than was necessary.

[Before returning] to normative theory, ... we need to go further in discovering how positive theory has approached these problems. For in helping to understand how the world is, it may provide a better theory of how the world might be. In particular, we need to look at alternatives to the economist—rational model of explanation.

Alternative explanations: Allison's three models

In his classic study of decision-making during the Cuban missile crisis of 1962, Graham Allison (1971) looks at the same piece of historical reality in three ways, each of which approaches a different level of reality. His model 1, the *rational actor paradigm*, corresponds closely to the rational model we have just considered. It assumes that action results from choice by a unitary object, called a nation or a government. Such a rational actor has a single set of goals (his utility function), a single set of options and a single set of consequences of alternatives. The actor reaches a static solution through analysing his goals and objectives, setting out his options, calculating benefits and costs of each, and reaching a choice that gives maximal excess of benefits. But Allison shows convincingly that, applied to the American–Russian confrontation at that time, the model 1 paradigm fails to account for a great deal of observed behaviour.

So Allison tries another approach. Model 2, the *organizational process paradigm*, assumes that most decision-making behaviour results from established routines within organizations. Here, the actors do not form a unity, but rather a constellation of individuals in organizations, with government leaders at the top. Problems are factored into sub-problems and are then acted upon by individuals with constrained powers. Organizations, developing a collective view, develop stable perceptions and procedures; their reactions thereby become predictable. Goals are dominated by the need to maintain the health of the organization and to avoid threats to it. Problems are tackled one by one as they arise, using standard procedures; uncertainty is avoided as much as possible. If unexpected problems are faced, the search for an answer will be biased by tradition and by the training of the actors. Dramatic changes will occur only in an organizational crisis involving personnel changes, or perhaps collapse of the entire organization. If any attempt is made from the centre to get a better integrated process, it will be found almost impossible to maintain the necessary continuing process of monitoring and control. Thus government is an established conglomerate of organizations, each with goals and programmes; change will be marginal and incremental, and long-range planning will be disregarded; solutions will not be adopted, indeed they may not be considered, if they depart from existing programmes or demand cooperation with other rival organizations.

Yet even this approach, Allison argues, still fails to catch the whole reality. Therefore he uses another mode of analysis: model 3, the *governmental (bureaucratic) politics paradigm*, assumes that decision-making by government is a political resultant from conflict, compromise and confusion among individuals whose behaviour must be understood in terms of game-playing. The players in these games each have positions; they may be chiefs, or their immediate staff, or Indians, or *ad hoc* players on the fringe (such as legislators and press). They have parochial perceptions and interests, especially organizational ones (a throwback to model 2). Their interests are represented as stakes, on which they may take stands; these stands are forced by deadlines, set by routines, by crises or by political actions. Each player will affect results depending on his power, which in turn will stem from a combination of bargaining advantages, skill and will in using them, or his perceptions of these things. Power must be invested wisely, otherwise the result will be a loss of reputation, and hence a loss of power. The game will be played through action channels, which government lays down for action of specific issue. The rules will be set by the constitution, by statutes, by regulations, even by culture; they may range from the very clear to the very hazy. Action then becomes a political resultant; politics is the mechanism of choice, and each player struggles for outcomes that advance his perception of his national, organizational, group or personal interests. The roles of players vary according to action channels; thus chiefs make decisions but Indians must implement them (and may fail to do so); Indians also frame most problems and propose most solutions. Solutions are reached by immediate responses to problems; deadlines impose quick decisions and a false air of confidence in them. Perceptions and expectations differ; communication is often poor; and decisions can be obtained through vagueness, with different actors understanding different meanings.

Allison's three models are distilled from many different insights in sociology, psychology and political science. Using them as a starting point, we can now look more critically at some of these elements of rational-positive theory.

Economists' explanations and sociologists' explanations

A critical starting point is a fact already noted: the rational mode of analysis or explanation, Allison's model 1, rests fundamentally on philosophical premises that are basic to economics. Indeed the central methods (assessment of uncertainty and comparison of utility) are economic techniques. In contrast, model 2 draws on insights from sociology and social psychology. Model 3, clearly, also draws on psychology, but at its interface with political science.

Here we can notice a fundamental difference: between what Daniel Bell (1973, pp. 283–4) and Mancur Olson (1965, pp. 110–17) call the economizing and sociologizing models. In the economizing mode, the focus is always on the individual; his satisfaction (or utility) is the unit in which costs and benefits are reckoned. In the sociologizing mode, the focus is on the individual in society. The economic ideal is Pareto optimality ... in resource allocation, so as to get the most efficient use of scarce resources. In contrast, the classical (or Parsonian) sociological ideal is to integrate society so that it forms a community with common norms and values and group associations and affiliations; in such a society, formalized groupings (including pressure groups) are particularly valuable. For Olson, these two models are normatively in conflict: an economically oriented society will have great dynamism but little social stability (as in many developing nations today), while a (Parsonian) sociologically-oriented country will have great stability but little economic growth (as, perhaps, Britain today). The choice between the two models, Olson stresses, has to be made by the political system ...

But, just now, it provides a useful insight into our positive models. Sociologists of the Parsonian school stress mutual adjustment; but in contrast; sociologists of a Marxist or neo-Marxist kind stress conflict between groups. Thus Ralf Dahrendorf's model shows us that a society is exposed to change, with ubiquitous and permanent social conflict, and with constraint of some groups by others; there will always be a dominant and a dominated quasi-group, and these two groups will organize themselves into groups with manifest interests, which will then fight over the preservation or removal of the status quo.[8] Similarly, John Rex questions the assumption that society is organized around common values; instead, he argues, social systems have built-in conflict situations, in which the parties will have unequal power giving a ruling and a subject class, struggling for legitimacy.[9]

We can say that Parsonian sociology has been the basis for one kind of alternative model, with both positive and normative aspects, but that conflict sociology has surely been the foundation for radically different alternatives. In the rational-economic model, by way of contrast, there is no conflict between one individual and another; there is competition, but in the end it serves the greatest good of the greatest number. Producers compete to make profits, consumers compete to get bargains; they mutually adjust their supply and demand levels until the market is cleared. In contrast, sociological theory sees bureaucracy as serving its own ends. And a whole group of social psychologists-turned-organizational analysts, especially at the Carnegie-Mellon school in Pittsburgh, has developed a general theory of conflict resolution within organizations. It was this group which first suggested that organizations work by reducing general goals to sub-goals, to which individuals and groups could then become attached. Out of this came the behavioural theory of the firm; it treats the firm as a conflict-solving organization, constantly dividing and reforming itself into coalitions which form for particular problems or particular times with temporary organizational goals.[10] Clearly the Carnegie-Mellon theorists have influenced both Allison's second and third models.

Models of game-playing behaviour, on the other hand, draw on theory developed by economists, but use it in a quite different sense from the rational-economic models, allying it to experimental work on the assessment of risk. Thus the stress is again on the individual rather than the organization; but now, there is no assumption that the outcome of the activity will be necessarily optimal in any way. In fact, the theory of games in its original form is quite incapable of application to these kinds of problem, since it cannot yet be extended to cover games with many players where the outcome may be better or worse for the whole group of players. But, as Bower (1968, p. 142) suggests, it may be used in non-rigorous formulations to describe a variety of complicated decision processes in conditions of uncertainty.

The conclusion might as well be stated in advance: none of these methods, in itself, will provide a touchstone to adequate understanding. But perhaps each of them can contribute something to an eclectic theory, still to be developed ...

A tentative positive theory

It may be tentatively stated thus. Decisions arise from a complex process of interactions among actors. All these people think themselves rational, and are trying to behave rationally for much of the time; but their conceptions of the rational differ. They have different goals, and different ways of achieving these goals. Some of them, particularly senior professionals and bureaucrats, have been trained according to rational modes and will try particularly hard to apply these in decision-making. Others, in particular politicians, will tend to follow more intuitive, adaptive, piecemeal methods. The most important definable groups are the *community*, or more particularly those members of the community who play an active role in various formal or informal organizations that try to intervene in the decision-making process; the elected *politicians*, who must promise certain policies to the electorate in order to gain re-election and who will be subject in office to pressures of events; and the professional and administrative *bureaucracy* which must administer policy but which invariably also plays a large role in shaping it. Each of these broad groups splits into *sub-groups* (different citizens' groups, often with contradictory purposes; political parties, and sub-groups within parties; divisions of bureaucracies, such as ministries or bureaux within ministries); any of these sub-groups is likely to have interests that in part coincide with the wider group, in part diverge. These sub-groups, and the wider groups, are to some extent bound by established perceptions and procedures. Members of groups or sub-groups, and even individuals, engage in strategic behaviour to gain what they perceive as their objectives. Their power stems from a variety of sources, including legal and institutional authority, reputation, skill in bargaining and acuteness of perception. They are bound by rules of the game, which may be extremely rigid (laws, established procedures) or fluid (custom) in different societies. No outcome is ever decisive, since it can be reversed or can wither away due to non-implementation. Thus the process of decision-making is not discrete, but is part of an ongoing complex of interrelated acts; and non-decisions may be as important as decisions.

Much of any such eclectic body of theory must derive from the United States, for that is where most of the work has been done. But in applying it to other countries, especially to Britain, caution may be needed. As Kenneth Newton (1975, pp. 11–22) has pointed out, in comparison to the United States Britain is more centralized, with a stronger national context; the role of bureaucracy and of political parties is certainly greater, and the role of voluntary organizations possibly so; a vital role is played by pressure groups, most of which are middle-class but at least one of which (the trade unions) is not. We need to reinterpret the theory in terms of different formal political structures.

Notes

1 Cf. Bauer (1968), p. 9.
2 Stewart (1971), p. 30; Dror (1968), p. 132; Chadwick (1971), p. 68; Churchman *et al.* (1957), pp. 118, 127.
3 Ackoff and Sasieni (1968), pp. 44–5.
4 Zeckhauser and Schaefer (1968), p. 107.
5 Etzioni (1968), p. 265.
6 Rittel and Webber (1973), p. 160.
7 Etzioni (1968), pp. 283–5.
8 Simmie (1974), pp. 59–60.
9 *Ibid.*, pp. 60–2.
10 Bower (1968), pp. 129–32.

SECTION 2

RATIONAL DECISION MAKING

One central problem of 'rationality' is that it has no precisely fixed meaning, as Carley points out at the beginning of his extract (2.2). Despite variations in the definitions, he believes that rationality has a common core of meaning which we can summarize as, *(a)* a distinction between ends/goals on the one hand and means to achieve those goals on the other, *(b)* some rules for evaluating the costs and benefits of each alternative means so as to *(c)* select the best or optimum solution to the decision problem in a way which could, in principle, be reconstructed and examined by an analyst. Such decisions can be *justified* to others who, particularly in an official or organizational context (rather than a private one), may require evidence of the decision-maker's 'proper exercise of judgement' as the Dictionary has it.

The need to justify decisions to others brings us to the normative or prescriptive nature of models, outlined in the General Introduction to this reader, since the labelling of a decision as non-rational raises doubts as to the quality of decisions which are also described. This is the first problem with rational decision-making models; frequently they are as much prescriptions of how decisions *should* be made as they are descriptions of what actually happens. One small aid is to clarify briefly the use of non-rational and irrational as they occur in these readings and in the literature generally. Non-rational is best regarded as describing decisions taken without the calculative or evaluative steps in *(b)* above. Decisions taken on impulse (some shopping decisions), to satisfy strong emotional drives (friendship), and for ritual needs (worship) are usually non-rational and of little interest to the analysts of decision-making, although they can be of great importance to other social scientists. Irrational decisions are of interest in the study of decision-making if they are regarded as rational decisions which have 'gone wrong' in some way, usually because what the decision-maker says he wished to achieve, and the means he selected to do so, do not fit according to accepted rules of calculation of means—ends relationships. Decisions 'go wrong' from the decision-makers' point of view either because they were wrongly calculated or, more importantly, because they cannot be calculated rightly because of the *uncertainty* which is characteristic of the decision-making process in most of the important areas of politics, of social problems as well as in economics. The key to the usefulness of rational-decision-making models is *(a)* finding the conditions under which human agents can calculate the consequences of their decisions with a reasonable degree of certainty, and *(b)* defining the rules of calculation which will choose the best alternative from the means available.

These two requirements of rational-decision-making models are clarified by Simon's distinction between substantive and procedural rationality (2.4). The strong meaning of 'rational' (substantive for Simon) is a way of modelling the outcomes of consequences of decisions so that the decision-maker has one and only one way of arriving at a 'best' decision — and what is best is itself defined by the model and the assumptions which it makes. Strongly rational models are common only in economics (and in applications of economic theories such as Barry's discussion of Downs's theory of voting (2.5)), where well-developed models of the perfectly competitive market were developed very early. Under conditions of perfect competition, the price which will maximize the producer's profits (his optimum solution) is the marginal cost of production or the cost of the last item to be produced. Decision rules like this are *objective*, the decision-maker's private beliefs or calculations are irrelevant because if he does not decide his prices in this way he will be punished by the competition of the market where those who do follow the rules will be more successful. This is why Simon points out that economics using this strong or substantive rationality did not have to bother about *how* decisions were made. In the long run, decision-makers who did not follow rational rules would leave the market. But, as both Simon and Samuelson (2.3) make clear, the typical form of economic organization is not perfect but imperfect competition where the market does not always punish those producers who fail to follow the rules. Thus, rather than ignore how decisions are made we now have to examine the procedures by which even economic decisions are arrived at — procedural rationality (Simon).

Outside economics, the assumptions made for applying a strongly rational model have long been severely criticized. The capacity of individuals to select and process and obtain the information required in such models is dubious as Simon himself, Smith and May (2.7), Jabes (2.1) and Lindblom (2.8) all acknowledge. Furthermore, unlike the perfectly competitive market, decision-makers operate under conditions where both information itself and the consequences of decisions are characterized by *uncertainty* to some degree or other.

If the hallmark of the environment in which real decisions are taken is uncertainty (Jabes) then the consequences of any decision depend as much on what others will do as on the correctness or otherwise of the decision-maker's calculations. Thus a strongly rational — or 'rational-comprehensive' as Richardson and Jordan (2.6) call it — solution to a problem is simply not possible. Decision-makers must operate with 'bounded rationality' (Simon) in which only some alternative means and goals are compared and evaluated. These may be 'edited' from the large number of possibilities by a form of Lindblom's 'strategic analysis' which puts a premium on some one objective, e.g. maximizing votes, minimizing the opposition, maintaining market-share etc. Studies of how decision makers select and evaluate their choices become the focus of the analyst's attention, and rather than optimizing solutions we find what is known as 'satisficing', in which a 'successive limited comparison' (Lindblom, Smith and May) of choices is made, each time selecting the better one. The comparisons are limited because the costs of obtaining the necessary information frequently outrun the benefits to be gained, and the search for a good decision finishes when the decision maker has satisfied himself that a feasible solution is 'good enough' from his perspective i.e. his definition of the 'decision-space' (Carley).

Rational decision making under conditions of uncertainty and the real costs of obtaining and processing data, moves us away from substantive or strong rational decision making, towards 'rationalistic' decision making and converges with Lindblom's incrementalism, once put forward as the alternative model to rational decision making. Incrementalism, with its emphasis on limited policy changes and comparison of only a few rather than of all alternatives, has been widely held to describe, much better than rational-decision-making models, what happens when real decisions are taken. But Smith and May argue that the contrast between incrementalism and rational models has been overdrawn and the two models converge in practice. This is true if we accept Carley's general definition of rational action (his five steps of rational decision making) rather than the narrower substantive rationality of Simon or the substantive rationality in Samuelson's competitive market mechanisms for deciding what, how and for whom goods and services are produced.

Several authors in this section agree that Lindblom's incremental decision making (or muddling through as he disarmingly puts it) is a better description of how decisions are made than are rational-decision-making models. If we accept Carley's or Jabes' broader definition of rational decisions then models adapted from Lindblom's are likely to capture reality better than strongly rational ones. But two major problems remain. Even with incrementalism in a rationalistic form there is an inherent pressure on decision-makers to increase the 'rational' approach to decisions, perhaps at the expense of the 'muddling through' one, because of the value bias of rationality itself (Smith and May). The difficulty here is that to increase the rational selection between means, the agent needs to be able to order his goals in such a way that his 'utility function' (Carley, Simon) allows him at least to say that he prefers *a* to *b* and *b* to *c* etc., and, preferably, that he might prefer *a* twice as much as *b*. Studies of real decision takers show that they are rarely as clear as this and that few if any of them operate with well-defined utility functions of an ordinal or ranking type let alone of a metric or quantified type.

The second problem is related and concerns the evaluation of decisions from a societal point of view rather than from an individual or organization's point of view — that is, from an essentially political viewpoint. To use the economic term, we would need a single Social Welfare Function in which the utilities of all major objectives were at least ranked. We would need consensus on, for example, whether reducing unemployment is to be preferred to reducing inflation. But this is precisely what does not happen and, as Richardson and Jordan point out, the perspective of political bargaining between interest groups (partisan mutual adjustment) can rule out consensus on ends as well as on means. So political bargaining (Section 4) or routine organization processes (Jabes's 'programmed decisions', Section 3) require a different perspective or model than the rational one with an agreed utility function. It is rare for an organization (certainly for an individual) to list and order its objectives clearly; and if it were to do so it would probably find that different interest groups would then dispute both the goals of their organization and their relative rankings. The conclusion must be that there are strong limits to the power of even broadened rational-decision-making models to explain how and why certain decisions are taken.

2.1   J. Jabes

INDIVIDUAL DECISION MAKING

From Jak Jabes, *Individual Processes im Organizational Behavior* (Arlington Heights, IL: Harlam Davidson Inc., 1978), pp. 86–102. Reprinted by permission of the publisher.

A *decision* is a goal-directed behavior made by the individual, in response to a certain need, with the intention of satisfying the motive that the need occasions. All behavior involves at least simple decisions. For example, one decides whether to walk to work or not. Many decisions involve a choice between more than two alternatives. One can walk to work, ride a bicycle, take a bus, or drive his car. All alternatives bring about the same goal, getting to work. The process of decision-making becomes difficult because often the existence of equally attractive, unattractive, or competing alternatives makes many decisions an unpleasant exercise. One can become frustrated while making a decision because the available alternatives may generate conflict. Tension is produced if we are uncertain about the choice or if we are fearful of the consequences of a wrong choice. The needs of the individual, and his perception of the environment, are important determiners of decision-making.

The decision process starts with problem identification and ends with a choice. We shall explain how the process has traditionally been analyzed; we shall study most explanations of how we decide when we are uncertain about the probability of occurrence of each alternative.

Then two competing general approaches will be discussed, describing how man makes decisions. The traditional approach was developed by economists and sees a person as trying to do the best thing for himself while being aware of all his options. The second approach is the behavioral science view, where the person is seen as trying to satisfice some personal values while being pertially aware of all the options in the environment. We favor the latter view because we believe that man possesses limited capabilities for processing information and hence cannot fulfill the demands made by the economic model.

Decision-making models aim to *describe* how people make decisions. The models describing the decision-making process fit the data from the actual decision to the prescriptions of the model. Besides being descriptive, many models also are normative. They tell us how people ought to decide, or at least how the theorist who evolved the model thinks people ought to decide ...

Decision-making is one of the most important processes in life. When discussing organizations, Simon (1960) treats decision-making as synonymous with managing. In so doing, he underlines the fact that decision-making as a process should not be reduced simply to a choice among alternatives. Rather, this process involves conceptualization of the problem to be solved and the description of how that final choice is made. Before one can describe the process of decision-making, one must understand the psychological variables that enter the process. Our aim is to deal with the person as a decision-maker.

The decision process

The decision process begins with identification of a problem. The problem arises when a sought-after goal can be obtained via alternative and sometimes competing avenues. A person faced with investing money for some sort of return has alternative ways of satisfying this goal. Simon (1960) suggests that problem identification leads first to intelligence activity, which involves searching the environment for various conditions reflecting on the decision. Within the organizational context, problem identification is followed by design activity in which all options are analyzed. Choice activity is the final step in the decision process where an alternative is selected. Decision theorists have tried to delineate a systematic, step-by-step process for decision-making. This process is usually characterized as consisting of identification of the problem, specification of goals, searching for alternatives and evaluating them, and the selection of an action.

Identification of the problem produces a motivational state that induces action. The definition and clarification of the goals are needed so that satisfaction can be obtained through various actions and outcomes. The person who is going to make an investment decision wants a return on the investment as the outcome of his decision. This would satisfy him. But further questions are raised. How much satisfaction does he want, and how much return would bring this satisfaction? This leads to a discussion of the aspects surrounding a decision. To do this we shall explain how decisions are categorized and how outcomes are selected.

Certainty, risk, and uncertainty involved in choice

The environment surrounding a decision is not always known to the person. Often the person is forced to make a decision with limited information about the environmental conditions of the decision. There are three conditions under which decisions are made: certainty, risk, and uncertainty. *Certainty* exists when the outcome of alternative actions can be accurately predicted. In the certainty condition the decision process involves a rule which maximizes the outcome of one or a combination of variables. For example, profit could be such an index to be maximized in an economic context. *Risk* involves a state in which the outcomes of the alternative actions can be specified and a probability assigned to the likelihood of the occurrence of each. To understand choice under conditions of risk, we have to know: 1) how the individual appraises the probability of the occurrence of each outcome, and 2) what personal values the person wants to maximize (that is, what kind of satisfaction he wants to derive). *Uncertainty* exists when the probability of occurrence of alternative outcomes is unknown. Under the condition of uncertainty, outcomes of actions can be determined, but the probability for their occurrence cannot be assigned.

Decisions can be viewed as ranging on a continuum of uncertainty. Decisions for which most of the information is known or available are at the end of this continuum, and decisions for which no knowledge exists are placed at the other. In order to understand choice under uncertainty, we must make recourse to the perceptions, needs, and the belief system of the individual ... Availability of information helps in reducing uncertainty. However, information is helpful only up to a point. Miller (1956) has shown that human memory imposes severe limitations on the amount of information which humans can receive, process, and remember ...

Types of decisions

Within organizations, individuals make decisions which are sometimes compatible with their personal goals but occasionally are not. Incompatibility between personal and organizational goals can bring further conflict into a decision. Most decisions made in an organization are of a routine nature. Examples of routine decisions can be seen when the personnel officer hires someone new, the first-line supervisor changes a part of the operation, the sales manager apportions territory, or the accountant makes entries into his books. Some decisions in the organization are more important and basic. Deciding on a new union contract or the manufacturing of a new line of products is of greater consequence than a routine decision. Routine decisions more often involve certainty or risk, whereas important decisions involve uncertainty.

Simon (1960) distinguishes two types of executive decisions: programmed and nonprogrammed. *Programmed decisions* are routine in nature. A procedure for handling programmed decisions exists in the organization and the problem-solving process involves referring to past experience. The solution for a programmable decision can be computed. New and unstructured decisions are called *nonprogrammed* because the problem has never arisen before. Simon's terminology, borrowed from that used for computers, suggests that some decisions leave us with no guidelines (program) for a step-by-step solution. Table 2.1.1 shows examples of programmed and nonprogrammed decisions. It must be understood that decision types are not always this clear-cut. They range on a continuum of programmability. Most programmable decisions are made under conditions of risk or uncertainty.

Table 2.1.1   Programmed and nonprogrammed decision-making

Types of decisions	Decision-making techniques	
	Traditional	Modern
Programmed Routine, repetitive decisions Organization develops specific processes for handling them	1. Habit 2. Clerical routine; standard operating procedures 3. Organization structure; common expectations; A system of subgoals; well-defined informational channels	1. Operations research; mathematical analysis; models; computer simulation 2. Electronic data-processing
Nonprogrammed One-shot, ill-structured, novel policy decisions Handled by general problem-solving processes	1. Judgement, intuition, and creativity 2. Rules of thumb 3. Selection and training of executives	Heuristic problem-solving techniques applied to: *(a)* training human decision makers *(b)* constructing heuristic computer programs

Source: H. A. Simon (1960), p. 8.

The man who decides

Decision-making is of interest not only to behavioral scientists but also to those in economics and political science. We hinted that rationality cannot always be expected when making a decision. The term rational means different things to different people. The person who makes decisions in economics and the person who makes decisions in organizational behavior are the same. However, each discipline has developed its own model of the decision-maker. Economists conceptualize the person who makes decisions as a rational being who weighs each alternative. Behavioral scientists, on the other hand, have observed a decision-making man who simplifies the world, distorts it in accordance with his values, and often uses chance phenomena such as coin-tossing or consulting an astrologer to make a decision.

Economically rational decision-making
Economic models of man have their roots in the pleasure principle submitted by the British philosophers Jeremy Bentham and John Stuart Mill. Their hedonistic approach postulated that man tries to maximize pleasure

and minimize pain. These ideas formed the basis for postulates in economics as well as learning theory in the behavioral sciences. Shubik (1958) outlines the following premises made by the economic model: Economic man is aware of all the alternatives in a given situation and acts rationally to choose the most viable one ... This reflects a means-ends analysis of rationality. If the appropriate means are chosen for specified ends, then a decision is rational ...

Each decision for the economically rational man is programmable. However, we know that there are nonprogrammable decisions and some of the decisions of economics fall into this category. The classic model of economic man is a normative model which suggests how a decision *ought* to be made. At best it would apply only to decisions made under certainty ... Churchman (1968) suggests that the rational approach, although flawless in its axioms, does not tell us much of practical value about rationality and its application to real behavior.

Noneconomically rational man

Simon (1947) criticized the rationality and maximization aspects of the economic model of man by suggesting a model of decision-making man that matches reality. Rationality in economics implies a complete knowledge of the environment and the maximization of a value based on this information. Simon has argued cogently that, at any point in time, an individual has only limited information on the states of nature. It is impossible to know what each choice alternative may lead to in the future. In organizations we deal with men who have bounded rationality. Man has access only to a portion of objective reality and his behavior is in response to bounded rationality. Consequently, due to lack of economic rationality, what is maximized is not necessarily always that which yields highest utility, but an alternative acceptable to the person. A means–ends definition of rationality is also erroneous because ends are rarely objectively specifiable and they are often inseparable from means.

In opposition to the economic man, Simon proposes the administrative man who 'satisfices' rather than maximizes. Administrative man is unable to have complete and accurate information about the environment, so he searches through available choice alternatives until he hits upon one that is 'good enough'. A choice is made when an alternative meets the minimum standard of satisfaction that the individual expects. This choice rarely coincides with an optimal decision, such as suggested by the model in economics. The interest is in feasible solutions that meet a minimal standard of satisfaction. Optimal solutions may not be feasible. During the search for a satisfactory alternative, the individual may realize that he is unable to find any alternative that meets his standards. He then lowers his level of aspiration, thereby lowering the minimum acceptable standard. If search shows that available alternatives are very satisfactory, the aspiration level may be raised. The whole process implies that the individual has a psychological set from which he determines subjective rationality ...

Support for Simon's model comes from several areas of research ... [The psychology of perception suggests that, as in Simon's model, decisions are] ... taken within a construction of a simplified reality ...

Soelberg (1966) has shown that search ends when a satisficing alternative is found. His research demonstrated that graduate students questioned on prospective job decisions stopped looking for a job ten days or more before reporting their decision. In trying to explain the unprogrammed decision process, Soelberg found ... that the decision process followed steps outlined by Simon. He further added to the approach by saying that the decision process is one of decision confirmation. An alternative becomes satisfactory during search, other choices are compared to it, and this alternative emerges as the choice when a satisfactory decision rule is constructed which rules out all other alternatives.

Myers and Fort (1963) found that level of aspiration in betting was based on the preceding pattern of outcomes. If the bettor won, another win was predicted. This agrees with the success and failure notion that characterizes level of aspiration. Success leads to raising aspirations and failures lower them. The whole notion of satisficing is rooted in motivational tendencies. Search is geared for drive satisfaction ... If we view decision-making as goal-directed behavior, then our concern is with the reduction of tension that develops prior to making the decision. Psychological theory shows that this is done by choosing a satisficing alternative.

Administrative people operate on a simplified version of the real world. This is due to the information available on the one hand, and their capability to process information on the other hand. Complex models built by operations research can aid organization people in making decisions. But limits to information processing lead many individuals to simplify the models. Hirschman and Lindblom (1962) suggest that the decision-maker sporadically muddles through solutions, redefining goals along the way.

The noneconomically rational model stands against the objective explanation of the environment in which the decision is made. The decision is made in a subjective environment constructed by the perceptions and cognitions of the person. Objective descriptions of the environment may fail to predict the actual decision process. If we are to subscribe to rational choice, then we must rule out selectivity in perception. But selectivity exists in the perceptual process and may result in excluding from the decision environment many variables that would need to be specified when making a decision using the economic model. Hence the idea of subjective rationality becomes important when describing decision-making. The decision-maker's bounded subjective rationality, in an organizational context, is determined by his limited knowledge of the world and the organizational environment in which he lives (March and Simon, 1958).

Models of individual decision-making and judgement

The continuum of decision-making can run from those decisions for which science provides a normative solution (such as programmable decisions) to those that are totally intuitive. Interest in both descriptive and normative approaches to individual decision-making have led to careful descriptions of the individual and the environment in which the decision is made. Decision-making is a complex process, unique for each individual in accordance with his perceptual, motivational, and value makeup.

2.2   M. Carley

ANALYTIC RATIONALITY

From *Rational Techniques in Policy Analysis* by M. Carley, published by
Heinemann Educational, 1981.

Rationality: a first look

The Oxford English Dictionary defines the word rational as 'exercising
one's reason in a proper manner; having sound judgement; sensible, sane'.
Unfortunately the use of the word related to public policy formulation is
not as clear and there are a variety of definitions. Levine *et al.* (1975,
p. 89) point out that for some people rationality:

means achievement of goals, some associate it with individuals maximising
satisfaction, others conceive of it as a decision making process without
regard to how successful a person is in achieving goals, and still others
consider rationality to be broadly synonymous with intelligent and pur-
poseful behaviour.

In spite of this multiplicity of perspectives on rationality in general
there is, in fact, much in common among authors concerned with rationality when one considers the working definitions in use. All relate to two
very similar ideal types of the 'rational man'. First, in economic thought,
to be rational is to select from a group of alternative courses of action
that course which maximises output for a given input, or minimises input
for a given output. Secondly, in systems analysis, decision theory, or game
theory, to be rational is to select a course of action, from a group of
possible courses of action, which has a given set of predicted consequences
in terms of some welfare function which, in turn, ranks each set of consequences in order of preference. This second application of rationality
can also be applied to the concept of 'planning' in so far as planning 'is
that activity that concerns itself with proposals for the future, with the
evaluation of alternative proposals, and with the methods by which those
proposals may be achieved' (Simon, 1958, p. 423) and is considered 'a
process for rationally determining the framework of future decisions'
(Smith, 1976, p. 24). In all of these definitions rationality refers to consistent, value-maximising choice given certain constraints. This analytic
rationality is embodied in rational analysis and generally undertaken
by what we have termed rational technique.

In almost every case working definitions of rationality can be expressed
by five sequential activities undertaken by the idealised 'rational man':

(1) A problem which requires action is identified and goals, values, and objectives related to the problem are classified and organised.
(2) All important possible ways of solving the problem or achieving goals and objectives are listed — these are alternative strategies, courses of action, or policies.
(3) The important consequences which would follow from each alternative strategy are predicted and the probability of those consequences occurring is estimated.
(4) The consequences of each strategy are then compared to the goals and objectives identified above.
(5) Finally, a policy or strategy is selected in which consequences most closely match goals and objectives, or the problem is most nearly solved, or most benefit is got from equal cost, or equal benefit at least cost.

There appears to be widespread agreement that these five steps constitute the basic activities of the idealised model which underpins all the techniques discussed here. We will run into them time and again in different guises and we can safely assume that when authors talk about rationality they are talking about some variation of these activities ... For now it is worth stressing for the first of many times that these steps constitute an ideal, or a model, which is well defined as 'an abstraction from reality that is intended to order and simplify our view of that reality while still capturing its essential characteristics' (Forcese and Richer, 1973, p. 38). A model, therefore, is not reality. In so far as this rational model diverges from reality in its attempts at simplification it is bound to be open to criticism, and there is indeed a considerable body of critical literature. [However], it will be argued that the rational model is a valuable but *partial* perspective on policy problems.

The policy process and analytic rationality

For a simple model of the policy process we might assume that there is a problem to be dealt with which will eventually require a decision by one or more policy makers. Like the stone falling to earth which moves the furthest planets, this problem and the subsequent decision involves complex inter-relationships and extensive effects which ripple throughout the system. The first task for anyone must be to define the problem in a manageable form — no person can grasp the entire complexity of the system and so one must draw a line around the influences and effects considered relevant. These effects are contained in what we might call the decision space.

Isolating, or defining, a decision space involves the first of the value judgements which permeate the policy process. One possible way of isolating these effects is to consider the personal implications for the policy makers. For the politician this means looking to the future decisions of voters: a decision space might be defined in terms of those effects which will cause people to vote for the policy makers. For the civil servant the decision space may involve factors influencing the distribution of administrative power, or career promotion. This is rational thinking for the persons involved, that is personal rationality, but it is not analytic rationality which is born of a distrust of allocating resources by means of personal rationality. The rational analyst therefore proposes what might be a quite different decision space based on those factors which are amenable to consideration in the form of the five step model given above. But distrust of the politically defined decision space is no guarantee that some other definition, like the rational analytic one, is necessarily any better. Both might well ignore important factors which would be relevant if the decision were put in a broader form ...

General problems with the rational model

Before moving on to consider rational policy analysis it is worth considering briefly a few common and general criticisms of the rational model. Gershuny (1978) identifies two main threads in these criticisms. The first stems from the assumption that to be rational one also has to be comprehensive. At its extreme this view assumes that rational analysis must involve the collection of all data relevant to a problem and the ordering of all human goals and subsequent objectives to facilitate proper comparison of the consequences of alternative strategies. The need for comprehensiveness therefore makes it impossible to define a decision space. Lindblom (1968, p. 10) uses this impossibility as the basis for arguing that the rational model (as proposed by Simon) is too divergent from reality and that 'a concept of rationality appropriate for judging a complex political system cannot be defined'. Lindblom proposes instead incrementalism or the 'science of muddling through', which emphasises only marginal changes in policy, thus drastically reducing the number and complexity of policy alternatives, but also severely limiting the decision space.

It is obvious, however, that nobody is arguing for full-grown comprehensive rationality and that what is described is a limited or partial rationality − only *some* alternatives and *some* consequences are related to *some* objectives. This limiting is done by (i) the decision makers ignoring consequences which are of no interest (ii) decision makers 'learning' from past decisions and thus adjusting the scope of their concern accordingly; and (iii) 'satisficing', which means the decision makers pursue sufficient, satisfactory goals rather than some 'one best' goal (Simon, 1957). Such satisficing is rational because it follows rational procedures (the five steps), but it is a limited rationality. Many authors accept the notion of limited rationality under a variety of terms. Rawls (1971, p. 418) calls it 'deliberative rationality' which is:

an activity like any other, and the extent to which one should engage in it is subject to rational decision. The formal rule is that we should deliberate up to the point where the likely benefits from improving our plan are just worth the time and effort of reflection. Once we take the costs of deliberation into account, it is unreasonable to worry about finding the best plan, the one we would choose had we complete information. It is perfectly rational to follow a satisfactory plan when the prospective returns from further calculation and additional knowledge outweigh the trouble.

... In summary, the criticism that rational behaviour is impossible because complete comprehensiveness is impossible is generally resolved by the concept of limited rationality, given that this basic limitation to rationality is made clear.

The second common criticism of the rational model is of the assumption that it is possible to develop a social welfare function (SWF), which can be defined as a preference ranking by society on some set of alternative strategies. In other words, if steps (4) and (5) of the rational man's tasks are to be applied by some group of people then this 'society' must prefer one strategy or policy over another based on the greater good (or social welfare) which accrues from choosing that alternative. If any two alternatives result in equal social welfare the society is 'indifferent' to the choice. A theoretical problem arises in that, while it is accepted that an individual (or rational man) can order a preference ranking, it may not be the case that a number of those rankings can be added up to some overall social ranking.

The best known form of this argument is that advanced by Arrow (1954) who demonstrates in the 'majority voting' paradox that aggregating individual preferences through democratic means always poses the possibility that no clear preference will emerge. *The Economist* (1978) gave a good example of this paradox in which a society consisting of three individuals attempted to rank three mutually exclusive policy alternatives: (*a*) environmentalism (*b*) efficiency and (*c*) goodheartedness. This was done in the hope that some social welfare function would evolve upon which policy decisions could be based. The ranking went like this:

	1st choice	2nd choice	3rd choice
Prof. Econut	(*a*)	(*b*)	(*c*)
Mr Tycoon	(*b*)	(*c*)	(*a*)
Rev. Goodchappe	(*c*)	(*a*)	(*b*)

The result is a 2 to 1 vote that environmentalism is preferred to efficiency, a 2 to 1 vote that efficiency is preferred to goodheartedness, but also a 2 to 1 vote that goodheartedness is preferred to environmentalism. In other words, (*a*) is preferred to (*b*), (*b*) is preferred to (*c*), but (*c*) is preferred to (*a*). No rational policy decision based on a social welfare function is possible in this hypothetical situation.

A second difficulty with the social welfare function is that there are situations where the results of actions taken by a group of rational individuals may lead to a non-rational outcome. For example, if all dairy farmers restrict their output of butter the price will go up and they will benefit. But each will assume that his output cannot affect the total price of butter so he will opt for full production. If each dairy farmer follows the same reasoning then full production occurs, the price drops, and they all fare badly.

Do these logical dilemmas preclude a role for rationality in the policy analysis process? Possibly in simple theory, but not in practice for a variety of reasons, which are discussed at length in Brown and Jackson (1978). First, the voting paradox assumes an individual self interest, direct voting model, but it may be that some public interest model or a representative government model more closely approximates the complex reality of the political process. To this we return shortly. Even, however, if one accepts the self-interest, direct-voting model there are still at least two reasons why the voting paradox does not hold in many cases. The first reason is that it is quite likely that the number of voters will be considerably more than three, in which case the probability of a unique majority outcome rises rapidly to over ninety per cent as the number of voters increases (De Meyer and Plott, 1970). Secondly, wherever there is a degree of consensus in a voting group the probability of a majority outcome also increases.

More importantly, however, is the fact that the political process is not the simple democracy put forward in the voting paradox but a representational system in which such elements as power wielding, vote-getting, argument, and party or bureaucratic maintenance are as important as simple choice. The role of government, which is in a sense determined by this process, also ensures that the simple 'free market' assumption of our dairy farmer example need not hold true in a mixed economy with government intervention. In such a system self interested voters will often have some means of expressing the intensity of their preferences, if not in the vote itself, then in the amount of resources they may put at the disposal of groups or parties espousing one alternative over another. Also quite common is what Brown and Jackson (1978, p. 77) call 'log-rolling', that is, a voluntary exchange of votes to the mutual benefit of different partisan groups. In other words, 'I'll vote for you on this issue, if you'll vote for me on that'. Such vote trading is quite in keeping with the economists' self-interest model and adds to the unlikelihood of a voting paradox. Tullock (1967), for example, argues that in the real world the probability of the voting paradox occurring is too small to make any practical difference.

Another possibility is that social welfare functions emerge, not as a result of aggregating individual self interests, but from some wider public interest which is the result of a process of political conflict which tries to produce agreement, establish consensus, and minimise instability. In this model political decisions are not reached simply by adding up preferences, but by a dynamic process which involves changing preferences towards a sufficient coalescence of opinion for action to take place. If a social welfare function does emerge it is a result of this dynamic process. Brent (1979) for example, argues that economists can construct social welfare functions based, not on individual preferences, but on values revealed in the political system related to particular social objectives. These values are ascertained by imputing motives to past government decisions and examining explicit policy statements. In fact, the public interest and the self-interest models of preference determination need not be mutually exclusive ... Both are valuable partial models of the reality of the policy-making process, which serve their disciplines of economics and political science for theory formation and which could profitably be integrated by policy scientists.

What about the social welfare function? It is possible to formulate one, and is it a necessary precondition for rational analysis? The answer to the first question, I would argue, is that it is not possible or necessary to formulate a unique, immutable social welfare function to the exclusion of all others on a particular issue, but that governments must continually have a series of 'working' social welfare functions upon which to base policy. As Cutt (1975, p. 226) argues:

We do not imply that there is a uniquely defined social preference function, but simply that for elected government there must be ascertainable, if there is to be meaningful policy analysis, a set of objectives and weights, in a continuing process of adjustment in response to changing government interpretation of public preference, and that the objective of public policy is the optimisation of that objective function. Alternative functions are the stuff of political opposition.

These functions are formulated in an iterative manner, and are subject to continuing reappraisal and modification as their impacts become apparent. At a general level in democratic societies where higher order goals and objectives are 'preference-ranked' by society the political process itself is certainly the mechanism by which individual value judgements are gradually translated into policy decisions. This is most often through representational politics, but also through such activities as lobbying, forming pressure groups, or 'log-rolling'. Here the guiding, if changing, SWF may well be implicit rather than stated.

As policy problems become more specific it may become possible to formulate an explicit objective function based on operationalised programme objectives, as a guide to social improvement through programme achievement ...

A second view is that the issue is not very critical because rational analysis has a valuable role to play in policy making whether or not an explicit social welfare function is identified. Gershuny (1978), for example, argues that even in the absence of a welfare function, rationality serves a valuable purpose in 'vindicating' the selection of particular policies over others to those 'losers' whose value judgements were not necessarily represented in the selected alternative. At one level, vindication constitutes the demonstration that the policy choice is a necessary consequence of the 'winners' value judgements and that there was no other alternative which might better serve the losers' value judgements without damaging the winners' interests. Vindication by rationality at this level promotes consensus in the sense that people accept policy decisions even though they may not agree with them. For example, Labour party members in the UK do not become revolutionaries when the Tories are in power because a rational view suggests that the best available alternative is not revolution, but rather waiting for a future Tory defeat. Rationality can also vindicate in the more specific sense of convincing a group of individuals to pursue some course of action. For example, trade unionists may accept an incomes policy in so far as rational analysis demonstrates to them that they should forego short term wage gain for longer term benefit in the form of less inflation. In addition, rationality may also vindicate in so far as it demonstrates to individuals the greater good of forsaking their particular interests for some larger interest of society. Any willingness on the part of the better-off to see their income redistributed through tax may be a case in point.

Conclusion

In many cases the role of policy analysis in policy making is not to identify the one single, optimal alternative which requires a unique, explicit social welfare function for its identification. Rather the role of policy analysis is to enlighten the policy process from its *particular* perspective, which is not expected to be completely comprehensive. Such enlightenment may take the form of espousing one explicit welfare function over another, based on its particular merits, or it may simply, but importantly, involve exposing new facts and details which fuel political debate. In either case, the possibility of the derivation of a unique social welfare function is not a critical issue for the policy analyst, and a role for rationality in policy analysis is not precluded.

2.3   P. Samuelson

PROBLEMS OF ECONOMIC ORGANIZATION

From *Economics* by P. Samuelson, 1976. Reproduced by permission of the publishers, McGraw-Hill Inc.

Any society, whether it consists of a totally collectivized communistic state, a tribe of South Sea Islanders, a capitalistic industrial nation, a Swiss Family Robinson, a Robinson Crusoe — or, one might almost add, a colony of bees — must somehow confront three fundamental and interdependent economic problems.

1. What commodities shall be produced and in what quantities? That is, how much and which of alternative goods and services shall be produced? Food or clothing? Much food and little clothing, or vice versa? Bread and butter today, or bread and grape plantings today with bread, butter, and jam next year?

2. How shall goods be produced? That is, by whom and with what resources and in what technological manner are they to be produced? Who hunts, who fishes? Electricity from steam or waterfall or atoms? Large- or small-scale production?

3. For Whom shall goods be produced? That is, who is to enjoy and get the benefit of the goods and services provided? Or, to put the same thing in another way, how is the total of national product to be *distributed* among different individuals and families? A few rich and many poor? Or most people in modest comfort?

These three problems are fundamental and common to all economies, but different economic systems try to solve them differently.

Custom, instinct, command, or the market

In a primitive civilization, custom may rule every facet of behavior. What, How, and For Whom may be decided by reference to *traditional* ways of doing things. To members of another culture, the practices followed may seem bizarre and unreasonable; the members of the tribe or clan may themselves be so familiar with existing practices as to be surprised, and perhaps offended, if asked the reason for their behavior. Thus, the Kwakiutl Indians consider it desirable not to accumulate wealth but to give it away in the *potlatch* — a roisterous celebration. This deviation from acquisite behavior toward taking turns at favor giving will not surprise anthropologists; their studies show that what is correct behavior in one culture is often the greatest crime in another.

In the bee colony, all such problems, even those involving an elaborate cooperative division of labor, are solved automatically by means of so-called 'biological instincts'. (Fair enough as a description, but not much of an 'explanation.')

At the other extreme, we can imagine an omnipotent benevolent or malevolent dictator who by arbitrary decree and command decides What, How, and For Whom. Or we might imagine economic organization by command, but with commands drawn up by democratic vote or by delegated legislative authorities.

The What, How, and For Whom questions in a so-called 'capitalist free enterprise economy' are determined primarily[1] by a system of prices (of markets, of profits and losses) ...

Every individual endeavours to employ his capital so that its produce may be of greatest value. He generally neither intends to promote the public interest, nor knows how much he is promoting it. He intends only his own security, only his own gain. And he is in this led by an INVISIBLE HAND to promote an end which was no part of his intention. By pursuing his own interest he frequently promotes that of society more effectually than when he really intends to promote it.
Adam Smith, *The Wealth of Nations* (1776).

How a free enterprise system solves the basic economic problems

In a system of free private enterprise, no individual or organization is *consciously* concerned with the triad of economic problems set forth above as What, How, and For Whom. This fact is really remarkable.

To paraphrase a famous economic example, let us consider the city of New York. Without a constant flow of goods in and out of the city, it would be on the verge of starvation within a week. A variety of the right kinds and amounts of food is required. From the surrounding counties, from 50 states, and from the far corners of the world, goods have been traveling for days and months with New York as their destination.

How is it that 12 million people are able to sleep easily at night, without living in mortal terror of a breakdown in the elaborate economic processes upon which the city's existence depends? For all this is undertaken *without coercion or centralized direction* by any conscious body!

Everyone notices how much the government does to control economic activity — tariff legislation, pure-food laws, utility and railroad regulation, minimum-wage laws, fair-labor-practice acts, social security, price ceilings and floors, public works, national defense, national and local taxation, police protection and judicial redress, zoning ordinances, municipal water or gas works, and so forth. What goes unnoted is how much of economic life proceeds *without* government intervention.

Hundreds of thousands of commodities are produced by millions of people more or less of their own volition and without central direction or master plan.

Not chaos but economic order

This functioning alone is convincing proof that a competitive system of markets and prices — whatever else it may be, however imperfectly it may function — is not a system of chaos and anarchy. There is in it a certain order and orderliness. It works.

A competitive system is an elaborate mechanism for unconscious coordination through a system of prices and markets, a communication device for pooling the knowledge and actions of millions of diverse individuals. Without a central intelligence, it solves one of the most complex problems imaginable, involving thousands of unknown variables and relations. Nobody designed it. It just evolved, and like human nature, it is changing; but it does meet the first test of any social organization — it can survive ...

The Invisible Hand and 'perfect competition'

Students of economics have to avoid the error of thinking that a price mechanism must work chaotically if it is not controlled by somebody. Having learned this lesson, they must not go to the other extreme and become enamored of the beauty of a pricing mechanism, regarding it as perfection itself, the essence of providential harmony, and beyond the touch of human hands.

Adam Smith, whose *The Wealth of Nations* (1776) is the germinal book of modern economics or political economy, was thrilled by the recognition of an order in the economic system. Smith proclaimed the principle of the 'Invisible Hand'; every individual, in pursuing only his own selfish good, was led, as if by an invisible hand, to achieve the best good for all, so that any interference with free competition by government was almost certain to be injurious.

Undoubtedly this was a valuable insight. But, on reflection and after two centuries of experience, we must recognize some of the realistic limitations on this doctrine. The virtues claimed for free enterprise are fully realized only when the complete checks and balances of 'perfect competition' are present.

Perfect competition is defined by the economist as a technical term: 'Perfect competition' exists only in the case where no farmer, businessman, or laborer is a big enough part of the total market to have any personal influence on market price. On the other hand, when his grain, merchandise, or labor is large enough in size to produce appreciable depressing or elevating effects on market prices, some degree of monopolistic imperfection has set in, and the virtues of the Invisible Hand must be that much discounted.

Actually, much of the praise of perfect competition is beside the point. Ours is a mixed system of government and private enterprise and it is also *a mixed system of monopoly and competition* ... The challenge is to work out laws and customs that help to improve the working of our less-than-perfect competitive system. The polar cases — laissez faire and totalitarian dictatorship of production — dramatize economic principles. Yet the relevant choice for policy is not a decision between such extremes, but rather the degree to which public policy should do *less* or *more* to modify the operation of particular private economic activities.

The price system

Just how does the unconscious automatic price mechanism operate? The bare outlines of a *competitive* profit-and-loss system are simple to describe.

Everything has a price — each commodity and each service. Even the different kinds of human labor have prices, namely, wage rates. Everybody receives money for what he sells, and uses this money to buy what he wishes.

If more is wanted of any good — say, shoes — a flood of new orders will be given for it. This will cause its price to rise and more to be produced.

On the other hand, what if more of a commodity — such as tea — becomes available than people want to buy at the last-quoted market price? Then its price will be marked down by competition. At the lower price people will drink more tea, and producers will no longer produce quite so much. Thus, equilibrium of supply and demand will be restored.

What is true of the markets for consumers' goods is also true of markets for *factors of production* such as labor, land, and capital inputs. If welders rather than glassblowers are needed, job opportunities will be more favorable in the welding field. The price of welders, their hourly wage, will tend to rise, while that of glassblowers will tend to fall. Other things being equal, this will cause a shift into the desired occupation. Likewise, an acre of land will go into sugar cultivation if sugar producers bid the most for its use. In the same way, machine-tool production will be determined by supply and demand.

The general-equilibrium system

In other words, we have a vast system of trial and error, of successive approximation to an *equilibrium system of prices and production.* We shall see later that the matching of supply and demand and of prices and costs helps solve our three problems simultaneously. Here are the bare outlines of competitive equilibrium.

1. What things will be produced is determined by the *dollar votes* of consumers — not every 2 or 4 years at the polls, but every day in their decisions to purchase this item and not that. Of course, the money that they pay into business cash registers ultimately provides the payrolls, rents, and dividends that consumers receive in weekly income. Thus the circle is a complete one.

2. How things are produced is determined by the competition of different producers. The method that is cheapest at any one time, because of both physical efficiency and cost efficiency, will displace a more costly method.

The only way for producers to meet price competition and maximize profits is to keep costs at a minimum by adopting the most efficient methods. For example, synthetic rubber will be made from oil rather than alcohol if the price of the one is in a certain relation to the price of the other; or electric power will be generated by steam rather than nuclear power if the price of coal is below some critical level. The large, tractor-operated farm will displace the family-size farm if this leads to lower costs of production ...

3. For Whom things are produced is determined by supply and demand in the markets for productive services: by wage rates, land rents, interest rates, and profits, all of which go to make up everybody's income — relative to everyone else and relative to the whole. (Of course, the character of the resulting distribution of income is highly dependent upon the *initial* distribution of property ownership, upon acquired or inherited abilities, educational opportunities, and presence or absence of racial and sex discriminations.)

Note this: Consumer votes do not by themselves determine What goods are produced. Demand has to meet with a supply of goods; so business cost and supply decisions, along with consumer demand, do help to determine What. Just as a broker may help arrange a match between buyer and seller, the auctioneer in the commodity market acts as the go-between who reconciles the consumer votes and business supplies that impinge on the market. The profit seeker is society's agent to determine How, seeking least factor-costs for producing each good and being punished by ruthless competition if he fails to use best methods.

A picture of prices and markets

... A competitive system is impersonal but not completely so. The consuming families face business enterprises on two fronts, with only prices in between. One front is the widely dispersed one, the retail market on which consumers buy thousands of small items from a score of different retail establishments: grocery, drug, and department stores; movie theaters; gasoline stations; and from electric-power companies, public post offices, landlords, railroad lines, and insurance companies.

On the other front — the market for labor and other productive services — relations are not always so peaceful. To the family breadwinner his wage is not simply another price; it is the difference between luxury and comfort, between comfort and privation. The laborer may feel inferior to the large corporation in bargaining power, and he may turn to collective bargaining through trade-unions. By doing this, he may at times be helping to restore competition, while at other times he may be causing conditions to deviate still further from perfect competition ...

Imperfections of competition

As we said earlier, one drawback to the picture of the price system as described above is the fact that, in the real world, competition is nowhere near 'perfect'. Firms do not know when consumer tastes will change; therefore they may *overproduce* in one field and *underproduce* in another. By the time they are ready to learn from experience, the situation may have changed again. Also, in a competitive system many producers simply do not know the methods of other producers, and costs do not fall to a minimum. In the competitive struggle, one can sometimes succeed as much by *keeping knowledge scarce* as by keeping production high.

The most serious deviation from perfect competition comes from *monopoly elements*. These — as we shall see later on — may result in wrong pricing, creation of distorted patterns of demand by repetitive advertising, incorrect and wasteful resource allocation, and monopoly profits. We shall be reminded again and again how strict is the economist's definition of a 'perfect competitor'. The mere presence of a few rivals is not enough for perfect competition.

Monopoly elements

The economic definition of 'imperfect competitor' is *anyone who buys or sells a good in large enough quantities to be able to affect the price of that good.* To some degree that means almost all businessmen, except possibly the millions of farmers who individually produce a negligible fraction of the total crop. All economic life is a blend of competitive and monopoly elements. Imperfect (monopolistic) competition is the prevailing mode, not perfect competition. A good approximation of perfect competition may be the most society can strive for.

Of course, as we shall later see, a businessman cannot see his prices completely as he pleases and still make profits. He must take into account the prices of goods that are substitutes for his own. Even if he produces a trademarked coal with unique properties, he must reckon with prices charged for other coals, oil, gas, and insulation.

Businessmen, farmers, and workers both like and dislike competition. We all like it when it enables us to expand our market, but we label it as 'chiseling', 'unfair', or 'ruinous' when the knife cuts the other way. The worker whose livelihood depends on how the market prices his labor may be the first to howl when competition threatens to depress wages. Farm groups, aware of what competition can do to agricultural prices, bring pressure on the state to restrict production and thereby raise prices.

In the idealized model of an efficiently acting competitive market mechanism, consumers are supposed to be well informed. They recognize low quality and avoid it; they never buy drugs that turn out to be poisonous or ineffective. Most important, their 'desires' are supposed to represent genuine 'wants' and 'needs' and 'tastes'. But in actual life ... business firms spend much money on advertising to *shape* — and, some insist, *distort* — consumer demands ...

Some of the basic factors responsible for monopoly-creating bigness in business may be *inherent in the economies of large-scale production.* This is especially true in a dynamic world of technological change. Competition by numerous producers would simply not be efficient in many fields and could not last. Trademarks, patents, and advertising are often responsible for still other market imperfections. It would be humanly impossible, therefore, to attempt to create *perfect* competition by law. The problem is one of achieving reasonably effective 'workable competition'.

We shall proceed later to a more microscopic examination of supply and demand. After that discussion we shall be in a position to appraise the workings of the price system more judiciously. A competitive system is one way of organizing an economy, *but not the only way.* Admiration should not inhibit reform. Still, it is of interest that some socialists plan to continue to use a price mechanism as part of their new society. A price system is not perfect, but neither are its alternatives.

Economic role of government

It was said earlier that ours is not a pure price economy but a *mixed economy* in which elements of government control are intermingled with market elements in organizing production and consumption. An outline of government's influence can be briefly indicated here.

Welfare minima

Democracies are not satisfied with the answers to What, How, and For Whom given by a completely unrestrained market system. Such a system, as already said, might dictate that some people starve from lack of income while others get inadequate or excessive incomes.

Therefore the citizenry through their government step in with expenditure to supplement the real or money incomes of some individuals. Thus, governments provide hospital beds for citizens, and monthly allowances for the needy in times of unemployment or old age. Minimum standards of life are widespread modern goals.

Public services and taxes
More than this, government provides certain indispensable *public* services
without which community life would be unthinkable and which by their
nature cannot appropriately be left to private enterprises. Government
came into existence once people realized, 'Everybody's business is nobody's business'. Obvious examples are the maintenance of national
defense and of internal law and order, and the administration of justice
and of contracts.

By and large, in its expenditure of money, government is behaving
exactly like any other large spender. By *casting sufficient votes in the
form of dollar bids* in certain directions, it causes resources to flow there.
The price system then takes over and performs much as if these were
private rather than public needs.

Actually, most government expenditure is paid for out of taxes collected. It is here that an important element of *coercion* enters. It is true
that the citizenry as a whole imposes the tax burden upon itself; also, each
citizen is sharing in the collective benefits of government. But there is not
the same close connection between benefits and tax payments as holds
when the individual citizen puts a dime into a gum machine or makes an
ordinary purchase. I need not smoke Winstons or buy nylon carpeting or
choose fried eggs, but I must pay my share of the taxes used to finance the
various activities of government.

Legal commands
Moreover, a second important form of coercion is involved in the universal
custom of passing governmental laws: thou shalt not sell false weight, thou
shalt not employ child labor, thou shalt not burn houses, thou shalt not
pour out smoke from thy factory chimney, thou shalt not sell or smoke
opium, thou shalt not charge more than the ceiling price for food, and so
forth. This set of rules gives the framework within which private enterprise functions; it also modifies the direction of that functioning. Together
with government expenditure and taxation, *the commands of government*
supplement the price system in determining the economic fate of the
nation ...

The market mechanism

[At the beginning of this extract I introduced the three basic problems
every economy must face: What to produce, How to produce it, and For
Whom shall goods be produced. I indicated that these decisions are taken
in a modern economy by a system of markets and prices. How does it
work?]

Let us take an example. You wake up this morning with an urge for a
new pair of shoes. You would not think of saying, 'I'll go down to the city

hall and vote for the mayor most likely to give me a new pair of shoes. Of course, I mean a new pair of size 9, soft-leather, dark brown shoes'.

Or, to take an actual case from history, suppose men begin to get prosperous enough to afford meat every day and do not have to fill up on potatoes. How does their desire to substitute meat for potatoes get translated into action? What politician do they tell? What orders does he in turn give to farmers to move from Maine to Texas? How much extra rent does he decide will be needed to bribe landlords to transfer land from potato production to cattle grazing? And how does he ensure that people get what they want of pork and lamb as well as beef? And who is to get the choice cuts?

Why belabor the obvious? Everyone knows it never works itself out that way at all. What happens is this. Consumers begin to buy fewer potatoes and more meat. *That raises the price of meat and cuts the price of potatoes.* So there soon results losses to the potato growers and gains to the ranchers. Ranch labor finds it can hold out for higher wages, and many a potato digger quits his job for a better-paying job elsewhere. In time, the higher meat prices coax out larger productions of beef, pork, and lamb. And the different parts of the cow — its horns, hide, liver, kidneys, choice tenderloin, and tough ribs — get auctioned off for what each part will bring ...

The purpose of this part of the chapter is to show how supply and demand work themselves out in the competitive market *for one particular good.* We shall define a demand curve and then a supply curve. Finally, we shall see how the market price reaches its competitive equilibrium where these two curves intersect — where the forces of demand and supply are just in balance.

The demand schedule

Let us start with demand. It is commonly observed: The quantity of a good that people will buy at any one time depends on price; the *higher* the price charged for an article, the *less* the quantity of it people will be willing to buy; and, other things being equal, the lower its market price, the more units of it will be demanded.

Thus there exists at any one time a definite relation between the market price of a good (such as wheat) and the quantity demanded of that good. This relationship between price and quantity bought is called the 'demand schedule', or 'demand curve'.

The table of Fig. 2.3.1 gives an example of a hypothetical demand schedule. At any price, such as $5 per bushel, there is a definite quantity or wheat that will be demanded by all the consumers in the market — in this case 9 (million) bushels per month. At a lower price, such as $4, the

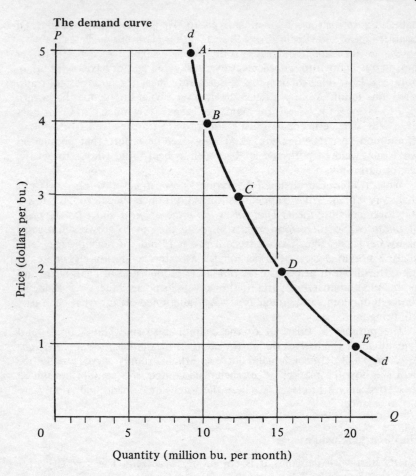

The demand curve

Demand schedule for wheat

	(1) Price ($ per bu.) P	(2) Quantity demanded (million bu. per month) Q
A	$5	9
B	4	10
C	3	12
D	2	15
E	1	20

quantity bought is even greater, being 10 (million) units. At lower P of $3, quantity demanded is even greater still — namely 12 (million). By lowering P enough, we could coax out sales of more than 20 (million) units. From Fig. 2.3.1's table we can determine the *quantity demanded at any price*, by comparing column (2) with column (1).

The demand curve

The numerical data can be given a graphic interpretation also. The vertical scale in Fig. 2.3.1 represents the various alternative prices of wheat, measured in dollars per bushel. The horizontal scale measures the quantity of wheat (in terms of bushels) that will be demanded per month.

A city corner is located as soon as we know its street and avenue, a ship's position is located as soon as we know its latitude and longitude. Similarly, to plot a point on this diagram, we must have two coordinate numbers: a price and a quantity. For our first point A, corresponding to $5 and 9 million bushels, we move upward 5 units and then over to the right 9 units. A dot marks the spot A. To get the next dot, at B, we go up only 4 units and over to the right 10 units. The last dot is shown by E. Through the dots we draw a smooth curve, marked *dd*.

This picturization of the demand schedule is called the 'demand curve'. Note that quantity and price are *inversely* related, Q going up when P goes down. The curve slopes downward, going from northwest to southeast. This important property is given a name: the *law of downward-sloping demand*. This law is true of practically all commodities: wheat, electric razors, cotton, Kellogg's cornflakes, and theater tickets.

The law of downward-sloping demand: When the price of a good is raised (at the same time that all other things are held constant), less of it is demanded. Or, what is the same thing: If a greater quantity of a good is put on the market, then — other things being equal — it can be sold only at a lower price.

Fig. 2.3.1 (opposite)   A downward-sloping demand curve relates quantity to price. At each market price there will be at any time a definite quantity of wheat that people will want to demand. At a lower price the quantity demanded will go up — as more people substitute it for other goods and feel they can afford to gratify their less important wants for wheat. Compare tables Q and P at A, B, C, D, E. In the figure prices are measured on the vertical axis and quantities demanded on the horizontal axis. Each pair of Q, P numbers from the table is plotted here as a point, and a smooth curve passed through the points gives us the demand curve. The fact that *dd* goes downward and to the right illustrates the very important 'law of downward-sloping demand'.

Reasons for the law of downward-sloping demand

This law is in accordance with common sense and has been known in at least a vague way since the beginning of recorded history. The reasons for it are not hard to identify. When the price of wheat is sky-high, only rich men will be able to afford it; the poor will have to make do with coarse rye bread, just as they still must do in poorer lands. When the price is still high but not quite so high as before, persons of moderate means who also happen to have an especially great liking for white bread will now be coaxed into buying some wheat.

Thus a first reason for the validity of the law of downward-sloping demand comes from the fact that *lowering prices brings in new buyers.*

Not quite so obvious is a second, equally important, reason for the law's validity; namely, each reduction of price may coax out some *extra purchases by each of the good's consumers*; and — what is the same thing — a rise in price may cause any of us to buy less. Why does my quantity demanded tend to fall as price rises? For two main reasons. When the price of a good rises, I naturally try to *substitute* other goods for it (for example, rye for wheat or tea for coffee). Also, when a price goes up, I find myself really poorer than I was before; and I will naturally cut down on my consumption of most normal goods when I feel poorer and have less real *income.*

Here are further examples of cases where I buy more of a good as it becomes more plentiful and its price drops. When water is very dear, I demand only enough of it to drink. Then when its price drops, I buy some to wash with. At still lower prices, I resort to still other uses; finally, when it is really very cheap, I water flowers and use it lavishly for any possible purpose. (Note once again that someone poorer than I will probably begin to use water to wash his car only at a lower price than that at which I buy water for that purpose. Since market demand is the sum of all different people's demands, what does this mean? It means that even after *my* quantity demanded stops expanding very much with price decreases, the *total* bought in the market may still expand as new uses for new people come into effect.)

To confirm your understanding of the demand concept, imagine that there is an increase in demand for wheat brought about by a boom in people's incomes or by a great rise in the market price of competing corn, or simply by a change in people's tastes in favor of wheat. Show that this *shifts* the whole demand curve in Fig. 2.3.1 rightward, and hence upward; pencil in such a new curve and label it *d'd'* to distinguish it from the old *dd* curve. Note that such an increase in demand means that more will now be bought at each price — as can be verified by carefully reading off points from the new curve and filling in a new *Q* column for Fig. 2.3.1's table.

The supply schedule

Let us now turn from demand to supply. The demand schedule related
market prices and the amounts *consumers* wish to buy. How is the 'supply
schedule' defined?

By the *supply schedule*, or *curve*, is meant the relation between market
prices and the amounts of the good that *producers* are willing to supply.

The table of Fig. 2.3.2 illustrates the supply schedule for wheat, and
the diagram plots it as a supply curve. Unlike the falling demand curve,
the *ss* supply curve for wheat *normally rises upward* and to the right, from
southwest to northeast.

At a higher price of wheat, farmers will take acres out of corn cultivation
and put them into wheat. In addition, each farmer can now afford the cost
of more fertilizer, more labor, more machinery, and can now even afford
to grow extra wheat on poorer land. All this tends to increase output at
the higher prices offered.

The law of diminishing returns provides one strong reason why the
supply curve would slope upward. If society wants more wine, then more
and more labor will have to be added to the same limited hill sites suitable
for producing wine grapes. Even if this industry is too small to affect the
general wage rate, each new man will — according to the law of diminishing
returns — be adding less and less extra product; and hence the necessary
cost to coax out additional product will have to rise.

How shall we depict an increase in supply? An increase in supply means
an increase in the amounts that will be supplied *at each different price*.
Now if you pencil the new supply curve into Fig. 2.3.2 you will see that it
has shifted *rightward*; but for an upward-sloping supply curve, this change
means the new *s's'* curve will have shifted rightward and *downward* (not
rightward and upward as in the case of a shifted downward-sloping
demand curve). To verify that *s's'* does depict an increase in supply, fill
in a new column in the table by reading off points from your new diagram
carefully.

Equilibrium of supply and demand

Let us now combine our analysis of demand and supply to see how competitive market price is determined. This is done in Fig. 2.3.3's table. Thus
far, we have been considering all prices as possible. We have said, 'If price
is so and so, *Q* sales will be so and so; if *P* is such and such, *Q* will be such
and such; and so forth'. But to which level will price *actually* go? And how
much will then be produced and consumed? The supply schedule alone
cannot tell us. Neither can the demand schedule alone.

Let us do what an auctioneer would do, i.e. proceed by trial and error.

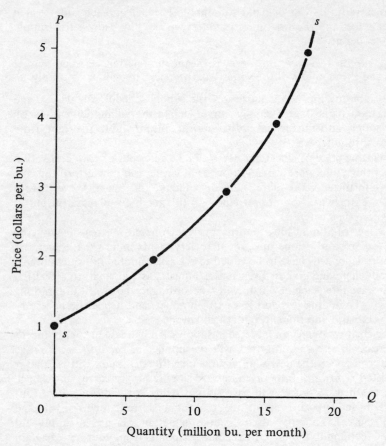

Supply curve for wheat

Supply schedule for wheat

	(1) Possible prices ($ per bu.) P	(2) Quantity sellers will supply (million bu. per month) Q
A	$5	18
B	4	16
C	3	12
D	2	7
E	1	0

Can situation *A* in the table, with wheat selling for $5 per bushel, prevail for any period of time? The answer is a clear 'No'. At $5, the producers will be supplying 18 (million) bushels to the market every month [Column (3)]. But the amount demanded by consumers will be only 9 (million) bushels per month [Column (2)]. *As stocks of wheat pile up, competitive sellers will cut the price a little.* Thus, as Column (4) shows, price will tend to fall downward. But it will not fall indefinitely to zero.

To understand this better, let us try the point *E* with price of only $1 per bushel. Can that price persist? Again, obviously not − for a comparison of Columns (2) and (3) shows that consumption will exceed production *at that price.* Storehouses will begin to empty, *disappointed demanders who can't get wheat will tend to bid up the too-low price.* This upward pressure on *P* is shown by Column (4)'s rising arrow.

We could go on to try other prices, but by now the answer is obvious:

The equilibrium price, i.e., the only price that can last, is that at which the amount *willingly* supplied and amount *willingly* demanded are equal. Competitive equilibrium must be *at the intersection point* of supply and demand curves.

Only at *C*, with a price of $3, will the amount demanded by consumers, 12 (million) bushels per month, exactly equal the amount supplied by producers, 12 (million). Price is at equilibrium, just as an olive at the bottom of a cocktail glass is at equilibrium, because there is no tendency for it to rise or fall. (Of course, this stationary price may not be reached at once. There may have to be an initial period of trial and error, of oscillation around the right level, before price finally settles down in balance.)

Fig. 2.3.3's diagram shows the same equilibrium in pictorial form. The supply and demand curves, superimposed on the same diagram, cross at only one intersection point. This point *C* represents the equilibrium price and quantity.

At a higher price, the bar shows the *excess* of amount supplied over amount demanded. The arrows point downward to show the direction in which price will move because of the competition of excess *sellers.* At a price lower than the $3 equilibrium price, the bar shows that amount demanded exceeds amount supplied. Consequently, the eager bidding of excess *buyers* requires us to point the arrow indicators upward to show the pressure that they are exerting on price. Only at the point *C* will there

---

Fig. 2.3.2 (opposite) The supply curve relates price to the quantity produced. The table lists, for each price, the quantity that producers will want to bring to the market. The diagram plots the (*P, Q*) pairs of numbers taken from the table as the indicated points. A smooth curve passed through these points gives the upward-sloping supply curve, *ss*.

**How supply and demand determine
market price and quantity**

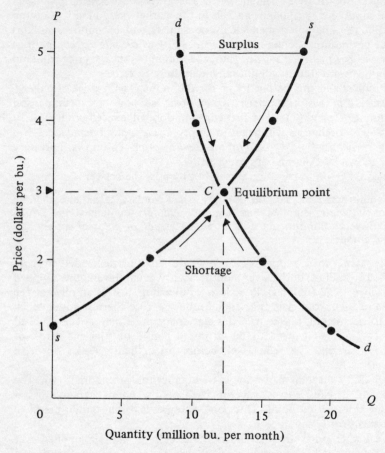

Quantity (million bu. per month)

Supply and demand schedules for wheat

	(1) Possible prices ($ per bu.)	(2) Quantity demanded (million bu. per month)	(3) Quantity supplied (million bu. per (month)	(4) Pressure on price
A	$5	9	18	Downward
B	4	10	16	Downward
C	3	12	12	**Neutral**
D	2	15	7	Upward
E	1	20	0	Upward

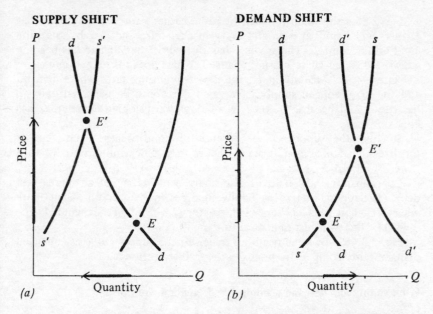

SUPPLY SHIFT   DEMAND SHIFT

Fig. 2.3.4. When either supply or demand curve shifts, equilibrium price changes:
(a) If supply shifts leftward for any reason, the equilibrium-price intersection will travel up the demand curve, giving higher *P* and lower *Q*.
(b) If demand increases the equilibrium will travel up the supply curve.

there be a balancing of forces and a stationary maintainable price.

Such is the essence of the doctrine of supply and demand.

Effect of a shift in supply or demand

Now we can put the supply-and-demand apparatus to work. Gregory King, an English writer of the seventeenth century, noticed that when the harvest was bad, food rose in price; and when it was plentiful, farmers got a lower price. Let us try to explain this common-sense fact by what happens in our diagrams.

Fig. 2.3.3 (opposite) Equilibrium price is at the intersection point where supply and demand match. Only at the equilibrium price of $3, shown in the third row, will the amount supplied just match the amount demanded. In the diagram, at the *C* equilibrium intersection the amount supplied just matches the amount demanded. At any lower *P*, the excess amount demanded will force *P* back up; and at any *P* higher than the equilibrium, *P* will be forced back down to it.

Fig. 2.3.4a shows how a spell of bad weather *reduces* the amount that farmers will supply at each and every market price and thereby raises the equilibrium point *E*. The *ss* curve has shifted to the left and has become *s's'*. The demand curve has not changed. Where does the new supply curve *s's'* intersect *dd*? Plainly at *E'*, the new equilibrium price where demand and the new reduced supply have again come into balance. Naturally, *P* has risen. And because of the law of downward-sloping demand, *Q* has gone down.

Suppose the supply curve, because of good weather and cheaper fertilizers, had *increased*, instead. Draw in a new equilibrium *E''* with lower *P* and higher *Q*.

Our apparatus will help us also analyze the effect of an increase in demand. Suppose that rising family incomes make everyone want more wheat. Then at each unchanged *P*, greater *Q* will now be demanded. The demand curve will shift rightward to *d'd'*.

Fig. 2.3.4b shows the resulting travel up the supply curve as enhanced demand raises competitive price (to the *E'* intersection) ...

What supply and demand accomplished: general equilibrium

Having seen how supply and demand work, let us take stock of what has been accomplished. The scarce goods of society have been rationed out among the possible users of them. Who did the rationing: a board? a committee? No. The auctioneering mechanism of competitive market price did the rationing. It was a case of 'rationing by the purse'.

For Whom goods are destined was *partially* determined by who was willing to pay for them. If you had the money votes, you got the wheat. If you did not, you went without. Or if you had the money votes, but preferred not to spend them on wheat, you did without. The most important needs or desires for goods — if backed by cash! — got fulfilled.

The What question was being *partially* answered at the same time. The rise in market price was the signal to coax out a higher supply of wheat — the signal for other scarce resources to move into the wheat-production industry from alternative uses.

Even the How question was being *partially* decided in the background. For with wheat prices now high, farmers could afford expensive tractors and fertilizers and could bring poorer soils into use.

Why the word 'partially' in this description of how the competitive market helped solve the three problems? Because this wheat market is but one market of many. What is happening in the corn and rye markets also counts; and what is happening in the market for fertilizer, men, and tractors obviously matters much.

We must note that the pricing problem is one that involves *interdependent markets*, not just the 'partial equilibrium' of a single market.

There are, so to speak, auctioneers operating simultaneously in the many different markets — wheat, rye, corn, fertilizer, and land; labor, wool, cotton, mutton, and rayon; bonds, stocks, personal loans, and foreign exchange in the form of English pounds or German marks. Each ends up at the equilibrium intersection point of his supply and demand schedules — wheat, rye, corn, fertilizer prices, and land rent; labor wage, wool, cotton, mutton, and rayon prices; bond price and its interest yield, stock prices and dividend yield, interest charges on personal loans, an exchange rate of \$2.43 per pound or $3\frac{1}{8}$ marks to the dollar.

No market is an island unto itself: when wool P rises (because, say, of sheep disease abroad), it pulls up the Ps of domestic labor, fertilizer, and land needed for expanded domestic wool output; and it raises the Ps of rival goods like cotton that some demanders will now turn to; and it might well lower the P of wool spinners and of suit-company stock shares, since the latter must now pay more for their raw materials and must bid less eagerly for spinning labor.

The new 'general-equilibrium set of interdependent prices' adjusts to the new situation. The price system meets the problem posed by the basic definition of economics: the study of (1) how *scarce means with alternative uses* — limited land and labor that can be switched from one industry to another — are allocated, and of (2) how to *achieve ends or goals* — as prescribed by the tastes for wool, nylon, food, and housing of sovereign consumers, possessed of factors or production that give them money-income votes for the marketplace. Each separate market, with its supply and demand curves, is doing its bit toward creating the general-equilibrium set of prices, which in a mixed economy largely resolves the basic economic problems of What, How, and For Whom.

Perfection and imperfections of competition

Our curves of supply and demand strictly apply only to a *perfectly competitive* market where some kind of *standardized* commodity such as wheat is being auctioned by an organized exchange that registers transactions of *numerous* buyers and sellers.

The Board of Trade in Chicago is one such example, and the cotton exchanges in New York or Liverpool are others. The New York Stock Exchange, while it does not auction goods and commodities or productive services rendered by factors of production, does provide a market where shares of common stocks such as those of General Motors and Royal Dutch Petroleum are auctioned at each moment of the working day. Many corporate bonds are also bought and sold in its bond division.

The economists' curves of supply and demand are important ways of *idealizing* the behavior of such markets. The curves do not pretend to give an accurate microscopic description of what is going on during each

changing moment in such a marketplace, as various brokers mill around on
the trading floor while frantically giving hand and voice signals to the
specialist who serves as auctioneer for each grain or company stock. None
the less, the tools of supply and demand to summarize the important
average relationships resulting over a period of time from such organized
trading ...

Perfection of competition as a limiting pole
Needless to say, the requirements for absolutely perfect competition are as
hard to meet as the requirements for a perfectly frictionless pendulum in
physics. We can approach closer and closer to perfection, but can never
quite reach it. Yet this fact need not do serious damage to the usefulness
of our employing the idealized concept. Actually, it matters little to the
economic scientist that different grades of wheat will call for slight
variations from the quoted market prices. Nor does it matter in the case of
standardized cotton goods, so-called 'gray goods', that they are sold and
bought in an informal way by many competing firms: so long as there are
numerous buyers and sellers on each side, *well informed* about quality and
about each other's prices and having no reason to discriminate in favor of
one merchant rather than another and no reason to expect that variations
in their *own* bids and offers will have an *appreciable effect* upon the
prevailing market price — so long as all this is true, the behavior of price
and quantity can be expected to be much like that predicted by our supply
and demand curves.

Note

1   There never was a 100 per cent purely automatic enterprise system,
    although Victorian England came close. Certainly in present-day
    systems, the government has an important role in modifying the
    workings of the price system. This is what is meant by saying we live
    in a 'mixed economy'.

2.4   H. A. Simon

FROM SUBSTANTIVE TO PROCEDURAL RATIONALITY

From *Method and Appraisal in Economics* ed. S.J. Latsis, published by Cambridge University Press, 1976.

1. Substantive rationality

Behavior is substantively rational when it is appropriate to the achievement of given goals within the limits imposed by given conditions and constraints. Notice that, by this definition, the rationality of behavior depends upon the actor in only a single respect – his goals. Given these goals, the rational behavior is determined entirely by the characteristics of the environment in which it takes place.

Suppose, for example, that the problem is to minimize the cost of a nutritionally adequate diet, where nutritional adequacy is defined in terms of minimum intakes of certain proteins, vitamins, and minerals, and minimum and maximum intakes of calories, and where the unit prices and compositions of the obtainable foods are specified. This diet problem can be (and has been) formulated as a straightforward linear-programming problem, and the correct solution found by computational procedures. Given the goal of minimizing cost and the definition of 'nutritionally adequate', there are no two ways about it – there is only one substantively rational solution.

Classical economic analysis rests on two fundamental assumptions. The first assumption is that the economic actor has a particular goal, for example, utility maximization [see Introduction to this section] or profit maximization. The second assumption is that the economic actor is substantively rational. Given these two assumptions, and given a description of a particular economic environment, economic analysis (descriptive or normative) could usually be carried out using such standard tools as the differential calculus, linear programming or dynamic programming.

Thus, the assumptions of utility or profit maximization, on the one hand, and the assumption of substantive rationality, on the other, freed economics from any dependence upon psychology. As long as these assumptions went unchallenged, there was no reason why an economist should acquaint himself with the psychological literature on human cognitive processes or human choice. There was absolutely no point at which the findings of psychological research could be injected into the process of economic analysis. The irrelevance of psychology to economics was complete.

2. Procedural rationality

Behavior is procedurally rational when it is the outcome of appropriate deliberation. Its procedural rationality depends on the process that generated it. When psychologists use the term 'rational', it is usually procedural rationality they have in mind. William James, for example, in his *Principles of Psychology* (James 1890), uses 'rationality' as synonymous with 'the peculiar thinking process called reasoning'. Conversely, behavior tends to be described as 'irrational' in psychology when it represents impulsive response to emotional mechanisms without an adequate intervention of thought.

Perhaps because 'rationality' resembles 'rationalism' too closely, and because psychology's primary concern is with process rather than outcome, psychologists tend to use phrases like 'cognitive processes' and 'intellective processes' when they write about rationality in behavior. This shift in terminology may have contributed further to the mutual isolation of the concepts of substantive and procedural rationality.

(a) The study of cognitive processes

The process of rational calculation is only interesting when it is nontrivial — that is, when the substantively rational response to a situation is not instantly obvious. If you put a 50p piece and a 10p piece before a subject and tell him that he may have either one, but not both, it is easy to predict which he will choose, but not easy to learn anything about his cognitive processes. Hence, procedural rationality is usually studied in problem situations — situations in which the subject must gather information of various kinds and process it in different ways in order to arrive at a reasonable course of action, a solution to the problem.

Historically, there have been three main categories of psychological research on cognitive processes: learning, problem solving, and concept attainment. Learning research is concerned with the ways in which information is extracted from one problem situation and stored in such a way as to facilitate the solving of similar problems subsequently. Problem-solving research (in this narrower sense) focuses especially upon the complementary roles of trial-and-error procedures and insight in reaching problem solutions. Concept attainment research is concerned with the ways in which rules or generalizations are extracted from a sequence of situations and used to predict subsequent situations. Only in recent years, particularly since the Second World War, has there been much unification of theory emerging from these three broad lines of research.

(b) Computational efficiency

Let us return for a moment to the optimal diet problem which we used to illustrate the concept of substantive rationality. From a procedural standpoint, our interest would lie not in the problem solution — the prescribed diet itself — but in the method used to discover it. At first blush, this appears to be more a problem in computational mathematics than in psychology. But that appearance is deceptive.

What is the task of computational mathematics? It is to discover the relative efficiencies of different computational processes for solving problems of various kinds. Underlying any question of computational efficiency is a set of assumptions about the capabilities of the computing system. For an omniscient being, there are no questions of computational efficiency, because the consequences of any mathematical statements are known as soon as the premises are stated; and computation is simply the spinning out of such consequences.

Nowadays, when we are concerned with computational efficiency, we are concerned with the computing time or effort that would be required to solve a problem by a system, basically serial in operation, requiring certain irreducible times to perform an addition, a multiplication, and a few other primitive operations. To compare the simplex method with some other method for solving linear programming problems, we seek to determine how much total computing time each method would need.

The search for computational efficiency is a search for procedural rationality, and computational mathematics is a normative theory of such rationality. In this normative theory, there is no point in prescribing a particular substantively rational solution if there exists no procedure for finding that solution with an acceptable amount of computing effort. So, for example, although there exist optimal (substantively rational) solutions for [combinatorial] problems of the travelling-salesman type,[1] and although these solutions can be discovered by a finite enumeration of alternatives, actual computation of the optimum is infeasible for problems of any size and complexity. The combinatorial explosion of such problems simply outraces the capacities of computers, present and prospective.

Hence, a theory of rationality for problems like the travelling-salesman problem is not a theory of best solutions — of substantive rationality — but a theory of efficient computational procedures to find good solutions — a theory of procedural rationality. Notice that this change in viewpoint involves not only a shift from the substantive to the procedural, but a shift also from concern for optimal solutions to a concern for good solutions. I shall discuss this point later.

(c) Computation: risky decisions

But now it is time to return to psychology and its concern with computational efficiency. Man, viewed as a thinker, is a system for processing information. What are his procedures for rational choice?

One method of testing a theory of human rational choice is to study choice behavior in relatively simple and well-structured laboratory situations where the theory makes specific predictions about how subjects will behave. This method has been used by a number of investigators ... to test whether human decisions in the face of uncertainty and risk can be explained by the normative concepts of statistical decision theory. This question is particularly interesting because these norms are closely allied, both historically and logically, to the notions of substantive rationality that have prevailed in economics, and make no concessions to computational difficulties – they never choose the computable second-best over the non-computable best.

Time does not permit me to review the extensive literature that this line of inquiry has produced. A review by Rapaport and Wallsten (1972) covers experimental tests of SEU (subjective expected utility) maximization of Bayesian strategies for sequential decisions [see Introduction to this section], and of other models of rational choice under uncertainty. I think the evidence can be fairly summarized by the statements (i) that it is possible to construct gambles sufficiently simple and transparent that most subjects will respond to them in a manner consistent with SEU theory; but (ii) the smallest departures from this simplicity and transparency produce behavior in many or most subjects that *cannot* be explained by SEU or Bayesian models ... I will illustrate this statement by examples, which I hope are not atypical.

The first is the phenomenon of event matching (Feldman, 1963). Suppose that you present a subject with a random sequence of X's and 0's, of which 70 per cent are X's and 30 per cent 0's. You ask the subject to predict the next symbol, rewarding him for the number of correct predictions. 'Obviously' the rational behavior is always to predict X. This is what subjects almost never do. Instead, they act as though the sequence were patterned, not random, and guess by trying to extrapolate the pattern. This kind of guessing will lead X to be guessed in proportion to the frequency with which it occurs in the sequence. As a result, the sequence of guesses has about the same statistical properties as the original sequence, but the prediction accuracy is lower than if X had been predicted each time (58 per cent instead of 70 per cent) ...

(d) Man's computational efficiency

If these laboratory demonstrations of human failure to follow the canons of substantive rationality in choice under uncertainty caused any surprise to economists (and I do not know that they did), they certainly did not to experimental psychologists familiar with human information processing capabilities.

Like a modern digital computer's, Man's equipment for thinking is basically serial in organization. That is to say, one step in thought follows another, and solving a problem requires the execution of a large number of steps in sequence. The speed of his elementary processes, especially arithmetic processes, is much slower, of course, than those of a computer, but there is much reason to think that the basic repertoire of processes in the two systems is quite similar. Man and computer can both recognize symbols (patterns), store symbols, copy symbols, compare symbols for identity, and output symbols. These processes seem to be the fundamental components of thinking as they are of computation.

For most problems that Man encounters in the real world, no procedure that he can carry out with his information processing equipment will enable him to discover the optimal solution, even when the notion of 'optimum' is well defined. There is no logical reason why this need be so; it is simply a rather obvious empirical fact about the world we live in – a fact about the relation between the enormous complexity of that world and the modest information-processing capabilities with which Man is endowed. One reason why computers have been so important to Man is that they enlarge a little bit the realm within which his computational powers can match the complexity of the problems. But as the example of the travelling-salesman problem shows, even with the help of the computer, Man soon finds himself outside the area of computable substantive rationality.

The problem space associated with the game of chess is very much smaller than the space associated with the game of life. Yet substantive rationality has so far proved unachievable, both for Man and computer, even in chess. Chess books are full of norms for rational play, but except for catalogues of opening moves, these are procedural rules: how to detect the significant features of a position, what computations to make on these features, how to select plausible moves for dynamic search, and so on.

The psychology of chess-playing now has a considerable literature ... These studies have told us a great deal about the thought processes of an expert chessplayer. First, they have shown how he compensates for his limited computational capacity by searching very selectively through the immense tree of move possibilities, seldom considering as many as 100 branches before making a move. Second, they have shown how he stores in long-term memory a large collection of common patterns of pieces, together with procedures for exploiting the relations that appear in these patterns. The expert chess player's heuristics [see Introduction to this section] for selective search and his encyclopedic knowledge of significant patterns are at the core of his procedural rationality in selecting a chess move. Third, the studies have shown how a player forms and modifies his aspirations for a position, so that he can decide when a particular move is 'good enough' (satisfices), and can end his search.

Chess is not an isolated example. There is now a large body of data describing human behavior in other problem situations of comparable complexity. All of the data point in the same direction, and provide essentially the same descriptions of the procedures men use to deal with situations where they are not able to compute an optimum. In all these situations, they use selective heuristics and means—end analysis to explore a small number of promising alternatives. They draw heavily upon past experience to detect the important features of the situation before them, features which are associated in memory with possibly relevant actions. They depend upon aspiration-like mechanisms to terminate search when a satisfactory alternative has been found ...

Contrast this picture of thought processes with the notion of rationality in the classical theory of the firm in its simplest form. The theory assumes that there is given, in addition to the goal of profit maximization, a demand schedule and a cost curve. The theory then consists of a characterization of the substantively rational production decision: for example, that the production quantity is set at the level where marginal cost, calculated from the cost curve, equals marginal revenue, calculated from the demand schedule [see Chapter 2.3 and the Introduction to this section]. The question of whether data are obtainable for estimating these quantities or the demand and cost functions on which they are based is outside the purview of the theory. If the actual demand and cost curves are given, the actual calculation of the optimum is trivial. This portion of economic theory certainly has nothing to do with procedural rationality.

3. Economics' concern with procedural rationality

While economics has traditionally concerned itself with substantive rationality, there has been a noticeable trend, since the Second World War, toward concern also with procedural rationality. This trend has been brought about by a number of more or less independent developments.

(a) The real world of business and public policy
The first of these developments, which predated the war to some extent, was increasing contact of academic economists with real-world business environments. An early and important product was the 1939 Hall and Hitch paper 'Price theory and business behavior', which advanced the heretical proposition that prices are often determined by applying a fixed mark-up to average direct cost rather than by equating them with marginal cost. [See Chapter 2.3 and the Introduction to this section.]

I am not concerned here to determine whether Hitch and Hall, or others who have made similar observations, were right or wrong. My point is that first-hand contact with business operations leads to observation of the procedures that are used in reaching decisions, and not simply the final outcomes. Independently of whether the decision processes have any importance for the questions to which classical economics has addressed itself, the phenomena of problem solving and decision-making cannot help but excite the interest of anyone with intellectual curiosity who encounters them. They represent a fascinating and important domain of human behavior, which any scientist will wish to describe and explain.

In the United States, in the decade immediately after the Second World War, a number of large corporations invited small groups of academic economists to spend periods of a month or more as 'interns' and observers in their corporate offices. Many young economists had their first opportunity, in this way, to try their hands at applying the tools of economic theory to the decisions of a factory department, or a regional sales office.

They found that businessmen did not need to be advised to 'set marginal cost equal to marginal revenue'. Substantive norms of profit maximization helped real decisions only to the extent that appropriate problem-solving procedures could be devised to implement them. What businessmen needed — from anyone who could supply it — was help in inventing and constructing such procedures, including the means for generating the necessary data. How could the marginal productivity of Research and Development expenditures be measured? Or of advertising expenditures? And if they could not be, what would be reasonable procedures for fixing these quantities? These — and not abstract questions of profit maximization in a simplified model of the firm — were the questions businessmen wrestled with in their decisions ...

(b) Imperfect competition [see Chapter 2.3]
More than a century ago, Cournot identified a problem that has become the permanent and ineradicable scandal of economic theory. He observed that where a market is supplied by only a few producers, the notion of profit-maximization is ill-defined. The choice that would be substantively rational for each actor depends on the choices made by the other actors; none can choose without making assumptions about how others will choose.

Cournot proposed a particular solution for the problem, which amounted to an assumption about the *procedure* each actor would follow: each would observe the quantities being produced by his competitors, and would assume these quantities to be fixed in his own calculations. The Cournot solution has often been challenged, and many alternative solutions have been proposed — conjectural variations, the kinky demand curve, market leadership, and others. All of them rest on postulates about the decision process, in particular, about the information each decision-maker will take into account, and the assumptions he will make about the reactions of the others to his behavior.

I have referred to the theory of imperfect competition as a 'scandal' because it has been treated as such in economics, and because it is generally conceded that no defensible formulation of the theory stays within the framework of profit maximization and substantive rationality ...

If perfect competition were the rule in the markets of our modern economy, and imperfect competition and oligopoly rare exceptions, the scandal might be ignored. Every family, after all, has some distant relative it would prefer to forget. But imperfect competition is not a 'distant relative', it is the characteristic form of market structure in a large part of the industries in our economy.

In the literature on oligopoly and imperfect competition one can trace a gradual movement toward more and more explicit concern with the processes used to reach decisions, even to the point — unusual in most other areas of economics — of trying to obtain empirical data about these processes. There remains, however, a lingering reluctance to acknowledge the impossibility of discovering at last 'The Rule' of substantively rational behavior for the oligopolist. Only when the hope of that discovery has been finally extinguished will it be admitted that understanding imperfect competition means understanding procedural rationality ...

For example, under conditions of imperfect competition, one can perhaps speak of the procedural rationality of an investment strategy, but surely not of its substantive rationality. At most, the statistical studies of investment behavior show that some business firms relate their investments to output; they do not show that such behavior is predictable from an objective theory of profit maximization. (And if that is what is being demonstrated, what is the advantage of doing it by means of elaborate statistical studies of public data, rather than by making inquiries or observations of the actual decision processes in the firms themselves?)

(c) Expectations and uncertainty
Making guesses about the behavior of a competitor in an oligopolistic industry is simply a special case of forming expectations in order to make decisions under uncertainty. As economics has moved from statics to dynamics — to business cycle theory, growth theory, dynamic investment theory, theory of innovation and technological change — it has become more and more explicit in its treatment of uncertainty.

Uncertainty, however, exists not in the outside world, but in the eye and mind of the beholder ... We are concerned with how men behave rationally in a world where they are often unable to predict the relevant future with accuracy. In such a world, their ignorance of the future prevents them from behaving in a substantively rational manner; they can only adopt a rational choice procedure, including a rational procedure for forecasting or otherwise adapting to the future ...

Once we become interested in the procedures — the rational processes — that economic actors use to cope with uncertainty, we must broaden our horizons further. Uncertainty not only calls forth forecasting procedures; it also calls forth a whole range of actions to reduce uncertainty, or at least to make outcomes less dependent upon it. These actions are of at least four kinds:

(i) intelligence actions to improve the data on which forecasts are based, to obtain new data, and to improve the forecasting models;

(ii) actions to buffer the effects of forecast errors: holding inventories, insuring, and hedging, for example;

(iii) actions to reduce the sensitivity of outcomes to the behavior of competitors: steps to increase product and market differentiation, for example;

(iv) actions to enlarge the range of alternatives whenever the perceived alternatives involve high risk.

A theory of rational choice in the face of uncertainty will have to encompass not only the topic of forecasting, but these other topics as well. Moreover, it will have to say something about the circumstances under which people will (or should) pursue one or the other of these lines of action.

Confronting a list of contingencies of this sort fills many economists with malaise. How can a unique answer be found to the problem of choice if all of these considerations enter it? How much more attractive is classical economics, in allowing strong conclusions to be drawn from a few *a priori* assumptions, with little need for empirical observation!

Alas, we must take the world as it is. As economics becomes more concerned with procedural rationality, it will necessarily have to borrow from psychology or build for itself a far more complete theory of human cognitive processes than it has had in the past. Even if our interest lies in normative rather than descriptive economics [see the General Introduction], we will need such a theory. There are still many areas of decision — particularly those that are illustrated — where human cognitive processes are more effective than the best available optimization techniques or artificial intelligence methods. Every Class A chessplayer plays a far better game than any existing chessplaying computer program. A great deal can still be learned about effective decision procedures by studying how humans make choices.

The human mind is programmable: it can acquire an enormous variety of different skills, behavior patterns, problem-solving repertoires, and perceptual habits. Which of these it will acquire in any particular case is a function of what it has been taught and what it has experienced. We can expect substantive rationality only in situations that are sufficiently simple as to be transparent to this mind. In all other situations, we must expect that the mind will use such imperfect information as it has, will simplify and represent the situation as it can, and will make such calculations as are within its powers. We cannot expect to predict what it will do in such situations unless we know what information it has, what forms of representation it prefers, and what [calculation rules] are available to it.

There seems to be no escape. If economics is to deal with uncertainty, it will have to understand how human beings in fact behave in the face of uncertainty, and by what limits of information and computability they are bound.

Note

1   The salesman has to combine or sequence his calls in such a way as to minimise the total distance travelled. As the number of calls increases, the complexity of the problem mounts disproportionately. There is not thought to be any single 'best' solution. (*eds.*)

2.5   B. Barry

THE DECISION TO VOTE

From *Sociologists, Economists and Democracy* by B. Barry, published by Macmillan Collier Ltd, 1970.

1 The decision to vote: Downs and Riker

Let us begin by examining the 'economic' approach to a simple question: why do people involve themselves in political activity? There are three advantages in studying this question. First, it is hardly possible to deny its importance for the understanding of politics. Second, an 'economic' style of analysis is able to show that the question is not as easy to answer as one might at first glance suppose, and that some answers which appeal to common sense are fallacious. Thus, the power of the 'economic' approach to clarify thought can be illustrated, even though its claims to produce interesting deductions that are also true must be judged more dubious. And, third, in following the attempts of economic theorists to answer the question 'why participate?', we can see in a relatively clear form some of the conceptual difficulties about the definition and scope of the 'economic' approach that have up to this point been skated over.

Two treatments of the question will be discussed in this chapter: first, Anthony Downs's analysis of the decision to vote (as against not voting) in his book *An Economic Theory of Democracy* (1957), and then Mancur Olson's more general theory of rational participation in 'collective action', as set out in his book, *The Logic of Collective Action* (1965) ...

Downs constructs a theory of politics in which there are, basically, only two kinds of actor. There are the parties, and there are the voters ... There is a clear analogy with the conception of the profit-maximising entrepreneur of classical economic theory. The voters correspond to the consumers. But, whereas there is not much point in asking why consumers do *anything* with their money (as against throwing it away), it is a perfectly serious question why voters should use their vote.[1] For one has to make some effort in order to cast a vote, yet what is the benefit to be derived from so doing? If we wish to apply an 'economic' analysis, an obvious line to take is that with which Downs begins: the value of voting is the value of the expected effect it would have in changing what would otherwise happen.

But what are the components of this calculation? When there are only two parties, the matter is fairly simple. The citizen faced with the question whether it is worth voting or not first computes his 'party differential', that is, how much better off he would be (not necessarily in purely financial terms) if his preferred party won the election, and he then multiplies it by the probability that his vote for that party will change the result of the election so that his party wins instead of losing. Obviously, this means that he has to reckon the probability of the election's turning on a single vote, and in an electorate of millions this probability is so small that the value of voting will be infinitesimal, even for someone who has a large party differential. Thus, it seems to follow that rational citizens would not vote if there are costs involved – and it always takes time and energy to cast a vote. But in fact it is notorious that many people do vote. Even low turnouts of, say, 25 per cent are, on this analysis, clearly inconsistent with rationality.

In an article, Riker has criticised Downs as if this were his last word on the subject. He says that 'it is certainly no explanation to assign a sizeable part of politics to the mysterious and inexplicable world of the irrational' (Riker and Ordeshook, 1968, p. 25) ... Riker proposes a reward for voting consisting of such satisfactions as 'compliance with the ethic of voting', 'affirming allegiance to the political system', 'affirming a partisan preference', 'deciding, going to the polls etc.', and 'affirming one's efficacy in the political system' (Riker and Ordeshook, 1968, p. 28).

Now it may well be true that much voting can be accounted for in this way, and one can of course formally fit it into an 'economic' framework by saying that people get certain 'rewards' from voting. But this *is* purely formal.[2] And it forces us to ask what really is the point and value of the whole 'economic' approach. It is no trick to restate all behaviour in terms of 'rewards' and 'costs'; it may for some purposes be a useful conceptual device, but it does not in itself provide anything more than a set of empty boxes waiting to be filled. The power of the 'economic' method is that, in appropriate kinds of situation, it enables us, operating with simple premises concerning rational behaviour, to deduce by logic and mathematics interesting conclusions about what will happen. Whether a situation is 'appropriate' or not depends on the extent to which other factors can safely be ignored.

Thus, the classical model of 'competitive equilibrium' in a market does approximate what happens in various 'real world' situations especially where profit-maximising traders make a living by dealing in some homogeneous commodity. But in a situation where, for example, all the participants believe in a 'just price' which is independent of supply and demand, the 'competitive equilibrium' model of price-determination will have no application ... Explanatory attention must shift to the question how people came to believe in a 'just price', how the belief is transmitted and maintained, and what determines the level of price which is believed right for each commodity. In other words, there are no interesting deductions to be drawn from the interaction to given 'tastes' in a market; the price can simply be read off from the universal 'taste' for a certain price. The question is how that taste arises, and this is a question that cannot be answered within the 'economic' framework.

The relevance of this example to voting decisions will, I hope, be clear. Riker says that people vote because they derive satisfaction from voting for reasons entirely divorced from the hope that it will bring about desired results. This may well be true but it does not leave any scope for an economic model to come between the premises and the phenomenon to be explained. Instead, the question shifts back to: 'Why do some people have this kind of motivation more strongly than others?'

Obviously, the utility of an 'economic' model in a given situation is not an all-or-nothing question. Thus, we might find that expectations about the closeness of the election result and beliefs about the importance of one party winning rather than another had a fairly big effect on the probability of a man's voting (though this itself would be hard to explain in 'economic' terms), and that the sheer satisfaction in voting as such was somewhat less important. But some data given by Riker suggest that this is not so. He presents a table showing, for the U.S. Presidential elections in 1952, 1956 and 1960, what proportion of respondents voted of those who were, for example, high on 'citizen duty', low on expecting the result to be close, and high on thinking it important who won ...

And he then cites Chapter 3 of Downs. In fact, in his discussion he lumps together, under the heading 'expected differential', both Downs's 'party differential' *and* the factor by which it is to be multiplied, namely the chance of one's vote altering the election result. But the trouble is that the 'expected differential' in this wide sense is, as we have seen, almost certain to be negligible. So the 'self-evident proposition' put forward by Campbell does not help much in explaining ... The perceived probability that one's vote will alter the result significantly *may* of course be quite irrationally high, ... but I seriously doubt whether the answer lies in this direction.

2   The decision to vote: limits of the economic approach

Downs himself allows for people getting a satisfaction from voting which does not depend on the possibility that their vote will alter the result of the election, though one would gain a contrary impression from Riker. But whereas Riker leaves the phenomenon unexplained, Downs boldly tries to cover it from within his economic model. His attempt is, I think, ulti-mately unsuccessful, but its failure is itself interesting, because it turns on the criterion for rational behaviour. According to Downs, the citizens in a democracy always consider that they benefit heavily from the continuance of the system, as against its replacement by some other; but the system must collapse if too few people vote. Therefore at least some people will incur a 'short-run' cost (voting) in order to help to secure the 'long-run' gain of the continuance of the system (Downs, 1957, pp. 266–71).

But to say that what we have here is a question of short-run versus long-run benefits for any given individual is a misleading way of putting the matter. It is quite fair to say that 'rational men accept limitations on their ability to make short-run gains in order to procure greater gains in the long-run' (p. 268). But the long-run gains must depend *for a given individual* on himself foregoing the short-run gain. Such is not the case here, as Downs himself admits: 'of course, he will actually get this reward (living in a democracy) even if he himself does not vote, as long as a sufficient number of other citizens do' (p. 270). And, by the same token, if the system is going to collapse because too few people vote, his one additional ballot-paper is unlikely to prevent it. But, in the next sentence, Downs commits a common fallacy in social thought which most of the book turns on his avoiding, when he adds that our citizen 'is willing to bear certain short-run costs he could avoid in order to do his share in providing long-run benefits' (p. 270). 'Doing his share' is a concept foreign to the kind of 'economic' rationality with which Downs is working. It requires our citizen to reason that since the benefits he gets depend on the efforts of others, he should contribute too. This may be good ethics, but it is not consistent with the assumptions of the model, which require the citizen to compute the advantage that accrues to him from his doing *x* rather than *y*; not the advantage that would accrue to him from *himself and others* doing *x* rather than *y*, unless, of course, his doing it is a necessary and sufficient condition of the others doing it ...

It looks, then, as if we have to abandon as unfruitful the attempt to explain the decision to vote as the unfolding of 'economic' rationality, because its most important component cannot usefully be discussed in those terms. Does this mean that the whole discussion up to this point has been a waste of time? I would say not, and adduce two kinds of understanding that we can carry away from it: substantive and methodological. In terms of substance, our main result, although in negative form, is surely not without considerable interest. Especially when we add a parallel analysis of the decision to vote for one party rather than another, we have an idea which is disturbing for the normative theorist of democracy in that it calls into question the foundations of the edifice. Nor is it true to say that the demonstration of non-rationality is without significance for those who wish to explain political phenomena, for it makes a great difference to the range of possible explanations if a whole family of them, namely those in terms of rational 'economic' behaviour, are dismissed ...

In spite of our mainly negative results, we have gained some insight into the way the 'economic' mode of analysis operates. And we have learned the crucial importance of always relating the costs and benefits of any action to each individual actor. It is of cardinal importance to hold fast to this conclusion as we move into areas of greater complexity. Note, however, what is *not* being said. There is no intention of denying that we will sometimes want to allow for the possibility that a given actor's costs and benefits are partially constituted by the happiness or unhappiness of other people whose interests he has at heart. We insist only that they must still figure explicitly as *his* costs and benefits. And when we do allow for this sort of altruism, we must recognize that we weaken the deductive power of our 'economic' model. Thus, we could have said that voters took direct account of the interests of others in deciding to vote, and this increased the reward of voting. But to do that would not be very different from saying that they felt guilty if they didn't vote and this was a cost of not voting. Even so, there is still a big difference between slurring over the difference between self-interest and collective interest by saying they coincide in the same action for a given individual, and saying that a person may prefer to follow the collective interest rather than his own self-interest.

We can also begin to surmise something about the limitations of an analysis of behaviour in terms of economic rationality. It may well be that both the costs and the (suitably discounted) benefits of voting are so low that it is simply not worth being 'rational' about it. Thus habit, self-expression, duty and other things have plenty of room to make themselves felt. Might we not reasonably expect better luck in analysing situations where more is at stake, and perhaps especially situations of a kind which recur frequently for a given individual and where he gets some feedback from each decision he takes, that is to say, situations where we may expect adaptive learning to take place? Let us turn to a more general formulation of the economic logic of participation, and see whether the 'economic' method of analysis can explain more of the details of behaviour in some other kinds of decisions about participation.

3 The basic logic of Olson's theory

We have examined a two-sector model (political entrepreneurs and ordinary citizens) in connection with a specific form of political activity, voting. We shall now move to an assumption of one sector, in other words an undifferentiated population, though we shall ask later what difference, if any, would be made to the system by the introduction of entrepreneurs. We shall also leave for the present the relatively trivial action (from the point of view of the ordinary citizen's psychic economy) of casting a vote in an election and consider more costly activities, in time and money, such as contributing money or energy to an organization devoted to altering the state policy on some matters. We shall take this up by following the argument of *The Logic of Collective Action* by Mancur Olson, Jr. (1965) ...

The discussion so far will enable us to present Olson's central point very quickly, for it is essentially a generalization of the idea that the reward of voting (in rational 'economic' terms) is the party differential times the probability that one vote will alter the outcome of the election. Olson's argument is intended to apply wherever what is at stake is a 'public good', that is, a benefit which cannot be deliberately restricted to certain people, such as those who helped bring it into existence. A potential beneficiary's calculation, when deciding whether to contribute to the provision of such a benefit, must take the form of seeing what the benefit would be to him and discounting it by the probability that his contribution would make the difference between the provision and the non-provision of the benefit. Where there are large numbers of potential beneficiaries, and especially when none of them stands to gain a lot, Olson argues that the total contribution made to the provision of the benefit will be much less than it would be if the beneficiaries were all rolled into one person who did the best possible for himself. In many cases, he suggests, there will simply be no contributions at all.

An excellent example of a 'public good' is a state policy — for instance, a particular piece of legislation on tariffs or the labelling of consumer goods. Someone who stands to be benefited by this legislation will not automatically be advantaged by paying to support a lobby in its favour. He has to ask not whether an extra pound spent on campaigning will bring in more than a pound's worth of benefit to the potential benefici- aries taken all together, but whether an extra pound contributed by him will bring in more than a pound's worth of benefit to him. And on this basis he often will not contribute. He will not reason: 'If everyone fails to contribute, we'll all be worse off than if we all contribute, so I'll con- tribute'. For whether all, some or none of the others contribute will not be affected by whether or not he does, and it is therefore irrelevant to ask what would happen if they all acted on the same principle as himself ...

There are, then, two general results if people apply an individually rational calculation to the decision whether to contribute to the provision of a public good. First, the total contribution will be 'too low'; and, second, the contribution of the greatest beneficiaries will be disproportion- ately high. The latter will tend to come about in conditions of independent decision as well as the interdependent case discussed. Suppose the total benefit is £1,000, and that one potential beneficiary stands to gain £100 while 90 others stand to gain £10 each. The first man should think it worth spending £25 on promoting the benefit even if nobody else co- operates, provided he thinks that this expenditure has a better than one in four chance of bringing about the benefit. But it would not pay any of the others to contribute £2.50 unless he thought that £2.50 had one chance in four of bringing the benefit about.

4 Application of Olson's theory

The bulk of Olson's short book cosists of applications of the basic ideas to various kinds of social organization. His analysis has a destructive and a constructive side. The destructive part consists of pointing out that a common explanation of organizations providing 'public goods' to the members is fallacious. This is the explanation that it pays them to belong because by contributing to it they help it to succeed and thus increase the benefits to themselves. The question is whether the contribution that the individual makes increases the benefit *he* gets enough to make it worth while, and where there are many beneficiaries the discounted pay-off[3] from the organisation's success is unlikely to be significant. The fallacy arises from treating 'the beneficiaries' as if they were a single individual deciding how to allocate his resources to the best advantage. Thus one must reject all conventional explanations of the existence of trade unions or pressure groups in terms of the self-interest of members stemming directly from the collective benefits provided. Similarly, if Marx's theory of class was intended to move from an assumption of individual self-interest to the 'rationality' of pursuing one's *class* interests once one realises what they are, then, Olson argues, it breaks down in precisely the same way.

The constructive side of Olson's work lies in his insistence that wherever we do find an organisation providing a public good and supported by the beneficiaries we must look for, and will normally find, motives other than the provision of the public good keeping people contributing to the organisation. Olson calls these 'selective incentives': that is to say, they are benefits which (unlike the public good) can be provided for members and effectively withheld from non-members, thus providing a particular gain to offset the cost of belonging.[4] Olson suggests that trade unions do not gain members by preaching their advantages to the working class as a whole, or even to all the workers in a particular industry, but by providing selective incentives. These may in the earlier stages be such things as sickness and death benefits but, once established, the union may succeed in getting a 'closed shop' (i.e. make union membership a condition of employment enforced by the firm) or bring about the same result by informal social pressures. Another possibility is that the function of representing individual workers who have grievances against management may be to some degree a selective incentive offered by the union to its members. Again, Olson argues that pressure groups do not rely for membership on showing that they are doing a good job in promoting measures to benefit all members (since these would equally well benefit potential members who do not join) but, as predicted by his theory, their staffs tend to devote a great deal of energy to providing specific benefits — information and other services — on an individual basis to members.

How convincing are these applications of the basic idea? Let us divide this into two questions, one involving its application to the arguments of other writers, and the other involving its use in explaining actual social phenomena. It seems to me quite clear that Olson has succeeded in finding arguments in various writers which make sense only if one supplies the premise that it is in an individual's interest to support collective action that would be to his interests. Thus, D.B. Truman, in his influential book *The Governmental Process* (Truman, 1951), really does seem to claim that wherever there is a common interest among people similar in some respect we have what he calls a latent group, and this group will be transformed from latency to actuality if its common interests are infringed. This is, of course, a very comforting notion for one who supports a group-dominated polity (as does Truman) because it suggests that if there are interests with no organisation this must show that they are being adequately catered for already. Olson is surely right to argue against this that 'latent groups' are latent not because there is no collective action that would advance the interest but because conditions are unpropitious for getting it organised ...[5]

Turning to Olson's examples of successful and unsuccessful organisations, I think one has to say that he tends to pick the cases which support his thesis rather than start by sampling the universe of organisations of a certain type within certain spatio-temporal boundaries. This is especially significant in the matter of explaining the levels of success of different organisations. Olson seems on fairly safe ground when he suggests (with examples) that an organisation which starts offering selective incentives at a certain point in its history will find that recruitment increases. But can we hope to explain the generally higher levels of unionism in Britain than in the USA by saying that there are more selective incentives? Can we explain the variations in union membership between industries by selective incentives? And can we explain the rise of mass unionism in Britain in the 1880s and the decline in union membership after 1926 by this means? On the face of it, these seem more related to such things as the perceived prospects for the success of collective action: the 'new unionism' was reinforced by successful industrial action, while the fiasco of the General Strike led to disillusionment. Likewise, the more similar the positions of a large number of workers are, the more they are likely to see a chance for collective betterment by unionism (Lockwood, 1958). Yet these are precisely the kinds of consideration that are ruled out by Olson, on the grounds that it is not rational for anyone to incur a cost where the increased amount of a public good that will thereby come to him personally is negligible.

5 Participation in collective action: some explanations

We thus arrive at a somewhat curious position. Downs tries to argue for the discounted value of the additional collective benefit (in this case the prospect of averting the collapse of the system) as an adequate explanation of voting. Olson, on the other hand, in accounting for membership of trade unions and pressure groups, dismisses the extra bit of collective benefit as an inadequate motive and insists on 'selective incentives'. The actual situation seems to be the same in both cases. In neither case would the marginal bit of collective benefit normally be sufficient to motivate an economically 'rational' person. Here Downs is wrong and Olson right. But, equally, in both cases a belief in the efficacy of the process does look as if it is related to participation, though not necessarily via an ill-calculated judgment of private self-interest ...

Finally, a 'sense of duty' appears to be an important factor in voting, and perhaps it is in some voluntary associations too. To take a pure case, it is difficult to see what 'selective incentive' or personal benefit comes about from sending a cheque to Oxfam. It is, of course, true and important that organisations providing selective incentives (e.g. shops) and those raising money coercively to provide public goods (e.g. the government) succeed in getting hold of a lot more of our incomes. But the example shows that other factors must be allowed for somewhere.

Now, as we have already seen, we can fit anything into a loosely 'economic' framework, if we are sufficiently hospitable to different kinds of 'reward' and 'cost'. Thus, we could say that the sense of guilt at not contributing to some altruistic organisation provides a 'selective incentive', since the guilt is obviously not incurred if one contributes. Or, where an organisation is expected to provide collective benefits for its members (but, by definition, not exclusively to its members), a man might be said to feel the pangs of conscience if he shares in the benefits without contributing time or money to the organisation himself. It is interesting to notice that this is a moral position, in that it does not reflect pure self-interest, though at the same time it depends on the belief that one will benefit personally from the activities of the organisation ...

6 Selective incentives as explanations

Obviously, the constant danger of 'economic' theories is that they can come to 'explain' everything merely by redescribing it. They then fail to be any use in predicting that one thing will happen rather than another. Thus, if an organisation maintains itself, we say 'It must have provided selective incentives'; and this is bound to be true since whatever motives people had for supporting it are called 'selective incentives' ...

Suppose, however, that we fall back on making the theory a tautology.

It is still a quite potent tautology, because it can be combined with empirical assertions to produce significant implications. Thus, it is possible to say, as Olson does, that many 'latent groups' (people with common interests in a certain kind of collective good) will not turn into organised groups because of the difficulty of getting selective incentives to operate. Consumer protection by law is to everyone's benefit, but organisations pressing for such legislation cannot count on economic rewards and sanctions, social pressure or moral principle to attract members in the millions ...

Again, it is an important fact that, in the absence of economic or social 'selective incentives' which might make it 'pay' to join an organisation providing a public good, the reason for joining *has* to be altruistic. This surely throws light on the notorious difficulty of organising the poor and generally socially disadvantaged to press for improvements in their lot. Sometimes this is described as 'apathy' and regarded as something irrational, which might be expected to disappear with more information and more self-confidence. But since it is not rational from a self-interested point of view to contribute to a widespread collective improvement, one way of looking at this 'apathy' would be to say that the poor cannot afford the *luxury* of collective action ...

7 Leadership and collective action

The relevance of the economic line of analysis is twofold. First, it shows that in certain circumstances the pursuit of collective interest cannot be explained in terms of individual interest; so, in as far as the pursuit of collective interests does occur in such circumstances, the explanation must require that some other motive be invoked. And, second, an 'economic' analysis suggests that if 'class consciousness' (or, more generally, 'group consciousness') requires an identification sufficiently intense to enable it to overcome the cost to each individual of participation, it may not be easy to sustain over a long haul. Self-interest can operate quietly, but mass altruism tends to require a succession of dramatic and well-publicised events to keep it going. Severe action against some members of the movement outside a context of extreme and general repression may, for example, keep the rest of the following in a militant mood, thus bearing out the general relevance of the saying that the blood of the martyrs is the seeds of the Church.

Thus, in any organisation that lasts long, we tend to find leaders who are held by selective incentives such as money, power or status. This still leaves the followers outside the theory. If selective incentives are out, we cannot in general expect the followers to incur severe costs for a long haul, but they can be got to contribute smaller ones. Thus, the introduction of leadership into the picture (the return of a two-sector model) does not mean that the economic approach can be completely rehabilitated, as one writer has enthusiastically suggested (Wagner, 1966). Wagner argued that, with a division of labour between the political entrepreneurs and their customers, we can solve the 'Olson problem', since the would-be leaders get their 'selective incentives' as a consequence of success in competing for the support of the ordinary citizens. Unfortunately, however, this simply evades the question how, if the only benefits they have to offer are collective goods, the leaders can get followers to provide cash and compliance for themselves ... The answer, as Wagner points out, lies in the fact that these are interests which can be expressed in voting, and politicians therefore have an incentive to offer legislation which will further them. But they are still collective goods, so we are thrown back to our old question why people vote, and it is now surely clear that an 'economic' analysis cannot explain it ...[6]

8 Conditions of economic rationality

Is it possible to carry any further forward the question raised earlier in the chapter: when is the 'economic' approach likely to work and when isn't it? The best lead in still seems to be the one mooted then, that the size of the cost is crucial. Olson himself suggests that 'there is a "threshold" above which costs and returns influence a person's action and below which they do not' (p. 164). But he apparently places the threshold very low: he contrasts voting for a union shop (below) with paying dues to a trade union (above). Where the threshold comes, if indeed there is one, must, of course, be an empirical matter.

Perhaps, rather than saying there is a threshold below which calculation has no place, we might suggest that where the cost is low it will take little to overcome it. Due to the opportunities for idiosyncrasy to operate, this may make it more difficult to predict whether action will be taken or not. But we can at least make the prediction that inertia will be a powerful force. Thus, when a positive effort is needed to join — sending off money, for example — organisations offering collective benefits may be expected to enjoy little success. But as soon as action is required to avoid joining, inertia will tend to work the other way. An excellent example of this is the 'political levy' which many trade unionists pay unless they contract out. The big increase in the numbers paying this levy when the basis was changed in 1946 from contracting in to contracting out is a vivid illustration of the fact that inertia is itself a powerful factor.

It might be argued that asking to contract out invites social sanctions from fellow-workers, and this may sometimes be so; but failure to contract in might equally do so. In any case, this argument merely invites us to push the question further back, for a work-group is itself too small a unit to benefit *collectively* from the increased probability of union control over the Labour party and/or electoral success of the Labour party. In other words, we cannot say that it would pay the work-group to institute a tax on itself, and that social sanctions are a substitute. (This might be true at the level of the union as a whole, if it is a large union, but it is not the union as a whole that exercises social sanctions.)

We might suggest that the main relevance of 'economic' reasoning here is to explain why it should matter so little to a Conservative trade unionist that he is paying a political levy to support the Labour party, as many apparently do. Just as it is not worth contributing if it involves a cost, neither is it worth not contributing if that involves a cost. Another slightly less obvious example is the lack of protests by share-holders against proposals by the directors to pay sums of money to the Conservative party or satellites of it, or to engage directly in political advertising. This is in effect a charge on the shareholders from which there can be no contracting out (except by selling the shares) but the cost to each is negligible ...

Individual membership of a political party, as against inertial contribution to one, requires that one should take the initiative in joining or at least allow oneself to be recruited. Thus, in Britain, individual membership of both major parties is much lower than the 'affiliated' membership of the Labour party; and the one with more 'selective incentives' (Conservative clubs and business contacts, and, of course, the heavily social emphasis of the Young Conservatives) has many more members (Blondel, 1963). But we cannot avoid the recognition that many individual members cannot be explained in terms of 'selective incentives' unless we stretch the concept so as to lose any distinctive meaning and include sentiments ranging from fairly unreflective party loyalty to an elaborated set of political beliefs ...

When the cost is small, it does appear that, though the economic model can account for some variations, its prediction of total failure for an organisation can be falsified rather easily either by 'selective incentives' (such as inertia) which are rather dubious, or by the 'moral' considerations which, in order to give the theory any teeth at all, we have decided to exclude. But can we say that, when the cost is great, the economic approach comes into its own? There is a certain amount of truth in this, in that the role of selective incentives tends to be much clearer in inducing participation.

Thus membership of a union may in some cases be pretty automatic; but attending meetings is rather more demanding than paying a subscription and, in the absence of selective incentives, few members go.[7] Strikes, finally, may well involve a substantial sacrifice by the worker and his family. But here 'selective incentives' come fully into play: ostracism and violence, verbal or even physical, may well be inflicted on the blackleg.[8] It is easy to see that these are essential to overcome the fact that it would otherwise pay any individual employee to continue work, even though he stands to gain if the strike is successful ...

These examples, however, raise in an acute form the question whether it is really true that where the costs are high the 'economic' mode of analysis comes into its own. Are not nation states and nationalist movements precisely the sorts of thing that are capable of eliciting action which incurs a substantial risk of very high cost without the presence of 'selective incentives'? I think the answer is that this is so, but that the qualifications already made apply here too. First, selective incentives still make a difference, though their absence (or at least their apparent inadequacy to offset the costs involved) does not reduce activity to zero. In Britain during the First World War the number of eligible men who volunteered to join the army was quite large; and, even if one recognises that many of the volunteers (especially in the earliest stages) did not expect to be killed and that there were social sanctions at work, we probably need to bring in other motives. However, it is significant that conscription was introduced later and that the selective incentives of penal sanctions did produce more men. Similarly with revolutionary movements: the amount of voluntary joining is above that explicable in terms of selective incentives, but tends to be only a minority of those who could participate. Again, coercion is often used to aid recruitment.

The second point is that not all ways of serving a state or movement are equally far outside the 'economic' calculus. Fighting, hardly surprisingly, is the furthest away, but at the other and economic dealings (in the ordinary sense of the word) are apparently difficult to dislodge from it. Even in wartime, states continue to rely on taxation rather than voluntary contributions for fiscal support, even if they can do without conscription for their armed forces; revolutionaries too seem to find food more difficult to obtain than men.

An attempt has been made (Coleman, 1966) to get the sense of national identification into the 'economic' style of analysis, by showing that it can be expressed in terms of self-interest, but I do not think the attempt is successful. National identification does, in my view, lead to certain kinds of action outside the 'economic' framework, and the most useful thing is to work out the circumstances and areas in which it does. Coleman's attempt is, however, interesting in that it falls down on the same confusion between individual and collective benefit that undermined Downs's demonstration of the economic rationality of voting. Just as Downs suggested that a democratic form of political system might be regarded as an investment, yielding a steady stream of utility but needing to be kept going by period acts of voting, so Coleman suggests that one might regard the whole country as something in which one has a certain investment, again requiring sacrifices (money at least, and perhaps more) from the investors to keep it going. The fallacy is the same in both cases (and Downs inconsistently admits the point), namely that the condition of the investment is so little affected by the actions of one ordinary person that it would not pay to contribute anything to its upkeep ...

In this chapter I have tended to emphasise the things Olson's theory cannot explain. When a theory is so simple and the claims advanced for it are so sweeping this may be unavoidable. But it should not be allowed to conceal the fact that, for such a simple theory, Olson's does explain a great deal. Although not all variations in strength between organisations can be accounted for by the theory (including the fact that certain organisations exist at all), much of the pattern of effective organisation over the long term in a society does seem broadly to correspond with the predictions we would draw from Olson. This is no mean achievement for the 'economic' approach.

Notes

1   Of course, a consumer may decide to defer expenditure on consumption and save money instead, but this course is not open to a voter. If you fail to vote in one election you have lost that vote for ever — you do not get an extra vote next time.
2   In so far as it includes voting as a purely expressive act, not undertaken with any expectation of changing the state of the world, it fails to fit the minimum requirements of the means—end model of rational behaviour.
3   Discounted pay-off means pay-off in real terms allowing for paying in advance and receiving benefits later. (*eds.*)
4   The word 'benefits', here, as normally in economic analysis, includes the absence of costs. Thus, for example, if a man would be ostracised or physically molested for not joining a trade union, we can say that belonging to the union provides the benefit of *not* having these unpleasant things happen.
5   For a development of this argument at a theoretical level, see Barry, 1965, Chapters 14 and 15. A full-scale treatment of the theme, with much supporting evidence drawn from the history of the USA is McConnell, 1966.
6   Olson himself recognises this and even goes so far as to say that the 'group theory of politics' would work well enough for the case of voting, as against that of pressure groups (p. 164).
7   Those that do are disproportionately made up of those motivated by ideological zeal, who thus fall outside the model. This again illustrates that it may be possible to give an 'economic' explanation of a *difference* in numbers (why *x* has a smaller membership than *y*) by adducing selective incentives, even though these cannot account for every feature of the situation (why *x* has any members at all).
8   The employer's optimal response, if he decides to try to break the strike, as few do nowadays, is to recruit from outside the community, ideally among people who do not speak the same language as the strikers.

2.6   J.J. Richardson and A.G. Jordan

POLICY-MAKING MODELS

From *Governing Under Pressure* by J.J. Richardson and A.G. Jordan, published by Martin Robertson & Co. Ltd, 1979.

If, as has been argued, groups play a central role in the various stages of the policy process, then what are the implications of this for the *style* of policy-making that political systems exhibit? Many theories of policy-making have been developed, but they have been conventionally grouped under two main headings: 'incremental' and 'rational'. Discussion of these models tends to present them as alternatives, and Herbert Simon (of the rational school) and Charles Lindblom (of the incremental) are usually regarded as the extremes on some theoretical continuum. In contrast, we choose to emphasise the remarkable agreement between both approaches on the description of how policies are actually made. The 'rationalists' might wish to change the policy-making process, but their description of existing practices is at times very near to that offered by Lindblom, Wildavsky and other incrementalists. The second theme ... is that policy-making in Britain can be described as 'incremental'.

With group theory there is a tendency for recognition of the explanatory value of the theory to be confused with uncritical approval of its consequences. So it is with incrementalism. A distinction between its descriptive and normative aspects must be made. Other parallels can be drawn between the group and incremental approaches. In their original sources they share what often appears as a deliberately provocative style of exposition. This common feature can probably be accounted for by their similar purposes: each was developed as a debunking exercise to counter a ruling orthodoxy; group theory was developed to question a legalistic and institutional tradition in political sciences; incrementalism was developed as an alternative to what Lindblom refers to as 'conventional' decision-making theory.

Rational model
Our brief account of rational policy-making models is primarily to provide a contrast with what we see as the more useful descriptive incremental model. There is, however, a second reason for examining models of rationality. While rational models may have had little or no impact on how policies have actually been made, the concept of rationality has actively influenced a whole range of attempts, particularly in the USA and UK, to improve the quality of the policy-making system. Policy-makers have

become aware of the weaknesses of the policy machinery and have there-fore looked for ways of improving the processes and institutions of policy-making ... It is important to note that there may be a fundamental conflict between a system that stresses the accommodation of group demands and a system of policy-making that stresses rationality in some objective sense.

The concept of rationality adopted by policy-makers in various govern-mental reforms was based on an intuitive and simple commonsense view of rationality rather than on the more refined concept of rationality as devised by, for example, Herbert Simon. Thus, if one looks at the rationality implied in experiments such as Programme Budgeting or Corporate Manage-ment, one can discern that the (implicit) rational approach is along the lines of the 'so-called rational' scheme, which was described by the incre-mentalist Lindblom (1968) as follows:

So-called rational model
1. Faced with a given problem
2. a rational man first clarifies his goals, values, or objectives and then ranks or otherwise organizes them in his mind;
3. he then lists all important possible ways of — policies for — achieving his goals
4. and investigates all the important consequences that would follow from each of the alternative policies,
5. at which point he is in a position to compare consequences of each policy with goals
6. and so choose the policy with consequences most closely matching his goals.

Lindblom, of course, rejected this pattern as being impractical: he is unconvinced that it is possible to perform operations such as clarifying goals, values and objectives and ranking them, or listing all important ways of achieving goals. However Lindblom's so-called 'rationality' model is akin to the means—end model whose weaknesses were earlier identified by Simon (1957). The means—end model also involves selecting appropriate means to each desired end. For Simon, such a conception of decision-making has limitations, and accordingly he claims that many arguments of 'the ends justify the means' type are futile because the means employed involve value questions. He makes his point by arguing that the *means* involved in enforcing Prohibition in the United States involved questions of personal liberty, proper police methods, etc. and these value questions soon overshadowed the 'ultimate' objective of temperance. Accordingly, Simon is essentially in sympathy with Lindblom in rejecting Lindblom's form of commonsense 'so-called rationality' outlined above. For example, he discusses the triangle of limits. By this he means that rationality, in practice, is bounded by the individual's unconscious skills, habits and reflexes: he is limited by his values and conceptions of purpose and by the extent of his knowledge and information. Simon (1957), rejecting the means—end distinction, constructs a preferred model of rational behaviour in decision-making. This rests instead on consideration of available alternatives and their consequences. In this approach the task of decision-making is seen to involve three principle steps.

Behaviour Alternatives Model (BAM)
1. The listing of *all* the alternative strategies;
2. The determination of all the consequences that follow upon each of these strategies;
3. The comparative evaluation of these sets of consequences.

Where Simon does differ from Lindblom and his colleagues is that he views the rationality implied in the Behaviour Alternatives Model as something worth pursuing — whereas Lindblom would argue that to engage in even such a limited exercise is to indulge in dangerous pseudo-rationality. We would add that to attempt something like BAM is in effect to challenge the group system. It may be possible, but it will lead to a lot of conflict. But again one must stress that Simon was very much aware of the gulf between the ideal of BAM and the necessary limitations of actual behaviour. For example, Simon has no sooner described BAM than he goes on to qualify it as follows; 'It is obviously impossible for the individual to know *all* his alternatives or *all* their consequences, and this impossibility is a very important departure of actual behavior from the model of objective rationality.'

As an observer of how decisions are made, Simon recognises the utility of the *satisficing* idea — that decision makers examine options until something satisfactory (probably less than the optimum) is discovered. If nothing satisfactory is found, the level of aspiration will be reduced until eventually what is desired matches what is available in policy terms. Simon, the observer, is much closer to Lindblom than he is often portrayed.

Incrementalism – Charles Lindblom

As hinted above, the main difference between Simon and Lindblom lies in their attitude to the practices they observe. For Lindblom, 'muddling through' or 'incrementalism' are processes to be commended and not condemned. Lindblom (1959) has aided his many interpreters by conveniently contrasting the main features of his 'incremental' or Successive Limited Comparison (SLC) approaches with his version of 'conventional' rationality ...

Rational comprehensive model	*Successive limited-comparison model*
Clarification of values or objectives distinct from and usually prerequisite to empirical analysis of alternative policies.	Selection of value goals and empirical analysis of the needed action are not distinct from one another but are closely entwined.

Policy formulation is therefore approached through means—end analysis; first the ends are isolated, then the means to achieve them are sought.	Since means and ends are not distinct, means—end analysis is often inappropriate or limited.
The test of a good policy is that it can be shown to be the more appropriate means to desired ends.	The test of a good policy is typically that various analysts find themselves agreeing on a policy (without their agreeing that it is the most appropriate means to an agreed objective).
Analysis is comprehensive; every relevant factor is taken into account.	Analysis is drastically limited; *(a)* important possible outcomes are neglected; *(b)* important potential policies are neglected; *(c)* important affected values are neglected;
Theory is often heavily relied upon.	A succession of comparisons greatly reduces or eliminates reliance on theory.

Lindblom argues that only a narrow range of possibilities is in practice seriously considered. The process of policy-making is one of selecting between the (comparatively) few alternatives that suggest themselves. In comparing these limited numbers of alternatives one does not dwell over-long on values or goals; instead one starts from the problem and considers a manageable range of alternatives. In choosing which option to adopt, one has reference to values, but (as in Simon's Behaviour Alternatives Model) the choice of policy instrument is combined with the ranking of values. In this approach there is a tendency for policy innovations to be small-scale extensions of past efforts with an expectation that there will be a constant return to the problem to make further extensions and to reconsider the problem in the light of new data, etc. In other words, successive limited comparisons — hence the SLC acronym.

The SLC concept leads on to another, which has even more direct connection with our interest in the role of groups in the policy process — that of Partisan Mutual Adjustment (PMA). One of the ideas underpinning SLC is that *policy-making involves achieving agreement between groups*. This is one of the reasons for avoiding a preliminary insistence on clarification of values or objectives — the probability of harmony at that stage is low. There is more chance of agreement on a specific proposal than there is of agreement on objectives. For example, the 'devolution' cause in Britain was supported by groups with very different — even incompatible — motivations and intentions. Some groups saw devolution as a step towards independence; others saw it as a means of *preventing* independence. The best policy is one that gains agreement. This emphasis on accommodation between groups explains why decision-making takes the form of comparison between pragmatic available alternatives. There is also an economy of effort principle at work. If agreement is sought it is unrealistic to consider too radical proposals as they are unlikely to have wide enough attractions for the various interests. This encourages only relatively minor changes to be put on the agenda. Discussion among varieties of minor increment is thus the realistic scope of consideration. Such limited alternatives also have two other benefits (other than realism).

The first of these is that consideration of a number of specific options is an intellectually manageable operation. It is possible to give reasonable attention to restricted options, but if the whole range of alternatives and the whole package of past agreements is open (as the conventional rationalists would prefer) then the scope is too demanding: the task is impossible. Thus there is an economy of effort involved in looking at the margins, where one reasonably expects the end-choice will come from. But, further, one looks at only the margins because, it is argued, one can only sensibly consider a relatively few possibilities. The third ingredient in this series of mutually reinforcing points is that what has been agreed in the past − what is the base − is not itself an arbitrary position but represents a negotiated balance. Current negotiations presumably involve similar interests, conflicts over values, preferences and demands, and accordingly it is likely that any current agreement will differ only marginally from the previous position, unless of course the balance of group power has shifted. This is an extension of the first point, but whereas that claimed agreement was almost certain to be only marginally different from what went before, and therefore there was little profit in looking at too radical options, this extension suggests that what was agreed before was probably a tolerably close approximation of the most satisfactory solution that is obtainable.

Lindblom (1959, p. 55) describes how policy is evolved in this system as follows:

In the United States, for example, no part of government attempts a comprehensive overview of policy on income distribution. A policy nonetheless evolves, and one responding to a wide variety of interests. A process of mutual adjustment among farm groups, labor unions, municipalities and school boards, tax authorities and government agencies with responsibilities in the fields of housing, health, highways, national parks, fire and police accomplishes a distribution of income in which particular income problems neglected at one point in the decision processes become central in another point.

... In our view, Lindblom's model of the policy process most accurately describes what actually happens. This is because groups are closely integrated in the process and this in turn usually leads to an incremental style of policy-making.

2.7   G. Smith and D. May

THE ARTIFICIAL DEBATE BETWEEN RATIONALIST AND INCREMENTALIST MODELS OF DECISION MAKING

From *Policy and Politics*, vol. 8 No. 2, pp. 147–61 (1980).

Introduction

... The notion of 'decision making' is indisputably central to studying the process, through which policies are both designed and implemented and this paper is about the components of that idea. Such analysis may be thought redundant for 'decision' is a common enough term ... But common sense notions in everyday usage tend initially to be rather blunt instruments when pressed into service as tools for research. And as any good craftsman knows, there are few things more dangerous than using blunt tools.

In the literature on public administration[1] a debate about the relative merits of rationalistic as opposed to incrementalist models of decision making has featured for some years now and although the terms of this debate are rather well known it has had comparatively little impact upon empirical research in the areas of either policy or administrative studies. However, an awareness of the limits to rational decision making in institutions has exerted a significant influence upon the direction of the more sociologically oriented work in the field of organisational analysis.[2] It is the purpose of this note to suggest that, when work from these several fields is considered together, it is apparent that (1) the components of 'decision making' in social policy are by no means obvious, (2) the rationalism versus incrementalism debate is in certain respects an artificial dispute and (3) this has implications for the design and conduct of empirical research on decision making which aspires to be policy relevant.

Two models of decision making

An essentially rationalistic approach to decision making has predominated in the study of organisations. This approach advances a definition of decision making which is described by Scott (1971, p. 19) as consisting of a process with the following components:

1. A search process to discover goals.
2. The formulation of objectives after search.
3. The selection of alternatives (strategies) to accomplish objectives.
4. The evaluation of outcomes.

These are the elements which are viewed as common to the making of all
kinds of decisions – and rightly so. That is, good decisions are those which
conform to this pattern. As Etzioni (1967, p. 385) observes:

Rationalistic models are widely held conceptions about how decisions are
and ought to be made. An actor becomes aware of a problem, posits a goal,
carefully weighs alternative means, and chooses among them according to
his estimate of their respective merit, with reference to the state of affairs
he prefers.

It is important to note that the approach purports to offer a framework
which is at one and the same time both explanatory and normative.[3]

The rationalistic approach, however, has been widely criticised. First, it
is regarded as being too narrow. It neglects the range of political variables
which limits the extent of choice available in the light of the power of
relevant vested interests. Most decision makers in policy contexts do not
work in an environment devoid of constraints. They are simply not free to
consider all possible options and often they are compelled to short list, if
not actually recommend, options that they would not even pretend to
justify as the most appropriate in terms of a simple means–ends schema.
This is the well known process of pressure group politics ...

Secondly, the rationalistic approach is seen as utopian. Most policy
decisions have numerous unanticipated consequences which are neither as
inconsequential nor disposed of nearly as readily as the model tends to
imply. The model represents, perhaps, the planner's dream but in the real
world it is argued, ends are not that clear, decisions are not that neat and
evaluation is not systematic ...

McCleery (1964, p. 161) sees the rational model as appropriate only to
those limited kinds of bureaucracy where the executive is given very precise
guidance. But in practice policy institutions of this kind may well be the
exception rather than the rule.

Thirdly, the rationalistic approach is accused of being value biased in
that rationality is itself a quality prized in varying degrees. There is by no
means consensus on the fact that rationality represents some universal
good nor even upon the definition of rationality.[4] Particularly in an
organisational context the model is accused of favouring management and
senior professions to the detriment of low ranking staff, clients and
patients, whose perspectives are in practice neglected. There is a tendency
to equate rationality with the smooth running of the organisation.
Although clearly we need to know a great deal about the way in which
claimants and clients, patients and the general public approach service
agencies, there is some evidence, in studies of welfare services for example,[5]
that the importance attached to the smooth running of different aspects of
a service may in significant respects differ between groups associated with
the agency.

Fourthly, rationalistic models are seen as too rigid in drawing sharp distinctions between ends and means, values and decisions, and facts and values. What counts as 'fact' is notoriously subject to the interests and values of the parties involved ...

As Lindblom, (1959) in his [original and] much quoted article, points out, means and ends are often chosen simultaneously within the administrative process. The frequent absence of any clear means—ends relationship is often particularly apparent when several of the stages of implementing policy are examined together ... Thus means often precede ends, become ends or even cause ends. Ends become means as one decision merges into the next. Values may rationalise rather than determine decisions and certainly actors are often unable to rank their values independent of specific choices. The ambiguity of means, ends and their relationship is substantially greater than rational models allow.

A final criticism of rationalistic models is that they are impractical. Even with the aid of computer technology a review and evaluation of all *possible* answers to a problem in order to select the optimal solution is seldom plausible and the cost of the search may well exceed the savings achieved by the solution eventually discovered. This is one of the dilemmas faced by policy makers in deciding whether or not it is worth commissioning research. The Seebohm Committee (1968, para. 115), for example, set up to examine the reorganisation of the personal social services in Britain, is only one of a number of government committees and commissions that have felt that the delay in producing their report which would be occasioned by awaiting the results of a programme of research, would not be justified ... Even if the savings of a novel policy option do exceed the search costs there is no way of knowing about that before the search begins. Inevitably, it is argued, at least some choices must be made without reference to the relationship between means and ends.

In reaction to these criticisms Lindblom (1959) has set out the alternative approach termed, provocatively, 'muddling through', or 'disjointed incrementalism'.[6] This model posits the decision maker as starting not with some ideal goal but with the policies currently in force. Decision making entails considering only incremental change, or changes at the margins. Only a rather restricted number of policy alternatives is reviewed and only a limited number of consequences is envisaged and evaluated for any given alternative. In empirical support of this view Jannson and Taylor, (1978) while commenting upon the virtual absence of studies which assess the effectiveness of planning procedures in social agencies, rank only one third of the sample of agencies which they studied, as undertaking extensive search activity for new policies. In contrast to the conventional view which sees means adjusted to ends, incrementalism promotes the opposite, allowing for a continuous and reciprocal relationship between means and ends. It is argued that in this way the problems of decision makers are rendered more manageable for what counts as 'the problem' is constantly subject to redefinition in the light of available means to solve it. Thus the very subject of the decision may be transformed and reinterpreted through the analysis. Evaluation is thus seen not as a separate activity but as taking place in series with decision making ...

Like the rationalistic model the incrementalist approach has also been subjected to important criticisms. It is accused of being conservative in that it copes with only remedial and short term change and reinforces inertia. Dror (1964) suggests that it is a valid approach only if the results of present policies are generally satisfactory, if the nature of the problem is relatively stable and if means for dealing with that problem are continuously available. Generally, however, he regards 'its [incrementalism's] main impact as an ideological reinforcement of the pro-inertia and anti-innovation forces prevelant in all human organisations, administrative and policy making'. Certainly there *are* major barriers to policy innovation. Booth (1978) for example, has described those factors in the machinery of local government in Britain which have inhibited the introduction of alternatives to residential care in the personal social services, in spite of a strong 'rational' case against the extensive supply of residential provision. Dror (1964, p. 155) concludes:

The 'rational-comprehensive' model has at least the advantage of stimulating administrators to get a little outside their regular routine, while Lindblom's model justifies a policy of 'no effort'.

Taken together, the limited validity of the 'muddling through' thesis and its inertia-reinforcing implications constitute a very serious weakness.

The incrementalist approach is also accused of being unjust since 'good' decisions are assessed not by their ranking on some objective evaluative criterion but simply by their acceptability in a particular situation. The approach is therefore thought to favour the interests of the most powerful and systematically to under-represent the interests of the underpriveleged and politically unorganised. Incrementalism, too, is felt to be more narrow and more limited than the model it seeks to replace. Incremental decisions take place within the context of more fundamental decisions and the approach has little to say about how decisions of this more fundamental kind are made. While it may afford a strategy for researching some of the more detailed workings of the decision making process it is incomplete as a framework for 'macro' analysis.

Finally it is argued that although much has been made of the practicality of the incrementalist approach in fact it is extremely costly. Although the costs of rational decision making are high the costs of failing to explore radical alternatives to existing policies may be even higher. Admittedly the optimal solution is not to be preferred if the costs of discovering it are greater than the savings incurred. But the incrementalist approach is accused of offering no way of informing participants that a sub-optimal solution which has emerged is so costly comparatively as to represent an outcome that decision makers would find unacceptable if the costs were apparent ...

Two 'third' approaches

Now this debate has generated important criticisms of both rationalist and incrementalist approaches and the study of decision making can hardly proceed without taking them into account. Certainly neither model has survived unscathed as the basis for research in social policy and both Etzioni (1967) and Dror (1964) have attempted to avoid the weaknesses of rationalist and incrementalist models by combining the strongest features of the two. Each offers a 'third' alternative. Etzioni describes the 'mixed-scanning approach' and Dror outlines what he calls the 'normative-optimum model for policy making'. But both have limitations.

Mixed scanning entails a decision making process in two phases. Initially a broad sweep is made of policy options and these are assessed against stated values in general terms. Then, within this framework, decision making proceeds incrementally in matters of detail. Etzioni (1967, p. 390) claims that:

each of the two elements in mixed-scanning helps to reduce the effects of the particular shortcomings of the other; incrementalism reduces the unrealistic aspects of rationalism by limiting the details required in fundamental decisions, and contextuating rationalism helps to overcome the conservative slant of incrementalism by exploring longer-run alternatives.

But in fact it is not clear that the unrealistic and conservative shortcomings would actually be avoided. They might merely be confined or moved to different sectors of the decision making process. There is no guarantee that within these confines they might not even be accentuated. We would need to examine mixed scanning in practice before we could judge. Other issues are sidestepped. For example Etzioni retains the presumption that decision makers can summarise and rank their values, at least ordinally [see the Introduction to this section] ...

However the central weakness of mixed scanning lies in the importance attached to a distinction between two different kinds of decision.

It is essential to differentiate fundamental decisions from incremental ones. Fundamental decisions are made by exploring the main alternatives the actor sees in view of his conception of his goals, but – unlike what rationalism would indicate – details and specifications are omitted so that an overview is feasible. Incremental decisions are made but within the contexts set by fundamental decisions (and fundamental reviews) (Etzioni, 1964, p. 390).

But just as the distinction between means and ends is flexible, as we have seen, so fundamental decisions in one context are incremental in another and vice versa. It is at least possible that decision makers would define decisions in different ways either quoting or ignoring detail and either exploring or neglecting alternatives as suited their purposes in particular situations. Without further empirical data the doubt remains that mixed scanning is just as utopian as rational planning and just as lethargic as 'muddling through'. The important point is that rationalism and incrementalism embody diametrically opposed principles which are not reconciled by 'mixed scanning' sampling of either side.

Dror (1964, p. 155) also seeks a model to 'increase rationality-content' in decision making while acknowledging that, 'Extrarational processes play a significant role in optimal policy making on complex issues'. Essentially his alternative consists of a recapitulation of some of the aspects of rational planning but with heavy caveats of the form, '*some* clarification of values' or '*preliminary* estimation of pay-offs' or 'explicit arrangements to stimulate creativity'. Lindblom (1964) has criticised Dror for offering no more than a series of discrete statements which do not connect and cannot be said to constitute a 'model' for decision making. However the weakest feature of Dror's statement is the role assigned to 'intuition' and 'experience'. These are disconcertingly vague variables and hardly more than residual categories for non-rational sources of information. The whole model borders on the tautologous as an extended restatement of the opening commitment to both rational and non-rational elements. Again the important point is that the central features of the dispute between rationalist and incrementalist models of decision making remain largely unmarred by this attempt to offer this 'third' alternative.

An artificial debate

These, then, are the terms of the argument. But in this note we are not proposing to come down in favour of one side or the other, nor indeed in favour of the attempts that have been made to construct a 'third' model of decision making as a compromise between the two. For in spite of prolonged dissension between rationalist and incrementalist models of decision making, both they and the several versions of a rapprochement, have in common epistemological[7] features the significance of which outweigh any specific points of variance. What we are proposing to do is to suggest that in certain respects the debate is somewhat artificial, firstly because it is not at all clear that the protagonists are actually arguing about the same thing and, secondly, because there is an important issue — of what it takes to act in accord with a set of rules about decision making behaviour — which is largely ignored on both sides. As policy research seeks clarification of the notion of 'decision making' it seems important initially to question some ground rules of the debate as it stands.

First, it is a mark of all the models that we have discussed that they should serve both explanatory and normative purposes ... We have already mentioned Etzioni's observation that rationalistic models are widely held conceptions about how decisions *are and ought* to be made. It is also an important aspect of Lindblom's thesis that incrementalism both describes decision makers' behaviour and formalises an account of how they should behave. Furthermore Etzioni (1967, p. 388) claims of the mixed scanning tactic that: 'Mixed-scanning provides both a realistic description of the strategy used by actors in a large variety of fields and the strategy for effective actors to follow' ... It is perhaps an indication of how deeply ingrained is this dual commitment within the disciplines of administrative and policy studies, that such a statement does not immediately stand out as odd, confused and confusing as a basis for empirical research.

However, it *is* anomolous to presume *a priori* that 'is' and 'ought' in modes of decision making correlate. Certainly the authors who adopt this position do not explain at all clearly how a model is supposed to serve simultaneously as an accurate description of how decisions are made and as a description of how they might be made differently by way of improvement. Can these decision making models serve both functions? The debate which this note has been reviewing suggests not. Indeed the frequency with which current practices are criticised and changes advocated indicates precisely the opposite; namely that quite different frameworks may be required for explanatory and normative discussion. We are not of course arguing that explanatory social research can have no prescriptive policy implications ... But to press either rationalist or incrementalist models into service for both functions at the same time is to risk 'ambiguities that defy clarification'. Certainly as the debate is currently structured concepts in use for analysis and practice are utterly confused and it is hard to see how lucidity can be distilled.

One way forward may lie in the suggestion that the protagonists in the 'rationalism versus incrementalism' debate are really arguing about different kinds of things and that the term 'decision making' is thus in danger of being applied insensitively to a variety of phenomena and to confusing effect. It may be helpful to make some distinctions.

It will be apparent from discussion earlier in this note that few commentators generally doubt rationalistic models to be rather accurate pictures of widely held images about ideal decision making procedures. Criticism centres on the fact that rationalistic models are empirically inaccurate, or unrealistic. *That is not the way things are.* On the other hand there is a degree of sympathy for the view that the incrementalist approach has much validity as an empirical model of how policies are made (or, as McCleery (1964) puts it, 'more often, not made'). Criticism here centres on the claims of this approach to be useful normatively. *That is not the way things should be.*

Now viewed in this light it can be seen that the debate between rationalistic and incrementalist models is artificial in the sense that it is based on what Ezioni (1960) elsewhere has pointed to as the confusion of comparing real with ideal states of affairs and expecting them to be the same. The two models are about different social phenomena and as such should seek to perform different functions. We should not expect them to agree. It certainly comes as no surprise to students of organisational behaviour to learn that the ideal accounts offered by organisational members of their practices are only a partial basis for explanation ...

And with a degree of consistency which is unusual in the social sciences, study after study has concluded that we require more than one account to describe the several facets of organisational life. The problem is not to reconcile the differences between contrasting rational and incremental models, nor to construct some third alternative which combines the strongest features of each. The problem is to relate the two in the sense of spelling out the relationship between the social realities with which each is concerned.

If this point is a valid one it has implications for policy related research. It means that more sophisticated accounts than those currently available are required of the impact of policy makers' ideologies, about the nature of decision making, upon the conduct and outcomes of the various stages of the policy process. In that sense what is called for is a data-based meta theory,[8] delineating more precisely the role and functions of existing decision making models within the machinery of policy and administration ...

A second general feature of the debate is that both incrementalist and rationalist models, again together with the proponents of a 'third' view, largely ignore the issue of *what it takes*[9] to constitute conformity to the rules of either rationalist or incrementalist principles. That is, insufficient attention has been paid to organisational members' own coding practice.[10] For activity which may be classified by the analyst in one set of terms may be described by the decision makers themselves, either prospectively or retrospectively, in another. What then is the relative status of the member's and analyst's coding manual? For instance, much apparent confusion of means and ends and objectiveless behaviour, from an incrementalist stance, may well be held by members as quite in accord with rational conduct. In the welfare services, for example, social workers are often accused by their critics of 'muddling through' yet persist in rational accounts of their own professional practices and decisions ...

If these points are valid they have implications for research. For they cast doubt upon the utility of expending any more intellectual energy in developing *a priori* 'models' of decision making. The way forward lies in producing more, and more carefully researched, data based answers to the following questions. What do relevant professionals, administrators, policy makers and laymen actually mean by 'decision making'? What activities do they include within these rubrics? What tactics do they employ? When? Where? How? And to what effects? ...

It is central to research in the field of policy and administration to understand not only how individual policy decisions are operationalised but also how decision makers at all stages of the policy process operationalise the notion of 'decison making' itself ...

Notes

1 Lindblom (1959); Dror (1964).
2 Salaman and Thompson (1973).
3 See the General Introduction for definitions of explanatory and normative, and for descriptive and prescriptive. (eds.)
4 Wilson (1970).
5 Mayer and Timms (1970); Sainsburg (1975); Rees (1978).
6 Lindblom refines his earlier views in his second major article on 'incrementalism', see Chapter 2.8; see also Braybrooke and Lindblom (1963). (eds.)
7 See the General Introduction. (eds.)
8 See the General Introduction. (eds.)
9 See especially on this point Zimmerman (1971).
10 'Coding practice': the rules and concepts (often implicit) which actors use to categorise their own behaviour — that is to say the *meanings* which they give to their actions. (eds.)

2.8 C. E. Lindblom

STILL MUDDLING, NOT YET THROUGH

An abridged version of an article first published in *Public Administration Review*, vol. 39, pp. 517–26 (1979).

For a people weary of their government, Abraham Lincoln asserted 'a revolutionary right to dismember and overthrow it'. Jefferson at least speculated on the possibility that occasional revolution was healthy for the body politic. It is not to dissent from them that I have been claiming that 'muddling through' — or incrementalism as it is more usually labeled — is and ought to be the usual method of policy making. Rather, it is that neither revolution, nor drastic policy change, nor even carefully planned big steps are ordinarily possible.

Perhaps at this stage in the study and practice of policy making the most common view (it has gradually found its way into textbooks) is that indeed no more than small or incremental steps — no more than muddling — is ordinarily possible. But most people, including many policy analysts and policy makers, want to separate the 'ought' from the 'is'. They think we should try to do better. So do I. What remains as an issue, then? It can be clearly put. Many critics of incrementalism believe that doing better usually means turning away from incrementalism. Incrementalists believe that for complex problem solving it usually means practicing incrementalism more skillfully and turning away from it only rarely.

Of the various ways of turning away from incrementalism, two stand out. One is taking bigger steps in policy — no longer fiddling, say, with our energy problems, but dealing with them as an integrated whole. The other is more complete and scientific analysis of policy alternatives than incrementalists attempt.[1] These two — big actions and comprehensive analysis — are obviously closely related and they come nicely together in conventional notions of 'planning'. Hence a choice is clearly posed. Is the general formula for better policy making one of more science and more political ambition, or as I would argue, a new and improved muddling?

I can now analyze the choice better than I did 20 years ago.[2] I begin with an apology for sometimes confusing incremental *politics* with incremental *analysis* and for inadequately distinguishing three versions of incremental analysis. In its core meaning incrementalism *as a political pattern* is easy to specify. It is political change by small steps (regardless of method of analysis). So defined, incrementalism varies by degree.

Raising or lowering the discount rate from time to time is extremely incremental. Making the original decision to use the discount rate [Minimum Lending Rate in UK] as a method of monetary control is still modestly though not extremely incremental. Reorganizing the banking system by introducing the Federal Reserve System is still incremental, though less so. Eliminating the use of money, as both the Soviets and the Cubans aspired in their early revolutionary years, is not incremental. Where the line is drawn is not important so long as we understand that size of step in policy making can be arranged on a continuum from small to large.

As for the three meanings of incrementalism as policy *analysis*, it now seems clear that in the literature and even in my own writing each of the following kinds of analysis sometimes takes the name of incrementalism:

1. Analysis that is limited to consideration of alternative policies all of which are only incrementally different from the status quo.
   Call this *simple incremental analysis.*
2. Analysis marked by a mutually supporting set of simplifying and focusing stratagems of which simple incremental analysis is only one, the others being those listed in my article of 20 years ago.[3] Specifically,
   a. limitation of analysis to a few somewhat familiar policy alternatives;
   b. an intertwining of analysis of policy goals and other values with the empirical aspects of the problem;
   c. a greater analytical preoccupation with ills to be remedied than positive goals to be sought;
   d. a sequence of trials, errors, and revised trials;
   e. analysis that explores only some, not all, of the important possible consequences of a considered alternative;
   f. fragmentation of analytical work to many (partisan) participants in policy making.
   This complex method of analysis I have called *disjointed incrementalism.*
3. Analysis limited to any calculated or thoughtfully chosen set of stratagems to simplify complex policy problems, that is, to short-cut the conventionally comprehensive 'scientific' analysis.[4]
   Such a practice I have now come to call *strategic analysis.*

Disjointed incrementalism is one of several possible forms of strategic analysis, and simple incremental analysis is one of several elements in disjointed incremental analysis. We can now examine each to see why it should be pursued as an alternative to the pursuit of conventional 'scientific' analysis, which I have usually labeled 'synoptic' in acknowledgement of its aspiration to be complete.[5] Let us begin with strategic analysis.

The case of strategic analysis

The case for strategic analysis as a norm or ideal is simple: No person, committee, or research team, even with all the resources of modern electronic computation, can complete the analysis of a complex problem. Too many interacting values are at stake,[6] too many possible alternatives, too many consequences to be traced through an uncertain future — the best we can do is achieve partial analysis or, in Herbert Simon's term, a 'bounded rationality'.[7] I need not here review the many familiar reasons by now recorded in the literature of social science for our inability to achieve a synoptic intellectual mastery of complex social problems.

Consider a continuum (Fig. 2.8.1) on which analysis is arrayed according to its *completeness* or synoptic quality. On it, we can indicate both hypothetical and real alternatives.

The continuum suggests several observations. We — policy makers, administrators, policy analysts, and researchers — usually do significantly better than the worst extreme that can be imagined. For complex problems, however, we never approach synopsis but remain instead at great distance. Some of us practice strategic analysis better than others — that is, we employ in an informed and thoughtful way a variety of simplifying stratagems, like skillfully sequenced trial and error.

Granted that, critics may ask: Doesn't the left end of the continuum, complete or synoptic analysis, represent the only defensible ideal? Should we not, therefore, continue to press toward it? To some critics the answers seem obvious, hardly worth reflecting on. Consider, however, a simple analogy. Men have always wanted to fly. Was the ambition to undertake unaided flight, devoid of any strategy for achieving it, ever a useful norm or ideal? Although the myth of Icarus stimulates the imagination, flying becomes a productive ambition only to those who accept the impossibility of flying without mechanical assistance and who entertain the thought of using fabricated wings and other devices. Achieving impossible feats of synopsis is a bootless, unproductive ideal. Aspiring to improving policy analysis through the use of strategies is a *directing or guiding* aspiration. It points to something to be done, something to be studied and learned, and something that can be successfully approximated ...

I suggest that, failing to grasp this point, analysts who think in the older conventional way about problem solving pretend to synopsis; but knowing no way to approximate it, they fall into worse patterns of analysis and decision than those who, with their eyes open, entertain the guiding ideal of strategic analysis. Again through a diagram, I can suggest what actually happens in policy analysis. We can array on the continuum a range of actually possible degrees of completeness of analysis.

For complex problems, tied to an unhelpful aspiration that simply admonishes 'Be complete!', an analyst unknowingly or guiltily muddles

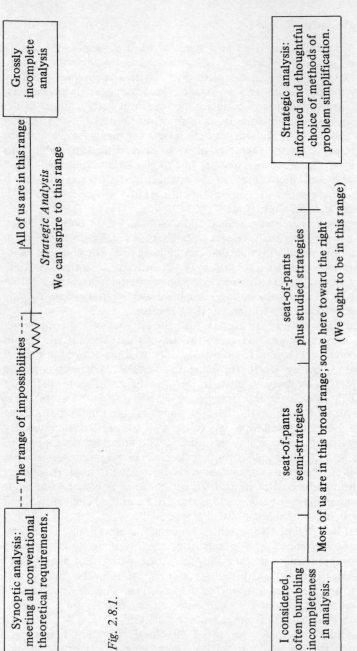

Fig. 2.8.1.

Fig. 2.8.2.

badly. Or, pursuing a guiding ideal of strategic analysis, he knowingly and openly muddles with some skill. Hence his taking as an ideal the development of better strategic analysis will be far more helpful than his turning away from strategic analysis in an impossible pursuit of approximations to synopsis (Fig. 2.8.2). Is the appropriate ideal for the commuter miraculously long legs or better bus service? What can actually be done in the pursuit of each of the two?

For complex social problems, even formal analytic techniques — systems analysis, operations research, management by objectives, PERT, for example — need to be developed around strategies rather than as attempts at synopsis. Some theoretical formulations of these techniques and all examples of their successful application to complex problems reflect this important point.

The case for disjointed incrementalism

It should now be clear why I endorse not only strategic analysis as a norm but disjointed incrementalism as one kind of it. Disjointed incrementalism is a strategy practiced with variable skill. Taking carefully considered disjointed incrementalism as a norm would improve the analytic efforts of many analysts, for the several now familiar reasons given in the article of 20 years ago. It would set them on a productive course of analysis while turning them away from conventional attempts at formal completeness that always lapse, for complex problems, into ill-defended makeshifts. A conventional synoptic (in aspiration) attempt to choose and justify the location of a new public housing unit by an analysis of the entirety of a city's land needs and potential development patterns always degenerates at least into superficiality if not fraud. A disjointed incremental analysis can do better.

The valid objection to disjointed incrementalism as a *practical analytical method* is that one can find better kinds of strategic analysis, not that one can turn to synopsis as an alternative. The valid objection to disjointed incrementalism as a *norm or ideal* for analysis is that better strategic ideals are available, not that synopsis is a useful ideal.[8] Are there other kinds of strategic analysis, or at least other hypothetic ideals of strategic analysis? More, I would reply, than we have taken the trouble to uncover; hence much exploration remains to be undertaken. A conspicuous early alternative, tapped in a concept with which disjointed incrementalism overlaps, is Simon's 'satisficing'.[9] Dror and Etzioni have also investigated alternatives.[10] Given the alternative strategies often available, disjointed incrementalism is of course not always necessary in analysis.

All analysis is incomplete, and all incomplete analysis may fail to grasp what turns out to be critical to good policy. But — and this is a 'but' that must be given a prominent seat in the halls of controversy over incrementalism — that means that for complex problems all attempts at synopsis are incomplete. The choice between synopsis and disjointed incrementalism — or between synopsis and any form of strategic analysis — is simply between ill-considered, often accidental incompleteness on one hand, and deliberate, designed incompleteness on the other.

Many specific weaknesses have been identified in disjointed incremental analysis: for example, that it will often do not better than find a 'local' optimum, a policy better than its near and only incrementally different neighbors but possibly much inferior to a more distant alternative policy never examined. Disjointed incremental analysis is much flawed, as are all alternative possible or concretely imaginable forms of policy making and policy analysis...

An aspect of disjointed incrementalism which I filed away years ago as unfinished business and to which I intend shortly to return is the relation between its remedial orientation — its concern with identifiable ills from which to flee rather than abstract ends to be pursued — and what appears to be the mind's need for a broad (and some would say 'higher') set of lasting ambitions or ideals. I am myself committed to some such ideals; that is, I make use of them. Yet they are often only distantly and loosely operative in the specific analysis of policy problems. At best they can only be incompletely analyzed — held in the mind loosely where they are beset by internal contradictions. They do not represent, as has been suggested, a distant synoptic guidance of incremental analysis, for synopsis on values remains impossible ...

The case for simple incremental analysis

Simple incremental analysis — which is analysis of no more than small or incremental possible departures from the status quo — cannot be defended in isolation from the more complex strategies, like disjointed incrementalism, of which it is a part. It is only an aspect of analysis and is or is not useful depending on circumstances and on the stratagem of which it is a part ... [The easiest point to make about simple incremental analysis] is that, in societies in which actual political change proceeds by incremental steps, it is difficult to deny the frequent relevance of simple incremental analysis. If political decision makers are going to choose among incremental alternatives *A, B,* and *C,* it would seem that some analysis of just those alternatives would often be helpful.

The most frequent and basic objection is not to simple incremental analysis of incremental alternatives actually on the political agenda; it is instead to the political practice of change only by increment. That is to say, the objection is not to incremental analysis but to the incremental politics to which incremental analysis is nicely suited.

Let us therefore explicitly digress from the appraisal of incremental analysis to the appraisal of incremental politics. Much can be said both for and against the latter, and I am increasingly impressed with what must be said against those forms of it that are practiced in Western Europe and North America.

Incremental politics

Abstractly considered, incremental politics looks very good. It is intelligently exploratory when linked with sequences of trial and error. It reduces the stakes in each political controversy, thus encouraging losers to bear their losses without disrupting the political system. It helps maintain the vague general consensus on basic values (because no specific policy issue ever centrally poses a challenge to them) that many people believe is necessary for widespread voluntary acceptance of democratic government.

Moreover, incrementalism in politics is not, in principle, slow moving. It is not necessarily, therefore, a tactic of conservatism. A fast-moving sequence of small changes can more speedily accomplish a drastic alternation of the *status quo* than can an only infrequent major policy change. If the speed of change is the product of size of step times frequency of step, incremental change patterns are, under ordinary circumstances, the fastest method of change available. One might reply of course that drastic steps in policy need be no more infrequent than incremental steps. We can be reasonably sure, however, that in almost all circumstances that suggestion is false. Incremental steps can be made quickly because they are only incremental. They do not rock the boat, do not stir up the great antagonisms and paralyzing schisms as do proposals for more drastic change.

None of this line of argument defuses the deep hostility that many people quite reasonably feel toward political incrementalism. Many people see the US, for example, as somehow trapped in an incremental politics that leaves its government incapable of coping effectively with big problems like environmental decay, energy shortage, inflation, and unemployment. I share their concern and would like to clarify its relation to political incrementalism.

American and Western European politics suffer from serious problem-solving disabilities. One, especially pronounced in the US, is the dispersion of veto powers throughout the political system. In addition to those veto powers to be found in the Constitution and in legislative procedures are those even more ubiquitous veto powers that reside in property rights. I refer not to rights you and I hold in our personal possessions but to the property rights of business enterprises, which permit, with the help of judicial interpretation, the veto of many forms of government regulation that 'might otherwise be attempted to cope with our problems. Even business property rights in information throw obstacles in the way of regulators who cannot obtain the necessary facts.

Perhaps a better way to put the point — simultaneously enlarging it somewhat — is to note a fundamental characteristic of politics in market-oriented systems. Having assigned many or most of the great organizing and coordinating tasks of society to business enterprises, then subjecting the managers of these enterprises to market inducements rather than commands (which the constitutional rules of these systems forbid in the main), the only way to get the assigned jobs done is to give businessmen whatever inducements will in fact motivate them to perform. That renders these political systems incapable of following many lines of policy that however attractive they might look for, say, energy conservation or environmental protection, threaten to undercut business inducements to perform.[11]

This particular structural feature of politics in market oriented societies, as well as other difficulties in policy making, is often confused with political incrementalism. To see our difficulties clearly, the problem is not incrementalism but a structure of veto powers that makes even incremental moves difficult and insufficiently frequent. (This same structure, moreover, makes drastic, less incremental moves even more difficult — ordinarily simply impossible.)

I think these comments rise above the dubious logic that many critics of political incrementalism have employed: US policy making, which is incremental, is inadequate. Let us therefore rid ourselves of incremental politics. My head, which is covered with hair, aches. I ought to shave my scalp ...

Perhaps then, short of revolution, we should attempt a comprehensive constitutional reform of American government? Such a proposal, if it could be made effective, falls into a category of big-step policies that strain or pass beyond the limits of incremental politics. Other big step examples would be the realization in actual operation of a comprehensive energy program, to which President Carter and many Americans aspire; or at the local level, a comprehensively planned actual rebuilding of a city, socially as well as physically; or one big integrated implemented solution to environmental decay; or an actually operative development plan for a developing country. For many people these are happy visions, but except in rare circumstances they remain impossibilities. Too many vetoes are cast against them. Too many conflicting interests pull them apart...

Moreover, among those who draw back from agreement will be many informed and thoughtful leaders and citizens who know that many of the specific elements embraced in the integrated program are bound to be mistaken. They believe that of any large sample of attempts at social problem solving, a large number will always turn out to have missed the mark or to have worsened the situation. They will prefer to see the political system act on the elements one at a time. Not that errors will be avoided, but each element will consequently receive greater attention and will be more carefully watched for feedback and correction.[12] Again, it is because we see reason to expect such big attempts to fail that we move incrementally in politics. It is not that incremental politics is the cause of our not making such attempts ...

Incremental politics is also a way of 'smuggling' changes into the political system. Important changes in policy and in the political system often come about quite indirectly and as a surprise to many participants in the system. That life has been heavily bureaucratized by the rise of the corporation and big government is a development that sneaked up on most citizens, who never debated the issues and who did not understand at the time that such a transformation was in process. Incremental changes add up; often more happens than meets the eye. If, on the one hand, this is an objection to incremental politics, this feature of it also suggests that a skilled reformer may learn paths of indirection and surprise, thus reaching objectives that would be successfully resisted were his program more fully revealed. This possibility of course raises important issues in political morality.

One last question about incremental politics: Is it true, as often suggested in the literature of political science, that democracies are for the most part committed to change by no more than incremental moves while authoritarian governments can move with bigger steps? It seems clear that authoritarian systems themselves ordinarily move by increments. Indeed, some authoritarian systems are relatively effective in suppressing political change of any kind. The pace of change in the Soviet Union, for example, incremental or other, is not demonstrably faster than in the US and may be slower. On the other hand, authoritarian systems are at least occasionally capable — apparently more often than in democratic systems — of such nonincremental change as the abrupt collectivization of agriculture in the Soviet Union and the Great Leap Forward and the Cultural Revolution in China (as well as the Holocaust and the recent destruction of Cambodia's cities and much of its population).

The most common reason alleged for democratic incapacity to act with comparable vigor on an equal number of occasions is that political change must not challenge the fundamental consensus which exists on the rules of the game and other basic values without which noncoercive democratic government is impossible. Small steps do not upset the democratic apple-cart; big steps do.

Although that argument may be valid, we have no solid evidence on it, and I am increasingly suspicious of it. It is too simple, assigning too much effect to a single cause. Whether a political community will be split in politically dangerous ways when larger issues, posing bigger losses and gains, move onto the political agenda depends, it would seem, on at least one other variable: how rigidly participants are attached to various causes, values, and perceptions of their own interests.

In contemporary societies, political participants are attached less by the flexible or adaptable bindings of reason than by the indoctrinations through which they have been reared: by parents and school and through the ever repeated media endorsements of the American way, private enterprise, the Constitution, and the like. It is easy to imagine a body of citizens more able than ours to cope with big issues because they are less indoctrinated, less habitual, and more thoughtful in their consideration of those issues — and, in particular, more open to alternative ways in which their needs can be met.

Hence, in a very distant future, bigger political steps may be possible — not large without constraint but perhaps significantly less incremental than at present. It is worth our thinking about, even if we cannot predict it.

Simple incremental analysis again

To return from our digression into incremental politics to the further appraisal of simple incremental analysis, we must meet the objection that simple incremental analysis, like disjointed incremental analysis of which it is a part, encourages political incrementalism. The analytical habit, found as it is in politicians as well as professors, encourages us all to think small, timidly, conservatively about social change. I agree, although the causation is in both directions, and the phenomenon is something like a vicious circle.

Yet the corrective is not the suppression or neglect of incremental analysis, which remains necessary and useful for all the reasons we have given above, but the supplementation of incremental analysis by broad-ranging, often highly speculative, and sometimes utopian thinking about directions and possible features, near and far in time. Skinner's *Walden Two*, Commoner's *Poverty of Power*, Fromm's *Escape from Freedom*, Shonfield's *Modern Capitalism*, Miliband's *The State in Capitalist Society*, Rawls' *Theory of Justice*, and Rousseau's *Social Contract* illustrate the variety of inputs, great and small, necessary to thinking about policy.

Some features of such analyses are especially pertinent. They are not synoptic — not even the most broadly ambitious of them, like the Platonic dialogues or Hobbes' *Leviathan* ... They are methods that liberate us from both synoptic and incremental methods of analysis ...

Some of these liberating analyses have the effect less of giving us information than of making us aware, and in that lies their great effect on our minds. They tell us what we know but did not know we knew; and what we know but had not before been able to make usable.

Of kinds of analysis that are neither synoptic nor incremental in intention, one modest kind frequently makes a highly valuable contribution to policy making. It is the analysis of some one or a few pivotal issues or variables critical to policy choices. To research the question, Why Johnny can't read, is to attempt neither synopsis nor incremental analysis. It is simply to try to ferret out some information or develop some understanding essential to good policy making. These modest but critical or pivotal research interventions in policy making perhaps represent professional analysis in one of its most fruitful forms. They make the kind of contribution to which professional research is well suited, and they leave most of the evaluation of policy alternatives in the hands of politicians, administrators, which is perhaps where it belongs.

Partisan mutual adjustment and pluralism

Some critics of incrementalism have failed to catch the distinction between political incrementalism and what in *The Intelligence of Democracy* is labeled and analyzed as partisan mutual adjustment. Partisan mutual adjustment, found in varying degrees in all political systems, takes the form of fragmented or greatly decentralized political decision making in which the various somewhat autonomous participants mutually affect one another (as they always do), with the result that policy making displays certain interesting characteristics. One is that policies are resultants of the mutual adjustment; they are better described as happening than as decided upon. Another is that policies are influenced by a broad range of participants and interests (compared to those of more centralized policy making). Another is that the connection between a policy and good reasons for it is obscure, since the many participants will act for diverse reasons.

Another is that, despite the absence or weakness of central coordination of the participants, their mutual adjustments of many kinds (of which bargaining is only one) will to some degree coordinate them as policy makers. In many circumstances their mutual adjustments will achieve a coordination superior to an attempt at central coordination, which is often so complex as to lie beyond any coordinator's competence. Such a proposition does not deny the obvious failures of coordination that mark government and are especially conspicuous in Washington. It merely claims that such coordination as, with difficulty, our governments achieve will often owe more to partisan mutual adjustment than to attempts at central coordination ...

'Partisan mutual adjustment' pins down one meaning of 'pluralism'. Objections to partisan mutual adjustment, often voiced as objections to pluralism, often begin with the allegation that not all interests are represented by participants in it, nor are participants influential in proportion to the number of citizens for whom they act. Who can deny so obvious a point? It is not, however, a persuasive objection to partisan mutual adjustment unless it can be shown that more centralized political decision making represents a fuller array of interests and does so more consistently with principles of democratic equality. In many cases it does not. For persons committed to democracy, the case for partisan mutual adjustment versus more central forms of policy making thus turns in part on which of the two can best cope with formidable inequalities in politics. A frequent opinion that the inequalities of partisan mutual adjustment are so great that more central decision making can simply be assumed to be an improvement is simply naive. Strong central authority can be — and historically is, in case after case — an instrument for protecting historically inherited inequalities.

A second major objection to partisan mutual adjustment, again expressed ordinarily as an objection to pluralism, is that it is fraudulent. The various participants do not in fact represent the variety of interests and values of the population. Instead they share dominant interests and values, and their relations with each other give the lie to those who claim to find in pluralism a healthy competition of ideas. In the extreme form, critics allege that policy is set by a ruling class with trappings of pluralist diversity.

I find it hard to deny a large core of truth in that criticism. Let us divide policy issues into two categories: those on the ordinary questions of policy, and those that constitute the grand issues pertaining to the fundamental structure of politico-economic life. The grand issues include those on the distribution of income and wealth, on the distribution of political power, and on corporate prerogatives. On the first set, the ordinary issues, partisan mutual adjustment is active (though not without defects of inequality in participation and disturbing tendencies toward corporatism). On the grand issues, partisan mutual adjustment is weak or absent. The treatment in politics of the grand issues is governed by a high degree of homogeneity of opinion — heavily indoctrinated, I would add. As has often been pointed out, the grand issues are, thanks to a homogeneity of opinion (i.e., the failure of a competition of ideas), simply left off the agenda.[13]

A third objection to partisan mutual adjustment turns out to be an objection to its particular form in many countries, the US included. It is a form in which, though none of the participants can on their own initiate a change, many or all can veto it. That is not essential to partisan mutual adjustment, but it is the way we do it in the US. That fact raises the possibility that a thoughtful response to the imperfections of policy making through partisan mutual adjustment might call for changing its form or governing rules rather than trying to suppress it ...

I have never well understood why incrementalism in its various forms has come to so prominent a place in the policy-making literature ... I always thought that, although some purpose was served by clarifying incremental strategies of policy analysis and policy making, to do so was only to add a touch of articulation and organization to ideas already in wide circulation. Nor have I well understood the frequency with which incremental analysis as a norm is resisted. That complex problems cannot be completely analyzed and that we therefore require strategies for skillful incompleteness still seem close to obvious to me.

I thought I ventured into territory not familiar to all social scientists and administrators only when I pointed out that fragmentation of policy making and consequent political interaction among many participants are not only methods for curbing power (as they are seen to be in a long tradition of thought incorporating both Montesquieu and the founding fathers) but are methods, in many circumstances, of raising the level of information and rationality brought to bear on decisions. That led me into examining policy analysis as itself a social process not limited to what goes on in the analyst's mind and thus to the concept of the 'intelligence' of partisan mutual adjustment.

I also thought that it was useful to elaborate the ways in which social problems can often be attacked (not well but with some reduction in incompetence) by 'resultants' of interaction rather than 'decisions' arising out of anyone's understanding of the problem at hand. If coin tossing can settle some problems better than can futile attempts at analysis of the unanalyzable (or futile attempts at analysis when information is wholly lacking), then it is not surprising that various forms of social interaction can sometimes handle problems better than analysis can when analysis at best is grossly incomplete. Understanding a social problem is not always necessary for its amelioration – a simple fact still widely overlooked.[14]

Rather than intending to stimulate a variety of attempts to question the usefulness of incremental analysis and of partisan mutual adjustment, I had earlier hoped that the *PAR* article and subsequent publications would stimulate attempts of colleagues to articulate other strategies that avoid the impossible aspiration to synopsis, to give a more precise formulation to disjointed incrementalism as one such strategy, and to model partisan mutual adjustment as a mechanism for social 'rationality' rather than as, historically, a mechanism for curbing central authority. On the whole, these hopes have been disappointed.

Some of my colleagues tell me they do not understand how – or whether! – I reconcile the benign view of pluralism to be found in my work on incrementalism and partisan mutual adjustment with the skepticism about pluralism expressed in the more recent *Politics and Markets* and its emphasis on an indoctrinated citizenry and the disproportionate political power and influence of business in politics. Do I deceive myself in believing that I have followed a consistent line of thought? As I have already noted, the policy issues that come onto the political agenda in what are called the Western democracies are almost entirely secondary issues on which policy making is indeed pluralistic, though grossly lopsided. On the grand issues that rarely come on the agenda, pluralism is weak to the point of invisibility.

To a disjointed incrementalist, there is never a last word; and these words are not intended to be a 'last word in incrementalism', which I have from time to time been asked to attempt. I have only a weak grasp of the concepts here discussed. Having for some years occupied myself with politics and markets and hence subordinated my interest in the further study of incrementalism, I have now returned to the study of knowledge and analysis in policy making and other forms of social problem solving.[15] I hope to muddle through – or along.

Notes

1 Specifically, the conventional steps, with appropriate refinements to deal with probabilities, are:
   a. Identify and organize in some coherent relation the goal and side values pertinent to the policy choice to be made.
   b. Identify all important policy alternatives that might realize the values.
   c. Analyze all important possible consequences of each of the considered alternative policies.
   d. Choose that policy the consequences of which best match the values of step *a*.

2 The only substantial deepening of the idea of incrementalism that I might be able to claim in the intervening period is an attempt to place incrementalism, as well as partisan mutual adjustment, in intellectual history by showing that it conforms with a long standing half implicit model of 'good' social organization and is challenged by another. See Lindblom (1975), subsequently revised as chapters 19 and 23 of Lindblom (1977).

   In the intervening years, I also spelled out disjointed incremantalism in more detail, including with the extended discussion an analysis of certain problems drawn from philosophical discourse, in David Braybrooke and Lindblom, *The Strategy of Discussion* (New York, Free Press, 1963). I also developed the related analysis of partisan mutual adjustment in *The Intelligence of Democracy* New York, Free Press, 1965).

3 And more fully in Braybrooke and Lindblom (1963) chapter 5.

4 For illustration, familiar stratagems include trial and error, bottle-neck breaking, limitation of analysis to only a few alternatives, routinization of decisions, and focusing decision making on crises, among others.

5 In the article of 20 years ago, synopsis was called the 'root' method (in contrast to 'branch', which was another term for incrementalism).

6 To which are added all the complications of value analysis arising out of the elusive character of values and their resistance to 'scientific' verification.

7 Herbert A. Simon (1957), p. 198.

8 In addition, an alternative to incrementalism as practiced is more skillful incrementalism: for example, more attention to monitoring policies for feedback and correction.

9 Herbert A. Simon (1955).

10 Dror (1968) and Etzioni (1967).

11 Developed more completely in Lindblom (1977) Part V.

12 That I am willing to claim, despite the obvious weaknesses of monitoring of results for feedback and correction that characterize most incremental policy making.

13 Bachrach and Baratz (1962).

14 Further developed in Lindblom and Cohen (1979), pp. 19−29.

15 As a beginning, Lindblom and Cohen (1979).

SECTION 3

THE PROCESS OF ORGANIZATIONAL DECISION MAKING

The theme of the preceding section, rational decision making, can be applied to the levels of both the individual or to the organization, or even to the State itself. To change the *level* of analysis from individual to collectivity does not change the form of the analysis, *in principle*. Organizations *could* have a single set of well-ordered goals to which its members are equally dedicated and which (by instruction or by the manner of their recruitment) are ranked in an official order, and where the set of feasible means to achieve those goals is a shared body of knowledge in the organization. In short it is possible to think of the organization as an individual, albeit a more knowledgeable and more consistent one than the real thing. Lindblom's 'disjointed incrementalism' (Section 2) could then be viewed as the result of the decision-making process amongst a number of officials whose work is smoothly coordinated (by the visible hand of the organization's leaders) and brought to bear on the agreed and publicly stated problems which the organization is expected to solve — be it efficient education, investment analysis or national defence.

Such a view *has* been held by theorists of organized decision making. But the central thrust of modern analysis of decision making in organizations is away from this simple view towards a descriptive and analytic picture of organizations whose members as a body necessarily value goals in policy making which are either indifferent to the organization's purposes as defined by its masters, or even hostile to them.

The analysts extracted here differ broadly on whether this indifference or hostility is because of intrinsic features of organizations as such or because of the monopolistic nature of bureaucracies which provide a service to society such as defence, policing or electricity generation.

The majority of authors share a common belief that the *organizational process* itself fundamentally changes the nature of the decisions which come from organizations rather than individuals. Their common point is that even if we imagined an individual with the knowledge-storing capacity and the information processing capacity of a large organization, the decisions which the individual would make would be different to the ones an organization would make even with the same inputs and the same initial definition of the problem. Why?

Steinbruner (3.1) provides the most general answer couched in the language of cybernetics (or systems of communication and control). The sources of information and the channels in which information flows interact with the limited information-processing capacity of real individuals to shape their basic thinking processes (cognition). To organize their decision-space (see General Introduction) the individual's thought processes become 'programmed' so as to give a continuity and predictability to their responses to the tasks the organization defines for them. In 'grooved thinking', symptomatic of the lower levels of any organization where the officials come face-to-face with an uncertain environment (the Social Security Offices and the claimants, for example), the decision maker drastically simplifies the complexity he meets by selecting out only a few variables as sufficient to classify and then process the 'case'. The decision-space is rapidly and crudely defined and thereafter purely routine or programmed decision making takes over. The organizational process in this is the 'culture' of the organization which teaches its members to categorize in similar ways; the new recruit's induction is to learn this 'hardening of the categories' which is absolutely necessary if he is to function effectively and considered to be in the control of the organization.

At higher levels of the organization the principles by which information is classified and acted upon become more abstract and policy-oriented rather than case-oriented and rather than functioning simply as the brain or central controller of the organization, the directorate is just as likely to be controlled by the *selection* of information by the lower cadres. To use the terms of less abstract approaches to organizational decision making (such as Garnett) the directorate is at the mercy of the *feasibility* studies which the organization sends up to define their nominal masters' decision-space.

When we turn to more concrete analysis of the organizational process, the pervading sense in which information is both the key resource of an organization and therefore a potential weapon in the hands of the organization against its masters comes through separately. Perlman (3.3) cites distortion of information in the Concorde project and Garnett (3.6) quotes instances of highly manipulated cost-benefit studies in defence planning which both led to gross irrationality from the Government's point of view.

The motives for this conscious and unconscious management of the information on which decisions are made are analysed by both Benveniste (3.2) and Perlman (3.3). Perlman rather crudely proposes, in the tradition of liberal-economic attacks on bureaucracy (Niskanen 1971, Tullock 1976), that bureaucrats seek to maximize the size of their organization or department and structure their analysis of policy options and the costs and benefits of alternative means so as to ensure their own interests as much as their masters'. Bureaucrats, says Perlman, have their own utility-functions (see Introduction to Section 2) which value organizational goals equally or even more highly than the utility or welfare functions of politicians and voters. In general, for bureaucracies, the bureaucrat will benefit from organizational growth more than he will from organizational effectiveness in providing services at minimum cost or maximum benefit. The author longs for an 'invisible boot' which will punish the bureaucrat for devaluing the public's interests in the same way that Adam Smith's 'invisible hand' led the individual pursuing rationally his private goals to contribute to the overall rationality of a free economy.

Benveniste distinguishes the 'games' which are played in organizations to protect or further the members' interests at the expense of the shareholders' or voters. He does not propose a simple rule such as size-maximization as Perlman does, but rather focuses on the way in which organization members protect themselves and survive in a potentially hostile environment. Benveniste stresses the pathology of organizational behaviour produced by *uncertainty*, where Perlman looks to the problem of the bureaucrat preferring his own goals to the organization's. Perlman would certainly recognize Benveniste's 'games' as examples of the pathology of organizations but his central focus is on the divergence of interests and goals, between bureaucrats on the one hand and the Government and public on the other, where Benveniste's analysis rests on the threats which uncertainty poses to the individual's survival in organizational life.

The organizational process of decisions begins to take shape then as a distinctive approach to decision making as it actually occurs in modern bureaucratized societies. It is a picture composed of organizational ends rather than public goals and of coping with the stresses of uncertainty in a way which benefits the individual rather than society. This is not the whole of the picture. Individuals in organizations develop corporate and professional needs for identity which are fundamentally social needs, requiring relatively non-hostile environments if the individual is to 'belong' and to cooperate with others. The need for cooperation between members in organizations can go directly against the pursuit of maximum organizational effectiveness and even subvert the ostensible nature of the organization itself.

The public myth of adversary justice, embodied in the popular conception of a 'fair trial', would threaten the mutual cooperation of court officers if carried out in every case. Furthermore, it would make the system of justice very expensive indeed. The *constraints* which Mohr notes for the Courts (3.4) are to some extent incompatible and have to be resolved at some level by the Court professionals. On the one hand there is the legitimacy of justice resting on the notion of defence versus prosecution, and the other is the less trumpeted but equally real need to keep costs down. Additionally the legal professionals have to cooperate in order to process cases in such a way that their potential hostility is minimized.

The outcome is a system of mutually defined cases, regarded as contestable or disposable rapidly by plea-bargaining, that Mohr analyses as a set of rules for deciding on the central classifying characteristics in an analogous manner to Steinbruner's 'grooved thinking' and 'uncommitted thinking'. The professionals, then, develop a common, mutually supportive, organization which runs counter to the official myth. They do this because the constraints inherent in the goal-set of justice represent an incompatibility of goals which have to be resolved. It is no accident that those with the greatest stake in the smooth running of the system of justice create the solution for they are the permanent members of the organization; for both political masters and accused persons pass quickly through.

Professional identity, commitment to mutual cooperation, and permanency are the characteristics of the members of an organization to an extent which sets them apart from politicians and the public. These social characteristics of organizations are further reasons why organizations do not make decisions in the same way that individuals do. The maintenance or aggrandizement of the organization becomes a new policy goal which is privately added as a new ingredient to the policy goals which are given to the bureaucracy. The steady growth of influence of the Department of Education and Science as a central decision-making body to the detriment of local autonomy in education is the focus of Salter's and Tapper's extract (3.5). The permanency of DES officials compared to local authority politicians (as well as to Secretaries of State) gives an enormous advantage to central decision-making and Salter and Tapper analyse the strategies adopted by the DES since the Second World War to try to monopolize the decision-space of educational decision-makers. By developing sophisticated planning mechanisms the DES both defined what information is relevant to educational choices and gave to itself a professional expertise in making decisions which enabled it to dominate local education authorities. But it has not been completely successful, since elements of bargaining and contestation remain between local and central government on education. The DES objective, as Salter and Tapper analyse it, appears to be the expansion of its organizational process to embrace local decision making. Overt conflict between interests in the decision-making process is a different and additional dimension to the study of decision making and is the theme of Section 4. Finally, the last extract by Keohane and Nye (3.7) takes the issues of organizational process and political bargaining within and between organizations to a more evenly balanced case than that of education where the DES is predominant as a single organization. The need for direct contact between parallel organizations in different countries because of the complexity and detail of negotiations and cooperation in such sensitive policy areas as policing and defence (for example) promotes the sense of professional identity on the part of organizational members which we noted as a social constraint on decision making in the administration of justice. Counterbalancing this transgovernmental organizational process which drifts towards common policy objectives more suited to the bureaucrats than the politicians is the attempt to recapture the definition of national policy by the organization's elected leaders. The 'structural' decisions, which Garnett calls the 'how to do it' type of decision, are the province of the organizational professional. Though such decisions have a low political input — left as they are to the organization to resolve — they frequently lead by a process of incrementalism (Lindblom, 2.8) to strategic decisions, or major decisions on central policy. The nuclear option in European War plans is clearly a result of incremental drift generated by a shared professional analysis of the different national militaries. Strategic review by politicians from time to time has simply confirmed what was mainly agreed, as Keohane and Nye would regard it, by transgovernmental and organizational processes.

To reverse the possible nuclear war in Europe decision would require a strong disruption of the web of later organizational agreements, requiring a major political initiative. The political bargaining (Section 4) needed for such a decision would threaten the cooperation within NATO built up since its foundation and for that reason if not for more overtly political ones could be effectively resisted by the organizational professionals who have a near-monopoly of the managerial skills and expertise required for such a complex change of military strategy.

3.1   J. D. Steinbruner

COGNITIVE DIMENSIONS OF ORGANIZATIONAL PHENOMENA

The basis for expanding cognitive theory to the collective level of explanation is provided by the fact that the principles are assumed to hold across the idiosyncratic features of men and cultures. If stable features of the mind encounter stable features of organizational settings, it should produce coherent, recurring patterns of behavior in the organizational decision process, other things being equal. The question then is what characteristics of the organizational setting affect cognitive operations?[1]

Among the more interesting features of the organizational setting for the cognitive theorists are: the natural information channels, the background of the personnel, and the level of organizational hierarchy at which various decision procedures operate. The natural information channels tend to determine the information input for the decision maker. His personal background gives some hint as to how his memory is structured. The level of organizational hierarchy determines the range of decision problems which the decision maker encounters, and the scope of those problems. All these factors affect the nature of cognitive experience men will have in an organization; and, as experience accumulates, they determine the structure of the minds which process information and make decisions.

A systematic approach to the problem would take these and other pertinent dimensions of organization and identify the important distinction within each dimension. Thus, for example, personnel backgrounds could be broken down by distinguishing professionals, substantive experts, and politicians. The intersection of the various dimensions with their internal distinctions could then be used, as in the familiar contingency table, to produce a categorization scheme. Such a project would extend beyond the scope of the current analysis, however, for the point here is not the full development of the theory of organization but rather an application of some of its principles to decision problems of special concern. Accordingly, a more limited approach is adopted. Three models of thinking are presented below, each of which represents a different resolution of the conflicting principles of cognitive processing and each of which seems clearly associated with a certain kind or organizational situation. These determinants are useful in the subsequent analysis of the nuclear sharing issue and ought to be useful in the analysis of other complex problems. It is not necessary to claim that these thought patterns are the only ones of interest or that the variables associated with them in the discussion are the only operative variables.

Grooved thinking

The first of the three patterns of thought is essentially the simple cybernetic process ... It is the operative mechanism of organizational routine. A person or organizational entity in such a mode attends to a small number of variables pertinent to the decision problem. Typically, the categories or concepts which the decision maker in this mode uses are determined by ranges of values on the critical variables; and his decisions are programed so that once he determines which category obtains, the decision follows without further question. The police patrol-man, for example, regularly faces situations where he is called upon to handle disputes between individuals or alleged disruptive behavior in order to maintain public order. His legal mandate in such situations is exceedingly ambiguous, as is the nature of the threat to order which he encounters. He is therefore a decision maker under uncertainty. Studies of the way police handle these situations indicate that they tend to develop such concepts as 'bad actor', 'hothead', 'liquored up', to distinguish between individuals they encounter and that variables such as race, sex, age, physical appearance, and tone of speech tend to determine which category is applied.[2] A person judged to be a 'bad actor' is treated harshly, and the patrolman is quick to use force with him. Persons judged to fall in the other categories receive less hostile, less coercive treatment. A person who readily submits to the authority of the police receives much more circumspect treatment than the person who verbally challenges the authority (which as a legal matter is often subject to challenge). The latter is likely to be seen as a 'wise guy', and there are rather tough routines for handling wise guys.

Grooved thinking characteristically occurs in organizations which are well established in the sense that they have been in existence for some period of time and have been conceded competence over a certain range of tasks. They have a regular load of business which repeatedly presents problems similar in character — the production line in a factory, the management of a sales department, the medical clinic, the traffic court, the small-loan department of a bank, the patrolman on his beat, etc. Grooved thinking occurs at an organizational level where the range of problems is narrow in the sense that the decision maker does not often encounter problems which do not readily fall into a small number of basic types.

It will be clear that this process is characteristic of the common bureaucrat who never seems to understand the special problem which the supplicant citizen sees in all its many dimensions. A casually selected newspaper story provides an example: A young, unwed mother gave her baby up for adoption. The adoption agency, following established procedure, matched the baby with a set of new parents on certain characteristics and initiated adoption proceedings. The young, unwed natural father of the child then petitioned to adopt his own child, arguing that he had a job, that his parents would provide shelter and a home atmosphere, and that he had, in fact, cared for the child for several months already. The agency found him unacceptable — he was a man, he was too young, he was unmarried, his job did not pay enough. The young father, the press, and several politicians were outraged. The father struck those who knew him as mature, responsible, devoted to the child and — the critical point — he was the *natural* father. The agency, however, would not budge. They had made a long sequence of such decisions, and their thought processes were well established. Moreover, they did not recognize a preeminent claim of natural parenthood; their business was adoption.

This sort of situation is repeated many times in everyday events. Those decision makers who repeatedly encounter complex decision problems and have the inescapable responsibility of taking some action develop these highly stable patterns of reaction. The fabled frustration of those who experience the results and find them inadequate to their special needs is a consequence of the fact that the decisions are actually taken on very narrow grounds and are determined by the execution of well-established decision rules. Rarely does this provide an outcome finely tuned to the particular needs of an individual case.

In cognitive terms the chief characteristic of a grooved decision process is that its stability is well established by long exercise over an extended sequence of decisions. This experience, recorded and weighted in memory, offers powerful analogues for new decisions and protection against the variance of new decision problems. The burdens of responsibility — uncertainty, political pressure, heavy workloads, potential controversy over the outcome — are handled unusually well by this sort of thought process, precisely because of the ready-made, well-anchored structure to which new problems can be fitted. The fact that this mode of thinking arises with repeatedly presented problems means that it is strongly determined by the reality principle. The variables which provide the focus of the process are likely to be the obviously pertinent, observable features of the situation — the apparent characteristics and immediate behavior patterns of those he encounters on the street, in the example of the policeman. This means that the grooved decision process operates in a very short-range time frame and with only a very low level of abstraction. The simplicity of such structures is preserved by this short time-horizon and by the narrowly limited sensitivity to information — a few variables out of hundreds of variables contained in the true state of the world. Moreover, there is a strong supposition that simplicity will also tend to produce problem conceptions organized around a single value.

It is clear that these features of the grooved thought process operate in such a way as to break a particular, short-range component out of a complex policy problem and to make decisions solely in that context. The result of this, repeated over many organizational entities (be they individuals or low-level offices and bureaus), is a fragmentation of a complex decision problem into small pieces which are essentially independently treated. This phenomenon becomes particularly important when high-level decisions are filtered through the low levels of a policy bureaucracy for implementation.

Uncommitted thinking

A second cognitive syndrome which operates in an organizational setting is what can be called uncommitted thinking. It appears in response to the problems of decisions at high levels in an organizational hierarchy. The natural information channels at the apex of an organizational hierarchy carry relatively abstracted, aggregated information. Since the apex of an organization represents the intersection of a number of different information channels, both the range of problems presented and the scope of individual problems is much greater than is the case at lower organizational levels. As a consequence, the decision maker experiences pressure to deal with problems more abstractly, and the decision process tends to operate in a more extended time frame. The decision maker will be much less able to adapt the short-term, highly specific focus of the grooved thinker. Moreover, this situation is further compounded by the intense workloads which are characteristic of high-level positions in the public sector. The sophisticated information processing which his position tends to demand takes time, and high-level officials experience many competing claims for their time.

The behavior of high-level officials is further affected by their backgrounds. In public-sector organizations, many high officials come to their jobs through political channels, and at any rate they are often reasonably unfamiliar with the organization and its business when they assume office. As a consequence, their beliefs are not stabilized by the weight of past experience. They are particularly vulnerable to uncertainty; and, for many of the problems which face them, they quite literally do not know what to think. Such officials naturally come to depend upon the problem structuring done by their personal staff, the organizations which they head, and/or outside experts. At any rate, the information channels to which they attend provide structured, generalized arguments, and coping with these — for a wide variety of problems — is their daily business.

The pattern of uncommitted thinking which tends to occur in this organizational situation has a number of notable features. First, the decision makers do adopt generalized concepts which are embedded in larger, theoretical belief structures and are not simply determined by a small number of specific variables, as in the case of grooved thinking. Such decision makers, in other words, will associate theoretical considerations about the state of the world with particular alternatives, and they will attempt to calculate the outcome which would result from each alternative. Second, for these non-expert high-level officials, their belief structures (relating an alternative and an outcome via a causal theory) will be associated with a sponsor (a utilization of the principle of social reinforcement to bolster belief strength). And finally, the critical point, the high-level policy maker, beset with uncertainty and sitting at the intersection of a number of information channels, will tend at different times to adopt *different* belief patterns for the same decision problem. Since his own experience does not commit him to a particular belief pattern, he will adopt several competing patterns, not at once, but in sequence.

The cognitive theorist lays out the principles involved in uncommitted thinking. Because of the organizational setting, the reality principle forces a more abstract intellectual framework than the highly specific focus of the grooved thinker. Abstraction, however, involving a set of interacting and reasonably extensive inferences cast in at least a medium time frame, is made difficult by uncertainty. The decision maker thus has difficulty in establishing his beliefs and protecting them against the pressures of inconsistent information. The use of social reinforcement provides some of the belief strength required, but does not eliminate inconsistency because of the normal structure of coherent belief patterns — i.e., their tendency to be organized around a single value and to project but a single favorable outcome. Such general belief patterns are prone to inconsistency ... because a complex environment is generally capable of producing a number of possible outcomes. The pressure of inconsistency then produces an oscillation over time between a number of belief patterns, each of which represents a psychologically coherent and consistent segment of the overall problem. The cognitive principles of consistency and simplicity prevent an overall integration of the separate patterns — that is, that inference mechanisms of the mind operate to keep them separate. However, new information and new argument received in organizational channels are not likely to allow any one pattern to dominate without some independent source of belief strength, because of the intrinsic complexity of the environment. And a principal source of independent belief strength — the corroborative judgment of other people — will not allow a dominant pattern either, because, at the intersection of organizational channels, 'sponsors' are diverse and likely to disagree. The overall effect, then, is an oscillation between competing belief patterns, a process which compromises stability to some degree, but not completely. The separate patterns of belief will be internally stable, and oscillation may occur only over two or three different patterns. Such is the syndrome of the uncommitted thinker.

The syndrome of the uncommitted thinker is one which the cognitive theorist readily observes in the behavior of Presidents. The common quip about Roosevelt – that he was of the mind of the last person he talked to – is an exaggeration which seems to reflect the process, as Arthur Schlesinger suggests in his description of the President in the winter of 1934–1935. With economic affairs still in a critical state and with growing radical political movements, Roosevelt faced policy choices between apparently conflicting demands of economic reform on one hand and recovery on the other. Schlesinger reports him vacillating between prescriptions for tightly controlled national planning, for economic orthodoxy to restore the confidence of business, for economic reform inspired by the antitrust sentiments of Brandeis, and for the use of public spending as a recovery device. Each position had its advocates, who at various times thought they had elicited favorable responses from the President. Schlesinger (1960, p. 263) in hindsight detects a gradual drift in one direction, but his qualifications are more significant:

Unconsciously, he was drawn in the new directions urged on him by Frankfurter, Corcoran, Cohen, and Eccles. But, as usual, he avoided ideological commitment. As usual, he even avoided intellectual clarity.

Thus his decision to send the holding companies' message to Congress in March did not necessarily mean full acceptance of the neo-Brandeisian analysis, any more than his support to the Eccles banking bill through the late winter and spring meant that he advocated (or even understood) the bold use of fiscal policy.

In fact, Roosevelt did not even resolve the situation on his own. The second New Deal emerged when the Supreme Court imposed an outside constraint on him by striking down the National Recovery Act, thus closing off a range of alternatives and the analysis associated with them. The pattern Roosevelt displayed of oscillating between groups of advisers – siding with one on one issue and with another on the next and then back again – is the signature of the uncommitted thinker.

Theoretical thinking

The final syndrome clearly suggested by cognitive theory is a mode of thinking in which the decision maker adopts very abstract and extensive belief patterns, patterns which are internally consistent and stable over time and to which he displays a great deal of commitment. One might label this pattern theoretical thinking, to reflect the generalized, highly deductive belief system which is its prime characteristic. The theoretical decision maker is an aggressive thinker who is very active in imposing an extensive pattern of meaning on immediate events. In the decision situation this means that he will connect concrete alternatives to an extensive pattern of calculations about the environment. Typically he is committed to one alternative which he invests with substantial significance in terms of very general values. In accord with the general cognitive pattern, his beliefs are organized around a single value, but in this case it tends rather clearly to be a dimension of value in which very general values ('peace' and 'world progress') are connected by a chain of inference to quite specific objectives (increased aid for Panama or additional conventional forces for Europe). The justification of the decision taken by a theoretical thinker is made in terms of the entire chain of inference and not simply its most specific component.

The characteristics of theoretical thinkers are most striking under conditions of uncertainty, since typically such a man has buffered himself from the impact of uncertainty by establishing his belief system on grounds relatively independent of the reality principle. Since the beliefs in question tend to extend well beyond what can be held on the weight of available information, some other basis of belief strength must be operative. (He is often called a 'theologian' in bureaucratic vernacular, to reflect the act of faith involved in his world view). With his beliefs established in a long-range framework and well anchored, his inference management mechanisms are able to handle the pressure of inconsistency in any short-term situation. Inferences of transformation and impossibility, the selective use of information, and other inconsistency management mechanisms are brought to bear for this purpose. Since the theoretical thought process is strongly deductive and thus relatively less dependent upon incoming information in order to *establish* coherent beliefs, incoming information can be molded and even ignored or denied with greater ease than is the case with other thought patterns. The theoretical thinker thus can act quickly and with great confidence in those fluid, chaotic situations of short duration which cause a great deal of distress to others operating in different modes of thought. Over longer durations, however, precisely because of the relative independence from incoming information and because of the tendency to structure beliefs around only a part of the complex policy problem, the theoretical thinker is likely to have trouble.

A particularly interesting example of theoretical thinking is provided by a prominent British staff officer at the outbreak of the First World War. Brigadier General Henry Wilson (later a Field Marshal) undertook, beginning in 1910, to formulate plans with the French Army for a British Expeditionary Force to aid the French in case of a German attack.[3] Wilson had become convinced of the necessity of British intervention by a set of calculations which foresaw a German attempt to dominate the Continent and which articulated the threat such domination would pose to the British world position and to the cause of British civilization. He constructed a military argument to show that a six-division British force would be a decisive factor in a French-German battle, a logic woven around assumptions that the German Army would attack through Belgium but without crossing the River Meuse. The limited number of roads in that area would limit the number of German divisions and allow the battle to be swayed by the British six-division force: Wilson's plans were elaborately laid out in close coordination with French plans; and in 1914, despite a great deal of reluctance in the British Cabinet regarding not only the wisdom of ground intervention but also Wilson's particular deployment, the plans determined the action which the British did in fact take. In the actual event, the German Army did cross the Meuse and swung wide on the British-French left flank. Though Wilson had available a fair amount of evidence that this was the way the battle would develop, he rigidly stuck to his original plan and managed to convince the British government. Wilson in the 1914 crisis is a clear case of the theoretical thinker. He connected his specific deployment plan to very general conceptions of value (British world position, the preservation of the empire) and overlooked specific evidence (of the wide German sweep) which represented grave difficulties for his conceptions.

The cognitive theorist is naturally interested in the particular way in which the extensive generalized belief system of the theoretical thinker comes about. Though this is particularly an area where a great deal is yet to be learned, cognitive theory is reasonably clear about two points: (1) that the development of such belief patterns takes time; and, (2) that even independent of duration the basic patterns must be established early in a person's maturational process. Regardless of whether belief strength is established by mechanisms of reinforcement or simply by the weight of stored information, it is clear that time must elapse during which the mind processes and stores information. Strong beliefs are thus the result of a gradual process of strengthening. The importance of early experience in a system biased toward stability is obvious, and it is established as an empirical matter that fundamental attitudes appear early and tend to persist throughout the life cycle. Established belief patterns cannot be uprooted without massive disruption to the highly interactive, well-structured system of memory characteristic of the mature mind ...

The most direct proposition is that the foundations of a theoretical belief system are laid down early in a person's professional training, or at that point in his career when he first becomes seriously concerned with the affairs of policy. The suspicion is that powerful, formative experiences of the young person in his twenties or early thirties or perhaps highly structured professional training (such as engineering or theoretical economics) are the sources of operative ideology. These 'early' attitudes, strengthened and reinforced through subsequent experience, provide the first grounds for the cognitive theorist to build his explanation.

It is also well to recognize immediately that early experience strengthened over time is not likely to be the only basis for theoretical thinking. The principles of cognitive theory underscore the proposition that the mind is a generalizing, inference-drawing machine in all its operations. A seminal historical event, a particularly compelling image, another man of great persuasive power are all capable of causing a given decision maker to adopt a large-scale, generalized conception of his situation and to act upon it. Undoubtedly, there are other critical factors as well. The important argument of cognitive theory asserts that when highly generalized conceptions do become established, they provide the mind (with its inference-management mechanisms maintaining stability and holding inconsistency below some criterion) with a basis for handling the uncertainty of the immediate decision problem ...

The organizational context which contributes to the theoretical thought patterns is primarily one which affords enough time for such patterns to become operative. Whether they must be created or merely connected with preferences for specific alternatives, theoretical patterns are not developed over short durations. Thus, a person who enters public service from a background closely related to his new responsibilities is more likely than others to display the pattern. So is the staff officer who remains in his job for some time and whose mandate concerns a rather specific area of policy. Unless some issue seizes high-level policy makers over a considerable period of time, theoretical thinking is likely to be removed from these positions at the intersection of channels and to be located within a particular information channel in an organizational unit, formal or informal, which has a restricted scope of concern. Moreover, theoretical thinkers are particularly likely to be found in small, closely knit groups which interact with one another about the issues of concern on a regular basis. This provides a stable source of social reinforcement to bolster their strong belief systems. Military officers and bureau chiefs are clearly prone to the syndrome on the issues which concern them. It is less likely to occur with Presidents and Cabinet officers.

These three patterns of cognitive operations in organizational settings — grooved thinking, uncommitted thinking, and theoretical thinking — provide the most direct and most immediately usable contribution of cognitive theory to the analysis of complex policy problems. As noted at the outset, the syndromes are sketched in general outline and become much more powerful when they can be used to structure data regarding specific situations ... The three cognitive syndromes state in the most concrete terms the general argument of cognitive theory as to how basic structure comes to be established for the complex decision problem. That argument holds that the inference mechanisms of the mind impose structure on uncertain situations in systematic ways under given organizational conditions, and that the cybernetic decision process operates within the structure thus established.

Some precautions need to be restated. First, the cognitive principles utilized are not idiosyncratic to individuals, as has been repeatedly emphasized. As a result, the three cognitive syndromes identified cannot be assumed to refer to personality types. It is reasonably clear that every person at different times and, most critically, *in different decision problems*, is likely to operate according to different syndromes. Many decision makers doubtless could be observed fitting all three patterns at one time or another. Second, in any actual organizational situation the various positions of power are likely to be held by people operating in different modes of thinking. Awareness of this fact is likely to aid analysis when details of the specific context can be supplied, but it is difficult at the moment to provide general propositions of any power. One cannot say with complete confidence what the consequences will be if an 'uncommitted' thinker with a 'theoretical' staff directs a 'grooved' bureau chief or division commander.

Notes

1   There is a limit, of course, to the power which can be claimed for such analysis, for it does not incorporate substantive variables – the values of an organization, the nature of its business, its peculiar historical experience, etc. – which unquestionably have a great deal to do with its character and behavior. The approach based upon cognitive principles does not counsel a neglect of these substantive considerations, however, and in fact it promises an analytic framework within which such specific information can be more systematically applied.

2   Wilson (1968).

3   Williamson (1969), pp. 168–72.

3.2   G. Benveniste

SURVIVAL INSIDE BUREAUCRACY

From *Bureaucracy*, Guy Benveniste, author, Copyright 1977 by Boyd & Fraser Publishing Company.

To understand the games played within bureaucracy, it is necessary to understand individual career motivations. Individual career paths determine some of the strategies that bureaucrats use to protect themselves. In some cases individuals are attempting to climb a status ladder; in other cases they seek to stay where they are. They are satisfied with their current situations. Without agreeing with the Peter Principle, which states that individuals in organizations climb the ladder until they occupy a position they are unable to perform and, therefore, move no further (Peter, 1970), it is correct to say that, for one reason or another, many position-holders are where they want to be or have no illusion that they can do better elsewhere. They have reached the top of their salary scale and there is no incentive for them to take any risk. But these individuals also need to protect their positions and so they too play games.

In this extract we describe how individual needs for protection result in several games. We discuss output measures, and such rules as bureaucratic insurance risk avoidance, excessive coordination, documented histories, and doing nothing.

Organizational careers

Members of organizations occupy successive positions in one or more organizations over time. The succession of positions one occupies forms an organizational career (Glaser, 1968).

Closed sector careers take place either in a single organization or in other organizations that are similar. Knowledge and experience with the organization or the sector are of first importance. Transfers from organizations in other fields of endeavor in different sectors occur only in rare instances. Once an individual initiates a career in such sectors as cinema, education, the military, banking, etc., the experience is most valued in the same area. A person may go from sales to production to assistant director for R & D to general manager. Moreover, in many such closed sectors, career paths are strongly determined by the status of the initial appointment location. If one is first appointed as an assistant professor in an unknown junior college, the probability of ever being appointed in a large university is low; but if one is first appointed at Columbia, there is a higher probability that one may end as a full professor at Harvard.

Open sector careers are skill-oriented. It is not the sector that matters (i.e., banking, education, etc.), but the kind of work performed. If one is a specialist in control system design or in public relations, the specialization may take one to different kinds of organizations as one acquires renown in the skill or profession: 'This person is very good; she worked with the teachers' unions – got them in order and then went to ...'

The level one occupies within an organization is related to the nature of the skill: 'She is a top-notch personnel manager – has a background in government service but worked several years with a private utility ...' Certain skills permit upward mobility within organizations: 'He started as a production troubleshooter for an electric firm, later became a negotiator in international sales and, ultimately, became their lobbyist in Washington, D.C. ...'

Location-dominated careers are controlled by desirable locations. It is not the sector or skill that matters. The relevant progression is from less desirable to more desirable locations: 'When I got out of school, I could not find a job. Finally, I started teaching in a small town in a rural area. ... Four years later, we moved to Boston, but we did not like it there. ... We came west to California, and I run a bookstore. ...'

'Career movement for the Chicago teacher is, in essence, movement from one school to another, some schools being more and others less satisfactory places to work' (Becker, 1952, p. 383).

Evaluations and evaluators

Each person in the organization plays the incumbent role according to his or her perception of the way the performance will be judged by significant evaluators. Those seeking advancement desire positive evaluations. Those who want to stay where they are seek to avoid negative evaluations.

Significant evaluators may be located within the same or in another or several other organizations; they can be a single person or they may be a multitude of persons who, in one way or another, are perceived to be important to one's career.

This point is particularly important because much of our current thinking treats organizations as units of analysis. We assume that behavior within organizations is explained in terms of the structure or the reward system of individual organizations. In fact, organizations operate in a larger environment, and that environment may be more important than the organization in explaining individual behavior.

Individual perceptions of evaluations may be vague and indefinite. To be sure, individuals who are pursuing closed-sector career paths often possess precise knowledge about how their performances are evaluated and by whom. But in some large organizations and at the higher levels of responsibility, individuals often do not have a clear perception of their evaluators. This lack of clarity occurs in large government bureaucracies, especially when the general environment is perceived to be threatening, but when the exact source of trouble or potential trouble is vague. Such ill-defined evaluators create fear. 'You never know who might be watching — who might send an anonymous report.' As one worker reported, the supervisor 'can push a button on this special console. Just to see if I'm pleasant enough ...[or] if I make a personal call. Ma Bell is listening. And you don't know. That's why it's smart to do the right thing most of the time. Keep your nose clean.' (In Terkel, 1974, p. 69).

In many organizations, there are no criteria of evaluation because there is no exact knowledge about how the role should be played. For example, this is true of teaching where it is not possible to know what makes a good teacher. In such organizations, pseudo-evaluations are often used; in education, it is possible to invent criteria of competency, but these are often considered meaningless by teachers. This imprecision tends to exacerbate the uncertainty of evaluations since no-one really knows what criteria are used in making decisions.

These fears are shared both by those who strive upward and those without ambition. In fact, fear may be more serious for the latter type. If individuals remain in the same position or the same line of work for many years, they may become obsolete for most other tasks. Such people recognize how vulnerable they are if their organization or department is embroiled in any difficulty and if, as a result, they fall into disgrace. If these people are middle-aged and have acquired responsibilities, they are doubly vulnerable. Even with strong unions or civil service protection, the fear prevails because everyone has heard, or seen at first hand, cases of individuals who were destroyed by events beyond their control. As a business consultant reports:

Fear is always prevalent in the corporate structure. Even if you're a top man, even if you're hard, even if you do your job — by the slight flick of a finger, your boss can fire you. There's always the insecurity. You bungle a job. You're fearful of losing a big customer. You're fearful so many things will appear on your record, stand against you. You're always fearful of the big mistake. (In Terkel, 1974, p. 531)

Closed-sector career paths

At the beginning of a career, closed-sector career path evaluations take place within subunits of the organization. As one starts a career, the relevant evaluator is the immediate hierarchical supervisor. As one's chances improve, and after a few promotions, the alternatives for future mobility become more restricted while the number of significant evaluators increases. To be promoted from sales manager to vice president for operations in Company X means that six or eight division heads have to agree not to oppose the appointment; the board, the president, and two other vice presidents have to agree to it. The significant evaluators include not only the person who has to make the final decision but all those whose opposition to the promotion might jeopardize it. The more important the position is in terms of the number of individuals affected by it, the larger the number of significant evaluators. Therefore, the more one advances in a closed career path, the more difficult it becomes to make the next progression upward and the more one becomes cautious and avoids risk.

In closed-sector career paths, the possibility of mobility from one organization to another decreases the longer one is identified with a single organization. Individuals who have served four to six years in one organization and who are still young may be able to move to another organization, but these opportunities tend to become scarcer the higher they move and the longer they stay within one organization. Therefore, such individuals are increasingly concerned about their lack of mobility and their excessive dependence on their position.

One result of this concern is that at the middle level, there is a tendency to maintain friendly relations with members of different organizations in the same sector. Contrary to expectation, there is considerable supportive behavior between members of competing organizations simply because one's competitors are also one's potential employers.

Since the rhetoric prevailing in all organizations is oriented toward innovation, risk-taking, and getting results, the cautious game is one that appears to innovate and appears to take risks, but really focuses on preserving the status quo. Perhaps a few errors are permitted, but not many. The strategy consists of looking good and conforming.

A New York management expert says that he would never promote into a top-level job a man who is not making mistakes − and big ones at that. 'Otherwise, he is sure to be mediocre.' (Proxy, 1969, p. 65)

In politics, as in surgery, a big mistake can be fatal. But in a fast moving, modern corporation, mistakes are inevitable. It's the number and frequency that makes differences on balance sheets. (Horn, 1964, p. 88)

Can business maverick survive in today's modern corporate structure? In a large company, the answer is yes but only at the relatively low levels of the management structure. The minute the business maverick reaches middle or top management, his jealous associates cut him down as a trouble-making non-conformist. (Lund, 1973, p. 109)

1.   You decide what it is you want to find out from this meeting and what you want to impart during it.

2. You decide what it is you want to press hard for.
3. You know the impression you want to create.
4. You know the particular problem you want to get solved.
5. You try to anticipate what most of the others in the meeting will do and say and how they will react. (Edgett, 1972, pp. 199–200)

These statements suggest that in closed-sector paths, the growth of one's organization is the stimulator of one's career progression. This process is particularly clear in new organizations, in which being at the right place at the right time can lead to greatly expanded role responsibility as the organization expands. Thus, the incentive for organizational spread and domination is also related to its resulting impact on the careers of middle and top echelon personnel.

Open-sector career paths

Open-sector career path evaluations are recognized as taking place both in one's organization and in other organizations. To the extent that outside evaluations are important, they include both the individual's performance and the performance of the organization. While in closed-sector career development one is not too concerned with the way one's organization is perceived, such perceptions are important in open-sector career assessment.

The principle strategy consists of 'being seen', of finding a way to do things that capture the imagination and attract attention to one's name. Open-sector career paths mean that individuals are less concerned with overall task performance and more with the way their organization – more specifically, *some aspect* of their organization – is perceived by significant outside evaluators. Inside evaluators, and clients, are of little relevance as long as outside evaluators think that 'something interesting is going on'.

Individuals in open-sector career paths do not disregard inside evaluations. It is not as easy to move from one organization to another if one is forced to move. Successful pursuit from the outside frequently depends on one's ability to wait. Therefore, inside evaluations must at least be positive. For this reason, individuals in this situation tend to be as conservative and cautious as their colleagues pursuing closed-sector career paths, *except* in a single narrow topic area where they pursue the limelight.

If accountability is the fashion, they will support accountability and seek to make accountability 'the thing.' If community participation is fashionable, they will attempt to be known as people who know how to make community participation work. If these individuals are talented, they will invent new approaches; they will be real innovators. If they are mediocre, they will only *seem* to invent.

The advantage of appearing to invent is that little change occurs. Such inertia has a double benefit. For some outsiders, you appear to be an innovator, and this is an advantage. For those in the know, however, you are really conservative, but you know how to appear to be innovative, and this duplicity may be a second advantage. Therefore, this mediocre approach tends to prevail. A copy chief reports:

There is a kind of cool paradox in advertising. There's a pressure toward the safe, tried and true that has worked in the past. But there's a tremendous need in the agency business for the fresh and the new, to differentiate this one agency from another. Writers are constantly torn between these two goals: selling the product and selling themselves. (In Terkel, 1974, p. 117)

Open-sector career paths mean one is more concerned with how one is percieved by people in the organizations one wants to move toward than with one's immediate co-workers and clients. A city manager in a small town, aspiring to move to a larger town, pursues policies and earns a reputation for handling those aspects of small-town problems that are more akin to the problems of the larger towns where he hopes to be in five years' time. He is grooming for his next assignment. He wants his work in his present assignment to look good to those who will hire him later. He does not really care about his present clientele. If the clientele belongs to one class (the poor) and the significant evaluators to another (upper middle class), we can expect him to be more attentive to the class to which the evaluators belong.

Open-sector paths also mean that one is more concerned with public relations than with task performance: even if the clientele is aware that the service is terrible, that the morale of the staff is collapsing, that the place is in disrepair, the public relations of the organization will continue imperturbably as if nothing were amiss. The rosy messages sent out are intended for people other than the clientele, for people who are unlikely to find out what is actually happening ...

Output measures as evaluation insurance

Output measures serve as evaluation insurance. When evaluators and criteria of evaluation are unknown, output measures are used to demonstrate performance. But different output measures can be used by different evaluators, thus causing confusion for those being evaluated. For example, legislative bodies wanting to control an agency may focus on one kind of performance evaluation while members of the agency may focus on another, thus placing the management of the agency in a conflict between the legislature and the professionals. Such conflicts are common in universities where funding agencies may be concerned with such measures as teacher—student contact hours and output of Ph.D.'s per year while the faculty evaluates itself on the basis of the quality and volume of its publications.

Nevertheless, while there may be some dispute about what output measures are relevant and should be used, there is a natural tendency for members of organizations to prefer output measures because they remove some uncertainty from evaluations. If it is not clear who is doing the evaluating or what criteria are used, there will be a preference for output measures that can be easily applied to one's own performance. These measures will be one's own outputs or, if one holds a middle-level position, the outputs of one's unit in the organization. This standard greatly limits discretion for cooperation with other parts of the organization and leads to the well-documented practice of non-cooperative bureaucratic empires having little, if any, relation to other parts of their organization.

It also leads to a narrowing of responsibility. Individuals are more concerned with the consequences of their acts during the period when they believe they are evaluated than with longer-term consequences which will not show up in the output measures. In many organizations, cost-cutting is a visible output easily attributable to the unit achieving it. Increasing productivity can be achieved by reducing costs per unit, and increases in productivity are a central concern of all modern organizations.

If there are no known ways to change a process or if change cannot be implemented because internal conditions are not amenable to change, it will not be possible to reduce costs through an increase in productivity. Therefore, one might be evaluated unfavorably even though one had no good way to act differently. A normal strategy in such cases would attempt to reduce costs without altering productivity. This alternative means reducing the quality of the goods or services produced.

The game of using cost reductions to protect one's career leads to mediocre service, particularly when the organization controls supply and clients have no alternative suppliers and so cannot exit. Organizations often produce mediocre products and services, not because clients really prefer mediocrity, but simply because individuals within the organization need to protect themselves, can only look good if they can reduce costs, and therefore reduce costs at the expense of the service as long as consumers do not balk ...

Rules as evaluation insurance

When output measures are unavailable or when it is not known how a different course of action might lead to different measures, members of organizations use the rules of the organization to justify and protect their behavior.

Suppose we have a department head in a large bureaucracy — a ministry in Ruritania. This person has no idea about how things are going to work out in the coming three years; there is conflict among the clients of her department; the politics are unclear; great energy is spent by eight different factions attempting to push the department in different directions. The top administration of the ministry is unpredictable; most of the directors and the minister have just been appointed. It is not clear how the president thinks, if he thinks at all, or how the department head perceives her evaluators or their criteria for evaluation.

Obviously, there are no guidelines to follow, and whatever this individual does will result in unknown outcomes. The individual does not have a clear basis for choice. It is not possible to relate actions to desirable evaluation results. What is left? When outcomes cannot be predicted, rules are used as protection: 'When in doubt, be sure to be clear; follow the rules.'

The more the environment is uncertain and the more it is difficult to predict outcomes, the more there is need for process rules to protect individual role performances, and the more rules will be established for this purpose. In addition, the more that rules are used to protect individual behavior, the more need for documented evidence; that is, the more bureaucrats produce forms, reports, accounts, and other written (or taped) documents. These are the defensive histories used to legitimate actions. In other words, when the environment is uncertain and the organization needs to be flexible, the members of the organization pursue defensive strategies that have exactly opposite consequences. They establish a barricade of rules which rigidifies performance and guarantees that service will be that much poorer than otherwise.

The game of risk avoidance

Taking risks results in positive evaluation *only* if the outcome is successful — that is, if the risk solves the problem at hand. Any innovation that fails implies bad judgment by the innovator, who is implicitly criticizing what was done previously.

Even if the outcome is successful, evaluators may react negatively. Any innovation that succeeds implies that the innovator exercised bad judgment by pushing herself too much; the innovator also exercised bad judgment in threatening others less successful than herself.

Not taking risks implies that the non-innovator feels that past procedures were correct, that past evaluations were reasonable. The non-innovator presents no threat to anyone. It is safe to evaluate such a person positively. Not taking risks means that the service continues to be mediocre, as it has been in the past, but at least it is predictable. No innovation also means that there is no need to keep trying to innovate, because there is no better way to provide service.

For these reasons, risks are taken only when past procedures are clearly inapplicable. For example, when the organization is in crisis, introducing innovations is not perceived as criticism of the old ways, especially when continuing in the old ways is perceived as too risky.

Risks are taken only when the situation has clearly changed and it is apparent that risks must be taken. But most individuals in organizations are not ready even for these risks. As far as possible, therefore, they attempt to avoid recognizing this condition. By contrast, however, the rhetoric of organizations emphasizes risk-taking. Therefore, there is a tendency for individuals in organizations to *appear* to be taking risks and to invent false risks.

In government, high-level appointments are made for political reasons and are usually of short duration. One is appointed Secretary or Assistant Secretary for an unknown term and is dismissed at discretion. High-level government appointees want and need to 'make a difference' either because it is possible to make a difference (this is exercise of personal power and is most satisfying to the ego), or because their high ambitions in open career paths require them to be highly visible. In these situations, risk-taking is part of the reward system and is an accepted way of life. Since dismissal or forced resignation is always possible, there is little time to act. Risks have to be taken immediately; there is a great hurry to bring about changes and innovations. It is no surprise that large government bureaucracies are continually being reorganized or announcing major new programs.

In contrast, the majority of individuals in the organization are part of the permanent hierarchy. They pursue closed career paths within the civil service and respond to a perceived reward system that deters risk-taking. It makes no sense for low- or middle-level bureaucrats to stick their necks out. Their aim is to remain quiet, to follow instructions, to stick to the rules.

This dichotomy is the basis for conflict. Individuals on the lower levels of the organization clearly perceive these differences. But they have to seek support outside the organization if they are to resist their hierarchical supervisors. To accomplish this goal, the public administration often reveals its conflict outside the organization where other arbitrators are available. Allies are sought in the permanent staffs of other departments or in the legislative bodies charged with the overall control of each agency. When allies are unavailable, the bureaucrats turn to the general public and leak stories to the press. Sooner or later, the ambitious masters realize the power of their minions, and the major reforms become small changes which may not be any reform at all.

Sending risks upstairs

Low- or middle-level bureaucrats prefer to send risky decisions upstairs. The top echelon — in government or private service — wants power, is anxious to intervene where it can be seen, and invites the upward flow of decisions. The top echelon may require the lower levels to channel all controversial decisions upward, particularly if it mistrusts its troops. But the top echelon receives more messages and is forced to deal with more issues than it can possibly handle. It therefore cannot spend as much time as it should on those decisions that are best taken at the top. The top echelon panics and decides to avoid risks. Big reforms become small adjustments, which may not be any change at all.

Inventing false risks

Lower and middle-levels respond positively to any suggestions from above that *appear* to be major innovations but do not alter any fundamental aspect of the way things are done. Since upper echelons are anxious to seek the limelight, since the easiest innovations they can introduce – that is, the innovations that the lower and middle levels will readily endorse – are those that are mostly appearance and little reality, it follows that most administrative reforms follow particular fads which provide legitimacy without affecting procedures.

When there is a change in the administration and a new government takes control, many of the new approaches of the previous administration are quickly forgotten; the new administration returns to normal before embarking on another set of innovations. The rapidity of these swings is well documented. For example, a study of the 1965 reform of the administrative unit of the Department of State showed that as soon as the Undersecretary of State for Administration resigned, his reforms were abolished:

Hence, within nine months of Crockett's departure, every experimental program in the former Office of Management Planning had been eliminated, eviscerated or totally redirected. MOP (Management by Objectives and Programs) had been mopped. (Warwick, 1975, p. 55)

Excessive Coordination

One function of coordination is to facilitate organizational spread. Another function is to protect members of organizations by providing a formal *sharing* of the responsibility for any decision. Coordination also has the advantage of creating the appearance that the house is in good order, that duplication is avoided and redundancy eliminated. But attempts at coordination do not alter the fact that most large organizations are composed of many independent empires that do not allow effective coordination to take place. Therefore much apparent coordination is not concerned with the rationalization of service but with providing protection for the members of organizations. We call it excessive coordination.

Excessive coordination is achieved through three processes: (1) lateral coordination via clearances; (2) lateral coordination via intra- or inter-committee work; and (3) hierarchical coordination. Two of these processes (committee work and hierarchical coordination) also serve other functions, such as providing visibility and mobility for middle-level staff (open career) and providing opportunities for defensive coalitions against top echelons and for hierarchical visibility (closed career).

Coordination procedures are rules that provide (2) documentation and (1) evidence of shared responsibility. If and when risks are taken, they are not taken by a single position-holder but by a long series of endorsers who agree to a decision and sign a document. This document becomes part of the evidence that is used to legitimate errors.

The more uncertain the environment, the more need there is for risk-sharing. This situation, in turn, reduces the extent of discretion and simultaneously creates a need for an increase in coordination procedures. But coordination takes time. Therefore, the more uncertain the environment, the more the organization is sluggish and slow to respond ...

We find therefore that when the environment is highly uncertain, organizations invent complex means of sharing responsibility among many members to reduce the possibility that any single individual might be blamed for errors.

Documented histories

Documented histories, as the name implies, are written or otherwise preserved documents that serve to protect individuals. Rules generate forms that confirm performance. Thus, individuals can document that they follow the rules; coordination clearance procedures provide documented histories. Coordinating committees write reports and memos providing proof of past individual behavior.

Documented histories are circulated to improve their defensive usefulness: 'How can you blame us now? You knew all along what we were doing; your office was kept informed of every decision; we sent your office copies of all our internal memoranda and of our correspondence.' Copies of documents are sent out 'for information' or 'for initial clearance'. Instructions are requested in writing. 'We would appreciate if your office would confirm these instructions in writing'.

Documented histories are the assets of a bureaucracy in fear. Files are jealously kept up to date. Even when conversations are not confirmed in writing, it is common practice to immediately dictate a memorandum for the file which can be used later as proof of one's original understanding. Most senior officials use a secretary to transcribe telephone conversations in shorthand, and the practice of taping conversations received much publicity during the administration of President Nixon.

A well-documented history can be used as both a defensive and an offensive weapon when difficulties arise. Therefore, all parties attempt to build histories that justify their actions. Since documented histories are used to share risks, bureaucrats resist becoming implicated in the documented histories of other departments or individuals. Officials who receive copies of decisions made elsewhere which they are supposed to clear or even concur in, defend themselves by suggesting changes, asking for additional information, or sending different points of view. One purpose is to show that the concurring unit never really approved the move. Another is to discourage others from involving one's unit in risk-taking.

Coordination meetings illustrate these processes. If several departments have to agree before a decision is taken, the originating unit seeks endorsements in order to share the risks with 'others'. But the 'others' seek to avoid responsibility. They lengthen the decision-making process and avoid participating in the discussions in order to protect themselves from future involvement. They insist on the most minute documentation from the originating unit to justify their own participation. 'We asked them to document their arguments, which they did, and we were reasonably satisfied that we could proceed'.

These bureaucratic processes easily become intolerable, and for this reason informal exchanges emerge: 'I'll gladly give you a clearance for this, but give me a clearance for that'. As a result, mutual trust emerges gradually. If and when trouble arises, elegant performances are appreciated. People who stand on their own feet and are not unreasonable in placing blame elsewhere acquire a reputation for 'playing the game fairly'. They become trusted members of the organization and acquire the ability to transact business. Trust is built gradually over the length of bureaucratic careers, and it is central to bureaucratic survival.

But trust is easily lost. When personal careers are at stake — when the issues are highly controversial — it is difficult for any one to be sure that others will behave elegantly. The card castle collapses as everyone attempts to protect his own interests. Accusations fly into the open; the scandal is leaked outside the organization, and trust evaporates. The organization is in crisis.

Doing nothing

Many persons in large organizations pursue a simple strategy: do nothing. Doing nothing is relatively safe because it is noncontroversial.

Doing nothing is not as easy as it sounds, because organizational roles have discretion; there are decisions to make; decisions are opportunities for controversy, and controversy can lead to negative evaluations. Moreover, the ideology of the organization calls for active innovations.

Doing nothing, while appearing to act, is accomplished as follows:

By greatly complicating the sequences of clearances, reviews, and reporting, so that considerable energy is spent by anyone attempting to do something within the organization. Careful procedures are established to guarantee that every attention is paid to make the new venture succeed. Proposals for new efforts are scrutinized indefinitely until their timeliness is past.

By starting small pilot projects that dissipate the energy of the innovators without committing anyone. Once the pilot project is completed, other pilot projects are initiated.

By encouraging competitive proposals for innovations from different portions of the organization and letting the innovators spend their energies competing against each other.

By introducing outside experts who are asked to assist in redesigning projects. The internal innovators enter into competition with the outside group. They spend their energies against each other.

By initiating a major review of existing activities and a massive reorganization. During the period of internal insecurity, when reorganization is under way, all new programs are postponed.

3.3 M. Perlman

THE ECONOMIC THEORY OF BUREAUCRACY

From *The Vote Motive*, ed. G. Tullock, published by the Institute of Economic Affairs, 1976.

Bureaucratic empires

'The Job Makers: Whitehall's Newest Empire' was a *Sunday Times* (7 Dec., 1975) 'Insight' report 'on the bizarre results of the Government's £30m. unemployment campaign'. The title gave some confirmation to the economic theory of bureaucracy; the contents are even more encouraging (for the theory, though not for the taxpayer!). It described the work of the Job-Creation Programme (JCP) organised by the Manpower Services Commission (MSC). It briefly described the birth of the MSC as a ' ... novel type of public agency' (bureau), its struggle for survival, its failure in competing with the private sector in previous ventures, and its successes in acquiring funds for the job-creation programme. It described how from the moment of its birth the MSC plunged into

... what one Department official called 'the most dramatic instance of empire building since Clive's arrival in India'. Prestigious offices were taken over in Piccadilly and Hyde Park Corner ... As unemployment rose, the Commission's staff rose to meet it. The Department of Employment's former group of functions is now administered by nearly 50,000 civil servants against some 35,000 in January last year, and the bulk of this increase is attributable to the burgeoning of the MSC and its subordinate agencies.

Job creation, like charity, plainly starts at home.

For the economic theory of bureaucracy, nothing in this episode should be surprising, except possibly how well it fits the theory. Economists working with a theory based on the idea that bureaucrats want to maximise the size of their bureau, its budget, and the non-pecuniary returns to the bureaucrats, are not particularly surprised when these things happen in practice. The JCP also exemplifies the difficulties in measuring and sometimes even defining the output produced by a government bureau — let alone evaluating its performance against its costs.

If by output is meant the achievement of the stated objectives of the scheme, the creation of jobs in regions of 'pressing needs ... designed to provide some vocational training', the project does not seem to have been very successful. According to the 'Insight' article

... The burden of the complaint [about the scheme] is that in view of the almost total absence of training, those youngsters involved ... are likely to be worse off at the end of it than they were at the start.

But is that really the correct measure of the output for which the JCP receives funds from its sponsors? After all, there is something strange about a situation in which one government bureau is telling local authorities to cut their expenditures while another wants to give them money to create jobs. Possibly the reported comment of Dr Gavin Kennedy from Strathclyde University that Job Creation is an 'exercise in window dressing' is a better guide to the real output of the project. From the point of view of the sponsor, its success must then be measured by how well it succeeds in this political aim. The report ends with 'Job Creation has already announced that it will require a further £100 million to continue its work beyond next year'. Obviously from the point of view of its government sponsor it has delivered the sponsored goods. In February 1976 Mr Healey announced in his special 'employment-creating' package an extra subsidy for the JCP of £30 million (in addition to the initial sum of £30 million (Sept. 1975) and a further allocation of £10 million (Dec. 1975).

The reticent bureaucrats: the information obstacle

'The Concorde Conspiracy' as described in the *Sunday Times* (8 & 15 Feb. 1976) is a fine example of the information obstacle to controlling bureaucracies. The political party acquires its information about costs and benefits of projects from the bureaucrats themselves. For a rational decision about a project like Concorde at least three pieces of information must be available: technical feasibility, costs of providing the finished product, and the expected benefit. The student of economics is taught that with such data he can begin to perform a cost-benefit analysis. It is understood, of course, that in any project of this kind there are uncertainties of all sorts. Predicting the future is not an easy task for economists or for bureaucrats. The political party making decisions, even in terms of the economic approach to politics, also makes a cost—benefit analysis. No political party gets many votes from squandering money. After all, even government works under a budget constraint and spending £x million on one project means that there will be less to spend on other projects, unless taxes are raised, bonds are issued, and/or the money supply is increased. Thus even in terms of the goal of maximising its votes, a political party will have to evaluate the costs and returns of any project, although it may well take account of electoral costs and benefits which the strictly economic approach may ignore.

The bureaucracy which will carry out the project also makes a cost-benefit analysis. But what variables enter into it? Assume the bureaucrats want to maximise the size of the bureau, their prestige, etc. Their constraints are the amounts of funds they can get from their sponsor, the government. This will depend on the government's cost—benefit analysis made on the basis of the information available to it. Many of the *variables* entering the several cost—benefit analyses may be the same, but what is being *maximised* is not necessarily the same. We therefore do not expect to have the same solution from the three sources: economists, government, and bureaucracy. The bureaucrats have however the biggest advantage since they control the information required for all the cost—benefit analyses.

... Concorde began as a dream among the boffins of Farnborough ... The project gathered momentum and adherents as ... enthusiasm spread to key civil servants ... Dissent within Farnborough itself ... was suppressed ... The 1959 report of the technical studies ... was presented with such enthusiasm ... that the difficulties were minimised. (A lobby was formed which) ... faked the first, ludicrously low, cost estimates to get them past the politicians [and] excluded the Treasury from the scrutiny of the early research and development costs. [*Sunday Times*, 15 Feb. 1976]

In 1962 the Mills Committee appointed to assess the project went away from its meeting 'believing that all the technical problems of building ... were already solved'. [*ibid.*] When realistic estimates for the project were required by the Treasure, it faced the typical kind of information problem in such situations:

The Treasury, of course, had no aviation expertise of its own. It could only cross-examine the experts from the Ministry. The guts of the costings were done largely by the enthusiasts at Farnborough and their ex-colleagues now promoting the project in the Ministry. [*ibid.*]

Step by step, the project was pushed through until recently it attained its well-deserved *technical* glory. But few believe that the rumoured opening line of the 1972 Rothschild (internal) report will have to be changed: 'Concorde is a commercial disaster ...' [*ibid.*]

If the politicians in power had had the available information at the time, it is doubtful whether Concorde would have 'got off the ground'. But they did not, because, to quote Niskanen,

... a bureaucrat has a stronger relative incentive [than the politician] ... to obtain the information relevant to his position (and to obscure information relevant to the sponsor) ... the relative incentives and available information, under most conditions, give the bureau the overwhelmingly dominant monopoly power. [Niskanen, 1971]

Bureaucrats and managers

The analysis of bureaucracy by Niskanen mainly applies to bureaux defined as 'non-profit organisations that receive a periodic appropriation or grant'. [Niskanen, 1973] This is not the everyday usage of the term 'bureaucracy', which is often applied to any large organisation. As the whole tenor of the economic approach to political decision-making is how to compare different institutional arrangements to allocate resources, it is useful to distinguish between large private firms and political bureaucracies. The former are run by managers, the latter by bureaucrats. Will they behave differently?

The analysis of bureaucracy is closely related to the analysis of large corporations. The latter raise problems of the relationship between shareholders as owners and ultimate recipients of residual profits, and the managers as decision-makers. Similarly, government bureaucracies raise the problem of the relationship between taxpayers as the ultimate recipients of the 'services' provided, the political party in power as the intermediary, and the bureaucrats as the decision-makers. In both situations it is assumed that managers and bureaucrats want to maximise their own utility functions[1] which may contain variables like the size of the bureau (or the size of the firm), the size of offices, a comfortable life, and other monetary and non-monetary advantages. If there are any differences between the two, it must be in the opportunities facing the bureaucrat and the manager.

In a world of perfect information and no transactions costs,[2] the manager would have to maximise the profit or utility of shareholders, otherwise he would be fired. The bureaucrat would have to do the same for the voter, otherwise the political party he serves would be fired. In a world in which information is costly to acquire, both the manager and the bureaucrat can divert some of the 'profits' to achieve their own goals rather than those of their respective sponsors. These returns can come by 'exploiting' either the consumer of the products or the ultimate recipients of residual profits. The distinction between the two, from which all others follow, is that the government bureaucracies have a higher degree of monopoly power over the goods and services they provide than do managers in industry.

Consider a firm that is badly run by its managers. To the consumers of its product the efficiency of the firm is not of much importance *as long as there are good substitutes for the product.* However badly the firm is run, the managers' powers to acquire resources so as to maximise their own utility do not extend over the consumer. The only way in which they can acquire the resources to increase their own utility is to divert some or all of the profits from shareholders to themselves. Since they cannot directly appropriate profits for their own use, this may be done in the form of exceptionally high salaries for beautiful secretaries, exceptionally high expenses for champagne lunches, etc. But although shareholders do not have information about these 'costs', they do have information about the profits left to them in the form of dividends and retained earnings. These yields can be compared with those from other shares in the same industry or outside and the shareholder can exercise the one power he always has if he is not satisfied with his managers – he can sell his shares. The existence of other companies (and potential competitors) means that there are prospective take-over bidders if the price of the shares falls low enough. Such bidders do have an incentive to acquire information on why profits are low and, if they discover it is because of the diversion of profits into managerial utility-increasing activities, they will replace the managers by taking over the company.

Consider a similar sitution in a government bureaucracy. The consumers of the service do not have many alternatives in the product market with which to make the comparisons made by consumers of market products. This means not only that the consumer (taxpayer) cannot buy the product elsewhere, but that he has no information on whether the high price charged is due to 'inefficiency' (from his point of view) or to real factors such as relative scarcities. Is the price of first-class post so high because the post office is inefficient or because real costs are high? Even if this information were available, what can customers do? They can protest, form pressure groups (like consumer associations), write to their MPs and send angry letters to the newspapers. But protests are not costless and the information must be available. However, the only source of the relevant information is the very group or organisation they want to affect. There are no takeover bidders either, and the taxpayer cannot as easily 'sell his shares', although emigration is, of course, always a possibility.

The economic approach to bureaucracy

Complaints about bureaucratic inefficiency are not new, nor are they confined to those whose approach to bureaucracy is 'economic'. However, most other approaches concentrate on bureaucrats, rather than on the institutions of bureaucracy. If there is a deep belief, not uncommon in Britain, that when ordinary people are turned into bureaucrats they acquire saintly virtues, or that the selection procedure is such that only saintly people are elected to the bureaucratic calling, the solution to any instance of failure is perverse. It is usually to create another bureau to oversee those who have lapsed into sin. Bureaux are piled on bureaux and the bureaucracy grows on. From the resulting mountain it is soon impossible to unearth the molehill that started it all.

The solutions suggested by the economic approach to bureaucracy are quite different. It does not accept that bureaucrats are especially virtuous (nor, let me emphasise, especially unvirtuous); the solution looked for by this approach is therefore how to set up constraints which will induce the bureaucrat to act in the social interest. The economist would like to introduce an 'invisible hand' to pat the bureaucrat on the back when he acts in the correct manner; and possibly an invisible foot for a different part of the anatomy if he does not. The deep-rooted belief in the exceptional virtue of the bureaucrat is the biggest deterrent to any such solutions. Few people are shocked, and most would approve, if a private company has an incentive scheme for its young managers based on their performance ('incentive schemes' sounds much better than 'efficiency tests'). Many MPs will make long speeches about the necessity of passing laws to force private companies to reveal all their accounts, the managers' salaries, shareholdings, performance, etc., all in the cause of protecting the shareholders. But these laws are seldom applicable to government bureaucracies. Why is it so difficult, for example, to get information about the performance in 'O' or 'A' levels from the bureaux controlling local schools? Those government bureaucracies considered to be part of the Crown are also exempted from many of the laws which apply to, and constrain private institutions, such as, for example, those regulating planning permission.[3]

Where there is, or may be, competition from private companies in the product market, the government bureaucracies are also protected. There are laws prohibiting private mail deliveries, or the private import of cheap coal. When rail costs rise there are demands for higher taxes on other means of transport. A recent case is a good example. Laker Airlines applied for permission to operate the Laker Skytrain to New York. This was to be a 'walk-on' service very economically provided by what seems from all accounts to be a very efficient private company. Recently Mr Peter Shore (the then Secretary of Trade) rejected the proposal on the ground that it would have had effects on British Airways which would lose customers. Similarly, any attempts to private bus companies to compete with British Rail for its commuter traffic are strenuously opposed by both British Rail and the National Bus Company. These prohibitions are, of course, never justified in terms of protecting a possibly inefficient government-subsidised concern. Their function, or so it would seem, is to protect the consumer from that terrible calamity of getting a better product more cheaply.

More disclosure: why not as much as companies?

Many of the problems of bureaucracy arise from the lack of information about the achievements of the bureaux. Why should not the bureaux be subjected to *at least* the same rules for revealing information to their 'shareholders' as private companies? I do not even mean information about how decisions are reached, about the debates and horse-trading going on behind closed doors (although that would also be welcome); I mean simply information about the achievements and failures, and the explanations for them. When an estimate of £1 million turns into £10 million, it is not enough to shrug and say 'We all suffer from inflation'. True. But even with a 100 per cent rate of inflation the other £8 million evoke a justified curiosity.

Similarly it would be very useful to have information about the quality of the products of bureaux (a bureaucratic *Which?* would be most helpful). For example, all schools should be required to reveal information relevant to their customers if asked: the number of 'O' and 'A' levels, the truancy rates, the qualifications of teachers, etc. Of course this would cause some problems, long waiting lists for some schools, disgruntled parents in others. But the underlying problem does not arise from the information but from the differences in the quality of output, and it is not beyond the ingenuity of men to solve queuing problems. The use of education vouchers is one suggestion that has been explored in some detail (Peacock and Wiseman, 1964). For those who are opposed to the introduction of filthy lucre into such a noble enterprise as education, there are alternatives. For example, a lottery to allocate the queues. This is very egalitarian; random numbers have no prejudices.

In the many activities where there is scope for competition by private companies, it should not be discouraged. Why should not government corporations be subjected to the same laws about competition as private companies? Why are 'good' government monopolies sacrosanct, while there is an open season on the 'bad' private monopolies? Both are equally bad from the point of view of excluding alternatives.

The costs of solutions

To avoid misunderstanding, one proposition should be emphasised. The approach described by Professor Tullock and taken here is one in which institutional arrangements are not taken for granted but examined to judge their efficiency in solving problems. Suggested solutions must be subjected to the same analysis. Incentive solutions may not be costless. To take one of Professor Tullock's examples it may be true that promoting the efficient police officer from one division to a higher rank in another will stimulate his efficiency. Exactly the same analysis which leads to that conclusion also predicts that if efficiency is measured by, say, the number of arrests, he will have an incentive to arrest more 'freely'. It may be necessary to set up other institutions which may not be costless. After analysis it may turn out that the incentive system suggested to increase efficiency results in even more inefficiencies. In that case, of course, it should not be introduced.

Summary

Problems are solved by people, not by institutions. How well they are solved depends on the people *and* on the institutional restrictions imposed on their behaviour. 'The government', like 'the market', cannot solve any problems. Both are institutional arrangements within which individuals operate. They both provide a different structure of incentives for some acts and of disincentives for others. Both are imperfect. Two hundred years of systematic economic analysis has provided us with a reasonable understanding of the types of incentives and sanctions provided by the market. It has given us some understanding of the problems posed by the imperfections of the market and sometimes even suggestions for possible solutions. The economic approach to politics is an attempt to acquire a similar understanding of government.

Notes

1　The utility function is a representation of peoples' tastes — how they evaluate different goods and services.
2　Information about all the activities of managers, and the transactions costs of changing managers.
3　For a discussion of the laws applying to government departments, see Griffith and Street (1952).

3.4   L. B. Mohr

ORGANIZATIONS, DECISIONS AND COURTS

From *Law and Society Review*, vol. 10 part 4, pp. 621–42 (1976). Copyright The Law and Society Association, 1976.

Courts are supposed in common law countries to operate by adversary adjudication, ... but lawyers, judges, legal-system personnel, and defendants have known for a long time that departures from adversary adjudication are common. In recent years, however, students of the legal system have recognized that such departures are not only common but firmly entrenched (see especially Heumann, 1976). Alternatives to the textbook method of handling cases are not anomalies; they are institutions in their own right. Studies of criminal courts depict not the adversary-trial institution as it exists in myth and movies, but an arena in which lower-class clients are hustled through the system just as they are in health care, welfare, public housing, and other meeting grounds of poverty with bureaucracy (Skolnick, 1966; Blumberg, 1967; Packer, 1968; Cole, 1973; Mather, 1974; Heumann, 1976; Eisenstein and Jacob, 1977). Defendants are presumed to be guilty, trials are exceptional, personal characteristics of the defendant and political pressures on the judge, prosecutor, and lawyer count more than evidence, and outcomes are decided more by bargaining than battling. Although it is not always explicit, this literature seems motivated by a desire to understand how such departures have taken place and taken hold.

The dominant analytic approach specifically suggested by Packer (1968, pp. 152–3), has been to provide 'models' of the criminal process, and in particular to contrast the normative model of adversary adjudication with models representing observed systems of processing. This approach has been illuminating, but it has fallen short of the goal of explanation. It helps us to understand what occurs in a given court, but it is of relatively little assistance in explaining why some courts follow one model and some another.

Organizations

Recently, there has been something of a movement to understand courts as 'organizations' (Blumberg, 1967; Feeley, 1973; Baar, 1973; Heumann, 1976; Eisenstein and Jacob, 1977). This is essentially a continuation of earlier modelling attempts, with the bureaucratic organization representing a well defined model that differs in many crucial respects from the normative adversarial trial court. But the analogy appears strained in some respects; it is doubtful that we can gain insight into a given court by applying rigorously the existing body of knowledge known as 'organization theory'. Furthermore, it is questionable whether organization theory helps us to understand why some courts are different from others ... I think it more productive to consider courts as decision-making systems than as organizations. This has led me to realize that it will be more productive to consider behavior in organizations as being 'decisional' rather than 'organizational'. ...

The crux of the problem is that courts do not have what organization theorists mean by a 'management'. In the early years, Luther Gulick (1937; pp. 3–45) presented the acronym 'POSDCORB' for what he called the 'functions of the executive' — Planning, Organizing, Staffing, Delegating, Co-ordinating, Reporting, and Budgeting. Most of mainstream organization theory applies to social units in which these functions are carried out and are important for determining organizational behavior. Courts do not fit easily within this group. Whereas POSDCORB has much to do with the way a car is made in a factory or a patient is treated in a hospital, it is relevant only in minor respects to the way in which a defendant is processed in a court. In short, although they could technically be classified as organizations, courts appear not to be comprehended by the dominant strains of existing organization theory.

On the other hand, there is a relatively recent theme of major importance in organization theory that does appear to be applicable in an interesting way to courts and that therefore deserves mention. This is the movement to consider organizational goals and structure as dependent upon technological and environmental forces rather than as properties to be manipulated at will by management (Burns and Stalker, 1961; Woodward, 1965; Perrow, 1967; Lawrence and Lorsch, 1967; Mohr, 1971, 1975; Duncan, 1972). Management is eliminated from consideration in this theoretical framework (see Child, 1972*b*, for an important and germane dissent). Courts do have goals that are interesting in organization theory perspective (Mohr, 1973; Baar, 1973) and they also have an organizational structure if this is defined (following Perrow, 1967, p. 195) as the forms taken by interaction among personnel in the process of getting the work accomplished. Technology, it is true, hardly varies from court to court, and thus would explain little variation in goals or structure, but courts do differ widely and significantly in their environments, both by type of court and by geographic area. I suggest that these two *dependent*[1] variables (structure and goals) as manifested in courts or organizations are worthy of further research by students both of judicial behavior and of organizations, and that adaptation to the environment presents a promising explanatory paradigm (Mohr, 1975).

The theoretical possibilities just reviewed, however, probably do not explain in fact why there has been a substantial temptation to consider courts as organizations. Through the eyes of an organization theorist, this temptation probably arises because actors in the judicial bureaucracies depicted by Blumberg, Cole, Eisenstein and Jacob, and Heumann behave in their decision making remarkably like actors in *A Behavioral Theory of the Firm* (Cyert and March, 1963). This book is rarely (if ever) cited by observers of the judicial process, but organizations scholars know that the theory is powerfully 'true to life'. Although highly formal in presentation, it seems to capture behavior in organizations as participants know it to be ...

But organizations may be characterized in quite different terms. To Dalton (1959), for example, an organization is a political arena in which actors struggle for advantage covertly with factions, lies, trickery, sabotage and opportunism. To Weber (1947), a bureaucratic organization is a structure in which predetermined rules and programs cover almost all contingencies and behavior is rational and predictable. Cohen, March, and Olsen (1972) talk about 'organized anarchies' — loosely coupled organizational structures in which solutions, problems, and decision makers meander from one choice situation to another, joining together here and there in 'garbage cans', i.e. collections of decisional elements bearing no compelling relationship to one another. The organizational behavior depicted in these studies may be less distinctive than the 'firm' of Cyert and March, but there is substantial agreement, I would say, that these characterizations are also 'true to life'. In short, all organizations are not alike in organization theory; therefore, it will not help the analysis of court behavior very much to say that courts are 'organizations'.

We might, however, suggest that *some* courts are 'firms'. To the extent that they are, organization theory would have been found to supply an excellent model for behavior within the judicial system. Still, this model, like the others mentioned, does not answer what I take to be an important kind of question; it needs to be embedded in a more general theory that provides a means of predicting *when* a court will behave like a firm.

At present, organization theory does not provide a way of predicting when a court might follow one model and when another ... There are, however, some good hints. The most prominent one is that the 'garbage-can model' offered by Cohen, March, and Olsen is not offered as a model of organizational structure, but of organizational *choice*. It is presented as a model of choice (or, equivalently, decision-making) behavior that is likely in a certain *context*, viz. the context of an 'organized anarchy', where preferences are ill defined, technology is unclear, and participation is fluid. In addition, the literature that links environment and technology with outcomes such as structure and goals constitutes an important precedent for considering the most prominent characteristics of organizations to be influenced by context (Burns and Stalker, 1961; Woodward, 1965;

Lawrence and Lorsch, 1967; Perrow, 1967). If we add modes of choice to this list of dependent variables, along with structure and goals, we might then consider all of the organizational models referred to above ('firm', political model, etc.) as different models of *choice* behavior, not of general *organizational* behavior, and look for the kind of context in which each is most likely to occur.

The distinction between these two terms is important for general organization theory as well as for judicial behavior. It suggests that we need not expect all behavior within an organization to conform to a single model — 'firm', or garbage can, or politics, or the bureaucratic ideal type. Rather, we may recognize that decision-making groups — even a single decision-making group — within an organization may well be subject to different contexts at different times and may shift, with changes of context, into different modes of choice. Within an 'organized anarchy' such as a large university, for example, many decisions follow the highly programmed, rational bureaucratic model; they are not all made out of garbage cans. Similarly, it is doubtless true that much decision making in the industrial firm is political, although much undoubtedly fits the model of Cyert and March. These are not competing hypotheses, in short, but categories of a dependent variable, one whose determinants can be uncovered. ...

Trial courts are instruments for rendering decisions. Their organizational product is a certain kind of decision. Not all such courts, however, are best characterized by the same model of decision making (cf. Mather, 1974; Eisenstein and Jacob, 1977). They differ among themselves and what is more important, even within themselves. The differences may perhaps be understood in terms of modes of choice and contextual profiles drawn from organization theory.

Decisions

The decision submodels

Let us consider four prominent modes of choice as values of a categorical dependent variable and four parameters of the decision context as interacting independent variables.[2] This analytic framework is meant to advance the general hypothesis that *the operative mode of choice, or decision making, is determined by the specific conditions under which the decision is made.* Each mode of choice, or process of decision making, is composed of a choice mechanism, together with the kind of preliminary, instrumental decision behavior that is typical of that mechanism. A 'choice mechanism' is defined as a criterion for selecting the levels at which the various goals relevant to a collective decision will be satisfied. For example, one such criterion might be the *maximization* of certain goals agreed upon by the participants. Each of the four modes of choice may be characterized by a submodel of decision making. (The term 'submodel' is now employed in preference to 'model' merely to emphasize that we are not dealing with four different theories of the way in which all decisions are made, but rather a single theory stipulating that decisions are made in at least four different ways.) In addition, I will refer to the independent variable in the hypothesis, the conditions under which the decision is made, as the 'context' of the decision. By this term, I do not mean the environment of the court or other organization as a whole, but rather the set of conditions that may be used as descriptors of a decision process and that may in principle vary from decision to decision within the same organization.

In concentrating on the context and the process of decisions, I emphasize two links of a longer causal chain that begins with the determinants of context and ends with the consequences of process. The whole is diagrammed in Fig. 3.4.1 with some examples of beginning and end points that seem applicable to decision-making in courts.

The four prominent decision-making submodels are the Firm, the Rational, the Garbage Can, and the Political ...

   a.   The *Firm* submodel. Here, the choice mechanism is *satisficing*, i.e. an alternative is selected such that all goals in the active demand set (Cyert and March, 1963, pp. 35, 39) are satisfied at least at minimally acceptable levels (this is opposed, for example, to satisfying some goals maximally and other not at at all. March and Simon, 1958, pp. 140–41; Cyert and March, 1963, pp. 78–80, 118). Because of the work of Cyert and March (1963) and others, this submodel is the most thoroughly elaborated of the four. It contains within it theories of search, estimation, and learning as

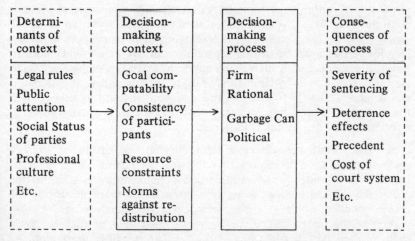

Fig. 3.4.1.   Causes and effects of variation in the decision-making process.

well as of choice, but these others need not concern us here. It is worthy of note, however, that in the Firm there is at least a tacit mutual search for a solution that will leave no participant greatly dissatisfied, and the typical mode of interaction among participants — the method by which final and true levels of aspiration in the active demand set are made known — is *bargaining* (Cyert and March, 1963, pp. 29–32). Department-store pricing decisions were shown by Cyert and March (1963, pp. 128–47) to be characterized by the Firm submodel. Municipal budgeting and Federal budgeting systems also exemplify the Firm in their mode of decision making (Crecine, 1969; Wildavsky, 1964). So, apparently, did national (U.S.) decision making in the Cuban missile crisis (Allison, 1971, pp. 67–100, 245–63). A board of directors or similar group is a Firm. In fact, because the profile of conditions determining this submodel is so very common, the Firm is probably the most prevalent mode of group decision making in Western societies. As we will show, many cases in criminal courts that are characterized by plea bargaining and simultaneous satisfaction of multiple competing goals are Firms in their process of decision.

b. The *Rational* submodel. In this case, the choice mechanism is *maximization*, i.e. logic and facts are adduced to discover and select the alternative that best attains a particular goal or weighted goal set.[3] For this submodel to operate, it is not necessary that the decisions that are made actually turn out to be 'best', but only that the maximization rule guides the process. Typical instrumental behavior features analysis and persuasion. Financial aid committees are often good examples, as are certain grant committees in Federal agencies.

Juries are often rational systems *par excellence*, with 'justice' being the primary goal, although if some jurors are strongly concerned about time constraints, or have divergent values, the rationality thrust can be significantly diluted. The decision stage leading up to submission to judge and jury for verdict must be treated separately. Initially, one would credit the Rational submodel with little if any applicability to this preliminary stage. However, the analysis by Heumann (1976) of the adaptation of presecutors and defense attorneys to plea bargaining suggests that at times the goals of the two are so completely consistent that the process of arriving jointly at a recommended disposition is Rational.

c. The *Garbage-can* submodel. Here, the choice mechanism is *'strategic agglomeration'*, i.e. a decision relative to a goal is rendered only if the latter happens to be under consideration when a choice on some other matter, call it the 'central choice', is actually made. Since there are usually too many appended problems to be solved or peripheral goals to be met in the making of the central choice, it is in general made only by 'flight' or 'oversight' (Cohen, March and Olsen, 1972) — that is, either most problems leave in search of a choice more likely to made ('flight'), or the central decision is made quickly — before other goals and problems have the opportunity to flock to it ('oversight'). A certain amount of politics, bargaining or rational analysis may take place, but these are not the behaviors with greatest importance for outcomes. Rather, the kinds of behavior that are typical and instrumental in the Garbage-can process of choice are going, coming, and waiting. For example, a new dean is to be selected. In the process, goals having to do with the hiring of women, neglect of the social science departments, antiquated data processing facilities, student rights, pass-fail grading, weak athletic teams, falling enrollments, and interdisciplinary programs become attached to the choice as problems to be resolved. Rational attempts are made, but it is clear that there is not enough energy available to solve all of these problems in the context of this particular choice. Gradually, problems wander off voluntarily in search of other choices. The dean is selected when only a few such problems remain, perhaps none. Cohen, March and Olsen tell us that the Garbage-can submodel is typical of 'organized anarchies', such as universities and other large, loose organizations. This may well be true, but the fact that a university is an organized anarchy does not imply that decisions within it will necessarily be characterized by the Garbage-can submodel. Many other kinds of decisions are taken in universities. The point is that an attribute such as fluid participation is more applicable to some decision-making situations in universities than to others. It may also be applicable more frequently to decisions in universities and similar organizations than to decisions in local welfare departments, small manufacturing firms, or criminal courts. But it is as parameters of a *decision context*, not a whole organization, that such attributes determine whether or not a process of choice is characterized by the Garbage-can submodel.

This submodel is presented more for its contribution to the broader theoretical framework proposed than for its applicability to courts. Its irrelevance to courts, however, is not a foregone conclusion. It may be pertinent to governmental decision making *about* courts, for example, or to decision making about what to review in appellate courts, or to other judicial activity not necessarily centered around individual cases.

d. The Political submodel. I use the term 'political' here in a narrow sense that is familiar and comfortable to organization theorists. It is meant to connote contention, struggle, and the attempt to overpower with superior force (whether this be force of money, arms, or argument). In this submodel, the choice mechanism is *domination*, i.e. the goals most satisfied are those most favored by the conqueror. Complete domination is not necessarily the outcome, just as a Rational process does not necessarily yield the most rational decision; stalemate is possible, for example, and selective losses and gains are common (see Kidder, 1974, for an elaboration of such outcomes with specific reference to litigation). Wars are often good examples of the operation of this submodel, as are many typical decision processes in the General Assembly of the United Nations ...

Many court cases are excellent examples of the operation of the Political mode of choice. This is not to suggest that judicial decisions are influenced by the current political regime. To say that what goes on in the courtroom is Political in this sense is essentially to say that normative[4] adversary adjudication obtains with no holds barred (cf. Skolnick, 1967) ...

For example, although there are many exceptions, the typical civil suit is Political. The goals involved are generally simple. One party wishes to obtain a lot of money (or some other value) and the other wishes to surrender very little. There can be no joint maximization because the goals of prime importance to both sides are on the same dimension with opposite sign.[5] Negotiation takes place and compromise or settlement may be reached before or during the court proceedings, but the negotiation is not of the same type as mutual search for a satisficing solution. Instead, it is essentially a struggle with all feasible weapons in which initial money and power differentials, the uncertainties of a trial, the desire to minimize losses, the facts of the case, and the skill of the lawyers determine the outcome. The suit itself, in fact, may be but a weapon in an underlying political struggle, which could conceivably be settled without reference to governmental authority at all.

The contextual variables

The four submodels discussed in the previous section are utilized as the column headings in Table 3.4.1, to which the reader is referred as a schematic rendering of the paradigm which follows. We may now turn to the contextual variables which comprise the row headings and fill in the matrix by specifying the ways in which approximate values of the latter lead toward one or another of the choice mechanisms. As will be noted, the various characteristics of context operate causally by providing incentives to and constraints upon the individual participants in the process of choice. The contextual variables are drawn from organization theory, particularly from Cyert and March (1963), Cohen, March and Olsen (1972), and Dalton (1959) ... and have been culled from a larger set of possible determinants implicit in the relevant literature and are offered here as parts of an integrated hypothesis. At a minimum, this set conveys the thrust of the paradigm and, as a synthesis of disparate strands of organization theory, represents a viable theoretical start.

a. Goal Compatibility. Following Cyert and March (1963, pp. 35, 39), we assume a set of latent demands (i.e. ends desired by participants and relevant to the decision, but for various reasons not pressed at a given time) and a set of active demands, or goals, attached to any choice. The active demands of each participant are pegged at specific aspiration levels,[6]

Table 3.4.1.   Decision submodels

	Firm	Rational	Garbage can	Political
Choice mechanisms	Satisficing	Maximizing	Strategic agglomeration	Domination
Typical instrumental behavior:	Bargaining	Analysis, persuasion	Going, coming, waiting	Contention struggle, force
Contextual variables				
1. Goal compatibility	Mod	High	Low	Low
2. Consistency of participants	High	Low-Mod	Low	Low
3. Resource constraints	High/Mod	Low	High	Low
4. Norms against redistribution	High	High	Mod	Low

although neither the goals themselves nor the aspiration levels need be clearly or openly avowed by their holders at any time during the choice process. Goal compatibility here refers to compatibility of the active demand sets of the various participants.

If goal compatibility is extremely low, then the choice must be made either by the flight of some participants or the domination of some by others — the third or fourth submodels — because the joint satisfaction of a number of mutually inconsistent goals is impossible. If compatibility is high, the tendency is strong to employ a Rational choice process, maximizing all demands in the set. If compatibility is moderate, there is a powerful incentive to bargain and satisfice; the demands are not so inconsistent that it is necessary to fight in order to obtain a favorable outcome, nor are they consistent enough to permit maximizing all simultaneously.

b. Consistency of Participants. This contextual variable has two sub-dimensions that operate multiplicatively (that is, both must be high in order for overall consistency to be high): (1) the extent to which the choice process involves face-to-face interaction (unlike, say, formal debate in a large legislature), and (2) the extent to which the cast of participants recurs in successive instances of choice.

This variable contributes substantially to the demarcation of the Firm submodel from the other three. If consistency is high, there is great pressure to satisfice, at least in Western societies; it is difficult for participants to tolerate repeated loss of face, by oneself or by another, in any *long-term face-to-face* group. If consistency of participants is low, there are several possibilities. If at the same time the goals are incompatible, then Garbage-can and Political processes will predominate. In other words, when goals seem to be divergent at the outset, and when there are also no personal ties and no possibilities for trading on demands in future choices, the incentives are either to leave or to fight. Low consistency of participants can also lead to Rational decision making, primarily when the goals of participants are compatible, as is the case with a jury. Moderate consistency might also lead to Rational processes, as in a financial aid committee, but whenever the consistency is greater than zero, a strong incentive to bargain is introduced. Even in groups that might otherwise be Rational, consistency of participants undermines the maximization dynamic by allowing the otherwise latent goals of individuals to creep into the active demand set.

   c.   Resource Constraints. This contextual dimension refers to time, energy, and other resources that may be necessary to support a given decision process (i.e., the transaction costs). Specifically, it is defined as the amount of resources it would take to reach a decision relative to the amount of resources available for the purpose. Thus, we would say that the constraints are high when there are relatively meager resources available.[7]

   If the resource constraints are low rather than high, the Rational or Political submodels become more probable, since there is incentive to keep on spending time, energy, money, lives, etc., until a maximizing solution is found, in the former case, or until one side is vanquished, in the latter. If the constraints are high, on the other hand, either the Firm submodel is encouraged, or the Garbage Can, that is, participants would either search for alternatives and bargain on the resources available until a satisficing solution is discovered, or, if this is infeasible, would simply have to give up and leave the field.[8]

   d.   Norms against redistribution. Decisions commonly allocate values. It is entirely possible to reach a decision that leaves one of the participants or constituencies worse off than before (even if only by losing face or reputation or by wasting resources). Choice processes differ importantly from one another in the extent to which they operate under norms that discourage such outcomes, a dimension that is conveyed here by the term "norms against redistribution."

   If there are no such norms in operation (denoted by 'Low' in Table 3.4.1), then the winner-take-all type of Political process is encouraged. If the norms against redistribution are strong, however, participants will be constrained to seek either a maximizing or a satisficing solution. If such norms are only moderately operative, the Garbage-can submodel is strongly suggested, i.e., if there is a bit of risk of losing significant ground in terms of one's goals, than one seriously considers leaving the fray for more likely opportunities, rather than hang around and make oneself perilously obnoxious to other participants by holding up the entire process. Although norms against redistribution might arise in many ways, they would almost always be strong in long-term, face-to-face groups, and this is one reason why consistency of participants leads to satisficing solutions.

Courts

Having offered a general paradigm for the determination of mode of decision making by conditions of context, it will be useful to conclude with a brief examination of courts in light of the theory presented.

The ordinary felony case that is common in a criminal court is a prototype of the Firm as a decision-making submodel:

Goal compatibility in such cases is moderate. Judges wish to save time, keep things simple, avoid certain undesirable images, and maintain political favor (Blumberg, 1967, pp. 120, 127). Prosecutors wish to maximize production, maximize convictions and guilty pleas, avoid over-leniency in the more serious cases, and earn favorable recommendations from superiors (Blumberg, 1967, p. 46; Alschuler, 1968). Defense lawyers wish primarily to earn a fee quickly (since it cannot be large) and keep clients satisfied (Blumberg, 1967, pp. 95–116; Alschuler, 1975). The public defender wishes to relieve the time pressure of his caseload, maintain a good reputation for the office, and obtain certain resources (e.g. confidence, prosecutorial information) that are necessary to the job (Alschuler, 1975, pp. 1206–55). Thus, goals are not highly compatible, in the sense that there is no possible way in which they can be jointly maximized. But they are not highly incompatible, either. Basically, the prosecutors and judges need a certain level of convictions and guilty pleas, but most often it does not matter crucially to what charges, with what sentences, and with what arrangements for bail, probation, etc. Defenders and lawyers need to do well for their clients, but this is measured much more in terms of penalties than in terms of formal outcomes of guilty or not guilty. Compatibility is to be found, therefore, in a plea of guilty to *some* charge and negotiated or tacit arrangements on the rest of the outcomes, especially the sentence, that do not mock the law but that are better for the defendant than he or she, and the family, might otherwise have expected. This is the very definition of plea bargaining (Alschuler, 1975, pp. 1180–81; Heumann, 1976, p. 64).

Consistency of participants, the second contextual variable, is extremely high in this sort of decision. The same few judges, prosecutors, and lawyers or defenders meet each other over and over again.

The *resource constraints* are also extremely high. Often, this is manifested in the pressure of a huge caseload, but I am sympathetic to the arguments of Feeley (1973, 417–9) and Heumann, (1976, pp. 64–82) that caseload *per se* is not the real villain (see Blumberg, 1967, p. 22 for the pro-caseload argument). Rather, the resource constraints inhere in two inescapable facts. First, neither the society nor the defendant is willing or able to expend nearly as much on minor criminal cases as on major ones, yet the costs of properly gathering information and conducting a trial are nearly as great. Second, the courtroom participants are personally disinclined to devote their energy and creativity to the great bulk of these routine criminal cases, where practically nothing is in dispute (Heumann, 1976). Thus, the resource constraints would remain just as high even if staggering caseloads were moderated, and would not be noticeably eased unless very few crimes were committed in the society.

The *norms against redistribution* are high.[9] The participants all have bargaining advantages and they meet again and again. To damage the reputation of one participant, to defeat him conspicuously or consistently, would simply lead to retaliation that could not be easily tolerated. Under these circumstances, the norms of playing the game are inevitably and firmly established and new personnel are socialized by the system to observe them scrupulously (Blumberg, 1967, pp. 73–94).

Given these characteristics on contextual dimensions, the Firm submodel is clearly suggested; the profile of characteristics just described adheres closely to the profile given by column 1 of the Table.

On the other hand, consider a case that came up in my own town several years ago, in the same court that settles case after case by plea bargaining. A man was accused of murder and was suspected to be the individual responsible for the sexual violation and brutal killing of more than ten young women. First, the lawyer for the defense was not a court regular but someone from out of town who had probably never appeared in our county building before. Thus, consistency of participants was low. The nature of the crime was such that very little flexibility existed in specifying the charges, and in addition, the public, watching attentively, would have been actively incensed if these murders had been labelled anything but murder. Thus, the defense attorney needed a finding of innocent and the prosecutor badly needed either a plea or a verdict of guilty. Compatibility of goals, then, was extremely low. The resource constraints were also low, since the county was obviously willing to spend whatever might be needed to administer justice in this case. The defendant and his family were not rich, but were willing to expend substantial sums for the defense, since the stakes were so very high. Energy resources were also available in abundance from judge, prosecutor and lawyer, since the case was unusual, challenging to all sides, and in the public spotlight. Finally, given the attention and expectations of the community, the norms favored whatever redistribution might result from an intense, all-out battle of evidence and argument. The profile of contextual characteristics therefore closely typifies the Political decision-making submodel and, despite the abundant familiarity of this court with plea bargaining, the case unfolded as a text-book example of adversary justice.[10]

Much of the literature on models of criminal justice and courts as organizations has tended to view individual courts as quite homogeneously representing either one or another category (e.g., Aubert, 1963; Nader, 1965; Blumberg, 1967; Baar, 1973; Feeley, 1973). I have argued that the mode of choice pursued not only varies from case to case within a given court, but varies predictably (the studies by Mather, 1974, and Eisenstein and Jacob, 1977, are within this latter spirit). To be sure, some courts do overwhelmingly represent a single submodel. Some, however, clearly represent both the Firm and the Political submodels, intermingled from day to day and from case to case. The clearest documentation of this is the analysis of Baltimore's Criminal Court by Eisenstein and Jacob (1977). Such courts are not confused, nor are they volatile, nor exceptions to some rule. They behave in this fashion simply because submodel of choice depends upon context of decision, and measures on the contextual dimensions may vary appreciably in such courts from case to case. The variation in context is not random, but is composed of events determined by prior causes, as suggested in Fig. 3.4.1. Some causes are to be found in courtroom structure and tradition itself and some in the surrounding community (Abel, 1973). Such courts, then, do not follow a model; they follow at least two models.

In general, individuals are motivated by profiles of conditions to adopt different decision-making strategies in different situations. I propose that such strategies tend to be uniform across participants in a given instance or tend to become integrated with one another in such a way that institutions, also, are ever ready to shift gears in response to contextual variation and slip unceremoniously into alternate modes of choice.

In sum, as an organization theorist I feel that although the fit between courts and organizations is not an altogether comfortable one, there are some themes in organization theory that may be helpful in the study of courts. The hypothesis linking structure and goals with organizational environment is one. When the idea of 'interorganizational analysis' is more tightly developed theoretically it will be another. Most importantly, I suggest, organization theory does have a small but special contribution to make in the area of models of choice; behavior in courts can be illuminated by analysis of processes of choice and contexts of decision. In these terms I have utilized incipient ideas in organization theory to propose a paradigm, patterned on discriminant function analysis. It rests on the assumption that choice behavior varies significantly both within and across individual courts and individual complex organizations and its goals are to classify and to render intelligible the striking behavioral variation in decision making that exists in both milieux.

Notes

1 A dependent variable is one which is the effect of one or more causes, or independent variables: independent variables determine dependent variables. (*eds.*)

2 The statistical model used here is one where a qualitative variable (e.g. acquit/convict) is predicted by a number of causal or independent variables which the author defines as context-variables; these variables may or may not be qualitative themselves. The general, theoretical, model of explanation being used is the idea of several independent causes adding their effects to determine an outcome or dependent variable. (*eds.*)

3 See Introduction to Section 2. (*eds.*)

4 See General Introduction. (*eds.*)

5 The zero-sum conception of decisions, see General Introduction. (*eds.*)

6 I.e. the subjective importance to an actor of achieving his demand. (*eds.*)

7 There are many different ways in which this dimension could be operationalized. One that suggests itself as particularly productive is, 'the resource constraints upon the least constrained participant'. The ratio referred to in the text then becomes, for each participant, the resources available to the participant divided by the resources required to reach a total solution which includes maximizing the goals of that participant. In many civil cases the resource constraints vary substantially among participants, so that one of them frequently has a highly favorable ratio and there is strong incentive to attempt to dominate (cf. Galanter, 1974). Studies indicate that in the bulk of criminal cases, the resource constraints are uniformly high on all participants, which encourages bargaining.

8 The choice between bargaining and leaving, given high resource constraints, would depend on goal compatibility—bargaining when there is moderate compatibility and leaving when compatibility is so low that, given the constraints on energy available, there is no hope of fulfilling the goals. In the same way, the choice between the Rational and Political submodels depends on goal compatibility when resource constraints are low — maximization is evoked when the goals are compatible and struggle is selected when they are not ...

9 It is interesting to note that bargaining toward a satisficing solution and conducting Political negotiations outside of court, instances in which the norms *against* redistribution are quite high and quite low, respectively, are seized upon as alternatives to a process (i.e. adjudication) in which the norms strongly *favor* redistribution. In court, the norms direct the judge and jury to measure the facts against pre-established standards and decide who wins; it is normatively illegitimate for the judge to encourage bargaining, compromise, or "working something out" (see Coons, 1964; and Ross, 1970).

10 So extreme a case as this one is not generally required to 'cue in' the Political submodel rather than the Firm. The study by Mather (1974) is most informative in this regard. In the court that she analyzed, 87% of the cases not dismissed were settled either through implicit or explicit plea bargaining. The analysis strongly suggests that, by tradition, *certain types* of cases were expected to be the exceptions — to go to trial. These were the types in which the goals of the prosecutor and the defender would understandably (by all concerned) be least compatible. The prime example is the case that must be considered 'serious' and that also contains an element of reasonable doubt as to guilt. Because of local tradition, the resource constraints and the norms against redistribution were also lower than usual in such cases, just as was the compatibility of goals: it appears to have been understood by all major participants that the limited time and energy available for adversary (redistributive) trials would be reserved for *just such cases*. The process of selection of cases for trial was not random, nor arbitrary, nor even, for the most part, unilateral. The same flavor is imparted by many of the examples scattered throughout the studies by Eisenstein and Jacob (1977) and by Heumann (1976).

3.5   B. Salter and T. Tapper

POLICY MAKING AND THE STATE APPARATUS

From *Education, Politics and the State* by B. Salter and T. Tapper, published by Grant McIntyre, 1981.

Educational policy making is the process whereby the various pressures for educational change are translated into formal governmental expression. In becoming policy, the dynamic for change takes on specific form and is endowed with whatever legitimacy and power the dominant political structure commands. That much is not in question. Where the difficulty arises is in exploring how the pressures derived from the social control, economic and personal consumption functions of education, on the one hand, and the input from demographic shifts and the political parties, on the other, come together to form policy. What are the structures which regulate, if that is the right word, this process and how do they do it?

Here we argue that the forum in which these pressures for change are politically negotiated is, increasingly, the educational state apparatus: the Department of Education and Science. Furthermore, that this struggle over educational policy takes place in a bureaucratic context which is far from passive in its policy preferences, and which, in fact, sets the parameters within which the policy debate is conducted. We therefore begin with a brief review of existing approaches both to more general and to specifically educational policy-making. This is followed by a consideration of the bureaucratic constraints within which educational change is negotiated and the limitations placed on different types of possible policy outcomes. Do the planning techniques of the British educational bureaucracy bolster the power of the professional civil servant both at the LEA and DES level of decision making? Thirdly, even assuming that the command posts of educational change are being captured by an ambitious bureaucracy, how well-equipped is it to ensure that the resulting policy is effectively executed? Fourthly, how does the expansion of bureaucratic power square with education's ideological and legitimating functions? Do the two always go neatly together or does the management of educational change present its own problems for the generation of the ideology necessary to mask education's underlying social functions?

Studies of policy making

... Three frequently quoted studies of educational policy are those by Jennings (1977), Saran (1973) and Kogan (1975) and in different ways they illustrate the difficulties of the area. The first two concern themselves with local authority education and Kogan deals with the national perspective. Although both Jennings and Saran claim to be using the decision-making approach to educational policy and although both employ the same methodology, that of the case study, the content of their work contradicts these superficial similarities. While Jennings' notion of decision making is explicitly derived from Agger's seven stage model (1964; see Dahl 1962), Saran relies on the administrative arrangements she finds to exist in the case study for her conceptual framework. Hence Jennings tends to impost a 'rational', and foreign model which leaves one with the uncomfortable feeling that facts have been crunched into place and Saran rarely raises her head above the details of procedural decision making.

Meanwhile, in his national study Kogan (1975, pp. 74–7) applies a model of interest group theory whereby policy is seen to emerge from the activities of a number of groups (e.g. local authority associations, teachers' unions) with the DES acting as eventual arbiter in the situation. Despite the empirical thoroughness of this approach the dynamic of policy formation remains elusive. Thus the initial assumption is that once the interests of the major educational groups have been identified the way is cleared for an explanation of how a consensus emerged to become policy. This is the normal tenet of such an equilibrium model. However, as Kogan (*ibid.*, p. 23) himself admits, such a framework is not adequate for the purpose of analysing the complexities of educational policy making.

The sources of policy generation are so difficult to locate, let alone place in any logical pattern, that detecting the changes in values, or the pressures by which change is effected, is more a matter of art than of analysis. The imagery of political science suggests too much precision: such words as 'power', 'structure', 'pressure', 'leverage' all suggest that political activity is analogous with predictable engineering. Softer and more modest imagery is needed.

The primary difficulty lies with the inability of interest group theory to incorporate the forces which lie behind the apparent balancing of rival group interests: hence the issues of process and change over time remain enigmatic. The result, as Kogan (*ibid.*, p. 235) observes, is that there is 'no adequate explanatory framework of how local pressures and decision-making add to the national aggregate', 'no clear or linear process of change' (*ibid.*, p. 236). Rather, educational change is like a kaleidoscope, 'Colours in a changing pattern move out of view, or get stuck, or change position when the box is tapped' (*ibid.*, p. 237).

This then leaves us in the position of asking, with Kogan (*ibid.*, p. 238),

'But, how does the DES aggregate the knowledge, feelings, resistances and resource feasibility of the 30,000 institutions, the complex political system that we have described, the press and the intelligentsia?'

One answer could be that the DES does not have this 'aggregating function' at all; or at least, not on any significant scale. Again, the DES may aggregate but only after it has decided which viewpoints should be selected for aggregation. The point to be made is that the adoption of the interest group model by Kogan has placed him in the position where he is obliged to try to make sense of educational policy in terms of its being an output produced as the result of a complex of interest group inputs, or policy preferences. According to this model, the main problem lies in discovering the equation which, it is assumed, governs the way in which inputs are 'balanced' and policy calculated. As we have shown the absence of such an equation then leads to the use of that 'softer and more modest imagery' in order to make sense of what is happening.

Recognition that less easily accessible, but nonetheless influential processes are at work in the formation of educational policy often appears as a discussion of vague concepts such as the changing 'climate of opinion' or 'public opinion' ... Comments such as these are usually linked to a consensus model of policy formation which presents 'policy making in education as a cumulative process, where change rarely occurs until a consensus is reached' (Parkinson, 1970, p. 122) and the government as the recipient of the inevitable: 'Public opinion, and especially opinion in the educational world, will usually have been moving in favour of such [policy] changes for many years before they are sanctioned officially by government' (Fowler, 1974, p. 21).

The advantage of such a diffuse idea as 'climate of opinion' is that it ostensibly plugs the gap between cause and effect in the group—policy relationship: groups influence, and are influenced by public opinion which in turn influences policy. However, although the felt need for such a concept is a valid one, this particular answer to that need merely raises the generality of the discussion without telling us how and why one type of 'climate of opinion' rather than another is formed. It is a kind of conceptual sop that leaves the question of the nature of the policy dynamic unanswered. It is to this question that we now turn.

The bureaucratization of educational power

British educational policy is increasingly produced in the context of bureaucratic developments which, we will argue, represent preferred policy directions. These developments have, in turn, to respond to the pressures generated by education's functions as an agent of social control and servant of the economy (however badly performed) as well as to the more demands imposed by demographic shifts and changing party governments.

As the manager of the arena in which these demands are negotiated, the state apparatus (the DES) is in a position to arrange not only the agenda of the negotiations but also to advise on the financial considerations involved in particular policy outcomes and the changes in the state apparatus required in order to implement certain policies. So although it cannot ignore the social and political pressures to which it is inevitably subject, the Department can nonetheless interpret these pressures in ways which suit its own bureaucratic ambitions. While the bureaucratic medium within which policy emerges very much constrains the content of the policy message produced, we are not arguing that this is a total process – if only because the bureaucratic developments in question are relatively recent and are occurring within a decentralized education system. They nevertheless have an internal logic, are progressive in their encapsulation of the policy-making arena and can in no way be seen as part of a rational balancing of opposing group interests.

An initial and highly visible indication of how the policy-making context in education has altered over the past thirty years is the changing position of the DES. 'For a long while after the 1944 Act', writes Kogan (1973, p. 171), 'the Department considered itself not as an educational planning department, or as leaders on policy, but primarily as a mediator between the "real" agents of educational government – the local education authorities, the teachers and the denominations and the government-wide network of control and economic policy led by the Treasury'. It exhibited a 'persistent reluctance' to take seriously its own role as promoter of educational policy (*ibid.*) and maintained the prewar functions of the Board of Education which were 'regulatory and quasi-judicial' (1971, p. 170). This passive and retiring posture has now changed. Today we see a far more interventionist-minded DES; one that is prepared to initiate and orchestrate the Great Debate, attack bodies such as the Schools Council, and raise questions about the curriculum and standards of teaching which had previously been regarded as well outside its preserve.

The change in the role of the DES from blushing handmaiden to prima donna has to be seen as the tip of the iceberg so far as the policy-making process is concerned. It is merely a surface indication of rather deeper sea changes in the educational bureaucracy which are reflected in the manner in which policy is shaped and controlled ... The more education is seen as an activity consciously directed by one group, the DES, as opposed to the impartial product of a consensus of wise old heads, the more it will need fresh legitimizing clothes to replace the discarded old ones. It is by no means clear that the DES appreciates that for the policy output to carry legitimizing weight it is essential that the policy-making process should itself be regarded as legitimate. Too much haste in changing the nature of that process could well undermine its credibility.

What aspects of educational policy formation do we need to examine to determine the extent to which the new DES stance is indicative of more fundamental shifts? The way in which policy is formed can be said to influence the shape of the policies produced in terms of both the range of structures which have access to the policy-making process and the values that dominate those structures. Together they constitute the parameters within which policy emerges. It is our contention that policy formation in education is becoming an activity encapsulated within a limited set of structures, permeated by bureaucratic values which emphasize the import-ance of scientific rationality, efficiency and professional expertise. These are the parameters which control the rate and direction of educational change ...

The DES

The origins of the Department's shift from 'holder of the ring between the real forces in educational policy-making' (local authorities, the denomi-nations, teachers and parents) to 'enforcer of positive controls, based increasingly on knowledge which the department itself went out to get' (Kogan, 1971, p. 30) can be traced back to changes in the DES–LEA relationship in the 1950s. During this period it became obvious that cer-tain basic processes of resource allocation within the educational system could no longer be subject to the whims of decentralized administrative procedures without complete confusion resulting. In particular, more effective centralized influence was seen to be necessary over capital spending on buildings and the prediction and supply of teachers. This led to the setting up within the department of the Architects and Building Branch and the Teachers Supply Branch. Referring to major developments in the Department's forward planning capacity in recent years, Sir William Pile (1979, p. 59) noted that 'These changes reflect the growing recognition than an essential function of the Department, over and above the perform-ance of specific practical and administrative duties deriving from the education Acts, is that of resource planning for the education service as a whole.' He elaborated:

that is, the formulation of objectives, the framing of national policies best calculated to meet these objectives, the undertaking of long term costings of policies in a way that enables ministers to choose their priorities, and the task of effectively presenting the consequential resource needs within central government.

Now there can be little doubt that, given the Department's final responsibility for the administration of education and the increasing demand for education and expenditure on it, the emergence of these more sophisticated kinds of planning mechanisms was inevitable. The question which concerns us is how far the theme of 'administrative necessity' was used to justify the enclosure of the policy-making process; how far the planning process has been internalized within the Department on the grounds that the Department alone has the planning know-how and that, within this, projections about capital expenditure and teacher manpower, for example, have an objective and unchallengeable validity of their own ...

The more that official estimates dominate the context in which policies are made, the more these estimates are likely to become self-fulfilling prophecies and, conversely, the more that opportunities to develop the system in different ways will be neglected. Official command of the type of information input for the consideration of policy makers (as in the case of a heavy reliance on the extrapolation of existing trends) will naturally prescribe the parameters of possible policies. There is also an easy symbiosis between the use of projections of student and teacher numbers by the DES and the financial procedures governing department spending organized under the Public Expenditure Survey Committee (PESC). This requires that early each year government departments submit estimates of what they expect to spend over the next five years of each of their programmes to PESC. Given that departments compete with each other for a share of the expenditure cake, the DES is naturally not going to lose the opportunity of supporting its case and its financial projections with parallel figures concerning student and teacher population trends. The 'hard' data culled from the latter thus have considerable political appeal for the DES in the annual round of interdepartmental budgeting warfare, and until it can find an equally authoritative substitute it is not likely to downgrade the importance of projections in the face it presents to the rest of Whitehall.

As a means of estimating the financial implications of existing government programmes the Public Expenditure Survey system obviously suffers from the weakness that it does not cost and compare alternative policy options, as the White Paper 'The Reorganisation of Central Government' (The Cabinet Office, 1979, para. 50) pointed out. In an attempt to remedy this problem, an output budgeting technique called Programme Analysis and Review (PAR), in many respects similar to the technique of corporate planning discussed earlier, was introduced into government planning in 1970, and the DES (1970b) has been one of the first departments to try and develop it. Like corporate planning, PAR seeks to systematize the process of policy analysis and policy formation along lines which place a premium on being able to assess the budgetary implications of different policy developments. The objective is to take a particular programme area such as nursery education and then to set out in a logical and informed fashion the alternative policies and their alternative costs.

Again it has that rational quality with immediate ramifications for the delimitation of the policy-making process. Firstly, some educational policies are going to be more easily costed than others and these are likely to be those already tried and tested and those which can be linked to trend data. Newer and less quantifiable policies are bound to appear experimental and hence more of a gamble. Secondly, the more confident that officials and ministers become that this management technique supplies them with the information required to make rational policy choices, the more policy formation will be internalized within the DES and the more outside interest groups will be excluded from it ...

Consultation with outside groups may take place, therefore, but in the context of choices already defined. Such consultation is consequently likely to be confirmatory rather than initiating in its objectives. However, what this argument does not deal with is the possibility that no matter how systematic the administration of PAR may be, and the indications are that it is not that systematic, that room still exists for the injection of values not sanctioned by the DES into policy making in the form of the education minister's role. How real is this possibility?

The most detailed evidence relevant to this question is Maurice Kogan's conversations with ex-DES ministers Edward Boyle and Antony Crosland in *The Politics of Education*. His general conclusion (1971, p. 41) is that the 'ability of even the most able Minister to create, promote and carry out policies is limited'. Both Boyle and Crosland emphasize the constraints under which a minister operates in terms of policies already in train or being explored, the amount of information to be digested and the continually evolving nature of educational policy. Crosland calculated that it takes about two years to fully master a department but that even so, within these two years 'there will be chunks of the Department and of Department policy which you have not really had time to look at at all' (*ibid.*, p. 158). Similarly Boyle felt that he did not have control over the vast range of policies of the DES — partly because he did not have time to understand all the various parts of education (*ibid.*, p. 137). This feeling is reinforced by the arguments of Lord Crowther-Hunt (a former Minister of State in the DES) concerning the gathering of influence by the bureaucratic elite. Crowther-Hunt maintains that the continual turnover of ministers of education (he estimates that in recent years their stay has averaged 17 months) means that they are rarely in the position of having sufficient independent knowledge to challenge the details of the policy aganda advanced by their civil servants. So when one of the Whitehall official committees (which ministers do not attend) or PAR reports (which are not published) produce their recommendations, it is increasingly difficult for a minister not to accept them (Crowther-Hunt & Kellner, 1980).

Probably the most influential role one can ascribe to a Minister, therefore, is that of arbitrator of competing policies within the DES rather than the initiator of completely new ones and the imposer of foreign values. This does not deny of course that department policies are heterogeneous rather then homogeneous. What Toby Weaver, ex-Deputy Secretary at the DES, has described as the 'dialectic within the office' ensures that such choice is available (*ibid.*, p. 123). However, it is our contention that the procedures on which the policy-making process is founded increasingly circumscribe the nature of its possible content and hence the range of choices available to a minister.

For those continually concerned with the generation of those choices, the civil servants of central government, it would seem that there would be little to object to in the enclosure and limitation of policy formation. Indeed, if Locke (1974, p. 71) is correct in his belief that the 'dedicated professional thinks of himself as fair and able to avoid self-interest in a way which representatives of localities or particular interests are not' then there would apparently be much to gain. The OECD report *Educational Development Strategy in England and Wales* was very forthright on this issue:

The feeling exists strongly within the Department that when it comes to planning leading to policy decisions for which resources have to be secured and allocated, such informal methods, utilised by sensitive and fair-minded government servants, are superior to highly structured formal procedures which invite half-baked and politically sectarian opinions, and encourage demagogy, confrontation, and publicity battles, leading to a considerable waste of time (1975, p. 31).

... The more activist definition of the educational administrator's role is a necessary corollary of the interventionist DES prepared both to take the lead in policy making and to prescribe its acceptable limits. Although the traditional conception of the department as aggregator and synthesizer of pressure group demands, responsive to the movement of the consensus, is still much beloved by many writers on education including the public self-presentation of the DES itself (see OECD, 1975; Pt. 1), it is a conception rapidly being rendered obsolete by the march of events ... And just as the Department shrugs off its passive policy stance so must those who administer it. But while shrugging off a self-conception is one thing, rearranging the relationships with others to fit that new conception is quite another and depends, firstly, on the amount of control the DES can exercise over its environment in the construction and execution of policy and, secondly, on its capacity to legitimize new policy. Changing the state apparatus can be a dicey affair.

Controls

Until recently, the department has been engagingly modest in its estimation of its own power. In its contribution to the 1975 OECD report, for example, it argued that the powers of the Secretary of State under the 1944 Education Act and subsequent Acts 'though important are not extensive' and that he 'relies heavily on non-statutory means of implementing his policies, by offering guidance and advice through the issue of circulars and other documents' (pp. 8–9). Phrases such as 'adequate consultation', 'foundation of assent' and 'general consensus' are scattered liberally throughout the DES section of the report as the Department insists that it is reflecting an aggregate of existing opinion rather than seeking to mould a new one. Its view of its controls are here fully consistent with its consensus model of educational policy making ... As it happens the Department's earlier promulgation of a public image where its powers were presented as limited and mainly non-statutory was in any case something of a false modesty.

All LEAs operate within an established network of national policies: the length of school life, salaries paid to teachers, minimum building standards and maximum building costs and pupil-teacher ratios. Any consideration of departmental control must in the first instance recognize that this framework exists and itself sets limits upon an LEA's capacity to deviate too far from central guidelines. Similarly, the much vaunted autonomy of the classroom teacher is regulated by the national system of curriculum control, namely the General Certificate of Education Examination at Ordinary and Advanced Levels, and the Certificate of Secondary Education Examinations in their various modes. Although the actual examinations are administered by autonomous examining bodies (eight GCE and fourteen CSE) the Secretary of State decided what changes will occur in the system after listening to the advice of an intermediary body, the Schools Council. Beyond this framework of controls, the DES has its financial controls, whatever overlap exists between local and central administrator values on policy making and last, but not least, Her Majesty's Inspectorate.

Although the department does not directly control the capital finance used by LEAs for educational building, it does decide ... which LEA projects will be given the go-ahead and which ones refused. The fact that local authorities must submit educational building plans to the Department for approval means that the DES cannot only apply the standing administrative requirements to the plans but can also use the opportunity, if it so wishes, to exercise political control over changes in local authority provision. The most notable clashes recently in this respect have been those over LEA plans for comprehensivization which have failed to meet DES standards, flexible though these are, on what precisely constitutes a comprehensive system. Given this method of financing the physical context in which education takes place, it is obviously in the interest of LEAs to remain sensitive to developments in DES policy both by keeping a close watch on the numerous circulars issued by the Department and by consultation with its local liaison officer, the HMI.

Even recognizing this ultimate control of capital investment by the DES, it would not do to conclude as a result that LEAs are the easy and obedient servants of the Departmental will. For although Crosland 'was

very struck by how much influence, control, power, or whatever the right
word is, the Department has' (Kogan, 1971, p. 169), Boyle pointed out
(*ibid.*, p. 124) that 'there can't be a straight, single control here for the
very simple reason that the Ministry directly controls so very little money'.
Boyle was referring to the fact that the majority of the expenditure on
education by local authorities, that is recurrent as opposed to capital
expenditure, comes to the LEA as part of the annual Rate Support Grant
(RSG) from which the government finances all local authority services.
The RSG is a block grant within which, until very recently, no funds were
separately labelled for the use of the education service alone: education
had to compete with the other services for its share. At first sight this
system may appear to have given LEAs substantial discretion in terms of
what they spend on education and how they spend it but, bearing in mind
the national guidelines within which LEAs must operate, the true situation
is much less clear cut and the arguments continue (see Boaden, 1971;
Byrne, 1974). The picture is further muddied by the 1980 Local Government Planning and Land (No. 2) Act which replaces the single block grant
with one awarded on a service by service basis. Precisely what effect this
will have on the DES–LEA relationship it is as yet to soon to say. What is,
nevertheless, clear, is that considerable variation exists in LEA provision of
books, equipment, furniture, in-service training of teachers, school transport etc., indicating that although the DES may control the broad parameters of education so far it does not substantially influence the quality of
the day-to-day provision within these parameters (see Taylor and Ayres,
1969) ...

At present, then, the fragmentation of the financial procedures on
which the DES relies in its attempts to construct policies leads to tensions
between the local authorities and the Department. However, it is worth
noting that both would agree on the diagnosis of the reasons for the
problem, that is the inefficiencies of the financing mechanisms, and the
need for more systematic cooperation. Whether this also means that they
would agree on who has what say in a more integrated planning system is
open to doubt. For our previous analysis suggests that the DES has already
defined what it means by more efficiency in central policy making and it
will be a question of how far local authorities are prepared to go along
with this definition once its structural implications begin to percolate
through. Despite the common professional concern that long-term planning
in education should be rationally organized the traditional central–local
differences are bound to pose problems. Thus Mrs Thatcher's rather abrupt
withdrawal of Circular 10/65 enforcing comprehensivization and its
replacement with Circular 10/70 allowing LEAs to decide against comprehensivization if they so wished drew unanimous protest from the local
authority associations. As Kogan (1975, p. 100) points out 'it was not what
she did but the way that she did it that was objectionable'.

If there is doubt this far about the Department's ability to orchestrate policy change, where does that leave its territorial force, Her Majesty's Inspectorate? How far can HMI be regarded as the willing tool of the DES in its attempts to impose central definitions of desirable policy shift and how far is HMI an independent body with opinions and values of its own? Its position in the educational system as authoritative supplier of information both to the LEAs and schools on the one hand, and the DES on the other, is undoubtedly critical. At the local level, HMIs have the functions of inspectors of schools and colleges, interpreters of Department policy to the LEAs, and are members of numerous committees such as examination boards and regional advisory council for further education ... At the central level, they act as professional advisers to the DES drawing on their network of local contacts, contribute to Department publications and staff Department courses for teachers. Any move by the DES to systematize further the process of policy construction is therefore dependent upon HMI to acquire and to disseminate the right information at the right time. This would imply that from the Department's point of view the closer the ties between itself and HMI the better.

Writers on Her Majesty's Inspectorate are frequently at pains to point out that HMIs are independent-minded people, if occasionally idiosyncratic. With some pride Blackie (1970, p. 52; and see Edmonds, 1962), an ex-HMI himself, argues that,

An inspector's essential independence is professional. In all educational matters he is free to hold and to express his own opinions, and no departmental control can be exercised upon them. This means that what he says to a teacher or writes in a report is what he really thinks, and is not in any way trimmed to suit government or departmental policy.

More realistically he subsequently admits that the 'Department could not tolerate a situation in which one of its employees was openly and explicitly hostile to a policy which it was implementing at the behest of Parliament' (*ibid.*). Other sources tend to confirm this image of HMIs operating within very severe constraints set by the Department and only exercising or voicing their personal judgement in situations not likely to offend. Thus the Select Committee on Her Majesty's Inspectorate (1968) concluded that the Department and the Inspectorate are in fact a very integrated body and the DES in its pamphlet *HMI Today and Tomorrow* (1970*a*) also down-played the significance of HMI autonomy:

HM Inspectors are a body of men and women who are ultimately answerable to the Secretary of State for Education and Science. They may well be given direct instructions by him. Their appointment is made on his recommendation. ... It is the duty of the Inspectors, as of other civil servants, to assist the central government in discharging the responsibilities that successive parliaments have laid down. (1970*a*, p. 9)

As the DES moves further in the direction of policy-making enclosure, so it must rely more on its internal means of information collecting rather than on information supplied by external groups. In this respect the role of HMIs as the field representatives and data collection agents of the DES is bound to be crucial in its efforts to sustain this move ... But suffice to it to say here that whatever the Inspectorate still retains is likely to be further eroded in response to the requirements of the new style of policy making; though the myth of autonomy may well be retained as long as possible since it enhances the supposed objectivity of the information on which the Department rests its policy proposals.

The legitimation of the state apparatus

The OECD report (1975, p. 28) on British educational development bravely stated that 'the evolution cf education in the United Kingdom cannot be charted without placing the planning function of the Department of Education and Science at the centre of the story'. It summarized DES policy formation as characterized by attempts to:

minimize the degree of controversiality in the planning process and its results; reduce possible alternatives to matters of choice of resource allocation: limit the planning process to those parts of the educational services and functions strictly controlled by the DES; exploit as fully as possible the powers, prerogatives and responsibilities given to the DES under the 1944 Education Act; understate as much as possible the full role of the Government in the determination of the future course of educational policy and even minimise it in the eyes of the general public. (*ibid.*, p. 42)

Our own analysis of the bureaucratization of educational power in Britain has so far reached similar, though probably less emphatic conclusions. However, our theoretical perspective leads us beyond the recognition that bureaucratic change has and is taking place in the management of education and takes us on to the further question of what ideological change is necessary to support these bureaucratic shifts in the state apparatus given education's central ideological function in society. Our theory insists that if educational change is to be acceptable to the populace at large it has to go through an ideological stage. There are, analytically speaking, two aspects to this stage: (*a*) the way in which policy is produced and (*b*) the policies produced. Both require ideological legitimation and, in practice, the nature of this legitimation may overlap the two aspects. Nevertheless, as we will show, the overlap is not so complete as to undermine the importance of the analytical distinction itself.

In the past the process of educational policy production was legitimated by the Department's claim that it aggregated and reflected the existing educational consensus. The major instrument reinforcing this claim was the work of the educational committees appointed either by the Central Advisory Council (CAC) on education, a standing statutory body, or by the DES itself. Major shifts in educational policy have, until recently, always been heralded by reports from such committees (e.g. Robbins, Crowther, Plowden) and their public hallmark has been their independence from the Department, the eminence of their membership, their sensitivity to the broad sweep of educational opinion, their increasing use of 'objective' social science, and, stemming from these others, the authority of their pronouncements. To a large extent these qualities are in fact illusory and the committees are, as Kogan documents, 'far more "in-house", far more a part of official review, than the outward forms seem to suggest' (Kogan and Packwood, 1974, p. 23). Committees generally have their terms of reference and membership determined by the Department and their secretarial and research data supplied by the Department (Robbins being a notable exception to the latter). This has meant that, up to now, they have performed the latent functions of enabling the Department to use them both as a jury against which Departmental policies could be tested as they emerged and as a centre for negotiations on policies which had, in any case, to be discussed with the main educational interests before reaching the public stage (*ibid.*, p. 23).

Nor is the DES in any way obliged to accept the policy implications of a committee's conclusions, though public opinion may force its hand. In his examination of the influence of prewar advisory councils on the Board of Education, Graves (1940, p. 89) cites the example of the report *Books in Elementary Schools* which was widely read, reprinted, yet comprehensively ignored by the board. He concludes that this well illustrates the impotence of an advisory body once it has reported: 'Unless the education authorities are willing to take the matter up, or public opinion is strong enough, a first-class report may disappear almost without trace.' And the Department is only likely to take the matter up if it fits a prior policy decision made internally.

Yet if education committees and their reports are such malleable material, to be promulgated by the DES as policy legitimating instruments as and when it thinks fit, why are such committees used less now than before? Why did Corsland deem it appropriate to disband the CAC after the publication of the Plowden and Gittins reports in 1967 particularly, since, as Kogan (1978, p. 135) underlines, 'since then there has been discontent at the way in which the recently created planning system within the DES seems to feed on its own expertise and knowledge rather than bringing in wider circles of expertise and knowledge', as it had done previously? Crosland's own explanation is revealing: he argues that there is a danger of too many and too lengthy reports — 'And they can slow up action, as Plowden would have done on comprehensivization if I hadn't been very firm' (Kogan, 1971, p. 174). In justifying the phasing out of the CACs, Sir William Pile (1979, p. 38) observed that if committees of inquiry are to be used then *ad hoc* ones which reach speedy conclusions are increasingly preferred by ministers. The difficulty with placing this premium on decision-making efficiency, however, is that the legitimating function of the committees is neglected. While it is one thing to take a decision swiftly, it is quite another to get it accepted by the rest of the educational system.

As the department adopts a more positive stance towards the rest of the education system, gathers its own information, internalizes its planning procedures and shrugs off its old service image, it has to face the fact that since policy can no longer be deemed to 'emerge' ... by some hidden but natural process of evolution, neither can the ideology necessary to support both the policy-making framework itself and the policies produced. At present the tendency is for the DES to attempt to legitimize its own dominance of the formation of policy by arguing that the planning techniques which it employs are in some sense 'objective' and 'scientific' and allow ministers a fair choice between a full range of policy options. This can be characterized as a low profile approach which will work so long as major educational interests are not unduly offended by the policy biases inherent in the Department's use of these techniques. Even so, the fact that the policies which are produced are directly the DES's responsibility alone, rather than that of a vague consensus, will increasingly place the Department in an exposed position.

If questions are raised about the legitimacy of the means of policy formation employed by the educational state apparatus, this is bound to have an effect in turn upon the DES's ability to manage the tensions between education's social control and economic functions. For these functions to be performed effectively by the educational system, it is essential that any change in their operation (i.e. any new educational policy) is both cloaked with the suitable ideological apparel and viewed as having been produced by legitimate policy-making machinery. As the forum in which these underlying pressures are politically negotiated, along with the inputs from demographic shifts and party policy, the Department undoubtedly comes under considerable institutional stress as it seeks to reconcile the policy implications of these demands with its own bureaucratic needs and ambitions. To relieve this stress, though not to remove it, the DES needs ideological protection: in order to implement successfully its social control and economic functions and to legitimize its policies. Merely claiming that the policies were produced by 'rational' planning techniques is not going to be good enough. We do not live in a rational world. What the CACs and the other committees were good at, and what the DES is still learning, was that assembling of broad societal values into patterns which carried authority — i.e. they were good at producing ideology. Until the Department acquires the art of developing ideological positions to match the policies it sponsors, it will not have fully worked out the implications of its own bureaucratic changes and education's social functions and will remain exposed to attacks such as that of the OECD report.

3.6 J.C. Garnett

SOME CONSTRAINTS ON DEFENCE POLICY MAKERS

From *The Management of Defence*, ed. L. Martin, published by Macmillan Publishers Ltd, 1976.

Sir David Kelly (1952) once made the dry observation that decision making – or is it decision taking? – in the Civil Service is a 'casual unreasoning action by ordinary men in positions of extraordinary power'. Now although government decisions do sometimes seem to have the quality of inexplicable arbitrariness to which Sir David referred, the assumption underlying this paper is that, for the most part at least, they reflect a deliberate and calculated response by officials to the situation in which they find themselves. In other words, it is assumed that defence decisions involve a reasoned choice from a number of perceived alternatives of that course of action deemed most likely to promote the state of affairs desired by the decision maker. As such, defence policy is susceptible to rational analysis, and although we may never quite get to the bottom of any particular decision, we can penetrate some of the mystery by identifying the constraints which pushed decision makers towards some choices and away from others. Much of the paper will deal with the human, organisational and political pressures which combine to force policy makers to take actions which, however curious to the outside observer, make sense when located in their proper context. Regrettably, other constraints of an economic and technological kind cannot be dealt with in a short paper ...

Whatever definition is accepted it is clear that policies involve decisions – decisions about *what to do* and about *how to do it.* Now this distinction may not stand up to rigorous examination, but it is useful because it suggests that there are two kinds of decision. Huntington (1961, pp. 3–4) has made a somewhat similar distinction between what he calls 'strategic decisions', i.e. 'those made in the categories or currency of international politics', and 'structural decisions', i.e. 'those made in the currency of domestic politics', which deal with procurement, allocation and organisation of men, money and material.

In general, decisions about 'what to do' are 'policy' decisions with a high political input. Whether to join NATO or the EEC, or whether to stay East of Suez were all issues involving the British government in defence 'policy' decisions. Decisions of the 'how to do it' variety are second-order decisions, micro-decisions if you like; they take place *within* the context of policy; they are more technical and in a sense more intellectually manageable. Whether to buy this weapon or that weapon; whether to opt for this mix of forces or that mix of forces. It is decisions like these which have received most attention in the defence field.

Today almost everyone is aware of the enormous strides made in developing and exploiting rigorous analytical techniques capable of improving these 'second-order' decisions. In the United States, particularly since the advent of Mr R. McNamara as Secretary of Defense, a lot of effort has gone into introducing to the defence field a whole range of sophisticated management techniques designed to save money, to use resources more economically and to produce better designed equipment. The McNamara revolution allocated a central role to the 'planning-programming budgeting system' of Mr Hitch, and it is fair to say that over the years it has changed the face of defence management in the United States. Operational research, cost-benefit analysis and systems analysis are now accepted tools of the trade in the defence business. And in many fields their value is proved ...

But a word of warning is appropriate. Defence management is not quite the same as defence policy making. There are a good many 'first-order' decisions to be taken in the defence field, and it is doubtful whether the various techniques of the programmatic approach have much to offer in the way of improving them. In the euphoria which followed the introduction of these management skills to the defence field there was, perhaps a tendency to believe that they could solve not just some defence problems but all. M. Desai has recently commented unfavourably on the tendency to apply the new economic techniques of optimisation to highly complicated 'messy' situations where they are quite inappropriate. He cites several incidents from the Pentagon Papers which illustrate the way in which the administration tried to reduce to manageable and quantifiable terms Vietnam war situations which were far too complicated for techniques designed fundamentally for relatively simple resource allocation problems. As Desai says, 'A complex phenomenon such as guerilla war demanding an analysis of many factors, most of them unmeasurable, even unimaginable, by the analyst, has to be reduced to a few variables because the method cannot handle many, and anyway the social scientist believes that the simpler the model the better it is' (Desai, 1972, p. 64).

This paper ... deals with defence policy making in its widest sense and has an explanatory rather than a prescriptive flavour. The aim is not to examine how defence policy making might be improved, but how it comes about that particular policies are chosen; and it does this by identifying some of the main constraints and influences which make themselves felt during the decision making process. Decision makers are seen as acting in 'a matrix of internal and external forces that affect their behaviour through pulls and pressures' (Wolfers, 1962, p. 37).

Perhaps the most obvious and intractable of the external forces which constrain the freedom of action of decision makers are to be found in the harsh realities of the decision makers' environment. The facts of international life and the pressure of events over which decision makers have no control inevitably narrow the area of manoeuvre available to statesmen. For example, as Lord Strang once pointed out, 'No British foreign secretary can get away from the fact that Great Britain is a small, densely populated island with wide overseas interests, inescapably dependent upon foreign trade for the maintenance of its relatively luxurious standard of living' (Frankel, 1963, p. 151). British vulnerability in terms of its economic strength, its dependence on trade for sources of food, raw materials and energy, is a powerful constraint on any foreign minister's freedom to act. There are limits to what small, densely populated islands can do in the world, and it is this fact of life which explains a good deal of British policy since the war. Those who cannot mould the international environment, must, inevitably, learn to adjust to it.

Think, for a moment, of the historic decision by Britain after World War II to undertake a firm commitment to the defence of Western Europe via the Dunkirk, Brussels and North Atlantic treaties. Given the grim international situation — the Soviet threat, a weakened and devastated Europe, an exhausted population, and the possibility of American withdrawal — what else could Britain do but throw her weight into a collective defence arrangement which reversed a long tradition of non-alignment? Statesmanship it may have been, but from another perspective it was determined by the whiplash of events, by the relentless pressures of the international environment, and, in a sense, it was inevitable. Similarly, Britain's withdrawal East of Suez can be interpreted as a response to a changed international situation and economic pressures which, for one reason or another, became irresistible.

And of course it is not only small or medium sized powers which find their choices effectively circumscribed by circumstance. The United States, as powerful a state as any, and more powerful than most, is almost equally chained by the facts of international life. Stanley Hoffman has described how after World War II, when the nature of Soviet power and policy and the erosion of British strength became obvious, the United States simply had to fill the power vacuum which was formed. As Hoffman puts it, 'the old choice between isolation and involvement is dead; there remains only the purely academic choice between historical sleep and the dangerous life of a great power. The fact that the latter often seems like a nightmare does not make escape into untroubled dreams a genuine alternative' (Hoffman, 1965, p. 162).

Decision makers who are constrainted by international circumstances and the events in which they find themselves caught up, are also constrained by their commitments and obligations and the web of relationships which they inherit. In this sense they are constrained by history and the decisions of their predecessors. Any alliance limits the freedom of movement of every member, even the most powerful. Every treaty obligation does the same. Even membership of the United Nations carries obligations. Some of these commitments may be purely residual, relics of a bygone era, as certain British commitments are, but however inconvenient they may be, they are legally binding, and their existence helps to determine the size, the shape and posture of Britain's defence effort.

Policy makers are constrained by the facts of international life and the web of relationships and commitments in which their country is enmeshed. But, because they are part and parcel of it, they are even more constrained by their domestic environment. They share its values and they are constantly exposed to the pressure of both organised and unorganised groups within it.

Some of these domestic constraints are scarcely felt at all by decision makers. Those who are reared in a particular value system rarely feel constrained by it even though it determines everything they do. So, those restrictions on decision making freedom which arise out of an unconscious compliance with a particular political style, for example, may not impinge on the decision maker at all. The British reluctance to think far ahead, to discuss abstract ideas, to see questions in terms of principles, to discuss hypothetical situations, are all characteristics of what is sometimes unfairly called the philosophy of 'muddling through'. This pragmatic tradition of policy making comes so naturally to civil servants reared in it that they are scarcely conscious of it as a constraint at all; but few would dispute the effect which it has on the way in which the Civil Service sees problems and handles them.

In the same way that a policy maker may be unaware of the constraints imposed upon him by the value system and style within which he operates, so may he be unaware of the way in which his own personality inevitably shapes the decisions he takes. But though he may be unaware of it, it is clear that the personal characteristics of the decision maker and the prism through which he looks at the world have something to do with the way in which he perceives problems and tries to solve them. P. Darby makes the point that between 1956 and 1959, many of Mr Duncan Sandys's problems in dealing with the Services can be explained by his own personal idiosyncrasies. 'Service grievances perhaps turned more on the personality of the minister and his method of taking decisions than on the doctrinal content of his policy' (Darby, 1973, p. 108). Apparently Sandys had the unfortunate habit of 'disregarding professional advice', a penchant for 'asking fundamental questions', and an unfortunate tendency to 'treat the Chiefs of Staff like schoolboys'.

Though policy makers may be quite unconscious of some of the constraints under which they operate, they are very much aware of others.

Public opinion, for example, is a domestic constraint which few government departments can afford to ignore. Of course, on most specific defence issues the public has no opinion, and, indeed, there is plenty of evidence of popular apathy across the entire foreign and defence policy fields. In almost every election since the war it has been questions of economic and social policy rather than defence which have dominated the political manifestos of the major political parties. But there is an important negative sense in which this lack of interest or enthusiasm for defence is an important constraint on governmental behaviour. As Franklin D. Roosevelt once said, 'I cannot go any faster than the people will let me,' and so long as the British public allocate such a low priority to defence, no British government can pursue anything but a low profile defence policy. In particular, the defence budget could not easily be raised during a period in which many people are reluctant to maintain even present levels of expenditure.

The economic constraint on defence policy is all pervasive, and it deserves much more discussion than it can be given in this paper. But it is worth saying here that fundamentally defence expenditure is determined not by economic, but by political constraints. If expenditure is cut back this is 'not because this is in some absolute sense necessary, not because the nation could not afford the previously planned effort, but because certain choices are made'. Now the choices which are made are political choices over which public opinion has some influence ...

It might be tempting to regard policies and decisions in the defence field as the results of considered reflection by omniscient and reasonable men pursuing clearly articulated and logically compatible goals. Roger Hilsman (1971, p. 4) has commented that 'we would like to think not only that policymaking is a conscious and deliberate act, one of analyzing problems and systematically examining grand alternatives in all their implications, but also that the alternative chosen is aimed at achieving over-arching ends that serve a high moral purpose'. This view that decisions are taken by unitary, high-minded individuals who are seeking to maximise the national interest is a travesty of reality, but it is implicit in much writing in the defence and foreign policy field. It is also an unconscious paradigm in the minds of ordinary men and women who, when confronted with some inexplicable piece of government behaviour, shrug their shoulders with the words, 'I suppose they know what they are doing.' Graham Allison (1971) has caricatured this notion of decision making as the 'rational policy model' which draws an analogy between a government and a reasonable man and assumes that government behaviour can be explained in terms of the means which a rational man, confronted with the same situation, would adopt to achieve his goals. This mode of analysis can produce plausible but by no means adequate accounts of international behaviour ... For example,

Soviet—American rearmament programmes during the 1950s are usually 'explained' on these lines:

When, in 1954, the Soviets demonstrated the capacity to produce medium and heavy jet bombers, this led to fears in the USA of a 'bomber gap' and an accelerated B.52 programme. In 1957, the Soviet announcement of an ICBM capacity, plus the orbitting sputnik, led to American fears of a 'missile gap' and increase in US missile expenditure.

Those who favour this kind of analysis — and to some extent all of us do — appear to think that an action in international politics is rather like a move in a complicated game of chess, to be explained entirely in terms of a desire to win (promote the national interest), and as a rational response to an opponent's moves. Explaining policy is simply a matter of showing how, given their national interests and a particular situation, governments could rationally choose such policies.

This way of thinking has a lot in common with what Charles Lindblom has described as the 'synoptic approach' to problem solving, according to which decision makers first sort out and order their objectives and values, then survey and evaluate the various means of achieving them before finally choosing those means best calculated to maximise the objectives attained (Lindblom, 1965, p. 137).

What is wrong with this approach ... is that it fails to recognise that the decisions of governments are not made by rational individuals but by complex, interrelated organisations. Much of what follows is about the way in which these government organisations constrain decision making in the defence field.

The flavour of policy making activity in these vast bureaucratic organisations has been brilliantly described by Allison (1971):

Hundreds of issues compete for players' attention every day. Each player is forced to fix upon his issues for that day, fight them on their own terms, and rush on to the next. Thus the character of emerging issues and the pace at which the game is played converge to yield government 'decisions' and 'actions' as collages. Choices by one player, outcomes of minor games, outcomes of central games, and 'foul-ups' — these pieces when stuck to the same canvas, constitute government behaviour to an issue.

Another illuminating metaphor in the context of organisational decision making is that of a canoeist on a fast flowing river. The canoeist's choices about where he travels are severely circumscribed, and his main activity is not so much deciding where to go, but how to survive the rocks and currents which threaten his safe passage.

In short, decision making, like life, is one damn thing after another, and the term policy taken in the normal sense of implying rational goal orientated activity, is perhaps not an entirely appropriate description of the curious mixture of chance and choice that we are talking about. As

Hilsman (1967, p. 5) explained it. 'Very often policy is the sum of congeries of separate or only vaguely related actions. On other occasions it is an uneasy, even internally inconsistent compromise among competing goals or an incompatible mixture of alternative means for achieving a single goal.'

In other words, instead of dealing with a rather high-faluting activity in which powerful men decisively change the course of human affairs, we are discussing the much-maligned philosophy of 'muddling through', of fumbling forwards in mini-steps without much knowledge or confidence but in the vague hope that we are moving in the right direction. Charles Lindblom (1965, p. 144) has analysed the process of disjointed or incremental problem solving according to which policy makers confronted with a problem simply devise tactics which involve only very small or incremental changes from their existing policy. 'In short policymakers and analysts take as their starting point not the whole range of hypothetical possibilities, but only the here and now in which we live, and then move on to consider how alternatives might be made at the margin.'

Within the Ministry of Defence the question of whether Britain should remain a nuclear power may not be raised, but the question of whether to MIRV Polaris or go for Poseidon is certain to have been discussed. Now it may be argued that choosing between Polaris and Poseidon assumes a prior decision to retain the nuclear deterrent; but if the problem did not come up in that form it is unfair to see it in that way. What was required was an incremental decision to replace one weapons system with another. Of course, that incremental decision, by foreclosing other alternatives, inevitably implies a major policy decision. As Brzezinski and Huntington (1965, p. 222) have suggested, even 'the grand choices are often made more by accretion than by selection'. The decision to move to the next generation of deterrent weapons effectively settles the issue of whether Britain will remain a nuclear power, but if those are not the terms in which it is considered, then that is not the decision that is taken.

What this interpretation of the decision making process does once and for all is to destroy utterly Lindblom's 'synoptic approach' and Allison's 'rational policy model' with their inbuilt assumption that policy making is a purely rational phenomenon. Decisions are now seen, not as 'discrete acts with recognisable beginnings and sharp, decisive endings' but as outcomes of a much more messy process. In particular, policy is not seen as being made by isolated and rational leaders and imposed downwards on the organisations for which they are responsible, but as the outputs of organisations which finally receive a stamp of approval by those who lead them.

Now the fact that decisions originate within organisations means two things. First, that the process by which they are reached is to some extent a political, rather than a reasoning process, and that is to say, it is a process

in which the interplay of power and interest on the part of various individuals and sections is at least as important a determinant of policy as
the arguments about the merits of particular courses of action. Decisions
emerge, not so much as a result of argument and reflection about the
problem in hand, but as a result of organisational strife between rival
departments, sections and individuals. The point is that in a given situation, organisations and the individuals within them, though not unaware
of the national interest, are in fact pursuing more complicated goals in
which organisational prosperity and survival and individual promotion
may figure prominently. Of course, organisational success is not necessarily incompatible with the national interest. What is good for General
Motors may indeed be good for the United States; but there is no in-
evitability about it.

It is difficult to estimate the importance of bureaucratic politics on
defence decision making, but even a casual perusal of the literature suggests that it has played a significant part in a variety of important
decisions. The history of inter-service relationships both in Britain and the
United States is full of inter-service clashes in which the national interest
seemed to get lost in a more parochial struggle for organisational survival.
In Britain, for example, the issue of whether or not to abandon the aircraft
carrier may be regarded as a struggle between the Navy and the RAF for
limited funds. And whatever the merits of their respective arguments, few
would dispute the bitterness with which each side pursued its interests.
In the event, as Sir Frank Hopkins ruefully revealed, the RAF were better
at the 'politiking' than their rivals. In a very revealing passage he described
the way in which the RAF conspired to show that the carrier force could
be effectively replaced by shore-based aircraft.

Many devices had to be resorted to ... such as assuming the existence of
bases which were not there and never likely to be; crediting the F−111
with a performance in which even its most ardent supporter could scarcely
believe, and in the event never materialized; assuming almost super-human
achievements in logistic support by the RAF; assuming overflying rights
of countries in Europe, Africa and Asia which were unlikely to be allowed
in the event; and even, in one study, moving Australia 600 miles to the
North-West in order to bring certain targets within the already elastic
radius of action of the F−111. (Hopkins, 1972).

... The fact that decisions are made by bureaucratic organisations also
means that policies inevitably reflect the habits, prejudices and perspectives
of those organisations. So pervasive is this limitation that it affects not
only the policies which emerge, but even the way in which problems are
formulated in the first place. Anyone interested in explaining decisions in
the defence field, therefore, is forced to consider the way in which the
MOD procedures by which they are reached rubbed off on them. Clearly,
any large organisation needs set procedures and detailed rules in order to

work at all, and yet these administrative conventions, which are designed to promote efficiency by reducing work to a routine, inevitably inculcate many of the vices of bureaucracy in the minds of those who operate them. To some extent, rigidity of mind, or 'hardening of the categories' as one professor so aptly called it, lack of imagination, absence of creativity, operating by the book instead of thinking for oneself, are all vices inherent in bureaucracies, but the effect which these traits have on policy making cannot be overstated even if it cannot be nicely calculated.

The cancellation of the TSR–2, for example, has led to some speculation about the way in which the accounting procedures operated by the Ministry of Aviation may have influenced the decision. It is suggested that one of the reasons why this aeroplane looked expensive was because a good deal of general R and D expenditure which ought to have been costed separately, was, for the sake of convenience, lumped in with the TSR–2. A good deal of the electronics research was relevant to both the Phantom and the Harrier, and it was certainly not wasted. As the authors of RUSI publication on the subject pointed out 'a significant proportion of the estimated £280 million research and development bill for the TSR–2 may have been assigned to it as a result of fairly arbitrary Ministry of Aviation accounting conventions'. If this is the case, it provides a classic example of how standard operating procedures may distort a problem, and significantly affect decisions relating to it.

An equally revealing example of how policy can be affected, if not determined, by organisational procedures is described by Admiral P. Gretton (1965). Apparently during World War II the mine barrage laid between the Orkneys and Scotland was a waste of effort in the sense that it made no discernible difference to the passage of enemy surface ships or U-boats. What is so depressing, however, is that 'we had laid a similar type of barrier between Norway and Scotland in 1917–18 with similarly ineffective results. But due to the misuse of the rules of secrecy, the planners of the World War II minefield were informed only of the war propaganda magnified claims of success, and the true figures — three U-boat losses only — were kept in the "top secret" safe'. As K. Booth has commented, the Rosengarten minefield 'is an instructive example of the way in which an organisational standard operating procedure (classification) can severely affect policy' (Booth, 1974).

A more recent example of the same phenomenon is described by Allison in his very influential analysis of the Cuban Missile crisis (Allison, 1971). When the United States Air Force was asked by the Ex-Com. Committee to spell out the details and implications of the 'surgical' air strike option, they started from an existing contingency plan for massive action, and they came up with frightening details of multiple sorties, likely casualties and collateral damage. The precise, 'surgical' strike was not considered for a whole week because, says Allison, according to US manuals, Soviet MRBMs in Cuba were classed as mobile and therefore required extensive bombing. Only when the Soviet missiles were re-classified as 'movable' was progress made and the surgical air strike given proper consideration.

The gist of the argument so far has been to suggest that policies and decisions 'are not the product of expert planners rationally determining the actions necessary to achieve desired goals. Rather they are the product of controversy, negotiation and bargaining among different groups with different interests and perspectives'. As such most decisions taken in the real world can best be described as 'extra-rational' or 'meta-rational'.

So far the paper has concentrated on the way in which *government* organisations may modify policy, but it is worth pointing out that other organisations and pressure groups can also exercise constraint on the freedom of policy makers. One of the most important of these is the political part of the government in power.

It has to be remembered that in any democratic political party, leaders walk a tightrope between leading and following, and those who emphasise the former at the expense of the latter run the risk of finding their power base dangerously eroded. The truth is that government authority rests with the leadership only 'so long as they retain the confidence of their political parties'. Leaders, therefore, are constantly engaged in consensus politics, in devising policies with sufficient appeal to carry the rank and file party members. Inevitably, though consensus building is sometimes costly in terms of compromising the policy's content, it is a prerequisite of effective policy. For that very reason the relationship between a government and the party it represents is best thought of as a continual dialogue, an uneasy partnership between those who have to govern in an intractable world, and their ideological supporters who expect them to implement political manifestos. Very rarely does the dialogue break down completely, though it is frequently strained. In general terms, as R. Butt (1967) puts it, 'the main lines of government policy are determined by the government but with some shading at the edges to maintain backbench consensus'. It is this 'shading at the edges' which this paper is interested in exploring.

In a perceptive study of the way in which intra-party wrangling has constrained the defence policies of successive Labour leaders, A. Walker (1973) describes a variety of occasions in which considerations of party unity pressed the leadership into policies not entirely to their liking. Whether the issue was German rearmament, nuclear deterrence, the MLF, the 'special relationship', overseas commitments, or defence expenditure, the influence of the left wing compelled successive labour leaders, both in opposition and in government, to trim their policies both in form and substance to accommodate the views of radicals who had no time for responsible *real politik*.

On the question of nuclear deterrence, the policies of the Labour Party have been consistently ambiguous because the leadership has had to be sensitive to criticism from the pacifist, unilateralist element in the rank and file. On the question of whether Britain should reduce her defence commitments both East and West of Suez, there is plenty of evidence that the Labour leadership was prepared to listen to backbench opinion. When, in the 1967 Commons debate on the defence White Paper there were sixty-two abstentions, Mr Wilson admitted that 'I now see more time and care should have been given to anticipating the trouble which broke when the vote was called.' Thereafter, he took steps to become more responsive to the party ... Verrier (1963) also commented that the weak position of the leadership within the party on defence issues led to the development of an 'intriguing bag of generalities' rather than a defence policy. These examples all indicate the constraining influence of intra-party debate on the formulation of defence policy. The need for consensus building within the party is an important constraint on the defence policies of all governments, but it is probably fair to say that it is most striking in the Labour party.

The importance of all this is clear. For years it has been fashionable to interpret decisions and policies in the defence field as being fundamentally rational responses to international situations and strategic problems. What is being suggested here is not that the international situation is irrelevant, but that internal factors are at least as important because policy makers spend as much time looking behind them as they do in front of them, and any adequate explanation of defence policy must take this into account ...

If there is any consistent philosophy underlying this paper it is that policy makers are rarely as free as their critics think they are. That does not mean that it is necessary to adopt a determinist philosophy which reduces all human action to that of puppets jerking to the whim of blind, impersonal forces, or actors going through the motions of a Greek tragedy. Perhaps it is the 'environmental possibilists' who have most nearly got it right with their view that men do indeed exercise freedom of choice but only within a framework prescribed by their environment — and sometimes the environment is very rigid. The constraints outlined in this paper all impinge on those who have to make policy, and, under their pressure, freedom of action may shrink to 'mitigating the bitterness of the unavoidable'.

3.7   R. Keohane and J. Nye

TRANSGOVERNMENTAL POLITICS AND
INTERNATIONAL ORGANIZATIONS

From *World Politics*, vol. 27, pp. 42—55 (1974). Copyright © 1974 by
Princeton University Press, reprinted by permission of Princeton University
Press.

1. Transgovernmental relations

During the last century, governments have become increasingly involved in
attempting to regulate the economic and social lives of the societies they
govern. As a result, they have become more sensitive to external disturb-
ances that may affect developments within their own societies. For instance, integration of money markets internationally, in the context of
governmental responsibility for national economies, has made government
policy sensitive both to changes in interest rates by other governments and
central banks, and to movements of funds by nongovernmental speculators.
These sensitivities are heightened further by the expanding decision
domains of transnational organizations such as multinational business
firms and banks, reinforced by decreases in the cost of transnational
communications.

As the agenda broadens, bureaucracies find that to cope effectively at
acceptable cost with many of the problems that arise, they must deal with
each other directly rather than indirectly through foreign offices.[1] Communications among governments increase. International conferences and
organizations facilitate direct contacts among officials of what were once
considered primarily domestic government agencies. In the words of a
former White House official, 'it is a central fact of foreign relations that
business is carried on by the separate departments with their counterpart
bureaucracies abroad, through a variety of informal as well as formal
connections.'[2] (That is especially true in alliance politics. But to a point, it
also applies elsewhere.) There have always been such contacts. What
seems to be new is the order of magnitude of transgovernmental relations,
as bureaucracies become more complex and communications and travel
costs decrease.

We define transgovernmental relations as sets of direct interactions
among sub-units of different governments that are not controlled or closely
guided by the policies of the cabinets or chief executives of those governments. Thus we take the policies of top leaders as our benchmarks of
'official government policy'. Lack of control of sub-unit behavior by top
leadership is obviously a matter of degree, and in practice by no means

free of ambiguity. The policy of the central executive is often unclear, particularly on details, and policy means different things at different organizational levels. 'One man's policy is another man's tactics' (Bauer, 1968). As one observer has put it, 'Central policy is always waffled; actors latch on to the waffled parts and form coalitions to shift policy at their level'. Nonetheless, to treat all actors as equal and to ignore the existence of a political hierarchy charged with 'course-setting' and maintaining some hierarchy of goals is to misrepresent both constitutional and political reality (Krasner, 1972). It is precisely because this central policy task has become more difficult in the face of greater complexity that both the opportunities and the importance of transgovernmental interactions may be expected to have increased.

It is quite conceivable that executives entrusted with responsibility for central foreign policy, such as presidents and prime ministers, will themselves attempt to collaborate with one another in ways that conflict with the behavior of their respective bureaucracies. Yet we will regard only the relatively autonomous activities of the lower-level bureaucracies, as opposed to those of top leadership, as being transgovernmental ...

In view of our interest in the opportunities that transgovernmental relations may create for international organizations, we will concentrate in this essay on *cooperative* behavior among governmental sub-units. It should be recognized, however, that conflict is not excluded from transgovernmental relations any more than from other aspects of world politics. Occasionally, direct contacts among sub-units may themselves be conflictual. A case in point is 'close surveillance' of each other's activities by the American and Soviet navies in the 1960's, which higher-level officials sought with some difficulty to control. Our emphasis on cooperative direct contacts does not, therefore, exclude the possibility of transgovernmental clashes of interests.

We will distinguish two major types of essentially cooperative transgovernmental behavior. Transgovernmental *policy coordination* refers to activity designed to facilitate smooth implementation or adjustment of policy, in the absence of detailed higher policy directives. Another process, *transgovernmental coalition building*, takes place when subunits build coalitions with like-minded agencies from other governments against elements of their own administrative structures. At that point, the unity of the state as a foreign policy actor breaks down. Although transgovernmental policy coordination and transgovernmental coalition building are analytically distinct processes, they merge into one another at the margin. While bearing in mind that the distinction is in some sense an artificial convenience, we will look at the two processes in turn.

Transgovernmental policy coordination

The most basic and diffuse form of transgovernmental policy coordination is simply informal communication among working-level officials of different bureaucracies ... Face-to-face communications often convey more information (intended or unintended) than indirect communications, and this additional information can affect policy expectations and preferences. It is well known that international organizations frequently provide suitable contexts for such transgovernmental communication. As one official said of INTERPOL, 'What's really important here are the meetings on a social level – the official agenda is only for show' (*New York Times*, Oct. 1 1972).

Where patterns of policy coordination are regularized, it becomes misleading to think of governments as closed decision-making units ... In the Skybolt affair of 1962, British complacency about American planning, before cancellation was announced, was reinforced by 'a steady stream of reassurances [that] flowed back and forth between the Air Forces. The USAF saw a staunch ally in Her Majesty's Government, and *vice versa*' (Neustadt, 1970, p. 37).

From regularized coordination over a period of time, changes in attitudes may result. When the same officials meet recurrently, they sometimes develop a sense of collegiality, which may be reinforced by their membership in a common profession, such as economics, physics, or meteorology. Individual officials may even define their roles partly in relation to their transnational reference group rather than in purely national terms. Thus, in discussing trade discrimination in the 1950s, Gardner Patterson argued that 'an important cost of discrimination was the necessity of reporting on it and defending it periodically in semi-public forums ... It was costly not just in terms of time and effort, but perhaps more important, in terms of the embarrassment of having many members of the "club" – professional colleagues – charge that another member was not living up to some of its international commitments' (Patterson, 1966, p. 36).

Regularized patterns of policy coordination can therefore create attitudes and relationships that will at least marginally change policy or affect its implementation. This has been evident particularly in relations among close allies or associates, for instance between the United States and Canada or among countries of the British Commonwealth. Even in relations among countries that are politically more distant from one another, policy coordination between bureaucracies with similar interests may occasionally take place. According to press reports, at any rate, United States and Soviet space officials who were engaged in technical talks on space cooperation in 1971 went considerably further than the National Security Council had authorized at that time (*New York Times*, Dec. 1971).

Patterns of regularized policy coordination have a significance that is not limited to the examples we have cited. As such practices become widespread, transgovernmental elite networks are created, linking officials in various governments to one another by ties of common interest, professional orientation, and personal friendship. Even where attitudes are not fundamentally affected and no major deviations from central policy positions occur, the existence of a sense of collegiality may permit the development of flexible bargaining behavior in which concessions need not be requited issue by issue or during each period. Coleman (1970) has suggested that the development of 'political bank accounts', where a mental reckoning of political credits and debits relaxes the need for all payoffs to be immediate, is dependent on the existence of small-group collegiality. When such behavior — once the prerogative of monarchs and diplomats — spreads throughout governments, the policy structure becomes more complex and decentralized. Some of the clearest examples of such behavior have been reported by students of the political processes of common markets, such as the European Community or the Central American Common Market, where the development of a sense of collegiality enables officials and ministers in many instances to press policy coordination beyond what would otherwise have been the case (Lindberg and Scheingold, 1970; Sheinman, 1966; Nye, 1967).

Transgovernmental coalition building
Transgovernmental policy coordination shades over into transgovernmental coalition building when sub-units of different governments (and/or intergovernmental institutions) jointly use resources to influence governmental decisions. To improve their chances of success, governmental sub-units attempt to bring actors from other governments into their own decision-making processes as allies. When such coalitions are successful, the outcomes are different than they would be if each coalition partner were limited to his own nationality. The politics of such situations are more subtle and the rules less clear than in the classical coalition theorists' cases of electoral coalitions where resources are directly transferable into influence through a set of generally accepted rules, or national bureaucratic coalitions in which players hold formal positions that legitimize their rights to participate.

Transgovernmental coalitions may be employed by sub-units of powerful states such as the United States as means by which to penetrate weaker governments. US aid agencies in the 1950s and 1960s frequently played a large role in writing requests for aid from the US on behalf of potential recipients, and on occasion even served a liaison function among several ministries of a foreign government. In Turkey, where the Planning Office and the Finance Ministry had equal authority but contradictory views on a US aid project to bring local officials together, a *de facto* coalition developed between AID officials and Finance Ministry officials. The Chilean military under Allende was willing to bear possible domestic opprobrium in order to receive American military aid. To some observers, the American strategy appeared to be an attempt to use transgovernmental politics to keep the Chilean Government divided (*New York Times*, Dec. 9 1972).

Transgovernmental coalitions, however, can also help agencies of other governments penetrate the US bureaucracy. In 1961, when the US Weather Bureau disagreed with the State Department's position at the United Nations on the control of the World Weather Watch, the Director of the US Weather Bureau telephoned his Canadian counterpart and they discussed the common interests of their respective weather bureaus. The position of the two weather bureaus became the official Canadian position, which led in turn to defeat of the State Department's proposals (Miles, 1970). In the late 1960s, a US Defense Department official, worried that delay in returning Okinawa to Japanese control might harm United States-Japanese relations, worked out with a Japanese counterpart how to phrase Japanese messages to ensure that they would enter the right channels and trigger the desired response in the US bureaucracy. In 1968, an Air Force general, to whom the responsibility for negotiating with Spain about military bases had been delegated, conferred secretly with his Spanish counterparts without informing civilian officials of the progress of his negotiations, and agreed to a negotiating paper that proved to be unacceptable to the Department of State. As this last case indicates, transgovernmental coalitions are not always successful: the agreement reached, which would have been favorable to the Spanish Government, was disowned by the United States, and a negative reaction against Spain took place in the Senate.[3]

It is obviously a necessary condition for explicit transgovernmental coalitions that sub-units of government have broad and intensive contacts with one another. In some sense, a degree of transgovernmental policy coordination is probably a precondition for such explicit transnational coalitions. A second set of necessary conditions has to do with conflict of interest among sub-units and the degree of central control by top executive leaders. For a transgovernmental coalition to take place, a sub-unit of one government must perceive a greater common interest with another government, or sub-units of another government, than with at least one pertinent agency in its own country; and central executive control must be loose enough to permit this perception to be translated into direct contacts with the foreign governments or agencies in question. Table 3.7.1 illustrates four types of political situations based on these two dimensions.

Sub-units in a governmental system of Type 1 are most likely to seek, or be amenable to, transgovernmental coalitions. High conflict of interest among sub-units of the government suggests that there may be sub-units of

Table 3.7.1   Conflict of interest and executive power in foreign policy:
four types

		1. Policy frag-	2. Nationally
Degree of conflict of	high	mentation	contained
interest among sub-units			conflict
or between sub-units and			
central foreign policy	low	3. National	4. Hierarchical
makers		coalition	structure
		low	high

*Extent of executive power to
control subordinates' behavior*

other governments with which advantageous coalitions can be made; low
executive power indicates that the central officials' ability to deter such
coalitions is relatively small. In the other three types, by contrast, the
conventional assumption of unitary actors is more likely to be valid for
external affairs, although for different reasons. In Type 2, conflict is contained by a strong executive; sub-units may perceive potentially advantageous transgovernmental coalitions, but they do not dare attempt to
consummate them directly. In Type 3, low conflict of interest among
domestic governmental sub-units ensures that the option of national
coalition generally seems more attractive than the transgovernmental
alternative, even in the absence of strong central control. Type 4, of course,
exemplifies the traditional situation: national coalition reinforced by
effective hierarchy.

Relatively frequent contacts among governmental sub-units, looseness
of governmental hierarchies (low executive control), and relatively high
conflict of interest within governments are all necessary conditions for the
development of explicit transgovernmental coalitions. But they are not in
themselves sufficient. In the first place, for coalitions to be feasible, actors
with common interests must be able to combine their resources effectively.
That means that political resources (such as funds, prestige, information,
and consent – where required, for instance, by the rules of an international
organization) of actors outside a government must be valuable to at least
some actors within it. This requires a political context that is relatively
open and free of xenophobia, since in a xenophobic society foreign resources are heavily devalued, or regarded negatively, by virtue of their
origin. Even in democratic societies, the borderline between legitimate
transgovernmental behavior and treason may be unclear.

The need for resources that can be aggregated suggests that transgovernmental behavior may be particularly important in issue areas in which
functionally defined international organizations operate. The procedures

of the organization itself, for reaching agreement among its members, insure that the resources of one actor — at least its votes — may be useful to another; insofar as the organization has a specialized, functional orientation, the activities of national representatives may not be closely supervised by top leaders or their agents. More generally, the greater the natural sensitivity of governmental policies and the wider the acceptance of joint decision making on issues that cross national lines, the greater the legitimacy of transgovernmental bargaining is likely to be. An international organization, by symbolizing governments' beliefs in the need for joint decision making, tends to strengthen the legitimacy of this activity.

2. International organizations and potential coalitions

Recurrent international conferences and other activities of international organizations help to increase transgovernmental contacts and thus create opportunities for the development of transgovernmental coalitions. The number of intergovernmental organizations more than tripled between 1945 and 1965. Nongovernmental organizations have grown even more rapidly. In Europe, the Commission of the European Communities has played a major role in the growth of such contacts, with the result that 'there is a steady flow of national economic and administrative elites to the seat of Community decision-making'. These elites are drawn from many sectors of national bureaucracies, by no means entirely from foreign offices. The pattern is not confined to Europe: In 1962, of some 2,786 people who represented the United States at international conferences, more came from other departments of the government than from the State Department (Beichman, 1967, p. 92).

Governments must organize themselves to cope with the fact that the flow of business, including such conferences, is often transacted under the auspices of international organizations. The organizations' definitions of which issues cluster together and which should be considered separately may help to determine the nature of interdepartmental committees and other arrangements within governments. In the long run, therefore, international organizations will affect how government officials define 'issue areas'. The existence of the International Monetary Fund and the General Agreement on Tariffs and Trade, for example, helps to focus governmental activity in the monetary and trade fields, in contrast to the area of private direct investment, in which no comparable international organization exists.

The fact that international organizations bring officials together should alert us to their effect in activating *potential* coalitions in world politics. Many sub-units of governments, which do not as a matter of course come into contact with each other, may have common or complementary interests. Indeed, we may speak of some potential coalitions as *de facto* 'tacit coalitions' if the independent actions of one member seem to serve the interests of others and vice versa. One of the important but seldom-noted roles of international organizations in world politics is to provide the arena for sub-units of governments to turn potential or tacit coalitions into explicit coalitions characterized by direct communication among the partners. In this particular bit of political alchemy, the organization provides physical proximity, an agenda of issues on which interaction is to take place, and aura of legitimacy. Informal discussions occur naturally in meetings of international organizations, and it is difficult, given the milieu, for other sub-units of one's own government to object to these contacts.

It is intriguing to ask specifically why some potential coalitions become active while others remain merely potential. It is easy to see why the parallel interests of the American and Soviet armed forces (in large military budgets) are not reflected in transgovernmental coalitions between military officers in the superpowers; but it may be more difficult to determine whether the common interests of central bankers in a stable currency system have been implemented as fully by transgovernmental contacts as they might have been. To take another example, the natural allies of the American farmer — and therefore of the Department of Agriculture — in seeking access to European markets are the European urban dwellers and European finance- and consumer-oriented ministers, rather than the European farmers and agriculture ministers. However, this kind of potential coalition between agriculture officials in the United States and non-agriculture officials in Europe is difficult to organize, since regular contacts have not been established. The contrast between the difficulty involved here and the close ties existing among European agriculture ministries, is instructive. Where analogous agencies with close patterns of working relationships have common interests and participate in the same international organizations, it is likely to be much easier to create coalitions on the basis of those common interests than where the potential coalitions include a variety of actors that are not used to working closely with one another.

Even without an active secretariat, therefore, international organizations are of considerable relevance in many issue areas of world politics because they help to transform potential or tacit coalitions into explicit ones. When issues are linked or dealt with in institutional arenas with broad mandates, heterogeneous coalitions can be formed. Narrow institutional mandates discriminate against such coalitions. Thus, by defining the issues to be considered together, and by excluding others, international organizations may significantly affect political processes and outcomes in world politics, quite apart from active lobbying by their secretariats.

The second important role for international organizations, however, is the active one. Most intergovernmental organizations have secretariats, and like all bureaucracies they have their own interests and goals that are defined through an interplay of staff and clientele. International secretariats can be viewed both as catalysts and as potential members of coalitions; their distinctive resources tend to be information and an aura of international legitimacy. As Robert Cox has put it, 'the executive head needs to fortify his position by alliance with domestic pressure groups. He must not limit himself to "foreign" politics but know how to make domestic politics work in favor of his policies' (Cox, 1969*a*). To the extent that the conditions enumerated in Part 1 of this article permit sub-units of governments to engage in transgovernmental coalitions, we would expect international secretariats or components of secretariats to form explicit or implicit coalitions with sub-units of governments as well as with nongovernmental organizations having similar interests.

Examples of alliances between parts of secretariats and governments are not hard to find. Many organizations have divisions that are regarded as fiefdoms of particular governments (Nye, 1973). In a number of cases, lower-level officials of a secretariat have lobbied with governments in efforts to thwart the declared policy of their secretaries-general.[4] Representatives of UN specialized agencies in developing countries often strengthen old-line ministries against their rivals in central planning offices (Gordenker, 1969). Chilean conservatives have used IMF missions to bolster their political positions (Hirschman, 1965). With reference to the World Health Organization (WHO), Cox and Jacobson (1973) argue that 'many government representatives to WHO almost can be viewed as the director-general's agents or lobbyists within country sub-systems'. In some cases, international organizations initiate the formation of transgovernmental coalitions; in others, they or their own sub-units are recruited to the coalitions by sub-units of governments.

It must be recognized, however, that this activist, coalition-building role of international organizations is usually closely circumscribed. By no means is it a sure recipe for success. Yet the alternatives of passivity or of frontally challenging traditions notions of national sovereignty are usually less attractive. Secretariat officials often find the only feasible alternative to be to help governments, or sectors of governments, to perceive problems differently and to use their own resources in innovative ways. For example, as Ruggie (1972) points out, the World Weather Watch is not a supranational operation but a set of national activities that the World Meterological Organization (perceived as an ally by most weather bureaus) helps to coordinate, and the distribution of whose results it encourages. Similarly, Maurice Strong has defined the role of the UN Environmental Office as one of stimulating the creation of new environmental units in member states, serving as an ally providing information and prestige for them, and thus encouraging a redefinition of 'national interests'.

Coalition building shades down into transgovernmental policy coordination in this example, as is frequently the case. On a long-term and somewhat diffuse basis, the communications that take place as a result of policy coordination and conferences may be as important as the coalitions that form on particular issues. As we have seen earlier, international organizations facilitate face-to-face meetings among officials in 'domestic' agencies of different governments who would have little to do with each other in traditional interstate politics. Strategically-minded secretariats of international organizations could very well plan meetings with a view toward this transgovernmental communications function. Recurrent interactions can change officials' perceptions of their activities and interests. As Bauer, Pool, and Dexter (1963, Ch. 3) have pointed out in their discussion of the United States politics of foreign trade, concentrating only on pressures of various interests for decisions leads to an overly mechanistic view of a continuous process and neglects the important role of communications in slowly changing perceptions of 'self-interest'.

Conditions for the involvement of international organizations

To the extent that transgovernmental relations are common in a given issue area, under what conditions should we expect international organizations, in the sense of intergovernmental organizations, to be involved in them? One set of cases is obvious: where the international organization itself has created the network of elites. Thus, both the International Labor Organization (ILO) and the World Health Organization (WHO), as described by Cox and Jacobson (1973) are characterized by extensive 'participant subsystems' that link national trade unions, employers, and government officials to the ILO secretariat, and health-care professionals to WHO's bureaucracy.

More generally, however, we would expect international organizations to become involved in transgovernmental politics on issues requiring some central point or agency for coordination. This implies that international organizations are likely to be most extensively involved on complex, multilateral issues in which major actors perceive a need for information and for communication with other actors, in addition to the traditional functions, as listed by Skolnikoff (1971) of '1) provision of services, 2) norm creation and allocation, 3) rule observance and settlement of disputes, and 4) operation'. Insofar as patterns of politics follow the transgovernmental mode, increasing the number of actors will tend to create greater demands for communication with other actors (often of different types), as well as for information about both technical and political conditions. International secretariats staffed with knowledgeable individuals, even without traditional sources of power, have the opportunity to place themselves at the center of crucial communications networks, and thereby acquire influence as brokers, facilitators, and suggestors of new approaches. They will continue to be dependent on governments for funds and legal powers; but the relevant agencies of governments may be dependent on them for information and for the policy coordination, by a legitimate system-wide actor, which is required to achieve their own objectives.

Notes

1   Karl Kaiser has been a pioneer in developing arguments about what he calls 'multi-bureaucratic politics'. See in particular Kaiser 1971 and 1972.

2   Testimony of Francis Bator before the Subcommittee on Foreign Economic Policy, Committee on Foreign Affairs, House of Representatives, July 25, 1972. *U.S. Foreign Economic Policy: Implications for the Organization of the Executive Branch*, pp. 110—11.

3   In the cases of the weather bureau and the Spanish bases, the United States Government was divided while the smaller state apparently had a relatively unified policy. In terms of coherence, these relationships were asymmetrical in favor of Canada and Spain, respectively. Spain, Nationalist China, Israel, and Canada are among the countries that have taken advantage of the size and diversity of the United States Government to create asymmetries of coherence in their favor to counter asymmetries of power in favor of the United States. See Keohane (1971); for Canadian cases see Swanson (1972, pp. 185—218) and Nye (1974).

4   Magee (1970) discusses a situation in which FAO bureaucrats conspired with African governments to thwart the director's decision to relocate two offices.

SECTION 4

THE POLITICS OF DECISION MAKING

Decision making has so far been explained either as the result of the rational evaluation of choices, or the product of organizational procedure and process. This third model borrows some analytical tools from both of these, but remains distinctive in its approach and substance. In arguing that there is a political dimension to decision making, analysts are using the term 'political' in its broadest conception, rather than the more restricted everyday usage of 'party political'.

To explain decisions as the result of political activity is essentially to introduce the elements of 'power', 'influence', and 'interests' into the equation. Decision making is thus to be considered an activity in which there are conflicting interests at stake, as well as conflicting perceptions of the substance of the problem which requires decision, amongst a variety of actors be they individuals, groups, organizations, or governments. In resolving this conflict of interests, the participants will bring to bear their relative resources of power, influence, and negotiating skill and in consequence the outcome, or decision, is the result of a complex bargaining process. This distinguishes it from the rational model, which explains decisions as the result of a single and objective calculation, and the organizational model, in which decisions are viewed as the outputs of organizations with specific goals and standardized procedures for attaining them. Within the political model a key set of questons is raised relating to the distribution of power and influence amongst the participants. In particular at the societal level the question of 'how decisions are made' sometimes interacts with the question 'who has the power to make decisions?'

The predominant explanation of decision making at the societal level has been that of the 'pluralist'. Smith (4.1) outlines exactly what pluralism means in the British context, with its emphasis upon the interplay of organized interests or interest groups, with government acting as final arbiter, or in some cases an interest in its own right. The outcome of the decision-making process is thus generally unpredictable, being dependent upon the resources each participant is willing or able to devote to its cause. And it is the question of the relative distribution of such resources which Newton queries in his extract on local government decision making in

Birmingham (4.2). Newton concludes by suggesting that some groups have greater access to the decision-making arena than others and he therefore distinguishes between such groups, which he labels the 'established' groups, and the remainder. Whilst Saunders would agree with Newton's conclusions his analysis is substantively different. In explaining the political flavour of decision making in Croydon, Saunders (4.3) indicates the existence of a 'political elite' which controls, together with the officials of the council, the process of decision. Although he does not deny the existence of other interests attempting to influence decision making, he does conclude that the overall process itself is under the firm direction of this single political elite.

However, the remaining contributions would not agree with Saunders that one single group (elite) could so pervasively control the process of decision making, nor with Smith when he suggests that government is simply a neutral arbiter between competing interests. Such judgements arise from a focus upon the relations between government and interest groups. For Williams (4.4) this relationship is dependent upon the underlying assumptions in the policy area in question. Thus, within education, whilst a consensus on the aims and objectives of education policy existed, the role of interest groups was quite institutionalized. However, as that consensus has been eroded, as a result of falling real levels of education expenditure, a greater degree of conflict has emerged between groups, each attempting to maintain an influence within the Department of Education and Science, and thus over education policy. But is it possible to make any further generalizations about such relations? Peters in his broadly based analysis (4.5) has developed a classification of these relations, distinguishing four major types in terms of their scope, influence, style, and impact upon decision making. The most effective form of relationship, from the interest group's perspective, is the 'legitimate', in which the group itself becomes legally instituted into the actual process of decision making and implementation. Within Britain this is evident in the Health and Safety Executive, and the Manpower Services Commission, in which the major sectional interests, such as the Trades Union Congress and the Confederation of British Industry, are legally incorporated alongside government representatives. This is also something which is apparent at the European level, in the Economic and Social Committee of the European Communities, which consists of representatives of national pressure groups.

There are, however, deeper implications which flow from such incorporation, particularly of the more powerful interests. Marsh and Grant (4.7) discuss these implications in relation to economic and industrial policy making in Britain. Within these sectors relations between government, the TUC and CBI appeared so close for a period that some analysts suggested the emergence of a new 'corporatist' system of decision making. What is meant by this is that decisions are reached by the mutual agreement of these three participants, and implemented through mutual cooperation. The decision-making system thus becomes a closed one; and therefore, consultation of interests becomes, in reality, a process of exclusion, in this case also excluding the membership of the respective sectional interests.

However, Marsh and Grant argue that the nature of the decision making process is less rigid than this and that the participants are far from being as cooperative as suggested. In fact they have significantly conflicting interests, and, moreover, within each there are internal clashes of interests between rival constituencies — different unions, large corporate enterprises and small business interests, or government departments. Thus, to explain decision making in the economic and industrial sectors it is vital, as Marsh and Grant indicate, to examine the political bargaining *within* the major interests concerned, as well as *between* them.

However incestuous the relations between interest groups and government become, it remains the case that certain rules structure their decision-making behaviour. If decision making is held comparable with a bargaining process then the implication is that this process must have certain behavioural rules. Richardson and Jordan (4.6) outline the nature of such rules, in their discussion of the role of interest groups, of both a governmental and non-governmental nature, in two key policy areas. In this bargaining game, decisions tend to be reached through a process of negotiation, which emphasizes the accommodation of conflicting interests, the achievement of consensus, and the maintenance of the existing form of relations between interest groups and government departments within the particular policy community. Changes in policy are thus always marginal and decision making becomes essentially incremental in character.[1]

Similar points are also made by Webb (4.8) in analysing the process of decision making at the international level, in particular within the European Communities (EC). Webb suggests that depending upon the issue involved, decision making within the EC can be explained either as a result of the bargaining between governments, in which the European institutions become marginal, or as a more complex set of bargaining relations which involve national and transnational pressure groups, coalitions of departments in different governments (transgovernmental relations), and the community institutions from the Commission (European bureaucracy) to the Parliament. But although the complexity of the process of decision making at the European level makes it distinctive, it remains essentially a bargaining process, which, she argues, is not entirely dissimilar to that in other, less mysterious contexts.

Decision making, portrayed in this section as a political activity which involves an intricate bargaining process amongst conflicting interests, has a convincing flavour since it conforms to what is superficially observable in the 'real world'. But even accepting this, the 'political' view should not be received uncritically since it reflects only one particular construction of what constitutes 'politics'. Hence, in the following section it will be necessary to unveil, and elaborate upon, some of its intellectual limitations.

Note

1   Incrementalism is discussed in the Introduction to Section Two.

4.1   B. Smith

PLURALISM

From *Policy Making in British Government*, published by Martin Robertson & Co. Ltd, 1977.

The pluralistic model ... has a number of interrelated elements, each of which corresponds to aspects of the British political system.

First, political equality and individualism are protected by the fundamental political rights to vote, to free speech and to association for political ends. Inequalities may ... result from the operation of the electoral system, but these are random in their effects and do not favour any one socio-economic group. Representative institutions and the rights of opposition protect individual and sectional interests from unfair or arbitrary discrimination. The narrow electoral margins which have separated the two main political parties since the war have contributed to the maintenance of a balance between social and economic interests. Access to government is guaranteed through electoral choice, through lobbying and other forms of pressure group activity and through the politically free mass media.

Secondly, the weakness of the individual citizen in a modern democracy is compensated for by the right and ability of all freely to organise groups and associations for political action. Interests can be mobilised and made politically effective by the processes of functional representation. In a pluralist society power is diffused between such groups. Their rough equality of power produces a balanced competition for resources leading to democratic policy-making. Equilibrium is maintained by the countervailing power of different groups with different power-bases ...

Thirdly, the state in a pluralist society is regarded as a neutral set of institutions for adjudicating between conflicting social and economic interests. The positive state is thought to protect all economic interests by accommodating and reconciling them. It does not defend the predominance of any particular class or show any marked bias towards a particular interest. No organisation or interest is consistently successful in obtaining its objectives across the whole range of public policies, and policy issues tend to be resolved in ways generally compatible with the preferences of the majority of the public ...

Fourthly, although every state has its elites, including a political elite, the pluralist state is characterised by a plurality of elites. The nature of mass democracy and large-scale organisations may be such that power is inevitably concentrated in the hands of political leaders rather than the mass electorate or rank-and-file members of political organisations ... Nevertheless this is compatible with democracy if positions within the elites are open to people recruited from diverse socio-economic backgrounds. Pluralism can exist when no single elite dominates the political system and when access to elite positions is based on merit ... Competition between the political parties is further evidence of elite plurality. Furthermore it is maintained that in Britain the different economic, social, political, professional, administrative and other elites lack the cohesion necessary to turn them into a ruling class.

In Britain pluralism is manifested in the decline of class and ideological politics and the rise of organised producer and consumer groups as the main channels of political communication between the people and the government. The pluralist character of British politics, and the relationships between groups and parties, has been most elaborately documented by Samuel Beer (1965). He concluded that in the post-war period the Conservative and Labour Parties moved away from their more ideological standpoints and class antagonisms towards a consensus based on acceptance of the welfare state and the managed economy. Their attitudes towards policy-making in these areas may still be conditioned by contrasting values about equality and political authority. Nevertheless party conflict and group pressures operate within a broad consensus of 'collectivist' values and beliefs which 'legitimated party government by two purposive, strongly united and elaborately organized parties – along with functional representation by similarly concentrated producer's organizations' (Beer, 1965, p. 388).

Finally, the picture which emerges ... of the techniques of policy-analysis in British government is also compatible with the pluralist conception of decision-making in democratic government ... The intellectual difficulties impeding rational behaviour fit neatly into the pluralists' model of politics as a process in which group competition within a broad consensus of goals serves to make marginal adjustments to the *status quo*. Consequently the organisational and political requirements of comprehensive, synoptic planning are rejected in favour of decentralised and dispersed decision-making powers: 'A spontaneous form of partisan mutual adjustment (PMA) among the various decision actors or centres is much to be preferred to the vain (but perhaps vainglorious) intellectual labours of central planners' (Self, 1973). 'Partisan mutual adjustment' is virtually another label for the pluralist political system in which consensus is maintained by a process of 'successive limited comparisons' in policy-making. 'Agreement on policy thus becomes the only practicable test of the policy's correctness' (Lindblom, 1959).

4.2   K. Newton

THE THEORY OF PLURALIST DEMOCRACY

From *Second City Politics*, published by Oxford University Press, 1976. Reprinted by permission of A.D. Peters & Co. Ltd.

According to one recent textbook on urban politics in the United States, 'The American model of democracy rests essentially on the doctrine of pluralism ... the application *par excellence* of the pluralistic model of democracy has been in the area of urban politics' (Stedman, 1972, p. 79).[1] Although pluralism has become the orthodox theory of American city politics, and to a lesser extent of politics in British cities also, and although the theory has been expounded and elaborated by some of the most powerful minds in modern sociology and political science, pluralism has rather shaky empirical foundations, primarily because there are so few systematic studies of the role and influence of organizations in the urban decision-making process.[2] This section of the work on voluntary organizations will compare some propositions drawn from pluralist theory with the data collected from the sample of voluntary organizations in Birmingham. Since the city is a large one, with a highly diversified economy and a population which is both relatively stable and mixed in terms of class, ethnicity, and religion, one would expect it to have a wide variety of organized groups and, therefore, to serve as a good case study of pluralist politics in action.

One of the most important planks of the whole pluralist case is that, although political resources are not distributed equally, the inequalities are not cumulative. This means that any individual or group with one important political resource, such as money, may lack other resources, such as voting power or the incentive to engage in prolonged political struggle. Robert Dahl has argued that 'a citizen who has less of one resource than another citizen may nonetheless gain greater influence because he has other resources. Though he may have less money, he may have more time, more energy, greater popularity, stronger ethnic ties.' (Dahl, 1967, p. 378).[3] Consequently, while political groups are not all equally matched, all have some resources which give them weight and leverage in the political system. As a result nobody is likely to lose out completely, and every group can get something out of the system, even if it cannot get most of what it wants. As Dahl puts it, 'few groups in the United States who are determined to influence the government — certainly few if any groups of citizens who are organized, active, and persistent — lack the capacity and

Table 4.2.1.   Birmingham City council grants to voluntary organizations,
1971

	Grant £
Social Services Committee	
Children's Department: voluntary organization grants	6,833
Residential accommodation provided by other bodies	154,174
Day nurseries: voluntary organizations grants	2,000
Family Service Unit grants	1,750
Mental Health Services: voluntary association charges	2,448
Temporary and emergency accommodation: Birmingham Friendship Association: Middlemore Homes	548
Welfare Department: grants to voluntary organizations providing residential accommodation	103,737
Services for the blind: voluntary organization charges and grants	1,838
Institute for the deaf	8,678
Services for the handicapped: voluntary organization charges and grants	5,274
Services for the aged: voluntary organization charges and grants	46,940
Sub-total	342,220
Finance Committee	
Housing associations:	
debt charges	2,481
Interest	247,310
Sub-total	249,791
Education Committee	
Nursery education: agency services	17,600
Special schools and hostels for maladjusted children, fees	138,614
Further education, technical colleges, etc.:	
Contribution to Student Union building	18,187
Charges by voluntary associations	1,102
University of Aston agency services	3,410
Other services rendered by voluntary associations	4,058
Grants to voluntary associations	1,986
Agricultural education: agency services	1,800
Youth services: grants to voluntary associations	28,098
Community centres: grants to voluntary associations	4,865
Other facilities: grants to voluntary associations	7,911
Play centres and adventure playgrounds: grants to voluntary associations	235
Supply of meals and refreshments to independent schools	2,591
Sub-total	230,457

	Grant £
General Purposes Committee	
Entertainments:	
Theatre Centre	6,461
Repertory Theatre	5,084
Grants to cultural organizations, etc.	74,117
Grants to:	
Birmingham Council of Social Services	12,725
Citizens' Advice Bureau	2,500
Visiting Service for Old People	7,148
Birmingham Retirement Council	1,000
Birmingham Settlement	1,000
Information service for the disabled	100
Civil Engineering Research Council	221
Balsall Heath Association	1,335
Margery Fry Memorial Fund	250
Marriage Guidance Council	1,700
Sparkbrook Association	385
Birmingham Yough Volunteers Trust	3,250
R.S.P.C.A.	250
St. John's Church Ladywood	250
Handsworth Community Centre	250
Birmingham Accident Prevention Council	833
Sub-total	118,859
Housing Committee	
Subsidies to private builders and housing associations	53,170
Sub-total	53,170
Health Committee	
Home nursing: grants to voluntary associations	731
Rehabilitation settlements: charges	443
Health education: grants to voluntary associations	165
Convalescent homes: charges	2,111
Family planning: payments to voluntary organizations	15,250
School health service: grants to voluntary associations	1,000
Other grants and payments	3,065
	22,765
Fire Brigade Committee	
Ambulance service: agency services and grants to voluntary organizations	519
	519
Airport, Baths, Establishment, Libraries and Museums, Markets and Fairs, Parks, Public Works, Salvage, Smallholdings and Allotments, Watch Committees	none
Total	£1,017,781

opportunity to influence some officials somewhere in the political system in order to obtain at least some of their goals' (Dahl, 1967, p. 386).

It is notable that the case for the unequal but non-cumulative distribution of political resources is illustrated in terms of individual citizens, and not in terms of the struggle between groups and organized interests. In this case, as in most of *Who Governs?* and *Pluralist Democracy in the United States*, the analysis deals primarily with individuals and assumes that political battles are fought out between different types of individuals rather than between organizations, groups, interests, or social strata. Individualistic assumptions are characteristic of the pluralist argument as a whole.[4] But even on the individual level, Dahl's arguments seem to run contrary to a great deal of social science research; this suggests very strongly that resources are not only distributed unequally, but are distributed with cumulative inequality. Research has shown over and over again that those with more money often have more time to give to politics, have more political skills, fill more political positions, have more information, more confidence, more effective organizations to defend their interests, and so on. Moreover, some research suggests that some of the tendencies are superimposed one on top of the other.[5] Dahl himself has pointed to cumulative inequalities when he says that 'money and influence have a certain interdependence. The poor man is not likely to gain high influence; but if he does, somehow on the way he is no longer a poor man' (Dahl, 1963, p. 245). He also points out that political participation and competence reinforce one another in a cumulative fashion (Dahl, 1963, p. 287).

Whatever may be the case with respect to individuals, there is certainly evidence in the Birmingham sample to show that the resources which are most closely associated with political activity are distributed among the groups with cumulative inequality. In the whole sample, one in every eight is a developed organization in the sense that it has a large membership, a large income, paid staff, and is well established. Another one in every eight has three out of four of these characteristics. Conversely, a quarter of the organizations have their disadvantages in one type of resource compounded on the other three as well. Another 13 per cent are poorly provided with three out of the four. Over all, therefore, 60 per cent of the organizations have either a high or a low ranking on three out of four resources. The tendency for politically relevant resources to be distributed with cumulative inequality is even more noticeable in the case of the most active sub-set of the sample, the city and local organizations. Among these groups there is a close association between membership size and income ($r = 0.65$), size and staff (0.61), and size and establishment (0.37), and between income and staff (0.72) and income and establishment (0.30) ...

Professional, trade, and manufacturing associations are heavily overrepresented among the best-developed organizations. They make up only one in ten of the total in the city, but almost one in three of the best-developed in the sample. Social welfare groups are also over-represented in this way since they make up one-sixth of the city total, but a quarter of the best-developed. Trade unions are the only other type of note, making up 1 per cent of the city organizations and 7 per cent of the best-developed. The remainder of the well-developed organizations are a mixture of churches, youth clubs, sports clubs, and health organizations. The value of this information depends on its being set in the context of its social and political meaning in the city. This presents difficulties, since it requires interpreting the social and political interests of the organizations concerned. In the case of professional and business organizations and trade unions the interests are reasonably clear; it is significant that the former seem to outnumber, and to be better equipped for the group struggle, than the latter. The interests of social welfare, youth, and health organizations are more difficult, and perhaps impossible, to judge in any objective way; however, at the risk of simplification, it does seem that the best-developed of these organizations are among the more conservative and cautious in terms of their activities and the people they are trying to reach. If one were to distinguish between the deserving and the undeserving poor, as indeed many in the city do, then they serve the interests of the deserving poor, and sometimes of the not-so-poor.

One could look at the same question from the point of view of those interests which are not well protected by well-developed organizations, or by any sort of organization at all.[6] The coloured population of the city, for example, is in need of strong organizations to protect its interests and rights, but not only are there few coloured organizations in the city as whole, but there are none whatsoever among the well-developed organiz-ations in the sample, even though coloured people make up about 10 per cent of the city population. In general, it seems that those sections of the population which have the most individual political resources, the middle and upper class, also have the best organizational resources to protect their interests.[7] The cumulative inequalities which mark off different social strata appear to be reinforced by the cumulative inequalities of the world of voluntary organizations. Trade unions are the major exception to this pattern, but even they take second place in numbers and resources to business and professional associations.

Another favourite argument of the pluralists, indeed one of their basic tenets, is that modern industrial society contains such an enormous diversity of organized interests that any given political issue is likely to attract the attention of two or more groups whose interests are involved, and who will then fight out the issue between them. Organized groups beget their own opposition, and hence the proliferation of groups proceeds in a long chain of actions and reactions. 'The growth of labour and trade associations, and of most others as well, exhibits a wavelike pattern; for the very success of one group in stabilizing its relationships creates new problems for others and makes necessary either new organizations or the extension and strengthening of existing ones.'[8] Pluralism involves the idea that society is divided into an enormous range of more or less well-organized groups, associations, and interests each of which is capable of defending its own interests against the threat of attack by other groups. Galbraith (1952) uses the term 'veto groups' to describe this situation. Dahl (1956, p. 150) argues that 'decisions, in fact, are made on the basis of seemingly endless bargaining ...', and Milbrath (1963) argues that the 'natural balancing factor', in which a vigorous push in one direction stimulates an opponent, or coalition of opponents, to push in the opposite direction, comes into play so often that it almost amounts to a law.

The Birmingham data are not consistent with these arguments. The organizations in the sample were involved in exactly one hundred issues, but in only three cases did secretaries know of any group which was acting in opposition to their own. Of course, the fact that secretaries knew of no opposition does not necessarily mean that there was none. Yet even in a city the size of Birmingham, the group world is a relatively small one (as will be shown below) and secretaries have a good knowledge of what is going on in their own area of interest. One would certainly expect them to know of opposition groups. If it is only a small minority of conspicuous and controversial issues that creates opposing groups, then it must be acknowledged that the pluralist model is based on a minute proportion of issues, the exception rather than the rule.

It might be argued that the system depends not so much on actual conflict but on the anticipation or threat of opposition. In anticipating such a reaction, groups will be careful not to overstep the mark. This argument is hard to accept, however, for group secretaries can scarcely anticipate the reaction of groups whose very existence is unknown. Besides, anticipating the reactions and power of others is a delicate and difficult business. If it were not, sociology and political science would be more scientific than they are. Given this high degree of uncertainty it is difficult to believe that over 90 per cent of the groups were able to calculate their actions so nicely as to avoid provoking the opposition of other organizations.

A second line of argument is more plausible. It could be pointed out that in most areas of political life in the city conflict is likely to be fairly indirect and diffuse. An organization which seeks public money to support a project is unlikely to be opposed by another organization demanding that public money should not be used for this purpose. There are, however, a number of organizations which play a general watchdog role over the city finances and bring as much pressure to bear as they can on the council to keep taxes down, irrespective of what the money might be spent on. In this general way it is probably correct to say that on many broad fronts there are a whole series of countervailing powers. But in many cases it is just as probable that the pluralist system of action and reaction, organization and counter-organization, proposal and counter-proposal is a very diffuse and underdeveloped one which fits where it touches, fails to touch in a number of places, and which may well have large holes in it. Without much difficulty one can think of areas where the pluralist system is puny or non-existent, and where some interests are well protected while others are only weakly articulated — the interests of coloured people as against whites, of pedestrians as against motorists, of users of public transport as against private transport, of old and infirm people as against the young and strong, of vagrants and gypsies as against permanent residents, of consumers as against producers, of environmentalists as against polluters.[9] There are organizations in each of these areas, it is true, but the pressure group system is not well developed or differentiated. Certainly in the hundred issues covered in the sample, organizations seem to operate pretty much on their own without any direct opposition or resistance.[10]

A third theme of the pluralist literature is concerned with the extent to which community organizations come together to form coalitions on a particular issue, but divide and reform to make up a different pattern on different issues. The particular formation of allies and enemies depends very much on the issue, the time, and the place. Yesterday's allies may be tomorrow's opposition, and today's allies may withdraw from active participation in the next issue. The pattern of power is said to be 'mercurial', or 'kaleidoscopic' and 'amorphous', and characterized by 'logrolling', 'wheeler-dealing', and 'coalition-building' ...[11]

If, as the pluralists hold, political resources are distributed with non-cumulative inequality, and if any given political issue is likely to engage the interests of different groups, each with its own set of resources, then it is almost inevitable that the search will start for allies to complement resources and to build up support. If, as this study suggests, political resources tend to be distributed with cumulative inequality, and political issues often involve only one interested party, and the need for coalition-building will arise fairly infrequently.

Respondents to the first-stage mail questionnaire were asked if they had sought the support of any other voluntary organization in their dealings with public bodies in the city. About a quarter said they had, and almost two-thirds said they had not. These figures were confirmed by the second-stage depth interviews with the secretaries of the seventy politically active organizations, who were asked if they had combined with any other voluntary organization in their political activity. On this occasion, a fifth said they had and three-quarters said they had not (see Table 4.2.2).

It seems that coalition-building in the world of community pressure groups is not especially common, and certainly not nearly as common as unilateral activity on the part of isolated organizations. As many secretaries pointed out, there was no need to complicate life further by bringing in

Table 4.2.2. Voluntary organizations seeking the support of, or combining with other voluntary organizations in their political activity

	Combined activity	No combined activity	Don't know Other	Total
	percentages			
First-stage mail questionnaire	28	63	9	100
(Numbers)	(47)	(104)	(15)	(166)
Second-stage interviews	20	77	3	100
(Numbers)	(14)	(54)	(2)	(70)

other organizations when most of the matters concerning them could be dealt with on a one-to-one basis with the relevant public body in the city.

However, the evidence presented in an earlier part of the chapter does suggest that organizations may begin to look around for the support of similar bodies if their initial moves are unsuccessful. If an organization does not get a satisfactory response from its opening activity, then it may well begin to look around for allies, but only a small minority of issues are pushed to this point, usually the most dramatic and controversial ones which arise only every now and again. The vast majority of more routine matters rarely involve coalition-building. Once again, the evidence suggests that pluralist theory applies to a relatively small number of special issues.

A fourth theme, or rather an assumption, which runs throughout the pluralist literature, is the idea that the great depth and diversity of the group world shows the extent to which different sections of the population are organized to protect their different interests. The gigantic number and diverse range of organizations is given as evidence of pluralism. Certainly Birmingham is densely packed with organizations. There are organizations for everything from abortion law reform, accountants, alcoholics, and accident prevention, to Zionists, zipfastener manufacturers, zoologists, and Zoroastrians. Yet as Lowi (1967) has pointed out, 'It is wrong to assume that social pluralism (which is an undeniable fact about America) produced *political* pluralism.'[12] The extent to which social pluralism creates political pluralism partly depends on the extent to which social groups are willing and able to engage in political activity. This study finds a 30 per cent political participation rate in a twelve-month period, but whether this is high or low, adequate or inadequate is a matter of personal judgement. Only comparative study can show what sorts of conditions are likely to produce a higher rather than a lower level of group participation, and hence what sorts of conditions are favourable and unfavourable to group participation in urban politics.

The connection between social and political pluralism also depends upon the extent to which a broad cross-section of different social and economic interests are organized. Although pluralists generally assume that the greater the number of groups the greater the diversity of interests represented among them, the assumption must be questioned. It is known that while a large minority belong to no organizations whatsoever, a small number belong to a great many. About a third of adult citizens in England and Wales are not members of any organization, a quarter belong to only one, another quarter belong to two or three, and 10 per cent are members of four or more.[13] A small minority of people tend to pile up a huge number of memberships between them. This sort of distribution would not matter if members were drawn from a cross-section of the population, but of course, it is known that joiners tend to be concentrated very heavily in the middle- and upper-class strata. Not only this, but middle- and upper-class people are even more heavily over-represented among the ranks of office-holders in voluntary organizations.[14] Joining and running voluntary organizations is pre-eminently, although not exclusively, a middle-class activity.

Seen from this point of view, voluntary organizations may have a broad scope in terms of activities, but a narrow scope in terms of their activists. Indeed, it has been said that community organizations in Britain are manned largely by a small stage army.[15] In one sense this overlapping and interlocking is conducive to democratic stability in so far as it leads to cross-cutting cleavages which contribute to compromise and moderation. In another sense the overlap may simply mean that a fairly wide range of decisions are being influenced by a narrow range of people who wear slightly different hats according to which organization they are involved in on what sort of issue. In this situation, a diverse range of groups involved in the political process may well give the appearance but not the reality of diverse social participation.

In order to gauge roughly how much overlap there is between organizations in Birmingham, secretaries were asked whether office-holders in their own organization held office in any other. Three-quarters were able to name at least one dual office-holder, and only 8 per cent could not do this, the remainder being uncertain. A large minority were able to name dozens of dual office-holders. Moreover, the groups which were best provided with money, members, paid staff, and establishment were also those most likely to overlap with other groups. These figures are not conclusive. They give no more than a vague and rough idea of the extent of organizational overlap; before any firm conclusions could be drawn it would be necessary to know more about the extent of the overlap, the size and class composition of the stage army involved, and the extent to which these interconnections are used on political matters. As they stand, however, the figures suggest that voluntary organizations are interconnected in a fairly close network, and that they are run by a rather small number of people ...

Issues, groups, and officials – the style of group politics

Four closely related factors seem to determine the style and effectiveness of pressure groups politics in Birmingham – the group, the matters of interest to it, the attitudes of elected officials to the group and the issue,[16] and the attitudes of appointed officials to the group and the issue. Established groups, such as the Law Society, the Royal Birmingham Society of Artists, or the Visiting Service for Old People, are respectable, reliable and responsible, and are able to build up a close set of relationships with public officials in the city, if need be. Other kinds of organizations, such as the Black Panthers or the Student Revolutionary Marxist Theatre Action Group, are not in this favoured position and are obliged to use different political tactics. Instead of friendly lunch-time meetings or official sub-committee meetings, these groups work through public meetings, leaflets, demonstrations, delegations to councillors, and the mass media.[17]

By their very nature established groups are unlikely to raise issues which challenge the fundamentals of the existing social and political order. Apart from anything else, they have a vested interest in the political status quo which encourages their special relationship with decision-makers. Moreover, because the established groups generally represent the more powerful and better-organized sections of society, they are often spared the necessity of defending their fundamental interests from attack by equally powerful but opposing political forces. As V.O. Key (1958, p. 150) has put it 'Groups well disciplined and amply supplied with the materials of political warfare are often countered by no organization of equal strength.' The more established the group, the more likely it is to have to deal only with piecemeal proposals affecting its interests, and the more likely it is to be in a position to handle these through its close and friendly relations with decision-makers.

Party politicians in local government are generally favourable to the involvement of voluntary organizations with government business. Since the majority of organizations are either not politically active at all, or else do not raise any fundamental political issues, and since a proportion of them provide a service which is of some value to the community, council members do not feel threatened by citizen organizations and are invariably inclined to support them. But some organizations, such as tenants' associations, some residents' associations, militant social welfare organizations, and various radical organizations of a political or para-political nature, are not of this kind, and members of the city council view them with anything ranging from scepticism to downright hostility. Such organizations often find it difficult to get access to elected or appointed officials, and if they do gain temporary access, they are less likely to be satisfied with the results than established organizations. So they are obliged to use different political tactics. Organizations of this kind are faced with a classic political dilemma

— either they become more moderate to gain acceptance with decision-makers, or else they preserve their policy but remain relatively powerless.[18] And yet established organizations have their problems too; becoming officially incorporated into the decision-making process, they run the risk of being captured by it. Alternatively, a strong, determined, and powerful group may capture the policy-making process.[19] Although it is extremely difficult to say what sorts of circumstances determine what sort of strategy, it is notable that the outcomes are generally favourable to the status quo. The group which challenges the existing order is unlikely to gain the special privileges of the system; groups with special privileges are given them because they do not challenge the existing order; and groups which capture the existing order are unlikely to try to change it. It is certainly not suggested that this amounts to an iron law of the preservation of the status quo, but it does seem a general tendency.

Lastly, local government bureaucrats play a role in directing the process of group politics. They have an extensive set of links and ties with established groups, and groups and bureaucrats can often settle a matter of an administrative or technical nature to their mutual satisfaction. The less well-established groups, or those raising issues of a more overtly political nature, are handled in a different way and politely referred to the politicians on the city council. However, if the bureaucrat is favourably disposed towards the group or the issue, he may be able to keep the matter within his own sphere of operations and out of the political arena. He can exercise his influence by presenting the group and the issue in a favourable light to his committee, and he can give the group advice about how to present its case to his committee chairman. Often the symbiotic relationship between groups and local government officers operates to exclude the politicians, especially where the professional interests of officers and the goals of the group coincide, as they sometimes do in the case of these social welfare organizations which are pushing for services which social worker professionals believe it is their duty to provide. In this case, a group which is not especially favoured by politicians may develop a special relationship with social workers and administrators. On major policy matters, however, the hands of local government officers seem to be closely tied and, although they have some room for manoeuvre, they cannot usurp policy-making powers.

In spite of exceptions to the rule, the local pressure group system seems to operate in such a way that the best-established groups, which usually possess the best organizational resources, press for the maintenance of the status quo or for small, piecemeal reforms in their own interest, and are able to work through their close ties with decision-makers, especially local government bureaucrats. Established groups with maximum power and control operate in a relatively quiet and unnoticed way, talking to local government officials, attending meetings, sending policy documents, and being consulted by public officials. Paradoxically, the noisier and more visible the group the greater the likelihood of its being powerless in the political system. These groups have relatively few organizational resources, and those which try to tackle fundamental social and political issues are often obliged to use less efficient, more time-consuming, and more expensive political tactics which involve mounting pressure group campaigns aimed at politicians and the general public.

The extensive, day-to-day use of administrative channels of communication means that a high proportion of pressure group activity is not immediately visible. Care must be taken, therefore, to search the appropriate channels of communication. Examination of the public arenas, most generally used by American pressure groups, such as the council chamber, the local newspaper, and the political parties, may reveal remarkably little group activity, but sampling a wide cross-section of voluntary organizations or talking to people in local government departments may produce a different conclusion. Yet the discovery of a large quantity of group activity does not necessarily mean the presence of a thriving pluralist democracy; rather we must ask questions about the active groups and the interests they seek to protect. The most visible part of the group world in Birmingham seems to operate fairly much as the theory of pluralist democracy suggests it should, but the less visible nine-tenths of the iceberg has a different set of political characteristics. One major difficulty with the pressure group literature is that it has tended to concentrate on the visible one-tenth of pressure group operations, and has tended to assume that this is practically the whole of the group world. Pluralist theory falls into much the same sort of trap.

Notes

1   See also Connolly (1969, p. 3); Smith and Freedman in Pennock and Chapman (1969, p. 43).
2   For a similar comment see 'Epilogue' in Pennock and Chapman (1969, p. 286) and Hutcheson and Steggert (undated), pp. 10–11, 15.
3   See also Dahl (1963, p. 85).
4   Not the least important is the assumption that formal organizations represent the interests of their individual members. This assumption cannot be examined here, unfortunately, but the literature on the iron law of oligarchy and on the way in which organizations develop goals of their own throws considerable doubt upon it. Barber, in Gouldner (1950), argues that the iron law of oligarchy may be even more cast iron in the case of voluntary association.
5   Allardt *et al.* (1958); Almond and Verba (1965); Rokhan and Campbell (1960).
6   See, for example, Parenti (1970).
7   For some speculations about this tendency see Warner in Horton Smith (1973, pp. 351–2).

8 Truman (1951, p. 107).
9 The same point is made by Lakoff (1973, p. 3).
10 The same point is made by Presthus (1964, p. 267) and by McConnell (1966, pp. 362–3).
11 Truman (1951, pp. 362–8); Presthus (1964, pp. 12–14); Polsby (1963, p. 137).
12 Given the scarcity of comprehensive research on the matter, it is open to doubt whether social pluralism is an undeniable fact of American life.
13 Committee on the Management of Local Government (1967, p. 114).
14 Bottomore in Glass (ed.), (1954, p. 374) and Brennan (1959).
15 Hill (1970, pp. 90–110); Stacey (1960, pp. 82–6).
16 On the importance of official attitudes towards groups see Zisk (1973).
17 A similar point has been made about group politics in New York city by Bornfriend (1969).
18 See Lipsky and Levi in Hahn (ed.), (1972, pp. 175–99).
19 McConnell (1966).

4.3   P. Saunders

THE POLITICAL ELITE

From *Urban Politics* (Penguin Education, 1980), pp. 216–26. Copyright ©
Peter Saunders, 1979. Reprinted by permission of Penguin Books Ltd.

The local council: internal relations

The policy-making process in most local authorities in England and Wales
has been 'rationalized' in recent years following various central government
initiatives, the most significant of which have been the 1972 Bains report
and the 1974 reorganization. This has produced two main consequences.
First, there has been an increased vertical integration of local, regional and
national levels of government. This has resulted in a fragmentation of
functions between the levels (e.g. the division between local and structure
planning), and in an overall increase in central regulation of local policy-
making. Secondly, the internal organization of local authorities themselves
has changed. This is not to suggest that before the 1970s local councils
were controlled by the elected members while today they are controlled
by the officers, for this would be too gross a simplification. Clearly there
has been a shift, at least as regards the formal structure of management
and policy-making, away from the members, and this is reflected in the
development of corporate planning teams (consisting of the heads of all
the main council departments) which tend to work closely with small
'inner cabinets' of leading members of the majority groups of the different
authorities. But this is only the culmination of a long term trend in local
government ... and, more significantly, it is a formal change in organizational structure which may not be directly reflected in organizational
practice. The point here is that it has become a sociological cliche that the
formal structure of an organization does not necessarily indicate what
actually goes on within it, and there is no reason to expect that local
authorities constitute an exception to this. Both functionalist (e.g. Blau,
1963) and interactionist (e.g. Silverman, 1970) approaches to the sociology
of formal organizations have stressed the need to examine how members
routinely accomplish their 'roles', and it follows that the analysis of the
formal organizational framework of local authority decision-making can
only be a first step in understanding how policies come to be made.

The formal decision-making procedure in Croydon is broadly similar
to that followed by most other local authorities in the country, and it is
summarized in Fig. 4.3.1. It can be seen from this that there are certain

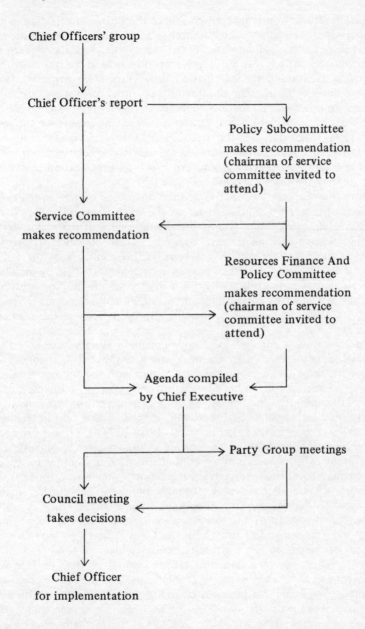

Fig. 4.3.1. Local authority decision-making: the formal structure.

strategic positions – notably membership of the Chief Officers' Group and membership of the Policy subcommittee – which would appear to provide the capacity for controlling virtually the entire policy-making process, for the lower-level participants are largely dependent upon them for both the original initiatives and for information about alternative proposals. However, we need to ask whether and how this potential control is exercised in practice. In other words, the formal model outlined in the diagram is little more than a 'script' which may guide to a greater or lesser extent what Gans (1967) has termed the decision-making 'performance'. As one Croydon Chief Officer observed, 'It's extremely difficult to describe the real decision-making practices. You can construct organization charts but these are only the theory and life isn't like that.'

From the perspective of the elected members of the council, the positions of greatest potential power are the seven seats on the Policy subcommittee and, to a lesser extent, the chairmanships of the major service committees such as education, housing and social services (although the chairmen of these committees are usually also members of the Policy subcommittee). All of these key positions, of course, are held by members of the majority party group, which in Croydon means the Conservatives, and they are filled by the leading and generally most senior members of the group. These individuals may nominally be defined as the council's 'political elite'.

Many previous studies of local government in Britain have noted the power which committee chairmen may come to enjoy over their colleagues. For a start, they have a privileged relationship with the appropriate Chief Officer and can draw upon his information and expertise to direct, initiate and curtail committee discussions. As Bealey and his co-authors suggest, 'A strong-willed and capable chairman who is well advised on the technical and legal aspects is likely to get his way' (1965, p. 369). Thus in Croydon, as in many other authorities, committee chairmen meet informally with the relevant officers before every committee meeting in order to discuss the agenda, resolve their strategies, and, as one councillor expressed it, 'to determine what shall be pushed through and what can be left to the committee to decide'. Furthermore, committee chairmen enjoy considerable delegated powers – inevitably since committees meet only eight times in any one year – and in liaison with the Chief Officers, such powers can be used 'on behalf of', yet without the knowledge of, other committee members. Sometimes, the decisions taken under these delegated powers can be reviewed by the committee at a later meeting (e.g. the closure of a children's playground can be reviewed and the decision reversed with little difficulty). At other times, however, the decisions are in practice irreversible (e.g. a land purchase where the decision is contractually binding). As one member put it, 'What's done is done.'

The power of most of the chairmen of the major committees is reinforced by their membership of the Policy subcommittee. This is the only one-party committee of the council – 'The tory caucus with the Town Clerk there' was how one Labour member described it. It is also the first committee to consider any proposal and, as its name suggests, it holds a wide brief to consider the development of council policy over the broad spectrum of the different departments and committees. It considers various proposals before the appropriate service committees meet, and although it can only make 'recommendations' to the other committees (and, through them, to the full council meeting), most councillors agreed with the member who suggested, 'It's a recognized thing that its recommendations are carried out.' This is not particularly surprising, of course, when we remember that its members are the leading figures in the majority group and that they tend also to be the chairmen of the major service committees to whom the recommendations are sent. It is no exaggeration to suggest that the seven men who comprise the Policy sub-committee recommend proposals in one role and then accept them in another.

Even in the unlikely event of a service committee rejecting a Policy sub-committee recommendation, the 'political elite' still has two other strings to its bow. First, its recommendation, together with those of the various service committees, are considered by the Resources Finance and Policy committee, of which Policy is a subcommittee. In other words, all seven members of the Policy subcommittee sit on the very committee which considers the various recommendations which have been made, and its chairman and vice-chairman occupy the same positions on Resources Finance and Policy. Furthermore, this latter committee, which does in-clude a minority of Labour members, always votes on strict party lines, and thus invariably endorses the recommendations of the Conservative group leaders. In short, service committee proposals are unlikely to be accepted where they conflict with those of the Policy subcommittee. Secondly, even where the Policy subcommittee is overruled by the decision taken in a full council meeting, it still retains an effective veto power since it controls the distribution of resources among the various departments of the council. In other words, the Policy subcommittee has the power to decide whether to allocate the necessary finance to a service committee which has resolved on a policy of which it disapproves. In 1972, for example, the council accepted a Health committee proposal for the introduction of a free family planning service in the borough. The Policy subcommittee, however, refused to allocate sufficient additional funds for the scheme to be put into operation, and the decision was therefore not implemented ...

This ability to 'persuade and dominate' is not simply a reflection of the strategic location of the Policy subcommittee in the decision-making process, however, for it also reflects the relationship between the 'political elite' and the rank-and-file of the majority party group. Sherman has argued that, 'In local government today, the group is more powerful and demanding than the party whips in Whitehall' (1973, p. 140), and although this may be something of an exaggeration, there is no doubt that, since the eclipse of the 'independent' councillor (which in Croydon can be dated effectively from the early 1960s although a handful of right-wing independents continued to gain election until the early 1970s), the party caucus has become a central element in the decision-making process. In Croydon, members of both party groups exhibited a marked reluctance to vote against group decisions; only 15 per cent of Labour members reported ever having voted against a group decision, the comparable figure among Conservatives being slightly higher at 20 per cent. Majority group decisions are thus tantamount to council decisions, and the power to control the majority group is thus crucial in determining the ability to control the council.

That the 'political elite' effectively controls the majority group in Croydon is beyond doubt. Conservative group meetings function mainly as a means of disseminating information on decisions which have already been resolved in committee, and as a way of determining voting strategies for forthcoming council meetings. The majority group meeting does not therefore serve as a vehicle for rank-and-file involvement in policy-formation, and in this respect, Croydon appears no different from many other authorities (e.g. see Bulpitt 1967). Because it meets after the agenda for the council meeting has been compiled (i.e. after the 'political elite' has made its 'recommendations'), all that usually remains to be done is to ensure that the members formally fall into line behind their leaders. This they invariably do with little trouble. The ideological commitment and political zeal of most Conservative members is relatively low compared with that found in the Labour group – only one quarter of the Conservatives, compared with half of the Labour members, cited 'involvement in decision-making' as their major concern as councillors – and this is reflected in their high level of compliance with the decisions taken by their leaders. As Harris (1971) has pointed out, there is perhaps less excitability and passion on the right of British politics than on the left, and this certainly appeared the case in Croydon where the Conservative rank-and-file was, by and large, fairly content with the passive political role it was called upon to play.

This is not to suggest that there have never been conflicts within the majority group, nor that the rank-and-file members have no control over the leadership. One particularly acrimonious dispute, for example, took place over the leadership's decision to accept the government's call to reorganize secondary education in the borough in the 1960s ... here we should note that it resulted in the resignation of the chairman of the Education committee following the mobilization of a right-wing faction against him. However, three points need to be made about this. First, the issue was somewhat unique in that most internal dissension within the majority group occurs around questions of personalities or parochial loyalties (mainly northern against southern ward representatives) rather than on a left–right split. Secondly, even in this fairly unique case where tory 'gut-feeling' was strongly opposed to the abolition of the grammar schools, the group leaders were still powerful enough to force the reform through. Indeed, ... the 'political elite' twice changed its policy on comprehensive reorganization, yet on both occasions was able to carry with it the support of the great majority of Conservative members. Thirdly, the successful coup against the Education committee chairman was only short-lived, and it resulted in 1974 in an important shift in the relations of power between the leadership and the rank-and-file. Until 1974, the major source of power for the rank-and-file members was their right to elect annually the chairmen of the different committees, but in that year the leader of the group announced that all chairmen would in future be appointed by him (although he was still to be elected by the group). 'It means,' he explained, 'the leader having more political control of the council, and that the load is shared as the leader would wish it to be. It's no good having the chairman of a committee who's opposed to the leader all the time.' Armed with these new powers, the group leader then proceeded to reinstate the former Education committee chairman to his old post, and since then the majority group has been reduced to a state of virtual impotence in relation to the leader and his appointees.

Although it is now firmly in control of its own majority group, however, the 'political elite' still depends for its power on its ability to negotiate two other crucial potential limitations posed by the internal organization of the decision-making process. One of these concerns its relationship with the Chief Officers of the council; the other concerns its ability to avoid direct and open confrontation with the Labour group.

The Chief Officers represent the strongest potential limitation on the power of the 'political elite', for not only do they initiate policy discussions (often as a result of central government or internal departmental stimuli, but also sometimes in response to members' own suggestions) and implement them, but they are also involved in the third and more contentious role of actively resolving them. The close relationship between a Chief Officer and a committee chairman, for example, is a two-edged sword, for if the latter uses the expertise of the former, it is also the case that the former can influence the latter through the information he chooses to make available and the way in which he does so. As Heclo (1969) points out, information and expertise constitute crucial power resources in the increasingly complex world of local government. Or as Weber observed, 'The question is always who controls the existing bureaucratic machinery. And such control is possible only in a very limited degree to persons who are not technical specialists' (1947, p. 338).

This point is not lost on the elected members themselves. As one Croydon councillor put it, 'In most things you're in the hands of the officers. They've got the information. Councillors are kept too busy to keep well informed.' This argument was reinforced by a Chief Officer who, citing Parkinson's Law, suggested that committees would sometimes talk for hours about where to locate a bicycle shed, and then accept a proposal involving vast council expenditure in a matter of minutes. Nor is the problem simply that of disparities of technical expertise, for the officers are in practice called upon, not only to 'advise' on policy options, but to make a host of routine decisions about what a policy actually 'means' once it has been decided. In other words, in administering council policies, the officers necessarily enjoy a wide area of discretion in which to draw their own interpretations, and this can substantially affect the impact of any given policy decision ...

There is a danger, however, in overemphasizing the power of the officers in relation to the elected members, and this follows from the failure to distinguish between the majority of the elected members and the small group I have termed the 'political elite'. As Newton concludes from his study of Birmingham council, 'Council members do have some resources to call upon when they confront expert opinion, and these resources are not by any means negligible for some sections of the membership. Most important, perhaps, they are least negligible for the members who generally fill the most important positions ... much of the current literature on officer–member relations overemphasizes the power of the officers and under-emphasizes that of the members' (1976, p. 164) ...

In Croydon there are strong grounds for suggesting that the relationship of the Chief Officers to the leading members of the majority group is more that of close allies than of daunting superiors. For a start, the 'political elite' can choose its men in its own image, for leading members dominate the Interviews and Appointments committee which selects Chief Officers. More significant than this, however, is the fact that the officers depend upon the leading members as much as the members do upon them; the relationship is symbiotic in that the 'political elite' needs the help, advice and information which only the officers can provide, while the officers in turn are obliged to address themselves to the ideological predispositions of the elite members if their proposals are eventually to be accepted by the council. Even where policies are initiated and formulated by the officers, in other words, they must generally reflect the values and overall objectives of the 'political elite', and in Croydon this is reflected in the lack of any observable tension over the years between bureaucratic advice and majority group preferences ...

The direction in which they are jointly headed is, needless to say, to the right, and given the long history in Croydon of right-wing domination of the council, first by 'independents' and later by the Conservatives, the compass needle has rarely wavered from this course. Two points arise out of this. First, it may well be that in authorities where a radical Labour group is in control (e.g. the so-called 'red islands' of local government), the bureaucracy does come to impose a strong constraint on the political actions of the members, but this does not appear to be the case in Conservative-controlled authorities like Croydon. This conclusion would seem to support the argument ... that constraints on policy-making are less severe when action is directed towards maintaining the status quo rather than fundamentally challenging it. The second point is that, despite professional claims to objectivity and political neutrality on the part of local state bureaucrats, it is clear that where their advice bears upon policy choices, it is and can be no more objective, rational or scientifically based than that of any other group ...

Poulantzas (1973) is only one of a number of writers who have identified the dominant political ideology in the western capitalist societies as that which stresses the neutrality of the state. In contrast to pre-capitalist societies where political power is recognized as explicitly class-based and is justified ideologically as the result of 'natural' or 'sacred' principles, Poulantzas suggests that the capitalist state is seen as the representative of the 'general interest', and that its policies are justified ideologically as the result of the application of rational principles: 'What specifically defines the ideologies in question is that they do not aim to be accepted by the dominated classes according to the principle of participation in the sacred: they explicitly declare themselves and are accepted as scientific techniques' (*ibid.*, p. 217). The consequence of this is that any challenge to the state which is premised on the existence of class antagonisms and which attempts to demonstrate the class-bias of state policies comes to be dismissed as 'utopian' in contrast to the scientific rationality of the state itself.

Poulantzas's insights here are directly applicable to the analysis of policy-making in Croydon, for not only is there the strong and pervasive assumption that the policy outcomes agreed by the political elite and the Chief Officers are in some way neutral and objective, but the response to those who challenge this assumption is invariably to define them as 'naive', 'irresponsible' and 'utopian'. It is in this respect that the Labour opposition constitutes an important factor in the policy-making process, for if the impression of rationality is to be sustained, it is necessary for the political elite to maintain a broad political consensus which enables it to represent its actions as 'sensible' and 'reasonable' rather than 'doctrinaire' and sectional.

The Labour leadership in Croydon has long aided them in this, and has been content to follow a policy of moderation and conciliation designed to create and maintain close and informal relations with the political elite. As one Labour leader expressed his philosophy, 'Half a loaf is better than none.' The older, more experienced and generally right-wing Labour leaders have in this way come to enjoy both the respect and the confidence of their Conservative counterparts (reflected in the fact that, while no Labour respondents identified their group leader as an influential man in the council, no less than thirty per cent of Conservatives did). The Labour leaders were quite happy to work with rather than against the political elite — 'I'm quite friendly with the other side ... I tend to respect more of the tories. On the whole they're in it to help the people of Croydon ... You can get a great deal done by private chats — far more than by shouting your mouth off' — and the elite, in turn, was quite prepared to listen to what the Labour leaders had to offer — 'When X speaks, you listen.' Indeed, the close and informal nature of the relationship between the two was such that the Labour leaders had at times been consulted over a proposal before many Conservative members had got to hear of it. One leading Conservative member, for example, having spent eighteen months in private and secret negotiations to secure the purchase by the council of a local independent school building, then sounded out a leading Labour member to gauge his reactions before he informed members of his own party.

Such close liaison between the two group leaderships brings benefits to both. For the political elite, it has traditionally meant that contentious opposition and public hostility to its policies and to its power have been avoided. By including the Labour leaders in its deliberations (if only somewhat superficially) it has ensured itself a quiescent opposition. For the Labour leaders themselves, of course, the relationship has provided for some degree of involvement in the decision-making process, and with it the possibility of gaining some minor concessions on policy. The relationship has thus been one of mutually satisfying back-scratching.

4.4 G. Williams

EDUCATIONAL PLANNING: PAST, PRESENT AND FUTURE

From *Education Policy Bulletin*, vol. 7 no. 2, pp. 125–40 (1979).

Introduction

There are broadly two extreme interpretations of the educational policy process. One may be called 'technocratic', the other 'political'.[1]

At one end of the spectrum is the technocratic model in which planning consists of the 'operationalising' of broad strategic objectives established by a dominant policy maker or policy making group or as a result of consensus amongst several groups. Examples of broad policy objectives are the meeting of national needs for qualified manpower, the establishment of equality of educational opportunity, the reduction of social inequality, meeting the wishes of private individuals for various kinds of courses or providing enough places for all the children for whom the law prescribes compulsory education.

In Britain the most clear cut example of such a model is the planning of higher education since the publication of the Robbins Report. The Robbins Committee proposed a broad policy objective that 'courses of higher education should be available for all who are qualified by ability and attainment to pursue them and who wish to do so'. The government of the day and all successive governments have accepted the objective. The planning problem was to convert this objective into operational terms. This involved first a precise definition of the terms 'higher education', 'ability', 'attainment', 'wish to enter higher education', and second a quantification of the various categories during a specific planning period. Such an exercise can be repeated periodically to take account of changes in underlying parameters such as the size of the relevant age group, or the 'willingness' of young people to obtain the necessary qualifications or to enter higher education once they have them. This approach to the planning of higher education was also prevalent in many other countries during the 1960s, for example, Germany, Sweden, Australia, Ireland and France ...

One aim of this paper is to consider why this technocratic model of strategic planning became so widespread during the 1960s and early 1970s and why it has come to be considered much less valid in recent years.

The 'political' model denies the existence of any easily recognisable group of policy makers. Instead 'policy' is a series of *tactical* decisions that emerge from the interplay of a universe of pressure groups and vested interests. Some pressure groups are obviously more powerful than others – the political party in power for example – but according to the model none is so powerful as to be able to impose its views on the others and hence to be identified as *the* policy maker or policy making group.

The best example in recent years in Britain of policy emerging from the interplay of pressure groups is the development of comprehensive secondary education. No objective comparable to the Robbins criterion for higher education has been agreed for secondary education since 1944. Instead there have been a variety of views, often contradictory; out of these, however, it can be said *ex post facto* that a policy of sorts has existed at any point in time ...

Where policy emerges from the interplay of opposing pressure groups the role of the planner becomes the tactical one of finding a way between the different interests involved. Usually this will result in some degree of compromise, with 'policy' being the 'resultant' of tactical pressures. It need not always be so. A carefully prepared plan can sometimes result in the implementation of a policy that has powerful opposition ranged against it. To be successful a planner must be well informed about the nature and strength of conflicting pressures. The construction of a plan is not a mathematical exercise as it is under the technocratic model but a matter of legal, administrative, diplomatic and political judgement. Nonetheless, governments in power are normally the strongest single pressure group and can do much of what they want provided they display a certain measure of subtlety.

In practice, of course, few educational policies can be said to be entirely the result of straightforward technocratic plans, nor are they the outcome of an entirely opportunistic balance of forces. It is not an outrageous oversimplification to say that the educational planner of the 1960s needed the skills of the systems analyst and engineer with a soupçon of statistics; while his counterpart of the late 1970s is more likely to be part administrator, part lawyer, part diplomat.

Educational planning in the past

The technocratic approach first became prominent in the late 1950s. It reached its zenith as a result of the enormous expansion of education during the 1960s. It has appeared less credible in the climate of increasing disagreement about the economic and social value of education in the 1970s.

Throughout the 1960s educational planning was closely linked to the economics of education and, though to a rather smaller extent, the sociology of education. The chance conjunction of two separate articles of faith – that expenditure on education would bring about in a relatively painless way both more rapid economic growth and greater social equality – was ultimately responsible for the great expansion that took place in the two decades of 1955–1975 ...

At the same time as economists were rediscovering education's role in promoting economic growth, sociologists were examining the function of education in promoting upward social mobility: enabling children to obtain 'better' (which usually meant better-paid) jobs than their parents.

These twin discoveries helped to provide three different kinds of rationale for educational expansion. First the belief that education was a major contributor to economic growth helped loosen the tight fists of Treasury officials. Second, as individuals became more aware of the role of education in promoting personal advancement the private demand for it increased. Third, it was argued somewhat ingenuously that if as a result of more education more and more people were able to achieve upward social mobility the outcome would be greater social equality. The net result was that very diverse strands in society, those of technocracy, meritocracy, and egalitarianism all agreed on the desirability of educational expansion. The planning process was seen essentially as that of setting quantitative targets for this expansion and removing administrative and financial obstacles of it. There were different methodologies for converting the general belief in expansion into specific targets through manpower planning, rate of return studies, studies of social class and educational opportunity, projections of individual demand and so on ...

This fortuitous consensus of different ideological view points, backed up by empirical research results from a variety of academic disciplines, provided ideal conditions for the development of technocratic methodologies of planning by small groups of specialist planners at the heart of national ministries of education. In England and Wales a small planning branch, staffed by economists and statisticians as well as by administrators, was set up in 1967, and by 1970 some of the results of its work became apparent with the publication of two education planning papers ...

Another major step forward that resulted from the expansion of the 1960s was the development of the concept of education as a system – or perhaps more accurately as a series of sub-systems that interact with each other and with wider social systems such as employment and social structures. It is possible that a systems approach to planning might provide the link between the strategic technocratic planning of the past and the tactical 'political' participatory approaches which are likely to be the key to future developments.

The present state of educational planning

It is not hard to see why the technocratic approach to educational planning was so widely acceptable in a period of rapid expansion. Although objectives differed between different interest and pressure groups in society, the policy implications apparently coincided. It was when doubts were felt simultaneously about the success of education in stimulating economic growth and about its role in the promotion of social equality that the simple strategic model which moved from well defined objectives to methods of implementation began to appear inappropriate.

The DES planning branch was wound up and new planning machinery was established. It rested on three principles:

(a) Planning must directly involve those who must administer the policies that have to be planned;
(b) Specialist skills must be brought into the machinery in such a way as to ensure that they can make a creative contribution to policy formation without being able to determine it single handed; and
(c) The planning machinery must keep close to Ministers, exploring amongst others, options that reflect their known views and seeking Ministerial guidance and endorsement from time to time.

On this basis, from 1971 to 1977 the Departmental Planning Organization (DPO) consisted of:

(a) A policy steering group under the chairmanship of the Permanent Secretary, the highest ranking official in the Department, and including the most senior officials on both the operational and specialist sides. The role of the group was to determine the planning programme in consultation with Ministers, to trigger off particular planning exercises, to ensure that the appropriate planning machinery exists for the jobs in hand and to receive and review the results prior to submitting them where appropriate to Ministers.
(b) Several policy groups, usually under the chairmanship of a Deputy Secretary, each directed to a major block of programmes. Each group comprised a mixture of the heads of the operational branches and specialists such as HM inspectors, statisticians, economists, architects and cost accountants.
(c) A small planning unit. The function of the unit is essentially to service the steering and policy groups, to take the lead in preparing papers in close cooperation with the operational branches and specialists, and generally to maintain consistency of methodology and co-ordination of efforts across the whole departmental planning organization. (Since 1977 this Planning Unit has been strengthened in the number and experience of its members and by being made the direct responsibility of a deputy secretary.)

In an enquiry by a House of Commons Select Committee into educational policy making in England and Wales in 1976, many witnesses expressed views that amounted to the claim that the main task of planners in the DES was to listen to the views of the representatives of various educational pressure and interest groups and to try to steer a path between them. The permanent secretary of the DES defended the current organisation of planning on the grounds that educational plans risked being unrealistic and impracticable unless they were closely linked to the real world of local education authorities and political parties and educational pressure groups (House of Commons, 1976).

This change in official attitudes towards the organisation of educational planning went only a small way towards meeting the claims of many individuals and educational interest groups outside government for a much greater degree of participation in the actual process of decision making. While the formal DES position was that interest groups were invariably *consulted* before decisions were taken, their protagonists often took the view that consultation was insufficient; what was needed was actual involvement in the decisions that were taken ...

The move towards political pragmatism in educational planning which was experienced at about the same time in other countries can be explained partly by changes in the economic and social climate surrounding the educational system and partly by radical changes in the prevailing opinions about the economic and social effects of education.

There was from the early 1970s onwards growing scepticism in the industrialised western world about the role of generalised education in promoting economic growth. Economic theories of the role of education in human capital formation were challenged by 'credentialist' theories which claimed that the principal economic function of education was to act as a 'filter', merely selecting those students who were intrinsically of highest ability for the more highly paid jobs in the economy. The extreme credentialist position espoused by some sociologists is that even this filtering function represents an *irrational* preference by employers for people with paper qualifications ...

At the same time declining birth rates since the mid 1960s have meant sharp falls in primary and later secondary school enrolments resulting in a chronic shortage of trained teachers being replaced by a chronic tendency to surplus supply. All governments have been faced with the problem of reducing the number of teachers in training. In this economic climate the natural reluctance of educationists to be subject to the technological disciplines of manpower planning has been reinforced by the vested interest that manpower forecasts seemed no longer to point in the direction of expansion.

The belief in education as an instrument for promoting social equality has fared no better than the faith in it as an instrument of economic growth. Just as the outcomes of the expansion of the 1960s have resulted in a dramatic reappraisal of the belief in education as an economic investment, so the persistence of wide social inequalities and disparities in access to education has rendered less and less credible any simple faith in the contribution of generalised education to the diminution of social and economic inequalities.

Finally and of course most dramatically in recent years, the attempts by governments to deal with the spectacular inflation of the mid 1970s by reducing public budgets have emphasised the need for choice between different claimants within the overall educational budget and between education and other public sector activities.

Almost certainly it is the empirically observable changes in the relationships between education and the socio-economic structure, combined with changes in the demographic and economic environment itself, that account for the changes in political attitudes to education which have resulted in the technocratic framework of educational planning and policy making being replaced by a political model.

Note

1   These terms correspond in some respects to what policy analysts call the 'consensual' and the 'conflictual' models of policy formation. However, 'consensus' and 'conflict' are better used as description of how objectives are arrived at than as an explanation of how policies and plans are formulated.

4.5 B. Guy Peters

INSIDERS AND OUTSIDERS: THE POLITICS OF PRESSURE GROUP INFLUENCE ON BUREAUCRACY

Reprinted from 'Insiders and outsiders: the politics of pressure group influence on bureaucracy', by B. Guy Peters, *Administration and Society*, vol. 9, no. 2, pp. 191–218, © 1977 Sage Publications, Inc., with permission of the publisher and the author.

We must suppose that the conflict between the demands of pressure groups and the role of the public bureaucracy in decision-making is, in most societies, one of the most basic in government. On the one hand, there is an institution of government, representing the authority of the state, impartiality, and even a judicial temperament. On the other side of the conflict are groups which, by their very nature, represent special interests seeking some preferential treatment from government for their members. This type of division of the role of the state and the role of interests is perceived differently in different political cultures so that the conflict may not be so intense in some systems (Sweden) as in others (France), but interestingly this conflict has been sufficiently ameliorated in most societies so that the two sets of organization — administration and pressure groups — are able not only to coexist but even cooperate quite effectively (Meynaud, 1962, 384–7; Weber, 1968) ...

Given the apparent conflict in the roles assigned to these two sets of political actors and institutions, how are they now able to cooperate so well and so often in making public policy? The simplest and best explanation is that they need each other. The administrators need the political support and influence of the pressure groups in their external relationships with other political institutions, and they further need the information supplied by pressure groups for making and defending their policies. We must assume that bureaucrats have some interest in maintaining or increasing their budgets and their autonomy in policy-making. Support from pressure groups before the right committees is crucial to these goals (Downs, 1967; Niskanen, 1971; Tullock, 1965). On the other side of the exchange, the pressure groups quite obviously need access to political decision-making and influence over the decisions taken. If for no other reason the leaders of the groups must produce enough differential benefits to be able to persuade members that it may be worthwhile to retain membership (Olsen, 1967; Frohlich, Oppenheimer, and Young, 1971). This need of both parties for the resources of the other can provide a general answer to the finding of frequent cooperation between bureaucracies and pressure groups.

We are, however, now left with the formidable task of describing how the two partners in this exchange between pressure groups and bureaucracy interact, and what are the effects of different patterns of interaction.

The basic purpose of this paper is to conceptualize the varying types of relationships that exist among pressure groups and bureaucracy in a number of societies. Second, we are interested in the possible relationships of those categories of interaction to the policies likely the emanate from the political system ...

Modes of interaction

We may again fruitfully begin the discussion by presenting a classification of types of interactions between pressure groups and bureaucracies, along with the presumed characteristics and effects of each type; this is presented in Table 4.5.1. This classificatory scheme places bureaucratic pressure group interaction into four broad categories. As presented, this constitutes an informal continuum from situations in which pressure group influence on policy is regarded as quite illegitimate to situations where it is legally accepted or even required. These four categories are themselves rather broad and may contain substantial variations, but it is still useful to use such a classificatory scheme to begin to understand the macroscopic differences in relationships between these actors.

Legitimate interactions
The first category of bureaucratic pressure group interactions is labeled 'legitimate'. This is to denote that in some political systems not only are pressure groups an accepted fact of political life, but they are also legally and officially involved in the process of making and implementing public policy ... More specifically, we can look at two forms of official or legitimate pressure group involvement in administrative activity: required consultation and direct administration of public programs on behalf of the government.

Required consulation. The required consultation mechanism for legitimating pressure group involvement in policy-making is, as the name would imply, the result of a variety of rules requiring administrative bodies preparing new regulations to consult with the relevant pressure groups as to their opinions, and to solicit advice and information from them. In some cases this will be done in the preparation of legislation to be sent to a legislative body for enactment, and in other cases it will be used for regulations which the administrative body can issue as a result of delegated legislative authority. In either case, however, this required consultation permits an interest group direct access to the making of administrative policies ...

Table 4.5.1.   Types of interaction between pressure groups and bureaucracy

Types	Scope	Influence	Style	Impact
Legitimate	Broad	Great	Bargaining	Redistribution/ self-regulation
Clientela	Narrow	Moderate	Symbiosis	Self-regulation/ distribution
Parantela	Narrow	Moderate	Kinship	Regulation/ distribution
Illegitimate	Variable	None/great	Confrontation	None/ redistribution

Other methods of required consultation use more personal methods.
Most notable in this regard is the use of advisory committees in Norwegian
administration (Kvavik, 1974). On each of these committees there will be
a variety of administrative and interest group personnel charged with
advising the respective administrative body on the proper course of public
policy. These committees then provide a forum for the interest group to
present their evidence and to make a case for their particular views on the
issue. Interestingly, however, the large majority of the representatives on
these committees do not view their role as that of an advocate of a particular position, but rather as more of a technical expert and manager (Kvavik,
1974; 110–15). This role conception is rather obviously useful in facil-
itating compromise on even the most difficult questions of policy ...

Implementation. The second major form of legitimate interest group
involvement in administration is the use of the groups as agents of implementation for public policies. The interest groups serve as quasi-official
arms of the political system in implementing some programs about which
they are assumed to have expert knowledge and skills ... One of the most
common areas in which administration of this type occurs is agriculture
where either commodity groups or local farmers organizations administer
regulations, or acreage allotments, or contractual relationships with the
government. In Sweden, the implementation of many portions of the labor
law is left to the individual groups most affected by the law (Castles, 1973,
33; Carlson, 1969, 125–8). Similarly, in The Netherlands much of that
country's complex system of economic regulation is administered by
boards composed largely of interest group representatives, charged with
the 'self-policing' of a particular industry in order to maintain the delicate
economic balance within the country (Abert, 1969, 56–7). In each of
these cases, the government essentially allows interest groups to engage in
activities in the name of the public with only indirect 'political' control
over their actions. They do tend to be somewhat restrained by having

competing interests represented on the same administrative boards, but this is obviously a manner in which interest groups can have a direct impact on the shape of public policy and its execution.

Institution pressure groups would appear to constitute a special class of legitimate pressure groups. By definition, these are members of an important social or political institution, or that institution itself, acting in the capacity of a pressure group seeking to influence the shape of public policy (Almond and Powell, 1966, 77–8). Some rather obvious examples are the church, the army, and the bureaucracy itself (Webster, 1961; Schmitt, 1972; Ambler, 1966; Johnson, 1962). Local governments, even in unitary regimes, may also act as institutional groups (Scarrow, 1971; Worms, 1966). These groups seek to obtain benefits for themselves or their members, and their actions are legitimated through the prestige of the institution, or perhaps the threat of adverse actions in the case of the army in some societies. Thus, although their position may provide them legitimacy they may actually be better conceptualized as a special class of *clientela* groups in that they have legitimate access when a number of competing groups may not, and tend to seek more special interest outputs than tends to be true in legitimate pressure group systems (Scarrow, 1971, 15–19) ...

Finally, the policy consequences of this interaction between pressure groups and administrators are generally confined to two types (phrased in terms of the Salisbury typology (Salisbury, 1968)): redistribution and self-regulation. That is, in situations in which administrators are capable of imposing the choices made by groups through a bargaining and negotiation process, the decisions taken are likely to take from one group and give to another. This means of policy-making is, however, a relatively safe manner in which to adopt redistributive policy since it ensures the participation of both winners and losers, as well as assuring the application of technical knowledge to the choice (Peters, Doughtie and McCulloch, 1977) ... Elvander notes that in Sweden the inclusion of all competing groups is important for the smooth implementation of policies adopted by pressure group representatives cooperating with the government (1966; Foyer, 1969). In addition, Heisler and Kvavik (1974, 27–89) point out that continued access to policy-making may be sufficient motivation in itself to produce compliance with the decisions taken, even in the face of adverse decisions in the short-run.

In other situations in which the elite may lack the cohesion and consensus necessary to implement a redistributive decision, these legitimate interactions between interest groups and administrators may result in policies of self-regulation (Sharpe, 1973). In these cases organizations are allowed generally to manage their own affairs and thereby essentially manage a sector of public policy for the government. One example of this type of policy outcome is in the area of agriculture where the conflict within the sector is relatively slight so that there may be little need for directly redistributive decisions, and where some policies — such as the allocation of acreage allotments — may have little effect on other groups (Salisbury and Heinz, 1970, 55—9). However, even here there is potential conflict between agricultural groups who would want high subsidies and therefore high food prices and labor groups who would want low prices and therefore lower subsidies. The choice between redistributive and self-regulative policies may depend therefore on the breadth of groups involved in any one decision as well as the integration of the elites making and enforcing the decisions. In other policy areas, one group may have such a monopoly of information and expertise that it is given the responsibility of self-regulation on the basis of that expertise. This has been especially true of the medical and legal interest groups in the United States, as well as similar groups in a variety of other political systems.

Clientela relationships
The second type of interaction between interest groups and administration is one of the two major types developed by LaPalombara. A clientela relationship is said to exist when:

an interest group, for whatever reasons, succeeds in becoming in the eyes of a given administrative agency, the natural expression and representative of a given social sector which, in turn, constitutes the natural target or reference point for the activity of the administrative agency (LaPalombara, 1965, 262).

Thus, this type of interaction is characterized by a perceived legitimacy on the part of administrators of *one* group rather than a formal statement of the legitimacy of all or virtually all groups. The consequences of this difference are, however, quite important. In the first place, the scope of interaction of pressure groups and administration tends to be rather severely constrained. Each agency tends to select a single pressure group as the legitimate representative of its particular social sector and to avoid most other groups seeking to present information and advice. Thus, whereas in the 'legitimate' arragement mentioned previously the agency might be able or required to consult a broad range of groups, in a clientela relationship they will receive a quite narrow range of information and advice. This narrowing is especially evident where two or more groups seek to organize a single sector of the society but where only one is accorded regular access to decision-making. This tends to skew the sources of information, generally in a direction toward which the administrators tended in the first place. Suleiman (1974, 338—9), for example, notes that in France 'legitimate' (or client) groups tend to be those whose economic strength is undeniable and whose demands are in general accord with government policy.

The second consequence of this form of interaction is that while the influence of one group may be increased, the overall influence of pressure groups on public policy will be lessened. Not having legitimacy in any formal sense obviously reduces the acceptability of special interest influence on policy to the general public, and the ability of the bureaucracy to accept advice is also limited. Each pressure group must expend relatively more of its organizational resources on the pursuit of access so that less is available for the information and influence functions. Furthermore, in this process of seeking access any conception of the 'public interest' — even as an aggregate of pressure group interests — will tend to be lost and replaced with a set of private interests each being represented in government by a single agency (Sharpe, 1973; Pizzomo, 1971, 90—92). Associated with the above is a fairly obvious need of keeping the negotiations and interactions of interest groups and administrators private and informal, thereby removing them even further from public scrutiny and accountability. All of these characteristics of the scope and manner of interaction indicate that the pressure group universe will tend to be less broadly influential over policies, despite the ability to capture single agencies. Any influence that does occur will have something of a taint of illegality among the general public.

The description of the interactions of interest groups and administration in clientela politics leads to the characterization of these relationships as being symbiotic. As in biological symbiosis, this relationship implies a mutual dependence of the two participants. The administrative agency depends upon the pressure group for information, advice, prior clearance of policy decisions, and, most importantly, for political support in its competition with other agencies for the scarce resources within government. The pressure groups, on the other hand, depend upon the agency for access to decision-making and ultimately, then, for favorable decisions on certain policy choices. For both sides the existence of a clientela relationship serves to regularize the political environment and to develop friendships in what might otherwise be a hostile political world. This form of pressure group relationship with administration which has been described by LaPalombara in Italy, has been used by several authors as a means of describing much of the politics of policy in the United States, and would seem to be prevalent in a number of other political systems which have strong interest groups but where the interactions of these groups and the government is at the margin of acceptability (Lowi, 1969; McConnell, 1966).

Finally, the policy consequences of the clientela arrangement are those of producing essentially self-regulative and distributive outcomes. LaPalombara (1965, 272—4) notes that regulation is one of the defining characteristics of a clientela relationship, but goes on to note that the regulative activities undertaken are not necessarily those which would promote the 'public interest'. Rather, they are activities which quite directly promote the interests of the regulated. This pattern of regulation has, as noted above, been referred to as 'self-regulation'. Again, this tendency toward self-regulation has been noted by a number of authors with respect to administrative agencies and especially independent regulatory commissions in the United States. Lowi (1969) has argued that 'interest group liberalism', or the appropriation of the power of the state for private ends, is in fact the dominant characteristic of contemporary public policy in the United States. McConnell (1966, 287) notes that the 'outstanding political fact about independent regulatory commissions is that they have in general become the protectors and promoters of the industries they have been established to regulate'. Evidence from other political systems, however, is that this phenomenon is not confined to the United States but is a more general feature of industrial societies. In a variety of settings the need for political support is sufficient to necessitate the replacement of regulation with clientelism and self-regulation. Administrators may lack the resources and the central political support to enforce programs of regulation in the face of opposition of powerful and well organized groups, so that in essence they must gain support from those groups.

As well as self-regulation, clientela relationships also tend to be associated with distributional outcomes, which may be merely more tangible types of self-regulative programs. In distributional policies, however, instead of being allowed to make one's own regulations one is granted certain continuing benefits. In Lowi's terms, these benefits, 'create privilege, and it is a type of privilege which is particularly hard to bear or combat because it is touched with the symbolism of the state' (Lowi, 1967, 19). The continuation of clientela politics can ensure that each of the clients receives something of value from the government, and that questions of redistribution and the need for adjustment of the relative benefits are rarely subjects for discussion.

This form of policy-making is in part a function of the peculiar politics and economics of public bureaucracies. Despite the arguments made which regard bureaucracy and bureaucrats as an integrated and homogeneous force, seeking to take control of the political system, bureaucracies are generally highly fragmented and divided political institutions. By being so fragmented, they are forced into competition, simply because there is rarely any effective central means of allocating resources with respect to the merits of programs or the needs of society (Niskanen, 1971; Tullock, 1965; Breton, 1974). Hence, the budgetary process becomes a competitive process in which agencies seek to maximize their budgets at the expense of other agencies. Part of this bureaucratic acquisitiveness may be a function of sincere commitments to policy objectives, but much of it appears to be a function of the rather fundamental need for bureaucratic organizations to grow and survive (Niskanen, 1968). The budgetary process then tends to force public bureaucracies to seek public support and to make distributive accommodations in order to gain that support. This outcome is further magnified by the division among the other actors in the budgetary process, and their needs for other types of benefits and accommodations. The clientelism that extends between the pressure group and the administration may extend to a type of clientelism between legislative committees and the administrative agencies they are ostensibly overseeing. This is in part a function of the stability of the actors involved in the process, as in the US Congress, but more generally is related to the joint need of administrators and legislators to serve a constituency. For example, legislators interested in agricultural matters tend to come from predominantly agricultural districts so that any attempt to curtail the activities of an agricultural agency would not be well received in their constituencies, thereby threatening their chances for reelection. We find then that there will often be a tight intermeshing of interests — groups, administration, and legislators, forming an 'iron triangle' (Seidman, 1980). All have something to gain by certain expenditures, producing patterns of policy quite similar to those predicted by Salisbury and Heinz (1970, 48) in such situations; the parceling out of goods and services available through the public budget in a manner which will provide each organized sector with some portion of the benefits.

Parantela relationships
This is the second of the types of administrative pressure group relationships mentioned by LaPalombara (1965, 306—7) in his discussion of Italian interest groups. A *parantela* relationship describes a situation of 'kinship' or close fraternal ties between a pressure group and the government or dominant political party. These relationships have been held to be most characteristic of preindustrial societies, but in our discussion they will be shown to occur in a number of political systems in which there is a single dominant party or faction, and in which pressure groups must gain access and legitimacy through their attachment to that particular party rather than through their ability to represent adequately a sector of the society.

Parantela relationships between pressure groups and bureaucracies involve an indirect linkage between those actors rather than the direct linkage as was discussed in the clientela relationship. The important added linkage is the political party — most commonly a hegemonic party — with which the pressure group must develop some feeling of consanguinity. In these cases, the pressure groups obtain access to administrative decision-making through the willingness of the party to intercede in their behalf with the bureaucracy and therefore in essence to control bureaucratic policy-making ...

The effects of parantela relationships tend to be quite pervasive. It is, in fact, one of the characteristics of these political systems that the hegemonic party will seek to impose its control over as much of the society and economy as is possible. One principle means of doing this is the fostering of parantela relationships in a number of social sectors through the co-optation of existing interest groups or through the creation of new groups directly allied with the party. ... A good example would be a party taking the side of an existing interest group in its struggle with other groups seeking to represent the same social interests, while the Spanish regime's organization of the workers into official or semiofficial syndicates is an example of a party creating its own interest group structure (Anderson, 1970, 30–34). In either case, this is an effective means through which the party can extend its scope downward into the society to control the nature of the inputs being generated, and regularize the behavior of that social sector in accordance with the dictates of the party. It also serves as a means of checking bureaucratic autonomy within that particular policy area.

The above would seem to imply that pressure groups involved in a parantela relationship are little more than the pawns of a dominant political party, and such an interpretation would be justifiable in many instances ...

To some degree the policies adopted by the participants in parantela relationships are a function of the idealogy and program of the hegemonic party and as such may vary from programs from the far left to the far right ideologically. In general, however, there is a tendency toward distributive programs. By this we mean there will be a tendency toward distributing various goods and services among the faithful, and having certain groups develop claims on certain public goods and services as the appropriate representatives of certain social sectors. In this sense, the party is acting as something of a 'canteen' for its adherents and for official groups by essentially subsidizing their existence in the market-place of pressure groups — and thereby depriving any competing, or potentially competing, groups (Riggs, 1964, 105–9). Thus, in some ways, the parantela arrangement may approach the idea of the corporate state in which societal sectors are represented as such rather than as individuals, and further receive policy benefits as members of the corporate entity rather than as a matter of individual right (Schmitter, 1974). Further, parantela relationships tend to be antithetical to the modern conception of universalism in the distribution of economic, social, and political benefits. Such benefits —even the most basic political benefits of the rights of organization and participation — are in parantela systems most definitely the function of having the proper political affiliations, and the influence which any group may expect to have over the outcomes of the decision-making process will be a function of this consanguinity.

A second effect of parantela relationships is rather obviously regulative. This is true not only of the attempts of the party to regulate the outputs of the bureaucracy through regulating the advice which they receive, but more broadly to regulate the society as a whole through the use of intermediary groups. These intermediary groups not only structure inputs but also may serve as a means of implementing the program of the regime. The parantela relationships then serve as two-way streets and information — and to a lesser extent, power — can flow in both directions. The extent to which power can flow upward is, however, ultimately determined by the willingness of the dominant political party to entertain modifications and challenges.

Illegitimate group processes
The final category of interactions between administrators and pressure groups is labeled illegitimate. This is to denote a variety of situations in which the interaction of pressure groups with bureaucracy may be defined as outside the pale of normal political actions, but where it occurs anyway. This may be a function of the political system as a whole which may attempt to suppress pluralism, or it may be a function of the nature of particular groups which are defined as being illegitimate as representatives of the social sector which they purport to represent. In the first three types of interactions discussed some or all pressure groups were accepted as legitimate spokesmen for some social sector or another. In the case of the illegitimate pressure groups neither the system as a whole nor the individual administrators are willing to accept the legitimacy of the inputs of certain interest groups.

As might be expected, influence from pressure groups of this type is not the normal pattern of policy-making. They tend to be indicative of some rather fundamental failures of the policy-making system in satisfying demands of one or more sectors of the society. Thus, these individuals feel constrained to go outside the bounds of 'normal' politics to seek what they want from the political system. We may, therefore, be talking in large part about the behavior of anomic pressure groups in their attempts to exert influence through protest, demonstration, and violence. We need not, however, confine this discussion entirely to violent groups, for there are a number of situations in which pressure groups declared as illegitimate in parantela or clientele arrangements may still seek influence, and may occasionally actually exert some influence on policies. The latter influences are, however, rare. As one of LaPalombara's (1965, 265) respondents noted on this topic:

I know of no policy within the Ministry of Industry and Commerce that says that there are certain groups in Italian society whose representatives will not at least be received. It is true that once this is done we will assign different importance or give varying weight to the proposals made to us by such groups, but they are free to approach us.

Likewise, Suleiman (1974, 340—46) notes that in France groups defined as *groups de pression* (in contrast to the acceptable 'professional' groups) may be received by the administrators but that they are unlikely to be able to produce the results they desire. The illegitimate groups continue, however, to play by the administrators' rules and politely present their petitions probably knowing all the while that their probability of success is nearly zero.

The above characterization of the interaction between illegitimate pressure groups and administrators is of a situation tending to produce high levels of frustration and alienation for those groups. This type of rather arbitrary categorization of pressure groups can be shown to take even in political systems generally receptive if not partial to groups' influences. The extent of frustration is therefore likely to be even more intense in political systems which suppress rather than simply ignore the activities of groups declared to be illegitimate. We can therefore better understand the characterization of the influences of these groups as coming essentially from extra-level activities — through some sort of conflict with the system — and their influence as being at best episodic. Likewise, the impacts of their activities on public policy are extremely difficult to predict, if they should occur at all. Despite these limitations, it is important to understand that these influences may occasionally be productive of important changes. The French student movement of May 1968 and its associated activities have been used as an example of virtually every political phenomenon known to man, but that should not restrain us from pointing out that this is one example of an essentially illegitimate pressure group having a substantial impact on a regime and on the shape of public policy in the future. The American students and the Vietnam war is, of course, another obvious example, while in some Latin American countries the argument can be made that to accomplish almost any type of policy change requires the type of fundamental challenge to the system which can be offered by illegitimate groups. When these groups are successful, the impacts of their activities tend to be redistributive, if for no other reason than they may force the system to recognize a set of demands which it could previously declare as being outside of its concern. Most illegitimate pressure groups seek to transform the existing political system and its output distribution sufficiently so that one would hypothesize that such effects as were forthcoming from their activities would be in the direction of a redistribution of privilege, be it political, social or economic.

To summarize what we have said about the interactions of pressure groups and administration, we should point to several of the more significant differences among these classes of interactions. First, the activities of illegitimate pressure groups are clearly the most distinctive. The other three patterns accord some legitimacy to the activities and influence of one or more groups, so that there are accepted patterns of interaction between the groups and the bureaucracy. In the case of illegitimate groups, such interaction – at least if it is to have any effect on policy outcomes – occurs almost by definition only in times of crisis. Thus, the three legitimate patterns imply a certain stability and institutionalization of influence while the illegitimate pattern implies episodic influence, or no influence at all.

Second, the legitimate pattern of interaction is the only one of the four in which there is little or no politics of access. In this arrangement, access exists for virtually any group which seeks it – even those which almost certainly would be declared illegitimate in other settings. By removing access from politics, such an interaction pattern may in fact make the pluralist's dream of a self-regulating universe of pressure groups making public policy a possibility if not a reality. So long as access remains a scarce and a regulated commodity, the possibility of finding the 'public interest' among a set of conflicting pressure groups is remote if not non-existent. Having legitimate interactions of pressure groups with administration – and perhaps more importantly, open interactions of pressure groups with each other in advising the administrators – by no means assures that such a mystical entity as the 'public interest' will emerge, but it is more likely to appear when a set of interests are forced to bargain than in a case in which each interest is able to capture its own portion of the administrative structure. This capture will tend to convert public policy into private policy. Likewise, unless one considers the hegemonic political party as an accurate representation of the interests of the population, the control of pressure groups and bureaucracy by such a party is also likely to produce distortions of outputs from what would emerge from a bargaining table, especially when many interests may be defined out of existence automatically by the dominant party. Serious distortions of policy from what would emerge from a single bargaining process among competing groups are likely to occur when the politics of policy-making cannot be removed from the politics of organizational survival.

We should note also that we have not been able to argue clearly that any particular pattern of interaction characterizes any one nation or another, although the examples used above do tend to point to some rather important patterns. In the first place, political systems with hegemonic political parties, be they ostensibly democratic or not, tend toward parantela relationships between interest groups and administrators, if for no other reason than that the hegemonic party is able to use these relationships as one means of social control and regulation. Second, legitimate interactions tend to be characteristic of the Northern European countries which have had long histories of the involvement of organized groups in social and political life, and whose leaders have also perceived a need to manage potentially divisive conflicts within the society, either ethnic or socioeconomic in origin. Third, clientela arrangements tend to be quite common in any number of societies, especially where there is a fragmentation of interests and a lack of overall coordinating mechanisms in the political system (e.g. a dominant political party or movement) that can regulate the competition among interest or among the competing agencies within the bureaucracy. Finally, illegitimate interest groups may arise in virtually any setting but paradoxically tend to be most important in settings where they are least likely, i.e. societies which seek to suppress interest groups, or at least a wide variety of interest groups. That is to say, these groups are most important in settings where they serve as a means of fundamental challenge to the regime. This means that their day-to-day interactions with administrators will be unfruitful if they should occur at all, but that they may at the same time produce quite substantial transformations of a political system.

Just as there is little pattern as to type of interest group bureaucratic interaction by political system, there is also little pattern by type of interest or policy area. There is some tendency for interest groups which can be clearly defined geographically to be able to establish clientele relationships with administration, perhaps because of the ability to readily mobilize political support. The most obvious example of this pattern is agriculture, which has been rather notoriously successful in clientele relationships in a number of political systems (Pennock, 1962). Likewise, interest groups which may be vertically integrated with political parties — frequently labor unions and labor parties — may tend to develop parantela relationships, even within the context of competitive political systems. Finally, groups which may be regarded as outcasts in normal social affairs, or who are not regarded as having differentiated political viewpoints by the dominant community — racial minorities, women, students — may tend to form illegitimate relationships with bureaucracies, if they are able to form any relationship at all.

Summary

This description of the modes of interaction of bureaucracy and pressure groups is by no means definitive but it does provide one conceptualization of the relationships between these two actors. It is hoped that further research can clarify the nature and determinants of the styles of interaction. This would seem a crucial question for our understanding of the policies of government as both the public bureaucracy and interest groups become increasingly important components of the policy process. One of the dominant features of postindustrial society is the return to pressure groups as a dominant input mechanism. Another is a growing influence of bureaucracy over policy. Thus, the correlation between these two institutional actors becomes crucial for understanding the nature of government in advanced societies.

4.6   J.J. Richardson and A.G. Jordan

THE POLICY PROCESS

From *Governing Under Pressure*, published by Martin Robertson & Co. Ltd, 1979.

The private management of public business

A superficial glance at the British policy process might suggest that characterisation of the process as 'private management of public business' is rather misleading. There are a number of examples where the government apparently behaves rather openly. For example, in April 1978 the Government announced that it was no longer certain that it had universal support for the introduction of metric units. The Minister of State for Prices and Consumer Protection wrote to more than 100 organisations representing the retail trade, wholesalers, industry and the consumer, asking if they supported the full introduction of metrication to an agreed timetable. One does not need to be a cynic to suspect that the purpose of this manoeuvre was to establish publicly that there was widespread group support for the Government's plans and to put into perspective the sniping ridicule that was aimed at the change-over. In a parliamentary answer in December 1977, the Under-Secretary of State for Trade stated that over 600 organisations were invited to comment on the consultation document *Airport Strategy for Great Britain*. The Departments of Energy and Education and Science were active in 1977 with 'great debates' on fuel and education policy. Conferences, ministerial tours, consultation papers were the apparent style of policy-making ...

Issues are handled in a multiplicity of fashions, but it is worth noting that there is a preferred relationship that Whitehall attempts to establish — and that generally very much suits the interests involved. Thus the decision on how much money is released each month by building societies to finance private building house purchases is made at the Joint Advisory Committee on Mortgage Finance where representatives of the government and the building societies reach 'understanding'. This is an example of a regularised, routinised relationship, which appears to be the normal response to problems that automatically reappear on the agenda. Our suggestion is that over time any governmental/interest group relationship on a matter of substance will evolve a special machinery — such as a standing committee, joint advisory committee, etc.

The reasons for the 'consultation' phenomenon in British government are various and include:

(*a*) a lack of confidence by civil servants in their own legitimacy to enforce decision;

(*b*) a realisation that implementation of policies is affected by a cooperation (or lack of it) by groups;

(*c*) a recognition that in other aspects of the subject or at other times the department will depend on the interests for political support, aid in policy implementation or the provision of detailed information;

(*d*) a desire to maintain professional relations with the officers of relevant groups.

For these and other reasons consultation takes place, and of course the development of committees is the extension of this consultative tide. By the use of committees with some continuity of existence there is administrative convenience — a process is established that obviates the need for decisions on procedure and protocol on each issue. But the formalisation of consultation has a greater importance. With a longer term perspective, the possibility of a gradualist solution becomes more likely.

One of the main points made elsewhere is that group competition is as prevalent within Whitehall as it is between Whitehall and outside bodies. But it is conflict constrained by an overall sense of community. This sense of community is illustrated by some of the chapter titles in Heclo and Wildavsky's (1974) study of the expenditure process — 'Kinship and culture', 'The Treasury', 'Village life in Civil Service society: Department—Treasury bargaining'. The essence of this present chapter is to extend their insights concerning the importance of 'community' within Whitehall to relationships outside Whitehall. For example, in their discussion of how the Treasury operates, they dwell not on intellect or ideas, but on emotions. They claim that the Treasury's 'supreme skill lies in personal relations. When the Treasury succeeds where others fail, it is due to the recognition of the over-riding importance of getting a personal commitment. Bringing colleagues along with you makes sense ...' This observation seems as important in understanding, say, DOE[1] local government relations as relations between the Treasury and DOE. Heclo and Wildavsky go on to say,

Ultimately, British Treasury men know that their desires cannot prevail unless they maintain a community to support them ... coercion has its uses and is not to be despised. Far better, however, to create a nexus of interests so that cooperation flows from a sense of mutual advantage ... You go along with the Treasury, then, because you must, because you expect to gain, and ultimately, because you are part of a civil service society that wants to do so.

We subscribe to this view and add that the 'community' is far wider: many other groups are bound into the policy process by this sense of respectability and responsibility.

In fact, not all groups are considered part of the 'community'. The question of whether a group is 'accepted' or not has been used as a basis of classification of groups. For example, Kogan (1975, p. 75) makes a distinction between legitimised and non-legitimised (non-accepted) groups. Change in this status can be a primary group goal. In 1978 the National Farmers' Union of Wales (formed in 1955) was formally recognised by the Government as having a *right* to be consulted on matters such as the annual review. This was hailed by the group as their major achievement.

Dearlove (1973, p. 168) in analysing the role of pressure groups at the local level, classifies groups into helpful or unhelpful — according to the perceptions that councillors have of them. However, as Grant has suggested, it may well be politically necessary for local councils, and indeed national governments, to consult, and bargain with, groups that are unhelpful or that, by challenging the government, cannot be considered legitimate. Indeed, this 'unhelpful' activity can be one means of gaining access.

Grant (1977, p. 16) chooses to make the distinction on the choice of strategy of the group.[2] 'Insider' groups actively seek consultative status and rely on a close relationship with government. 'Outsider' groups either reject, or cannot obtain, a close or even symbiotic position. There is, then, an important distinction between groups that are invited by central government departments to submit their views on topics related to their concerns and those that are at best tolerated to the extent that they are allowed to send occasional deputations. In the main, of course, such distinctions tend to merge and the major groups we principally discuss in this account are 'legitimised', 'helpful' and 'insider'. It is these established (and establishment?) groups that form the substance of the system we are describing. Groups such as the Trades Union Congress, National Farmers' Union, Association of Metropolitan Authorities, etc., enjoy an automatic right to consultation in their fields of interest. Necessarily the relationship varies with the precise subject. The TUC was not interested in detailed consultations with the Heath Government on their industrial relations proposals, but this breakdown on this (albeit important) front did not inhibit the 'normal' relations on wider business.

While our main interest is in the clientele type relations at the centre of the British policy system, one must acknowledge that other styles exist. Some groups perforce have to adopt outsider strategies: few would voluntarily use that channel. There have been attempts to make some systematic connection between the kind of policy in question and the style of relationship that emerges. Theodore Lowi (1964) has claimed that distributive policies produce different processes.[3] The proposition has some validity, but in the British context it is difficult to see the pattern working out so neatly as the theory suggests. One reason might be the breadth of involvement of groups. After all if the TUC enjoys one style of relationship on the detail of safety at work, it is unlikely permanently to accept a very different connection on old age pensions, pay policy or the length of the working week.

This chapter is about the 'operating understandings' under which the major groups are granted participation; the process by which and the atmosphere within which most policy-making is resolved. Groups have traded off certain rights to frustrate the government by all possible means — in return for the predictability, the insurance of consultative status and the 'standing' in the policy-making community that insider status confers. Notwithstanding the publicity that group non-cooperation obtains, in the pressure group/government nexus, a stress on conflict avoidance has developed. There are relationships that must be maintained. The task of the civil servant and his counterpart on the pressure group side is to minimise conflict. The civil servant who cannot 'manage' his group is a liability to his minister. It seems useful to begin by looking at a few concepts borrowed from other fields, but that appear to provide useful insights into group/departmental relations.

Negotiated order and negotiated environment ...

There is no escaping the tension between policy and community, between adopting actions and maintaining relationships, between decision and co-hesion, between governing now and preserving the possibility of governing later. To cope with the world without destroying the understandings their common life requires — this is the underlying dilemma facing the community of political administrators. (Heclo and Wildavsky (1974) p. xv)

'Negotiated order' is the concept that squares this circle. Strauss (1976) and his colleagues stress the importance of negotiation — the processes of give and take, of diplomacy, of bargaining, that characterise organisation life. They also suggest that social order must be continually 'worked at'. This is suggestive of the continuous reappraisal of problems implicit in 'incrementalism'. Parties to the dispute have to weigh up the risk of damaging long-term relationships if they adopt intransigent positions ... But it is useful in extending the negotiated order idea to departmental/ group relationships to observe the professionalisation of negotiations. Those involved tend to see their task as the efficient reconciliation of the dispute. If a committee has been created to deal with a matter, those operating the committee have some commitment to agreement. This is so when the negotiations are at a political level — (say) Minister of Agriculture and president of the NFU — but is reinforced when those involved are literally professional — civil servants and officers of groups. On both sides, then, it will be recognised that getting agreement is their prime role: the essence of their job. As we have seen above, not infrequently those negoti-ating have experience of the other side of the table, and because of their common situations vis-à-vis 'their politicians' they have an appreciation of each other's settings. A pattern of compromise is thus established. Neither side will push too far. Each will offer some kind of concession. To ignore these implicit rules is to infringe the professional ethic of negotiation.

A further dimension of negotiated order — at least as we extend its use — is a tendency to concentrate on small manageable problems. Part of the mode of negotiation is to translate large unbargainable conflicts into smaller negotiable items. Where there is unlikely to be agreement on the major aspects, specific points — perhaps details of implementation — can be put forward for discussion. This allows an impression of progress and permits concessions on detail that might undermine resistance to the overall concept. The negotiated order model suggests that the agreements reached in this complexity do not occur by chance: they are 'patterned'. The outcome becomes, to a certain extent, predictable. The re-constitution of this order can be conceived in terms of a complex relationship between the *daily negotiative process and a periodic appraisal process.* This seems a valuable insight into appreciating how groups and departments have constant contact over policy details, but this does not prevent, in the longer term, a change in the style of the relationship between groups and departments to emerge. The relationship between the Department of Transport (in its various manifestations) and, say, the motorway building lobby undoubtedly changed between approximately 1965 and 1978. The kind of understandings developed allowed business to be done but did not prevent other groups, other values, other priorities from gradually impinging so that ultimately the department/'motorway lobby' had a different relative position ...

Accommodation

A third concept that appears useful in understanding how policies are decided within the British policy system is Arend Lijphart's (1968) 'accommodation' — used to convey the process by which divisive issues and conflicts in the Netherlands are settled despite only a minimal consensus. He claims that pragmatic solutions are forged for all problems. His explanation of the origins of accommodation in the period from 1878 to 1917 suggests that this spirit is a product of the singular circumstances of the Netherlands. But his seven 'rules of the game' surely have a wider validity:

Rule 1: 'The Business of Politics'. Lijphart quotes Alan D. Robinson's (1961, p. 37) comment 'that doctrinal disputes should not stand in the way of getting the work done'.
Rule 2: 'The Agreement to Disagree'. The determination to reach agreement leads on to the second rule — there is a pragmatic acceptance of the ideological differences. Lijphart says that 'the fundamental convictions of other blocs must be tolerated, if not respected'. He concedes

that if this principle were always enforced paralysis in decision-making would follow. So on occasion it is infringed, but if a compromise cannot be reached, 'the other groups will go to great lengths in trying to avoid antagonising their opponents'. Winners should go out of their way to avoid antagonising the losers.

Rule 3: 'Summit Diplomacy'. Here Lijphart argues that the politics of accommodation entails government by elite ... This rule might be more particular to the Netherlands than the others he offers, but the British version of tripartism might approximate to the Dutch practice. In 1972 Sir Frank Figgures, director general of NEDO, Sir Douglas Allen, Permanent Secretary of the Treasury, Victor Feather of the TUC and Campbell Adamson of the CBI picked up the sobriquet 'the group of four'. When Sir William Armstrong, Head of the Home Civil Service, joined the talks as the Prime Minister's unofficial representative, the group became 'the five wise men'.[4]

Rule 4: 'Proportionality'. Lijphart offers the rule of proportionality as a procedural device capable of solving a host of troublesome problems. In three very important senses this extends to Britain. There is proportionality ('fair shares') in the allocation of financial resources. There is proportionality in the form of tripartite institutions such as the Manpower Services Commission and in the composition of various advisory committees. Various parts of the UK are also becoming very sensitive to their 'fair share' of regional aid, Civil Service jobs, miles of motorway, etc. Decisions are often justified (or attacked) on 'proportional' grounds.

Rule 5: 'Depoliticisation'. Perhaps we can interpret this rule in the British context as the attempt to solve matters by 'rationality' ... There has been an attempt to make matters subject to technical criteria rather than value judgements – though with little success.

Rule 6: 'Secrecy'. This point is akin to rule 3 on 'summit diplomacy'. As successful accommodation requires flexibility, the negotiations are best kept secret. Members are apt to confuse bargaining positions and realistic demands and they are best kept out of the discussion.

Rule 7: 'The Government's Right to Govern'. This rule is a useful corrective to parts of this book where we would argue that the government is just another group. It is a player in the game but it has special status. At times its special status will be ignored – as in the late 60s and early 70s, or in special cases where the Urban District Councillors of Clay Cross failed to implement the 1972 Housing Finance Act. The government can indulge in coercion, in 'elective dictatorship', and it is often important to realise that there is this right in the background.

Each of these rules implies that the policy system has a strong tendency to 'accommodate' interests wherever possible.[5]

The local government community

Our claim that policy is made within these professional communities, and is determined by a wish in the community to avoid direct conflict, stems from our assumption that most decisions are made without involving party politicians. Most issues are not politicised in the party sense. In the rest of this discussion we look in more detail at the 'communities' of local government and agriculture, but we would argue that the kinds of relationship described here are by no means unique. What has emerged in the local government case is the (inevitable) compromise whereby central government attempts to influence a nominally independent local government. Central government itself does not have the capacity to monitor the impact of policies at the local level, but what it can do is respond when its attention is drawn to difficulties. This response can follow direct bilateral links between a departmental section and an individual local authority, but it is here that the local authority associations are a particularly useful channel.

So 'consultation' between central government and the main associations – Association of Metropolitan Authorities (AMA), Association of District Councils (ADC), Association of County Councils (ACC) – is not a generous concession but is the inevitable response in a situation where the centre lacks detailed control. The associations act as filters, ranking matters according to importance, aggregating individual cases so that wider implications can be recognised. The frequency of contact between the associations and central government is impressive. The office diary of the AMA shows officer/officer level meetings occur practically every day of the year outside August and Christmas. Member/minister meetings average two to three meetings a month – and are of increasing frequency. Exceptionally contact is made between ministers and whole AMA committees. Contacts are then more or less continuous – particularly at officer level. Indeed, so routinised are relations that it is difficult to convey the frequency, but any meeting of the AMA Policy Committee is likely to be in touch with government departments on subjects as varied as population projections (and the implication for planning in metropolitan areas), finance, pay policy, industrial democracy, public sector pensions, employment of children, arts subsidies, etc.

The competitive group basis of central government means that the relations between central government and local government are complex. While the DOE is the main point of contact for the local authority associations, local government has much wider interests, and contacts are needed with the DHSS, the Department of Industry, the Home Department, etc. The Central Policy Review Staff report (1977, p. 21) on *Relations between Central Government and Local Authorities* argues:

Central Government is, in fact, a federation of separate departments with

their own Ministers and their own policies. The aims of the Treasury and
of the DOE in its capacity as the 'Department of Local Government' often
cut across those of the spending or service departments. They in turn
compete with each other for scarce resources. The development of an interdepartmental view about a local authority service is a rare achievement.

The CRPS report acknowledges some 'joint' working in central government
vis-à-vis local government, but their main argument is that it inevitably
follows from the 'plural nature of central government' that joint behaviour
is the exception. Most circulars, for example, relate to a single service and
are drafted and circulated by the single department responsible.

It follows from this that the contacts between central and local government are varied — with local government in contact with different departments and indeed different sections of departments. A feature of the
relationship is the multiplicity of committees and joint bodies between
central and local government — the Housing Consultative Council, the
National and Local Government Statistical Liaison Committee, Working
Group on the Management of Higher Education, Joint Working Party on
Local Authority Fees and Charges, Waste Management Advisory Council,
etc. The relations between central and local government provide confirmation for the theme of earlier chapters with regard to central government's departmental pluralism ...

While policy requests/demands might appear to the individual local
authority as sudden and arbitrary, it is often the case that the policy will
have been discussed exhaustively in the labyrinth of central/local consultative machinery. Consultation between government and the various
local government organisations is accepted as the regular convention, as
can be seen by a deviant case where sufficient consultation did *not* take
place. A circular in July 1970 was intended to give local councils greater
freedom over their pattern of secondary education. Although the contents
were broadly welcomed, complaints about the lack of prior consultation
were still made.[6] It can, then, be misleading to view the stream of circulars
from the centre as evidence of central government always attempting to
regulate local authorities. It can be seen in part as self-regulation by local
government. Various standards are agreed in the central organs of local
government in discussion with central government and then promulgated
by the departments.

The pattern of multiple contacts between specialist services of local
government and their relevant sections in various departments in central
government remains, but since 1975 a new instrument has been developed
to provide a more ordered and convenient forum for the vital financial
discussions. The Consultative Council on Local Government Finance
(CCLGF) was set up in May 1975.[7] It has no formal terms of reference
but its main work, as its name implies, concerns levels of expenditure and
grants. But given this useful mechanism, central government has been

unable to resist using it to discuss wider issues (such as the Health and Safety at Work Act).

The local government side of the Consultative Council broadly consists of the chairmen and some of the leading members of the local authority associations. Central government is represented by the Secretary of State for the Environment (who chairs the meetings). He is supported by the Chief Secretary to the Treasury and ministerial representatives from other interested departments — such as the Department of Education and Science and the Department of Transport. Much of the detailed work goes on in a parallel committee of officers and civil servants — the Official Steering Group (OSG). This is chaired by the DOE Deputy Secretary (Finance and Local Government) and is attended by officials of other departments and secretaries and advisors of the associations. Ostensibly the main purpose of the OSG is to filter out and deal with items of lesser importance and to clarify issues for the 'political' side. Of course, in practice, matters of substance can be dealt with in the technical setting. A second tier of officers' groups have specialised remits and report to the Consultative Council through the OSG.

Thus the relationship is developing along the lines suggested in the earlier part of this chapter — closer and more formal contacts, a predilection for policy to be passed to more technical levels for resolution, a reluctance to act without predigestion of the policy in the consultative machinery. This is not to say that the local authorities always welcome the results. The associations have differences between and within themselves. The DOE (or whatever department) sometimes fails to win a large enough budget to satisfy local authority demands. And plainly, on occasions, the DOE interest and attitude clashes with that of the associations. Even so, the type of arrangement that recurs frequently in association minutes is 'a small working group of officers from local authorities and the DOE have been working ...', or 'the Secretaries of the three local authority Associations have been discussing with officials of the DOE', or 'an officer level working group has been set up with the DOE' ...

The local government 'strike'

The idea of 'negotiated order' is useful in understanding the process that led to the Water Act in 1973. 'Negotiated order' helps explain why the Ministry of Housing and Local Government went to such trouble to consult the industry when it had its own clear policy preference with regard to water reorganisation in the period 1968–73. An internal Ministry working party in the summer of 1969 came out in favour of four to twelve regional, multipurpose water authorities. The extensive bargaining that nonetheless followed was a good example of negotiated order. The Ministry decided change was necessary, but attempted to avoid as much direct conflict with the groups as it could. Accordingly, it involved the interested parties in discussions, such as on the Central Advisory Water Committee, and in direct negotiations. These were intended to educate the groups as to the need for a change and most importantly to assuage resentment by those involved. 'Consultation' is one of the rules of the game and it would aggravate the matter if groups had not at least the courtesy of futile consultation ...

The core of the new scheme — the replacement of a local government by a managerial system — could not be compromised ... The relatively unsuccessful challenge by the local government associations meant that they were faced with the decision — how far could their 'pressure' escalate? And how much could they afford to embarrass general relations with Whitehall for the sake of one particular topic? The following incident also demonstrates the cooperation between the associations in a 'common cause' campaign.

It has been suggested to us by one participant that the strength of feeling engendered in local government by the proposed water reorganisation stemmed from the fact that 'water' was the end of a long list of local government functions 'lost' since World War II. The secretary of the then County Councils Association (CCA) expressed something of this in a letter to the Government in December 1971: 'It has been our hope, and indeed the Government's stated intention to use a strengthened local government for the devolution of powers from Central Government. The taking away therefore of further functions ... at this time is bound to be a matter of grave concern to the Association.' More materially, there was also the argument that with the loss of water supply and sewerage disposal functions, the viability of the proposed (post 'Redcliffe-Maud') district councils, from a technical services point of view, was questioned: there was not the work to maintain such a team.

The initial reaction of the associations to the Government's proposals in December 1971 was produced by the secretaries of the four associations involved. No formal coordination machinery was set up; informal collaboration — at secretary level — was sufficient. A joint memorandum was prepared in May 1972 that suggested a more 'evolutionary' transformation of the water industry. On 9 June the DOE asked the local authorities to participate in local working parties and steering committees to prepare the way for the setting up of the proposed Regional Water Authorities (RWA). The groups were to produce a report for the new RWAS with proposals for action. These innocuous sounding means and ends were not uncontroversial.

On 7 March 1973 a letter appeared in *The Times* from the vice-chairman of one of the RWA steering committees. Members of the standing committee considering the Bill in Parliament raised this anticipation of legislation in moving towards reorganisation before the Bill was through.

Graham Page (Minister for Local Government and Development) explained
that 'those so-called steering committees were set up, at the invitation of
the Department, by the British Waterworks Association (BWA). *Whilst
this action is in no way official* [our emphasis], we were glad that those
interested in such questions are getting together to consider the future ...
The Committees have been set up merely at the Department's invitation,
and are in no way departmental committees.'

In fact, when we queried this account with BWA they suggested to us
that the Department played a somewhat larger part in the creation of the
committees:

The water supply steering committees and working parties ... *have been set
up by the Department of the Environment* [our emphasis] to consider
certain aspects of the reorganisation proposals. The Associations' part in
this exercise was limited to providing facilities for water undertakings to
meet together to determine whether or not they should co-operate with
the Department of the Environment in setting up of water supply steering
committees and working parties, in advance of the publication of the
Water Bill.

The formula of a departmental invitation to BWA to arrange the initial
meetings appears to have been an administrative improvisation by the
Department to circumvent the restraints of the parliamentary timetable ...
It also, however, demonstrates how useful good relations with a group,
such as BWA, can be for a department.

That episode provoked a minor crisis of constitutionality in the standing
committee, but the local authority response proved another difficulty.
Initially, the associations recommended cooperation, but subsequently
their line changed. On 23 June the CCA wrote to the DOE that 'It would
be inappropriate for the local authorities to undertake detailed work on
the basis of the Department's present proposals until the general method
of reorganisation has been settled in the light of the ultimative proposals
of the four associations'. On 20 July the Association of Municipal Corporations (AMC) General Purpose Committee carried a motion that the
setting up of committees and working parties was premature, 'in view of
the fact that the Department's proposals are contrary to the advice of the
local authority Associations and that the Department's action in requiring
the setting up of the steering committees and working parties appears to
have been designed to pre-empt legislation on the subject'. By 28 July the
official policy of the associations had crystallised and a joint letter was
sent out advising constituent members to 'boycott work on the transfer of
water and sewage services out of local government'. This boycott was
confirmed at the end of August when concessions by the Department were
judged insufficient. A letter from the associations read; 'We think that we
should tell you that the preliminary response to our consultations indicates

that concessions which you are offering fall far short of meeting the associations' case.'

The Permanent Secretary of the Department wrote to the AMC on 27 October in an attempt to obtain progress at the working party level:

He [the Secretary of State] is also anxious that the difficulties of the transitional period are minimised. It is for this reason that he has proposed the establishment of Steering Committees of members of local authorities and of Working Parties of officers to prepare for the change. The British Waterworks Association and the Association of Joint Sewerage Boards have co-operated in these arrangements. The Secretary of State regrets that your Association together with other associations of local authorities have not felt able to do the same.

He argued that the work would be essentially similar whatever form of reorganisation was adopted and that delay could lead to a risk to public health. After this moral carrot, the Permanent Secretary ended with a thinly veiled stick: '... [Co-operation] is desirable if the discussions between the Department and the Associations on the substantive proposals to be enacted in legislation are to be helpful and fruitful.' This threat that concession would be withheld if cooperation was not forthcoming had no effect and the policy (described by the AMC as 'reluctant hesitation') continued.

The policy of non-cooperation was eventually rescinded on 9 March 1973. By that time the concession allowing district councils to undertake certain sewerage functions for the RWAS on a 'controlled agency' basis had been developed by the officers and civil servants. This followed a meeting of the officers with the DOE in September 1972 when it had been agreed that the Department would draft a compromise proposal. This was discussed at further officer/civil servant meetings. Another draft was (confidentially) sent by the Department to the association in December and further meetings were held in January and February ...

At first sight this breakdown of normal relations between the Department and the associations might appear to be an unlikely example of our argument that a 'local government community' exists. But, of course, the existence of community does not preclude conflict, and in following the dispute one was struck by the reluctance with which the associations pursued their tactics. It appeared to be recognised that such action was outside the 'rules'. The associations could have maintained their boycott to secure bigger concessions, but before that could happen the associations felt obliged to accept the Government's view — to accept the government's right to govern. The Department has claimed to us that the 'strike' had little effect, but there must at least have been some nuisance value as the period between the Royal Assent to the Act in July 1973 and the vesting of the new authorities in April 1974 was already very short. Our assessment is that non-cooperation was withdrawn, not because it was ineffective or because the authorities were satisfied with the concession, but because it was thought that it was an inappropriate form of behaviour in view of the normal central/local relationship.

The agricultural partnership

The relationship between local government and central government is not, we think, untypically close. Indeed, the view has been expressed that the relationship with the central authorities is insufficiently close. From the government side the suggestion was made in the November 1977 Green Paper on Local Government Finance that better consultation was yet possible. In turning to the relationship between the agriculture lobby and the Ministry of Agriculture, Fisheries and Food (MAFF), we are turning to what is often thought to be one of the closest departmental/pressure group partnerships. It is certainly one of the best-documented cases.[8]

There are approximately 188,000 full-time farm businesses in England and Wales. The National Farmers' Union of England and Wales claims a membership of approximately 85 per cent of full-time farmers. The most important link between the MAFF and the NFU follows from the nature of the annual review that takes place in February between the government and the union. This determines the anticipated level of profitability of farming in the next year. The Agriculture Act of 1947 obliges the government to consult 'such bodies of persons who appear to them to represent the interests of producers in the agricultural industry'. Until 1978 this meant the NFU, but from 1978 onwards the newly recognised Farmers' Union of Wales has also been consulted. Self and Storing (1974, p. 61) describe the reviews as having 'been shaped by a series of understandings (written or unwritten) arrived at by the two participants. The most significant, if least admitted of these, is that the final settlement (which, constitutionally is of course the Government's sole responsibility) shall be broadly acceptable to both parties.' By 1958 the union had disassociated itself from only one review, but since then it has disassociated itself from about half. Of course, the tendency to fail to agree to the price review does not necessarily imply that the NFU is unhappy at MAFF's attitude – but it means that the union is unhappy at the deal that MAFF has been allowed to give by the Treasury and other forces in Whitehall ...

Throughout the year the NFU is in constant touch with MAFF – 'almost hourly contact' as Graham Wilson (1977, p. 45) describes it. 'Thus it is only natural that a community of shared beliefs and attitudes should develop between the officials of the two organisations in such close contact.' He reports an acceptance of a form of neopluralism by civil servants within the Ministry ... He was told, 'We cannot worry about everything, so we leave some factors to other Ministries to worry about'.

Another said, 'The duty of the MAFF is to present the arguments for help for farming. Other Ministries will soon bring forth criticism based on trade policy implications for public expenditure'. Self and Storing significantly dedicate their book on agricultural politics 'to Partnership, properly understood'. The partnership they describe so fully seems consistent with the broad generalisations made at the start of this chapter — though they themselves might have been reluctant to put their case in such terms ...

The closeness of the Ministry/NFU embrace has been tightened by the British entry into Europe.[9] One Minister has told us that the union knows 99 per cent of the British information and arguments. The union can further these arguments in the COPA (Comité des Organisations Professionnelles Agricoles — the 'umbrella' organisation for the various national agricultural lobbies) or by its direct lobbying in Brussels. This means that when an agreement is reached not only does the Minister have to get it accepted in Cabinet, but the interest group leadership has to 'sell' it to its own membership. There is consequently a dilemma for the leadership — either it attacks a deal to which it was, in practice, a party or it is seen by the membership to be acquiescing to whatever the Ministry delivers. Domestically the lobby is very often 'making the bullets for MAFF to fire', and the European dimension has certainly reinforced this tendency.

Implications

These examples cannot prove the argument that policy-making is carried out in governmental sub-systems in an essentially co-operative and consensual atmosphere, but they may have illustrated the kind of practices that prompt the generalisation. The overwhelming proliferation of committees and regular meetings means that one cannot fully catalogue and describe what goes on. In local government there are so many bodies in specific areas — such as the Housing Consultative Council (HCC), which was set up as 'a forum for discussions between central and local government' and was intended 'to foster the concept of partnership between the two' — that listing is tedious. The HCC consists only of representatives of the department and the associations, and in turn relates to other machinery for consultation with the construction industry, the building societies and the housing association movement. The (relative) absence of such a number of committees on the agriculture side is because the relations are so close as to make such formalisation less necessary.

The Whitehall preference in the processing of policies is to internalise the required debate within some structure or institutions ... The possible combinations of the nature of the problem and the type of forum are presented in Table 4.6.1.

The regularised arrangements represent the more likely options. One can see a drift to the establishment of more and more of these instruments

Table 4.6.1.   Internalised processing of problems

Type of forum	*Nature of problem*	
	'One-off'	Recurring
Regularised	(1) e.g. Central Advisory Water Committee	(2) e.g. Joint Advisory Committee on Mortgage Finance
Ad hoc	(3) e.g. Fulton Committee on the Civil Service	(4) e.g. pay conflict

over a wider and wider range of policies. They can be used for recurring problems, but they can also be used to 'process' 'one-off' issues such as water reorganisation in the Central Advisory Water Committee or the Layfield Report in the Consultative Council on Local Government Finance. They are convenient for dealing with 'one-off' issues and they are also (ideally) imbued with the correct, cooperative atmosphere. Developments of the Fulton type are also part of the 'bureaucratisation' of problems that we have identified, but since there was no convenient forum that would be politically credible an 'ad hoc' body was created. We see discussions of pay conflict in the late 1970s as being fully compatible with this simple scheme. The common arguments for systematic bargaining, for kitty bargaining, for negotiation rather than strikes, etc., can be seen as an implicit attempt to accommodate the pay issue in machinery similar to that existing in other policy areas – subject to the same consensual values. The ambition appears to move pay from cell (4) to cell (2) ...

Of course, processing of problems in such a fashion does not mean the resolution of all issues. Some obviously spill over into the party/parliamentary/political area. But just as writers in the 1950s saw public campaigns by pressure groups as a sign of the breakdown – the failure – of group strategies, so we would argue that the need to bring in parties and Parliament to resolve an issue is a failure of both department and outside group strategies. Both 'sides' try to reach agreement *before* issues go to Parliament for formal ratification. So the cases where Parliament is called in to resolve a conflict are comparatively rare. These are instances when the normal processing system has 'blown a fuse'.

Notes

1   Department of the Environment.
2   See also Peters (1977).
3   See also Salisbury (1968).
4   See Grant and Marsh (1977).

5   For a discussion of the related concepts of network and linkage in
     public administration see Friend and Spink (1978).
6   See Redcliffe-Maud and Wood (1974), p. 121.
7   The CCLGF machinery is described more fully in Caulcott (1977).
8   For example Self and Storing (1962), and Wilson (1977). See also Self
     and Storing (1974). With EEC entry an 'Annual Review' replaces the
     'Price Review'.
9   See Grant (1978).

4.7   D. Marsh and W. Grant

TRIPARTISM: REALITY OR MYTH?

From *Government and Opposition*, vol. 12, pp. 194–211 (1977).

It is increasingly common to find analyses of Britain as a corporate state, or more circumspectly as developing a tripartite system of economic and industrial policy-making.[1] Unfortunately, such work is often marked by a lack of definitional rigour and an inadequate consideration of relevant empirical material. In view of these limitations in the literature our article has two aims. Initially it examines the relationship between corporatism and tripartism, showing that in many ways tripartism can be viewed as a variation on one strand of corporatist thought, and what is more that it is the strand which appears most relevant to discussions of Britain. Subsequently, against this background, we examine empirical evidence to establish how far Britain can be described as having a tripartite system of economic and industrial policy-making.

Schools of thought

Of course, as there have been many corporatist theorists, so there have been many varieties of corporatist thought. Nevertheless, Schmitter's (1974) excellent review of the history of corporatist thought makes it clear that corporatist theorists share an emphasis on unity, or more particularly class harmony, but differ substantially as to the role that they assign to the state in the corporatist system. Indeed Schmitter shows how the stress on harmony between classes in corporatist thought develops from its origins as a 19th-century reaction against the individualism and competitiveness associated with capitalist development. The corporatist theorists believed that although labour and capital might have superficially conflicting interests they shared mutual rights and obligations. The organic unity of society is preserved if the organizations representing capital and labour are aware of these mutual rights and obligations. As Pahl and Winkler put it, 'Society is seen as consisting of diverse elements unified into one body, forming one *corpus*, hence the word corporatism. These elements are united because they are reciprocally interdependent, each performs tasks which the other requires' (Pahl and Winkler, 1976, p. 7).

There is no doubt that this notion of unity or class harmony is crucial in corporatist thought, but how is this class harmony to be obtained and preserved? On this point a sharp distinction can be found between different models of corporatism in terms of their account of the role of the state. Indeed Schmitter establishes a crucial distinction within corporatist thought between what he terms 'state corporatism' and 'societal corporatism' ... In 'state corporatism' the state plays a directive role in the establishment of class harmony and the organizations representing the different economic interests within society are subordinate to and dependent on the state. In 'societal corporatism' the representative organizations are autonomous but cooperate with the state and each other because they recognize that they are mutually interdependent ...

The idea of 'liberal' or 'societal' corporatism stresses cooperation between the state and the functional groups, not domination by the state of these groups. At the same time the emphasis in corporate thought upon the need to promote class harmony inevitably directs attention towards the groups which represent capital and labour. Of course this in turn means that there is a close identity between 'societal' or 'liberal' corporatism and the idea of tripartism which has received a great deal of attention in Britain in the last decade. This seems evident as the doctrine of tripartism emphasizes the need for cooperation between government and the peak organizations representing both sides of industry, the TUC and the CBI, in the evolution of economic and industrial policy. Indeed, tripartism might best be viewed as a sub-type of 'liberal corporatism'. In a 'liberal corporatist' state the emphasis would be on the relationships between government and a wide range of functional groups, or at least between government and all organizations that represent capital and labour. In contrast the notion of tripartism emphasizes the relationship between government and the peak organizations. Nevertheless 'liberal corporatism' and tripartism do appear to be closely related and by examining how far Britain has developed a tripartite system of economic and industrial policy making we hope to throw considerable light upon arguments about the development of 'liberal corporatism' in Britain.

We hope that we have established a link between corporatism and tripartism. However, as yet we have offered only a cursory explanation of the notion of tripartism. Before we can examine the empirical problems we have set ourselves it is essential that we give a more precise formulation of that term.

It seems to us that an ideal-typical tripartite system would have a number of distinct characteristics:

1. Obviously it would involve three parties, here the government, the CBI and the TUC, interacting to evolve a commonly agreed industrial and economic policy within both formal and informal settings.

2. The system would be underpinned by a basic consensus: whilst there would be disagreement between the parties, such disagreement would be limited in its character and therefore capable of resolution. In particular, the parties involved would be willing to set aside any fundamental disagreements about ultimate goals in order to arrive at agreed solutions to specific problems. Without such a consensus there would seem to be little chance of arriving at policies which would be acceptable to all parties.

3. An effective tripartite system would not only involve elite accommodation. Such a system would involve the acceptance of decisions as authoritative by both leaders and members of the groups involved. The leaderships would have to be willing and able to persuade their memberships to comply with the agreed policies. Without acceptance of the policies evolved under such a system by the memberships of the groups, the chances of successfully implementing policy would be slight.

4. The three parties would each have similar degrees of influence on the evolution of policy, otherwise the system would be tripartite in name but not in effect. If one or two parties became dominant, then not only would the term 'tripartism' be a misnomer, but also the disadvantaged party or parties would feel under no obligation to accept the agreed policies.

If these can be agreed as the main characteristics of a tripartite system, how far do we have a tripartite system in Britain? Has the government involved the CBI and the TUC policy-making on a regular and continuing basis? Is there a consensus which can provide the basis for the formulation of economic and industrial policy? Are the CBI and the TUC capable of becoming pillars of some kind of British liberal corporatist state? How equivalent is the influence of government, TUC and CBI on economic policy making? In the rest of the article we shall examine these questions.

A developing tripartism?

Since the formulation of the CBI in 1965 both it and the TUC have enjoyed good access to government. However, there is no doubt that at present the continuing worsening of the economic situation in Britain has led the Labour government to attempt to involve both sides of industry more closely in the process of economic policy formation. The government has inevitably turned to the 'peak organizations' as the representatives of both sides of industry. All this might lead one to see tripartism both as a description of the current means of evolving economic policy and as a developing trend. However, a consideration of the changing nature of the relationship between the three parties since the formation of the CBI does little to indicate that any permanent basis for consensus between the three parties exists.

During the life of the Labour government from 1964 until 1970 relationships between the government and the CBI and the government and the TUC deteriorated. The Labour government's relations with the CBI had initially been reasonably good, indeed the government, and George Brown in particular, had pressed hard for the formation of the organization.[2] However, when the government introduced its statutory prices and wages freeze, relations quickly worsened. The CBI found the provisions of the 1968 Industrial Expansion Act so objectionable that they refused to talk about it to the Labour government. The CBI was even more disturbed by proposals announced by the government in 1969 for the creation of a Commission for Industry and Manpower which would take over the functions of the Monopolies Commission and the National Board for Prices and Incomes. The Commission would have been given powers to investigate situations of market dominance as well as of monopoly and would have been able to enquire into mergers retrospectively. The CBI felt that the proposals would lay the basis for an intolerable increase in government intervention in industry.

At the same time, relations between the Labour government and the TUC reached one of their lowest ebbs with the introduction of the government's proposals for the reform of industrial relations in January 1969. The government's proposals were, of course, subsequently withdrawn, but their introduction seriously damaged relations between the TUC and the Labour government for the rest of its term of office and beyond.[3] The notion of tripartism was hardly likely to be popular or practical while such conflicts existed.

There is little doubt that initially relations between government and the CBI improved considerably after the return of a Conservative administration in 1970. Indeed, although the Conservative government came to pursue interventionist policies, the CBI itself, as we have shown elsewhere,[4] came increasingly to accept, while trying to contain, government intervention in industry.[5] Nevertheless, relations between the government and the CBI were not without their troubles. So, although the CBI saw their former Director-General, John Davies, assume responsibility in 1970 for what to them was the key Department of Trade and Industry, they were faced two years later with the 1972 Industry Bill in which he proposed a more sweeping extension of intervention into industry than anything previously enacted. One of the most significant pieces of legislation for the CBI since its formation came as a very unpleasant surprise to the organization. This was hardly a situation likely to deepen trust and understanding between the CBI and the government.[6]

However, there can be little doubt that the real body blow to hopes of meaningful tripartism during the life of the 1970–74 Heath government came with the passage of the 1971 Industrial Relations Act. As Lord Watkinson (1976, p. 85), President of the CBI in 1976, has commented,

'No Prime Minister has ever devoted as much care and patience as Edward Heath did to seeking to bring about tripartite agreement ... on the cure for Britain's economic ills. Had the Industrial Relations Act not soured relationships, the initiative might well have succeeded.' Indeed, the Industrial Relations Act came close to marking an all-time low in government-trade union relations. The government may not have set out to confront the trade unions but there is no doubt at all that the unions, and the TUC, viewed the legislation in this way. This meant, that those who had taken a conciliatory line in the TUC, in the style of George Woodcock, were completely outflanked. It also ensured that for two years there was little, if any, meaningful contact between the TUC and the government at any level ...

The advent of a Labour government after the February 1974 election changed the picture substantially. After its defeat in the 1970 election the Labour Party reviewed its relationship with the trade union movement. The institutional aspect of the new relationship which developed was the TUC–Labour Party Liaison Committee established in 1972 which was composed of six senior members from the Parliamentary Labour Party, the National Executive Committee of the Labour Party and the General Council of the TUC. The liaison committee played a central role in the development of the social contract and in the shaping of the Labour Party's two 1974 election manifestos. Thus when the Labour government came into office relations were extremely close between the government and the TUC. This closeness was reflected in a number of pieces of legislation, notably the 1974 Trade Union and Labour Relations Act and the 1975 Employment Protection Act.[7]

In contrast the CBI's relations with the new Labour government began badly, but then improved rapidly to the extent that the CBI (1975, p. 7) could talk of 'reversing' the government's initial policies in the economic sphere. These changes in government economic strategy were matched by the development of an economic orthodoxy about the 'deindustrialization' of Britain which facilitated the development of some measure of consensus on economic policy between the government, the CBI and the TUC in the short term, a consensus cemented by common fears about the fate of sterling. At the same time, the three parties worked together in the tripartite agencies, the Manpower Services Commission, the Health and Safety Commission and the Conciliation and Arbitration Council. These agencies directly involved the CBI and the TUC in the executive operations of government.[8]

Our discussion so far indicates that, while there is evidence of improving relations between the government and both the TUC and CBI since 1974, there can be little confidence that a genuinely tripartite system exists. In the past relations have improved at various times but harmony has not persisted for long. One of the problems is that however good bilateral relations between the government and the CBI and the government and the TUC have been, there has rarely been a good working relationship between the CBI and the TUC. What is more, on those occasions when the CBI and the TUC have found a basis for agreement, they have often been at odds with the government ...

Even in 1976, when there was evidence that both parties had better contacts with the government, much of that contact was bipartite rather than tripartite in nature. The real problem, of course, is that while some degree of consensus on immediate measures may exist at any given time, as seemed to be the case in 1976, there is no evidence of consensus upon long-term goals. Indeed, even during 1975–6, there has often been considerable disagreement on the desirability of certain immediate economic measures, such as the possible use of import controls.[9]

There must be doubt, then, whether the first two conditions specified earlier have been fulfilled for whole, or even for part, of the period considered. Despite this, it is worth considering the other two conditions at some length, because such a discussion may help us to judge whether Britain is likely to become a tripartite state at some time in the future. In particular, it is important to establish whether the groups involved are sufficiently representative, well organized and in control of their memberships to operate as component parts of a genuine tripartite system.

Pillars of tripartism: the position of the CBI and the TUC

Both the CBI and the TUC are large interest groups with good access to the government. There are over 130 unions affiliated to the TUC and the latest available figures show that TUC membership is over 11 millions.[10] The TUC estimate that about fifty per cent of the working population is unionized.[11] These figures are impressive when compared with those for other major European countries.[12] The CBI (1976, p. 7) represents businesses who employ over 10 million people, one half of the total outside central and local government. As Lord Watkinson (1976, p. 146) has emphasized, the CBI 'primarily revolves at present around the pivot of the one hundred top manufacturing companies'. Indeed, approximately fifty per cent of the total income from the CBI comes from member companies in the top five hundred of *The Times* list of one thousand companies. As we can see from Table 4.7.1, the membership of the CBI has significantly declined since 1974. In Table 4.7.2, the membership pattern since 1970 is more clear.

However, the decline in membership is not as significant as might at first appear to be the case. The majority of firms who have discontinued their membership are smaller firms which seem unlikely to rejoin because since 1973 the membership subscriptions have been substantially increased. The small number of larger firms who left in 1974 because they

Table 4.7.1. Membership of the CBI

	At 31/12/1973	At 31/12/1974	At 31/12/1975
Industrial companies	11,242	10,234	10,112
Commercial companies	379	425	488
Public sector members	18	16	15
Employers' organizations and trade associations	196	172	163
Industrial/commercial companies	9	Not stated	

Table 4.7.2. Percentage change in total CBI membership

1970	+ 1%
1971	+ 1½%
1972	+ 2%
1973	+ 1%
1974	- 8%
1975	- ½%

believed that the CBI was accepting increased government intervention in industry too passively have almost all rejoined as we predicted in an earlier article ...[13]

Overall both organizations have substantial memberships which is one of the reasons why each has good access to government. Government can view them as representing important interests within society. Each group is a member of a large number of advisory bodies and is regularly consulted by departments on all major issues which concern it. In addition these two groups are the only ones which enjoy continuing access at the Cabinet level.[14] Strong memberships and good access might be taken to indicate that these groups are both representative and capable of becoming pillars of a tripartite state. However, both organizations have significant weaknesses.

Obviously, neither the CBI nor the TUC is fully representative of the interests which they purport to represent to government. The TUC has only about fifty per cent of the employed population in membership and no decision taken by the TUC General Council is binding on individual member unions ...

The TUC, then, cannot ensure that the leadership of individual unions acts upon General Council decisions. At the same time, the nature of British trade unions has changed considerably in the last two decades so that the individual union leadership cannot be sure that its membership will act upon *its* instructions. Indeed, as Fox (1976, p. 13) stresses,

'Britain has the strongest semi-independent shop-floor union organisation in the world; a fact which obliges us to formulate propositions about corporate control with some care, in so far as they apply to the trade unions'. Of course, at any given time, the trade union movement may be more or less unified and the TUC may be more or less able to persuade its members that a particular policy line is advantageous.[15] However, the TUC's financial resources are limited compared with its smaller European counterparts and the staff of Congress House is only around a hundred strong with thirty officials in the TUC's regional offices. The staff of the TUC is not really large enough to perform the range of tasks with which they are involved.

We have discussed the CBI's internal divisions in an earlier article and it would be repetitious to examine them in detail here. However, some new developments require emphasis. The organization's position in relation to the nationalized industries has been changed by the formation of a separate group from the chairman of the state industries (the so-called 'Group of 21') and by the resignation from the CBI of the Post Office, the largest employer among the nationalized industries. Moreover, the CBI has encountered increased competition from three reinvigorated organizations, the Association of British Chambers of Commerce, the British Institute of Management and the Institute of Directors.[16] There can be little doubt that these developments have weakened the CBI's position. It is also important to re-emphasize[17] that the CBI is an organization which represents industrial capital; although City institutions are members, this is primarily for liaison purposes, and the CBI cannot claim to represent finance capital.

Even the CBI's leadership admits the weaknesses of the organization's internal decision-making structure. Lord Watkinson (1976, p. 146) has admitted 'it is surprising ... that the CBI actually represents anything. Its structure of a Grand Council and a large network of internal and often overlapping policy committees is not well suited to the making of long-term policy or to instant reaction to events.' ...

Lord Watkinson (1976, p. 147) has made it clear that the 'old CBI tradition of "representing" the views of its members to government and reacting to events is no longer appropriate. In a world where militancy and industrial muscle counts, the CBI too has to become militant and activist when it suits the interests of its members.'

It is evident, then, that both the CBI and the TUC have weaknesses which make it doubtful whether they could function effectively as pillars of a tripartite system. They are strong groups with large memberships but they cannot purport to represent all important sections of society. Perhaps more important as far as the government is concerned, it is by no means certain that either group, once it has entered into an agreement, can ensure that its members accept that agreement as authoritative.

Neither group is more than a coalition of more or less diverging interests.

The balance of influence

Of course, even if no genuine consensus exists as a basis for tripartism, and if neither the CBI nor the TUC is really in a position to assume a role as a pillar of a tripartite state, this does not mean that the two groups do not have a substantial influence on industrial and economic policy.

Questions about a particular interest group's influence are difficult (and sometimes impossible) to answer, but this does not imply that they should not be posed. If a tripartite system existed or was imminent in Britain one would expect both the TUC and the CBI to be very influential. Yet the academic literature tends to play down the influence of these groups. For example, after a survey in 1973 of the role of the trade unions in modern British politics, May and Moran (1973, p. 573) conclude, 'the evidence suggests that for all their access to Whitehall [the trade unions] have been a relatively unsuccessful pressure group. No doubt their capacity to effect piecemeal changes in policy has been increased by frequent contacts with Government departments. But on the really important issues the unions have lost consistently.' However, if the unions have lost, one cannot really say that the CBI has won. After a review of the activity of the CBI between 1965 and 1974, we ourselves (1977, p. 217) concluded, 'although the CBI is always prominent and sometimes influential, it is in no sense politically dominant'.

It is clear that the situation has changed somewhat since 1974. We have already argued that the access of both trade unions and the CBI to government has increased. At the same time, the influence of the TUC increased dramatically with the accession of the Labour government. The development of the social contract meant that the trade unions were influential in the evolution of policy. The TUC–Labour Party liaison committee formed in 1972 played a major role in the development of the first two stages of the Labour government's incomes policy. In addition, the Trade Union and Labour Relations Act in 1974 which repealed the Conservatives' Industrial Relations Act of 1971, the 1975 Employment Protection Act and the 1976 Trade Union and Labour Relations (Amendment) Act were all products of discussions with the TUC, particularly within the liaison committee.[18]

However, it may also be argued that the influence of the CBI has increased. Thus, the tax relief on stock appreciation negotiated by the CBI has added some £2,000 million a year to corporate profitability and the series of changes in the Price Code made in 1976 could improve company profitability by as much as £1,500 millions. One might also contrast the 1972 Industry Act passed by the Conservatives with Labour's

1975 Industry Act. The 1972 Industry Act contained a number of unpleasant surprises for the CBI, particularly the proposals on selective
assistance contained in Part 2. Although the CBI (1972, p. 11) received
a number of 'welcome assurances' from the government, it cannot be said
to have influenced the contents of the Act in any substantial way. In
contrast, the CBI (1975, p. 13) felt that its campaign against the 1975
Industry Bill 'contributed towards amendments to the provisions for
compulsory disclosure of information and the Government's recognition
of the need for guidelines for the National Enterprise Board'. Both the
content of the guidelines and statements made by Eric Varley (1975),
Secretary of State for Industry, and Lord Ryder, chairman of the National
Enterprise Board, seemed designed to allay industrialists' fears about the
board's role ...

These substantial, specific concessions have to be set alongside the
change in the Labour government's overall economic strategy since it
came into office. Of course, it is difficult to estimate the extent to which
this change of policy was due to CBI pressure and to what extent it was
due to pressure from the City of London and the international financial
community ... Moreover, to understand what has happened between 1974
and the present, one needs to understand the nature of the British Labour
Party; one needs to know how its leaders see the world and what their
personal priorities are in relation to economic and social policy. In other
words, one has to take account of sources of pressure other than the CBI
and, above all, one has to consider the nature of the target of the pressure.

Perhaps the lesson the CBI has learned from its first ten years is that
'the Confederation is now seeing the necessity of acting more to influence
policy and events in advance and of taking a more political line where this
is necessary'.[20] Certainly, the CBI has been outspoken in its criticisms of
government policy since 1974. On its own admission 'during 1974 the CBI
was drawn much further into the political arena than most of us would
normally have wished' ...[21] As the government modified its policies, the
CBI's attacks moderated. However, it would seem that the organization is
paying more attention to influencing public opinion than was previously
the case. During 1975 the CBI (1975, p. 5) held over fifty press conferences and 250 industrialists have now been through its 'television
familiarization' courses. Lord Watkinson (1976, p. 148) has emphasized,
'the CBI must try successfully to influence the general public and the
electorate as a way of supporting the longer-term policy objectives which
it will be promoting in the NEDC and directly with government' ...

Regardless of which party is in power, when it comes to influencing the
broad shape of economic policy, both the CBI and the TUC are limited
by the way in which the state of the economy narrows the range of
possible policy options, by the government's determination to pursue
whatever happens to be its economic strategy at the time, and by the

government's need to secure the cooperation of other parties, including particularly foreign holders of sterling. So after its initially dramatic influence when the Labour government came to power, the influence of the TUC has substantially declined as the government has responded to other pressures. Thus, despite constant efforts, the TUC has been unable so far to persuade the government to introduce wide-ranging import controls, to take any reflationary measures designed to reduce unemployment, or to restrict cuts in public expenditure.

The crucial point is that it is the government which has the ultimate responsibility and is accountable to the electorate. Sectional groups may sometimes be able to frustrate government policy, but they cannot determine its course in the long run. Governments have to take much more than the views of the CBI and TUC into account when formulating economic policies, not least some estimate of likely electoral consequences (especially when the government has a slim Parliamentary majority). One also hardly needs to emphasize that a wide range of external forces and circumstances constrain the government in its choice of economic policy options. If the groups feel that they are getting little in return for their general support of government economic policy, they may become increasingly sceptical about the value of entering into tripartite arrangements. All this means that while at a time of economic difficulty the CBI and TUC may be incorporated increasingly into the process of governmental decision-making on economic questions, without a consensus on means and ends they are unlikely to become pillars of a tripartite or liberal corporatist state.

Conclusion

The belief that a tripartite solution to Britain's economic problems is possible has been a recurrent feature of political debate since 1964.[22] However, it cannot be said that Britain has at any time in this period experienced a tripartite system which approximates to the characteristics described at the beginning of the article ... This is not to say that tripartism is unimportant; at the very least, the attachment of so many decision-makers to the tripartite formula precludes the pursuit of other possible policy options.

If we accept that there is a close identity between tripartism and liberal corporatism our evidence seems to throw considerable doubt on the idea that Britain is, or in future will develop into, a liberal corporate state ... Undoubtedly there has been an increase in government intervention into industry and the economy ... The government may have more influence on the direction of economic policy than either the CBI or the TUC. However, this does not mean that Britain approximates to a system of state corporatism. Indeed, we have shown that the government's decisions are influenced by the CBI and the TUC. In addition, the government's autonomy is constrained by other British interests, notably the City and by actors external to the system.

Notes

1 Pahl and Winkler are prodigious writers on the subject: for example, Pahl and Winkler (1975) and (1976). See also Crouch (1976), Lehmbruch (1976) and Panitch (1976*b*).
2 Grant and Marsh (1970, p. 25).
3 See Jenkins (1970).
4 Grant and Marsh, *op. cit.*, pp. 156–68.
5 Although this policy met increasing resistance from the organization's membership.
6 Grant and Marsh, *op. cit.*, pp. 156–68.
7 The role of the trade unions is discussed more fully in Marsh and Smith (undated).
8 Their origins, structure and role are discussed more fully in Grant and Marsh, *op. cit.*, Chapter 7.
9 The joint CBI–TUC statement on important controls issued in 1976 amounted to little more than agreement on the necessity for a somewhat wider range of 'anti-dumping' measures than were being undertaken at the time.
10 *The Guardian*, 4 September 1976.
11 *Ibid.*
12 Smith (1972, p. 326).
13 Grant and Marsh (1975, p. 103).
14 Groups like the Retail Consortium have enjoyed access at this level, but their access has been less continuous.
15 For example, in 1976 the TUC was able to forestall the threatened seamen's strike.
16 For a discussion of these developments see Bruce-Gardyne (1975).
17 Grant and Marsh (1975, pp. 91–2).
18 See Minkin (1974).
19 For an apposite comment on this point see Crossman (1975, p. 155).
20 Watkinson (1976, p. 88).
21 CBI (1974, p. 4).
22 This is not to say, of course, that the notion of 'tripartism' first emerged in 1964. However, this article has been concerned with the period since 1964.

4.8   C. Webb

DECISION MAKING IN THE EEC

From *Policy Making in the European Communities*, ed. H. Wallace. Copyright © C. Webb, 1977. Reprinted by permission of John Wiley & Sons Ltd.

The European Communities as an 'intergovernmental' framework

... The underlying implications of an intergovernmental interpretation of the European Communities policy-making procedures can be spelled out fairly easily. The ... growing assertiveness of national governments, combined with the failure to make rapid progress in many policy areas, have stimulated a reassessment of the significance of the European Communities for national and international politics. Stanley Hoffman's (1966) analysis and, more recently, the views of Ralf Dahrendorf (1972), offer a radically different perspective on the procedures of the European Communities. Hoffmann has argued forcefully that governments ... are to be seen as the central actors in any process of international cooperation. This deference by Hoffman to the 'realist' school in international politics makes him sceptical of the success of any indirect assault on national authority ... According to his analysis, the EC (European Communities) may successfully create common procedures for resolving low key issues between states but it has made no impression, nor is it likely to in the future, on the issues and arenas of diplomacy and strategy where governments jealously guard their sovereignty.

Intergovernmentalism thus suggests a totally different picture of the Communities' policy context. It denies the uniqueness of the Communities as a framework for international cooperation, capable of exceeding existing international organisations in the undermining of governmental authority. It denies that the national political, economic and social systems of Western Europe are so interdependent and so penetrated by the Communities that governments cease to be sole arbiters of their country's external fortunes. The pluralist image of the network of participants in the EC's policy process is rejected in favour of a more conventional picture of governments carefully aggregating domestic positions at the national level. The Commission faces not a flood of separately articulated sub-national demands but a well-constructed dam, with the governments holding the gates between the Commission and their domestic politics ... The policy context of the European Communities, like OEEC[1] in the 1950s could be said to be one where governments are willing to take part in consultations to achieve limited economic objectives. Is there such a vast difference then, between the 'confrontation' method of intergovernmental consultation developed by OEEC and much of the consultation that goes on within the Council of Ministers and its subordinate network of intergovernmental committees? While there are clearly some aspects of the European Communities (the status of EC law inside member states, the provision for automatic Community financing etc.) which set them apart from other international organizations, the increasing predominance of the essentially intergovernmental Council of Ministers, with its failure to make any significant move to majority voting, work to lessen the differences between the EC and other international organizations. There are several reasons why an intergovernmental assessment of the EC's policy procedures is likely to prove more productive than the neofunctionalist perspective. The first and prime reason is that the institutional evolution of the Communities has strengthened and enlarged the role of national governments. The Commission–Council dialogue has been surrounded by a range of intergovernmental Committees, under the overall control of COREPER[2] and the Council, and these continuously filter over-ambitious Commission initiatives. Nor can these committees be seen as ultimately vulnerable to growth of a Community-wide administrative consensus which could threaten national governmental autonomy. Most of the officials participating in the functional committees under the Council are instructed by their governments and cannot depart significantly from their briefs. They are there, for the most part, to defend, rather than to bargain concessions freely. The net result of this mushrooming of intergovernmental committees is to produce hard and prolonged bargaining among governments rather than creative interchange among the Commission, national officials and interest groups. The process increasingly resembles a ... game with governments inclining to the definition of their positions in rigid terms. The classic interpretation of this form of bargaining in international politics is to view it in terms of the clash of 'national interests'. These national interests may or may not be of the same order as those traditionally associated with the foreign policy sector. However, if governments approach Community negotiations in a frame of mind in which very little can be conceded without the prejudicing of vital interests, then this surely reveals their continuing determination to play their role of guardian in the relations between the state and the international environment.

What role do national interests play in Community policy-making? The fact that the Luxembourg Compromise formula[3] leaves the definitions of 'national interests' entirely to the governments themselves indicates the impossibility of isolating a fixed set of interests for each government. It also shows the extent to which the very imprecision of the phrase allows governments to control the pace and scope of the policy process within the Communities. What is of interest here is what happens to the process when a government decides to respond to an issue or proposal in national interest terms — the Regional Development Fund for the British, compensatory payments in the agricultural sector for the Germans and so on. At least two broad effects can be hypothesized. Where an issue is seen as vital by a government it will seek to prepare its internal position so as to leave no room for exploiting differences, and attempt to settle any interdepartmental or interest group conflict at the national level. Secondly, governments will try to ensure that this vital interest is stubbornly defended in the policy formulation stage between national representatives and the Commission, and even more firmly adhered to when the issue enters the real discussion stage in COREPER. A government may even choose to strengthen its position by engaging in bilateral diplomacy with another government in a process which may totally exclude the Commission's representatives from playing any role at all.

A second reason for suggesting the utility of an intergovernmental framework is that stringent national policy-making procedures for developing positions on Community issues have accompanied the emergence of Community-level procedures. Far from witnessing the disintegration of governmental solidarity in those functional areas coming under the EC's jurisdiction, the EC has been witness, if anything, to an increase in government control as their political leaders seek to maintain a coordinating and directing role. As Lawrence Scheinman (1971, p.219) notes, 'Technical ministries have been victims of their increased importance and expanding competence in the sense that dealing with problems multilaterally has reduced the exclusivity and autonomy of these ministries ... What previously might have been done with little or no surveillance from internal political forces is now bruited and subject to stronger political control.'

The two most important structural mechanisms for exerting this political control within the EC are the coordinating machinery developed at the national level and the role of the Permanent Representations in Brussels ... Suffice it to suggest here that these, together with the Council itself, represent the most important components of the Community's policy-making process and yet all are governed by much more overt national considerations than [other images of] the policy process would lead us to expect.

In the intergovernmental approach much less weight is attached to the Commission's ability to exploit the overspill of functional loyalties amongst officials and interest groups, and its ability to define the terms of a problem in ways which will maximize its own authority. The key factor is the perception by governments of the issues and the assessment they make of their implications for the defence and promotion of vital interests, and for maintaining governmental control of a sector. Stanley Hoffman (1966) argues that governments distinguish between those areas where they are willing to concede part of their authority to international institutions and those in which the assertion of national control is seen as vital to national independence. He argues that the self-contained and elevated sphere of 'high politics' (foreign and defence policies) is not susceptible to the subtle undermining of governmental authority which is conceivable in welfare or 'low politics' areas. It is arguable, however, that even Hoffman's distinction between 'high' and 'low' underestimates the extent to which governments seek to preserve their role as national guardians. Thus there are plenty of examples of governments attaching special importance (for symbolic or domestic political reasons) to an apparently low-level political issue using Hoffman's criteria, which immediately elevates the issue into the status of a national interest for the purposes of negotiations with EC partners. The French Government's long standing determination to strengthen the role of gold in the international monetary system and the identification of this with French independence makes it very difficult for the issue to be thought of in purely technical terms. Hoffman's categories of 'high' and 'low' politics, in other words, are not fixed but change according to the perceptions of governments. While there may be a point at the higher end of the spectrum where all diplomacy and military issues are safely labelled 'high', in the experience of Communities no welfare or apparently technical question can be reliably labelled 'low' for all time, for all governments.

It ought to be apparent by now that much of the experience of the European Communities contradicts the ... model of a distinctive style of policy-making in which governments rarely act as rigid defenders of national interests as they are prone to do in other international organisations. Without empirical examination however, it is not possible to establish whether the EC is closer to an intergovernmental model in all functional sectors, at all times ... Since 1969 the holding of Summit meetings amongst Heads of Government in order to preserve a minimum of top-level political commitment to the continued development of the EC, has ostensibly strengthened the intergovernmental focus of the Communities. It is not only the Summit meetings themselves, with their tendency to highlight the confrontation of national positions and the uncertain contribution available to the Commission, which reflect this focus. Perhaps more significant have been the preparatory negotiations undertaken for the Summits, with COREPER and the political cooperation machinery increasingly blocking the Commissions's input into the policy process. Once an issue becomes caught up in this intergovernmental preparatory process and is discussed by Heads of State and Government, it is likely to become subject to rather different considerations than had the issue remained on a less charged level. The decision of the December 1974 Paris Summit to formalize the Summits into European Councils, is bound to deepen the penetration of intergovernmentalism as middle range policy issues, and not merely new initiatives, are presented with a final, explicitly intergovernmental forum for their adjudication. It is also possible that the European Councils, with their more intimate, club-like atmosphere, may well be adding a distinctly positive dimension to the policy-making process. Summitry in international diplomacy is frequently associated with the probability of misunderstandings and negotiation failures. In the context of the European Communities, it is acquiring a reputation for successfully overcoming protracted divisions among officials and ministers. Intergovernmentalism may not pose so great a threat to the Communities' development as it often suggested.

... In spite of the general increase in intergovernmentalism in the EC since 1965, it may well be the case, for example in the standardization of food regulations and in other areas of law harmonization, that governments have been willing to yield some control over these policing aspects of the common market. The discovery of a mixed pattern of policy-making in the EC would be entirely consistent with our argument that it is governments who decide the appropriate procedures for policy-making across the range of issues and not the issues themselves which objectively determine the processes.

A transnational ... transgovernmental framework

... Transnationalism suggests a view in which states remain important but have to share the international arena with multinational corporations, transnational pressure groups, international organizations and even 'transgovernmental' bureaucratic alliances. Such a mixed, cobweb image of the international system presents a [second] framework for examining the EC's policy-making process. It suggests that the policy interdependence and intensive network of interest group and bureaucratic consultations, created by the formation of the EC, represent a microcosmic reflection of transnational processes in the wider international system.

The development of a transnational perspective in studies of international relations stems from the view that the growing economic and technological interdependence of the world, and the rapidly increasing opportunities for global communication, transportation, movement of finance and persons, has 'increased the sensitivities of societies to one another and thereby altered the relationship between governments' (Keohane and Nye, 1972, p. xvi). The chain of reaction, leading from this heightened sensitivity of societies to one another to the loosening of governmental control over contacts between societies, is outlined by Keohane and Nye (1974, p.4). 'Transnational activity ... may lead governments to control this non-governmental behaviour. Such efforts if pursued by more than one government make government policies sensitive to one another; since one government may deliberately or inadvertently thwart the other's purposes, governments must design their own policies with the policies of others in mind. The result of this may well be attempts at coordination which will increase direct bureaucratic contacts among government subunits, and which may, particularly in a multilateral context, create opportunities for international organizations to play significant roles'.

They have distinguished two major subcategories of transnational activity which are identifiable within the policy framework created by the European Communities. The first is the formation of transnational, non-governmental alliances amongst interest groups, whose sectional interests attract them to similar groups inside other states and with whom they can identify more easily than with opposing or rival interests inside their own societies. The Community-wide interest groups bringing together farmers in COPA[4], industrialists in UNICE[5], specialized producers such as textile interests in COMITEXTIL[6] and the European organizations of trade unionists fit exactly this concept of transnational non-governmental alliances. These organizations have attempted to exert influence within the Communities' policy framework by seeking access to the Commission and mobilising their supporters against national governments when national priorities fail to coincide with transnational objectives. The second form of transnational activity is that which brings together subunits of government into transgovernmental coalitions. Such coalitions are formed when these subunits come together across national boundaries to resist the attempts of Cabinets to enforce coordination and curtail the pursuit of departmental objectives within governments. Within the EC framework national agricultural officials, for example, try to maximize their strength to resist the efforts of their national treasuries to limit expenditure by holding down price increases or pressing for reform of the CAP[7] itself. The degree to which transnational alliances are successful will naturally depend on an awareness of common goals, and a similar feeling of being disadvantaged by their national systems. The success of transgovernmental coalitions depends on two factors. One is the ability to bypass central coordinating machinery in the pursuit of departmental objectives. The second factor is the use of the Community arena as a resource for intra-governmental conflicts.

A transnational interpretation of the Community process presents a rather confused picture compared with the neat vertical lines of inter-governmentalism ... It suggests a mixture of role playing on the part of government officials in the network of committees under COREPER with some, at least, being influenced by the regular contact and communication channels to modify their attitudes. Face to face contact over a prolonged period may make explicit areas of agreement which, without such contact, might have remained merely latent. The convening of consultative meetings of national officials by the Commission can create, in the words of

Keohane and Nye, 'political alchemy', where 'the organization provides physical proximity, an agenda of issues on which interaction is to take place, and an aura of legitimacy' (Keohane and Nye, 1974, p.51).

At the same time as national officials are being attracted by the centrifugal pull of the Community network, they are also subject to the centripetal pressures of their own governments. The EC's policy formulation and implementative process necessitates an expanding network of contacts which governments seek to prevent escaping out of control. The transnational perspective does not exclude attempts by governments to assert their control over transnational contacts but it does suggest that these attempts are not wholly successful. Keohane and Nye picture the consequences. 'A continuing struggle between groups favouring transgovernmental policy patterns, and those supporting a return to strategies of national assertion or national protection is likely to ensue' (Keohane and Nye, 1974, p.61).

One reason why governments are not able fully to maintain their control in the EC lies in the inescapable consequences of increasing economic interdependence and the complex patterns of communication and exchange of information which such interdependence requires. Individual governments are no longer able to act as coordinators in sectors such as agriculture where the administrative centre has shifted to Brussels, or in managing the operation of common rules for competition throughout the EC. In these policy sectors the Commission is able to place itself at the centre of an increasingly complex communications network with governments being able to monitor only a limited area.

The prevailing image of transnationalism is one of growing decentralization with power slipping from the grasp of governments but not accumulating in any one place, certainly not totally in the hands of international organizations. Transnationalism is useful as a counterperspective ... to intergovernmentalism ... It is clearly, dependent on the existence of a minimum network of transnational relations and on the presence of groups, whether governmental or non-governmental, which are sufficiently mobilized and active to make an impact on governments. Such a network is discernible ... in the monetary sector where central banks illustrate the importance of transnational and para-governmental groupings to international monetary relations; secondly in the industrial sector, where one would expect transnational interests of both employers and workers to coalesce around a commitment to the more efficient management of economic interdependence in Western Europe.

The context for Community policy-making

... The weakness of the Community processes in generating genuine policy choices tends, in our view, to make 'comprehensive rationality' policy-making models less helpful in studying Community policy making. The policy context of the European Communities seems much closer to that identified by Lindblom (1959) in his 'muddling through' model of public policy making. Lindblom emphasises the tendency of policy makers to prefer maximizing security to radical and comprehensive innovation, and therefore for the policy process as a whole to be characterized by incrementalism and a high degree of continuity. Policy-making in the European Communities is more often than not distinguished by the repeated fudging of fundamental issues, deriving from the political fragility of Community bargaining. In agriculture, for example, the crunch issue is the search for an efficient mechanism for subsidising farming incomes which will not raise consumer prices too high, divert resources, induce surpluses or offend overseas suppliers. The Community policy process has consistently proved incapable of confronting directly the choices involved. The lack of transparency in Community bargaining makes it difficult to disentangle the motives and preferences of participants and link them to clearly enunciated policy goals. One of the central problems faced both by governments and students of Community policy-making is the difficulty of relating Community issues to the two broad categories of foreign policy and domestic policy, conventionally used to differentiate the policy processes of political systems. The Communities' major policy areas involving commercial, agricultural and general economic issues, are clearly those which in the past, have been part of a state's domestic concerns. Yet the presence of foreign ministers in regular Council meetings discussing non-foreign policy questions, and the involvement of national ambassadorial delegations in the day to day affairs of the Communities, suggests at the very least, problems of overlap and competing roles for national officials. In national capitals, foreign offices have attempted to assert their control over Community contacts in a reflex action born of traditional perceptions of their roles. However, Community negotiations demand the expertise and collaboration of 'home' ministries. For Ministries of Agriculture, for example, membership of the Communities transforms their working environment, while Ministries of the Interior and their equivalents are still only marginally affected. Pentland has noted that 'Community policy-making is unique in that it is made in an environment where the nature of the political game itself is more than usually ambiguous and where different groups see it in different terms' (Pentland, 1973, p.221).

While this is certainly true of the Communities, it is by no means evident that the blurring of the boundaries between foreign and domestic policies starts and ends with the EC. The IMF's[8] involvement in national monetary policies and the IEA[9] in national energy policies are two examples where governments have found that traditional distinctions of what is 'foreign' and what is 'domestic' break down. The presumed existence of a dividing line between foreign and domestic policy suggests two sorts of differences which are of interest to the policy-making process. The first difference is that policy issues are said to lend themselves to division into separate categories. Thus for governments, relations with other states clearly belong in one category, internal and law and order measures in another. The second difference lies in the assumption that different categories of issues give rise to different political processes in their handling by political systems. Traditional images of the handling of foreign policy by states accords an almost exclusive role to the executive branch of government. This executive dominance is seen to stem from the specialized nature of the issues, the need for secrecy and the link between foreign policy and statehood where governments see themselves as acting as the guardian of the national interest. In contrast the handling of domestic policy is viewed in more pluralistic terms, where competing demands for resources rule out readily definable national interests and where parliaments, political parties and pressure groups play active roles in the formulation of policy. Rosenau (1967), in distinguishing between foreign and domestic policy issue areas according to the interaction patterns characteristic of each, argues that foreign policy is typically carried out in a restricted, centralized decision-structure, whereas in domestic policy power and responsibility are dispersed amongst a number of centres.

The European Communities provide a particularly appropriate setting for exploring the differences between domestic and foreign policy with respect to both issues and political processes. It has already been suggested that governments find themselves unable to differentiate between domestic and foreign issues. International economic interdependence, of which the EC is a particularly intense example, results in a far wider range of issues becoming subject to international discussions. Whether the blurring of issue boundaries at the same time affects the way governments respond to them is another question. The intrusion of domestic issues into international bargaining may or may not mean that governments respond in a less rigid and more accommodating manner to one another's demands. It is also relevant to ask whether governments seek to monopolize the representation of their domestic interests at the Community level, or whether these interests are able to assert themselves independently ...

The implication of an intergovernmental interpretation ... is that governments seek to maintain their predominance in negotiations at the Community level on every issue at the expense of other participants. Thus, for example, the management of agricultural, industrial and internal market issues in a multilateral context is actually extending the reach of foreign policy processes.

... However, what is striking about the Communities is the degree to which both styles of policy-making − the gladiatorial and pluralistic − are reflected across a range of policy areas which fail to marry with any conventional domestic/foreign distinction. The policy process is as subject to unexpected changes in pattern as a child's kaleidoscope. Governments may be satisfied with a relatively minor role in some policy areas, as in competition policy where the interactions mainly occur amongst Commission officials, business enterprises and national and Community legal representatives, but vigorously assert their claim to be major participants in the development of a Community regional policy.

A clarity and uniformity of objectives within and amongst the member governments of the European Communities needs to exist in practice in order to maintain a sharp distinction between foreign and domestic policy responses. On the contrary, governments show considerable ambivalence in their utilization of the Community framework. This is certainly evident on the part of two of the new members. Both Denmark and the UK seem to be making deliberate attempts to limit the impact of the Communities on the exercise of their national sovereignty. Yet in both countries there are signs of acknowledgement that the Communities can act as a guardian of specific national interests when these are felt to be under threat ... The British Government in 1974 was relieved to have the Communities carry out the major part of the negotiations to secure access for Commonwealth sugar into the Community after 1975. At one and the same time the Communities are being regarded as a preferred policy-making forum and looked on with suspicion as an unwelcome intruder. This schizophrenia on the part of the national governments leads to a curious transience in the character of Community policy-making. The shape of a distinct Community process capable of generating output is discernible in some policy areas only to evaporate rapidly in others. The structure of the Community system is equally uneven. The supremacy of the legal rule-making and enforcement framework, headed by the Court of Justice, has not been seriously challenged, although it has quite substantially undermined the autonomy of specific parts of the legal systems in the member states. On the other hand, the political legitimacy of the Communities has not yet been fully conceded either by political elites or the general public, especially when comparisons are made with national political structures. Yet the Community framework is occasionally used as a political alibi by governments in search of justification for concessions made in Brussels at the expense of domestic interests.

Notes

1   OEEC, Organization for European Economic Cooperation.
2   COREPER, Committee of Permanent Representatives – national government officials of member governments.
3   It was agreed in 1966 to replace majority voting in the Council of Ministers with a national veto.

4   COPA, Confederation of Professional Agricultural Organizations
     (European-wide farmers' pressure group).
5   UNICE, Union des Industries de la Communauté Européene
     (industrialists' community-wide pressure group).
6   COMITEXTIL, Coordination Committee for the Textile Industries in
     the EEC (textile producers' pressure group).
7   CAP, Common Agricultural Policy.
8   IMF, International Monetary Fund.
9   IEA, International Energy Agency.

SECTION 5

A CRITICAL PERSPECTIVE

In the preceding sections the form has been to enrich the basic nature of each perspective by elaborating its specific contributions to the analysis of decision making. This has culminated in the propagation of three distinctive frameworks for analysing decision making, each of which not only focuses upon different sets of questions, the answers to which structure its interpretation of decision making, but each of which also retains its own intuitive criteria against which its explanation can be judged adequate or otherwise. Allison likens the use of such models to a fishing exercise, in which the models are the fishing nets, and each is designed only to catch certain fish, in certain ponds, and at certain depths. Thus each model is very selective in what it judges relevant to the explanation of decision making. However, to continue the analogy, by implication the design of the fishing nets may be such that they are unable to catch the fish that really matter. In other words, whilst each model is able to provide an adequate explanation of the process of decision making in its own terms, it is not doubted that each is selective and thus neglects evidence which could be vital to a fuller understanding. So the purpose of this section is to redress two of the more limiting aspects of this selectivity which apply equally to all three models.

The first relates to the general thrust of each of these models, which implies quite strongly that what requires explanation is only the process of decision making and not why certain issues never arise on the agenda of decision at the level of the group, organization, or society. Of course this point concerning non-decision making was dealt with in Section 1 by Parry and Morriss, who argued that the concept was expendable. However, Jenkins (5.1) takes issue with this diagnosis, firmly stating that if we are to understand the dynamics of decision making in society this will entail that: 'Non-issues, non-decisions, even non-politics are necessary and legitimate subjects for examination.' But having said that the study of non-decisions is both necessary and legitimate does not entirely answer Parry and Morriss's concern over its feasibility. Thus, to give credence to Jenkins' position, as well as those who agree with his general inclination, and also to validate the feasibility of the approach, Brogden's contribution (5.2) applies the concept of non-decision in one particular context.

Brogden's article examines the financial accountability of a Police force to its Police Authority, concluding that the issues which the Authority neglected, and the general manner in which it conducted its relationship with the Police, cannot be explained as choices or decisions but only by reference to non-decision making behaviour. The fact that discretion is implicitly left with the Police is itself an important political non-decision but one which has not been positively taken. What Brogden achieves, therefore, albeit indirectly, is the radical questioning of Parry and Morriss's view that non-decisions can simply be regarded as a form of routine decision, and this makes the initial sections of Brogden's article worthy of close reading.

Apart from the above, however, the three models also suffer from a lack of attention to the socio-economic context in which decisions are made, and the forces which influence changes in the nature of that context. And it is here that Cawson (5.3) and Morse (5.4) become significant. For Cawson, the debate between 'pluralists' and 'elite theorists' over whether decisions in society are the result of the interplay of organized interests or the dominance of one particular self-conscious social group is rather sterile since it neglects significant developments in British society. The central development, it is argued, has been that of the changing relationship between the State, crudely the organs of government, and society. Succinctly, Cawson argues that the requirements of an advanced industrial economy have forced governments into increasing involvement in the management of economic and social activity. As this has occurred, in order to make this management efficacious, the major organized interests in each sector have been incorporated into the very decision-making structure of government. The less important and powerful interests are thus marginalized. And for Cawson the result is the juxtaposition of a corporatist sector of decision making, in which the government and leadership of the major organized interests collectively take decisions in their mutual interests, and a pluralist sector, in which the normal interplay of organized interests and disinterested government occurs. Thus, to explain decision making in society it is necessary, Cawson suggests, to examine the broader socio-economic context in which decision making occurs, together with the forces which structure it.

This general point is also what Morse is concerned to elucidate, although his focus and argument differ from Cawson. Morse examines how the impact of modernization, which he regards as a complex amalgam of industrialization and its consequent effects (urbanization, bureaucratization, democratization), has transformed the nature of foreign policy, and in particular the process of foreign policy decision making. For Morse, the underlying forces of modernization structure the general pattern of foreign policy decision making in certain ways, yet this remains hidden to the analyst focusing upon the explanation of discrete decisions.

What both Morse and Cawson would, therefore, agree upon, is that the analyst can discern a general pattern or structure to decision making which is neither apparent to the decision maker nor to those concerned with explaining discrete decisions. Such a structure is itself a further analytical construct, devised by the social scientist, to explain the general processes of decision making in contemporary society. It is therefore also open to both methodological and substantive criticism.

These final four contributions then do not simply redress the more obvious limitations of our three models upon decision making but, together with the preceding contributions, act as a reminder both of the complexity of this field of social enquiry, and its intellectual 'colonization' by the varied disciplines which comprise the social sciences.

5.1 W. E. Jenkins

THE CASE OF NON-DECISIONS

From *Policy Analysis*, published by Martin Robertson Co. Ltd, 1978.

Some perverted priorities

At the crucial stage of Antonioni's film *Blow-Up* the central character, a young fashion photographer, struggles to find out whether he has unwittingly witnessed and photographed a murder in a London park. Did he see a figure with a gun in the park bushes or was it his imagination? What has his camera captured? What do the enlargements show? In his frantic quest to find out he runs his film through the enlarger until the grains almost separate from each other on the print. Technology, however, sets a limit on perception. Shadow or substance? Fact or fantasy? The final answer is unknown.

It is our argument here that as things stand the policy analyst, like Antonioni's photographer, is technically limited, controlled by his tools and only able to see indistinctly beyond the park railings. However, we will also argue that a focus on policy content, as reflected in arena or issue contexts writ large, is one way of curing this myopia. By adjusting the lenses we use we can increase our capacity for analysis to a point of greater resolution.

'Policy', argue Rackoff and Schaefer (1970), 'is the action and non-action of the system in response to the demands made on it': an interesting and provocative statement pushing us in directions we have touched on before but not examined in any great detail. We return to Crenson's (1976, p. 4) study of air pollution in Gary and East Chicago to note his general concern with cities and towns in the U.S. which ignored their dirty air. In analytical terms, their behaviour constitutes a case of non-action, a matter that is rarely studied in any detail: 'No attempt is made to account for seemingly important decisions never made, significant policies that are never formulated and issues that never arise.' Yet is this important? In terms of policy and policy analysis, does it pose any questions of either an analytic or a normative nature? We must look further.

Asbestos is a useful material; it provides cheap and efficient insulation against fire. However, when milled into fibre, it produces dust and this dust is a killer ... In the UK the Asbestos Act of 1931 specifically forbade any level of dust whatsoever in factories. Yet today, in Yorkshire and in

London, people employed in the asbestos industry since the Second World
War are slowly and painfully dying. Why? Because the legislation regarding
the permissible levels of dust was not applied, and because the Factory
Inspectorate empowered to enforce the legislation never brought a prosecution. This constituted a 'policy of non-enforcement'. There was a price
for cheap asbestos – human health. Dust could have been prevented in the
factories but it was not. Someone, somewhere, was unwilling to pay the
true cost of safety.[1]

The non-enforcement of the asbestos legislation may be an extreme
example, yet it has many parallels. As Duane Lockard (1971, Ch. 1) has
pointed out, the safety record in US coal mines is appalling, particularly
when one considers that the means for improvement are at hand. The
economic case against the application of such measures is simple: more
stringent safety laws may mean more unemployment through the erosion
of the market by other fuels. But, even granted this, should miners expect
the worst? Have they a right to safety legislation? On this issue Lockard's
position is clear. Some kinds of issue get into the political system with
ease; others are quietly suppressed or ignored. Mine safety is one of the
latter ...

'Everyone opposes pollution yet we find pollution everywhere ... the
explanation of the gap between intention and reality lies in the realm of
politics.'[2] Replace 'pollution' by 'asbestosis' or 'mine safety' and you have
the same problem: in many policy areas issues fail to appear or policies fail
to be implemented. Further, there are also, as Webb (1972) points out in
his assessment of Gregory's studies, 'decision-less decisions' – decisions
that ghost out of nowhere or are the product of nobody in particular. The
extension of this argument, as has been pointed out by Dearlove (1973), is
that in policy structures dramatic decisions and important activity are the
exceptions rather than the rule. Instead, 'policy maintenance' and hum-
drum routine may be the order of the day, so a central item of importance
is the extent to which policy making itself is avoided and resisted by those
in government. If this is the case, policy analysis may need to probe the
dynamics of the system more thoroughly than it has done, and one way to
do this may be to focus on policy content and its associated processes.
To examine policy content may offer a means for probing the internal
dynamics of the political machine. It may also underline the importance of
studying the process of setting the rules (who decides what the machine is
and is not used for?). An important question is: what leads to the presence
of conflict in a system and what leads to its absence? Should we research
not only decisions but also non-decisions? For policy analysts, are non-
decisions the figure in the park bushes?

Beyond pluralism – a move into the second dimension

So a concern with the presence or absence of items on a decision agenda and with the nature of issue or content areas may be linked through a focus on political power and conflict. Hence we are drawn into the theoretical debate that exists in this area. Who has the power? Does anyone have the power? What is power? These rallying cries that have echoed over political science for at least two decades lead one immediately to the camps of the élitist and pluralist forces which have spread from small beginnings (the analysis of community power) to theories of democracy itself. Here we can hardly hope to improve on, or even to capture, an extensive if repetitive debate. Yet an appreciation of its flavour is essential, since out of it have emerged both the concept of non-decision and the controversies that surround it.

The power élite theory has been with us for some time; indeed, power (key concept or dustbin?) is the pivot around which much of this debate sways. The ideas of C. Wright Mills, that power is concentrated in the hands of permanent, stable groups of political actors, aloof and impenetrable, who dominate all aspects of the social system, gave broader scope to an analysis developed a little earlier by Floyd Hunter in the area of community power studies. In Hunter's examination of Atlanta, Georgia, power lay with a tightly knit and coherent élite, whose web of influence spread out over all issues. There was limited access to the group and little opposition to its activities, consequently community influence on the political process was negligible. However, both the theory and the methodology of Hunter, together with the wider speculations of Mills, were opposed by Robert Dahl and others who formed the vanguard of what was to be termed the pluralist movement. Was the potential for control *actual* control? they asked; was there *always* a power structure in social institutions and, if there was, did it change over time? From extensive studies of a series of decisions (or key issues) in New Haven, Dahl formulated the pluralist model of power founded on the assumption that the political system is composed of a network of competing groups with differing power bases. In particular, the system is not closed, but open to all; channels of articulation are always available because the nature of the system allows individuals to influence political behaviour in a variety of ways.[3]

As Crenson points out, the pluralists contend that power exists only when it is being exercised; consequently the rationale of policy, as reflected in decisions, can be constructed only through an examination of political actions rather than opinions. Power is not concentrated in the hands of a single élite; rather, as it is issue-based, it is 'fractionated and fleeting'. Pluralist theory, therefore, rejects 'any subordination of the political system by the class system. Rather it embraces a more thorough subordination of the political system to its environment.' Given this thesis, it must quickly be apparent that pluralism as a theory has greater import than simply to explain the comings and goings in New Haven. It is, in essence, a normative theory of democracy: pluralism is a condition not only to be examined but also to be aimed for. As such, its influence has been considerable and pervasive. For example, Lindblom's theory of incrementalism depends heavily on a political theory of pluralism (i.e. a consensus decision is a 'good' decision), ... Indeed, the validity and widespread applicability of pluralism has excited a great deal of attention. Students have been concerned to learn whether it is generalisable or culturally specific. To what extent, for instance, is pluralism applicable to community politics in the UK ...? To what extent is the doctrine of pluralist democracy specific to the US ...? Again, a substantial literature beckons, posing interesting questions.[4] However, we must ignore this discussion, turning instead to some of the issues of theory and justice posed by a pluralist model which has special relevance for the policy field.

For those who would question and oppose a pluralist analysis, the key words are those of Schattsneider (1960, p. 71): 'All forms of political organisation have a bias in favour of some kinds of conflict and the suppression of others because organisation is the mobilisation of bias. Some issues are organised into politics while others are organised out.' So, in terms of theory, the argument is that the pluralist vision is limited. In dealing with political behaviour by centering on issues that generate open conflict of interest, it may tell only part of the story. As Bachrach and Baratz argued in their important article, power has two faces: one, the overt struggle seen by the pluralists, and the other, which the pluralists ignore, the mobilisation of bias within the system to keep issues suppressed or to prevent their ever being raised in the first instance. Pluralism may therefore be theoretically and morally wanting: theoretically deficient, since it fails 'to account for the way in which men define their own interests and the ways in which others perceive and respond to these interests'; morally deficient, since far from being open, the pluralist system may in fact be closed and exclusive – hardly a model for democratic justice. Hence Bachrach and Baratz argue that power and policy can only be understood through an examination both of decisions and of non-decisions, a perspective they refer to as the 'two-dimensional' approach to power.[5]

Non-decisions: opposed and developed

But what is a non-decision? Would we recognise one if we saw one? Is it more illusion than fact? If it is fact, is it possible to test for its presence? Such questions of evidence and empirical validity have been central features of the non-decision-making debate and therefore demand some consideration. To Bachrach, a non-decision is essentially a product of a decision, but a decision the results of which are difficult to detect. Such decisions are 'instrumental in preventing an issue potentially threatening to the interests or values of a decision maker from reaching the agenda of a decision-making body of the political system'. In these terms, non-decisions may be identified in several ways: through efforts to localise conflicts and control demands; through labelling demands so as to eliminate them from the system (e.g. by terming them 'illegal') or routinising them within the system (committees, enquiry procedures, etc.); through threats of sanctions (either positive or negative), or through co-operation ... But still, can the incidence of non-decisions be tested empirically? Bachrach's point is that they can, but only within the context of observable conflict. Pre-existing covert or overt power conflict among actors is a prerequisite for the occurrence of non-decisions. This constraint permits certain subtle formulations of non-decision to be examined (e.g. the fact that one party is unaware of the nature of a decision does not render the concept untenable), but it does not permit (on empirical grounds at least) investigation of one issue that has caused much controversy in this thesis, the possibility of a situation in which both parties accept the *status quo*.[6]

The writings of Bachrach and Baratz have clear normative implications. They are concerned with linking patterns of relative deprivation with specific decision-making mechanisms, a focus that may also be seen as a first step to alleviating such problems. In this their analytical interests are based on a conceptualisation that goes beyond pluralism and, in fact, attacks the basis of pluralist analysis by introducing into it a behavioural dimension. As Lukes (1974, Ch. 3) observes, they 'redefine the boundaries of what is to constitute a political issue' by identifying potential issues which non-decision making prevents from reaching the policy arena. 'Key issues', a central point of the pluralist analysis, become issues that may never get into the system and hence policy outcomes and overt political behaviour may constitute smokescreens obscuring much of reality.[7] This thesis is an aggressive one and, in the face of it, the pluralists were distracted from their demolition of the élitist perspective to defend their flank from what they termed the 'neo-élitist' attack. Non-decisions, they argued, were an unnecessary idea, an erroneous concept which it was impossible to test empirically. In empirical terms, data was difficult to gather and, even when gathered, difficult to apply ...

It was some years before Bachrach and Baratz took their theory to the field and, when they did, it was to focus on race relations issues in the city of Baltimore. How, over a period of time, did the power struggle shift? What determined the structure of policy arenas and changes in them? How did issues and process interact? Concentrating first on power outside the system, the authors argue that, due to non-decisions by political leaders in the white community, the black population was unable to generate a 'politics of conflict'. The inaccessibility of decision-making centres to the poor, and the absence of political machinery for the promotion of political issues in the ghetto, resulted in what was, effectively, a closed political system. Ghetto organisation has its own characteristics which render it peculiarly ineffective in political conflict and, in any case, the political system tended to avoid conflict. Further, other strategies and routinisations, such as recruitment policies for important positions ('a sustaining non-decision'), acted so as to prevent any direct challenge to established power distributions. However, following race riots in Baltimore in early 1968, substantial changes took place. Power struggles shifted to within the system and federal government programmes, part of the 'War on Poverty', provided the mechanisms to generate conflict and to politicise minority groups.[8] The authors, therefore, examine alterations in arenas of conflict and sources of power both within the immediate political system itself and as this was influenced by the wider environment. They concentrate on 'politics on confrontation' outside the system and 'politics of conflict' within it to interpret the complex and dynamic changes taking place. An examination of both decisions and non-decisions, they claim, makes it possible to observe, in a time of change, power relationships and political behaviour both inside and outside the system.[9]

Steven Lukes has a great deal of time for Bachrach's and Baratz's theory. However, he does not have much time for its application in Baltimore: 'The analysis remains superficial because it confines itself to studying individual decisions made to avert potentially threatening demands from becoming politically dangerous.' Rather, Lukes (1974, Chs 3, 7) argues, analysis should concern itself with 'the complex and subtle ways in which the inactivity of leaders and the sheer weight of institutions ... served for so long to keep the blacks out of Baltimore politics and indeed for a long period kept them from trying to get into it'. For Lukes, the neo-élitist thesis goes far in undermining the pluralists' case, but in terms of explaining activities in policy arenas it does not go far enough. First, the analysis of behaviour is seen as too limited ...; second, the insistence of conflict as a prerequisite for power is seen as too demanding ... So Lukes is unwilling to accept that actual conflict is essential to power; he claims, rather, that one of the most effective uses of power is to prevent conflict from emerging in the first place. From this Lukes moves to what he terms his 'three-dimensional view' which recognises that power (*a*) may be exercised through collectivities, (*b*) may involve inaction rather than observable action and (*c*) may be exercised unwittingly. By raising and exploring the question of an 'unconscious decision', he advances onto ground that the pluralists stare at with horror. Lukes, however, is undismayed. To a sociologist such a move presents fewer problems than to a behavioural political scientist. He advocates what he claims is a radical and more penetrative analysis of power relations, at once 'value laden, theoretical and empirical', a three-dimensional position which he sees approximated in Crenson's study of Gary and East Chicago.

... In his examination of the air pollution issue Crenson states that here, at least, political neglect is not a random phenomenon. 'In this field an element of policy consistency in the occurrence of non-decision making has been found.' Consequently any analysis which bases its research conclusions on the examination of decision-making events alone produces results contingent upon 'a politically biased sample of phenomena'. To establish why policy making concerned with air pollution varies in different urban areas, Crenson sets himself the task of carefully exploring the second face of power. What, he asks, are the elements that constitute the rationale for inertia? He argues that inaction is related to factors such as industrial presence, the structure of the local political system and the nature of the air pollution issue itself. That industry may act to suppress an issue that may threaten its profit margins is no surprise. But what is surprising in Gary is that US Steel manages to effect a good deal of suppression without lifting a finger. Industrial inaction, rather than industrial action, is the crucial form of behaviour, since US Steel's reputation for power acts as a sufficient deterrent. Second, are policy outputs modified by the nature of the political system? Possibly, but this may depend on the assessments of political actors concerning collective as opposed to specific benefits ... Third, what of the issues themselves (the policies, their advocates, their clientele)? May these, of their own accord, build biases into the system? 'Political issues create political consciousness, so, just as one issue may lead to another, may not one issue lead to the *avoidance* of another?' Crenson, therefore, argues against the pluralist conception of issue independence ...

The air pollution study raises to an empirical level issues developed by the neo-élitists and emphasised by Lukes: that it is both important and possible to examine how demands are prevented from being raised (do people really want to be poisoned?); that it is necessary to explore non-decision making outside perceived and overt conflicts (US Steel), and that one should consider institutional as well as individual power ... In particular, it enquires why often many matters of 'the greatest social importance are not the objects of anyone's decision at all'.[10]

Non-decisions: some implications

As a concept, non-decision is frequently much like quicksand. Both logically and empirically it poses problems. May it, at one and the same time, mean everything and nothing? Possibly, but like all other concepts, this depends on the care with which it is formulated.[11] As the work of Crenson and, to a lesser extent, that of Bachrach and Baratz shows, it is possible to raise the status of non-decision from that of a critical idea to that of a manageable concept applicable to policy studies. While recognising the caveats of the pluralist critique, we would argue that the adoption of a non-decision perspective offers scope for a wider and more searching analysis of the policy arena. In particular, it demands that the investigator step back and probe in greater depth 'the world taken for granted', without becoming ensnared in the false consciousness debate which a total acceptance of Luke's analysis might involve.[12]

A focus on non-decisions therefore links with, and extends a focus on, policy content or policy area by posing wider questions regarding actions and inactions within the political system, such as the extent to which process and content influence each other to establish ongoing constraints. Crenson's idea of an 'ecology of issues' is suggestive here, in that it shows, as Newton reminds us, 'why issues are likely to remain *underdeveloped* granted a certain combination of circumstances' ...

As Crenson's study demonstrates, a non-decision analysis allows comparative work to be instigated, and policy theory to be constructed, on a general level. It is also abundantly clear that other questions raised earlier, namely asbestos legislation in the UK and mine safety in the US ... are approachable on the same basis ... Non-issues, non-decisions, even non-policies are necessary and legitimate subjects for examination. So we are led to the issue of values and to the point that a focus on non-decisions is a clear way out of the dilemma described by Lowi (1970, pp. 318–19) as 'the technocratisation of policy analysis': that the analyst, in being instrumental and technocratic, becomes blinded to certain fundamental political patterns. A non-decision-making perspective is one way to clear this blindness, to gaze with Antonioni's photographer through the park railings, and to identify whether there is a figure at all and whether it is threatening.

Notes

1   An account of asbestosis in the UK and of the non-enforcement of the 1931 Asbestos Act was given in the BBC television programme entitled *The Killer Dust*, broadcast on 20 January 1975. The case was reported on by the Parliamentary Ombudsman in March 1976.
2   Davies (1970) quoted in Newton (1972).
3   The classic volumes in the community power debate are Hunter (1953) and Dahl (1961). For examples of opposing arguments in the debate see Castles *et al.* (1971).
4   On the applicability of the community power debate to the UK see Hill (1972, Ch. 11); also Newton (1969*a* and *b*). Also note Newton (1976). On issues of democracy, see Sharpe (1973).
5   The classic articles are Bachrach and Baratz (1962 and 1963). Also see Bachrach and Baratz (1971) and Bachrach (1969–70).
6   On this, see Bachrach, *op. cit.*, p. 60. To the critics of the non-decision school this issue is vital, since they see it as defying empirical investigation. Bachrach, however, argues that it is marginal to the total situation.

7 For a critical view see Bradshaw (1976) or Hindess (1976).
8 Again the literature on the subject is extensive. For cases that give further indication of the effects of US government programmes involved in the 'War on Poverty', see Moynihan (1969) and Marris and Rein (1972).
9 Bachrach, *op. cit.*, p. 186; also Bachrach and Baratz (1971) *op. cit.* The major importance of non-decisions in this instance is seen as explaining the situation in Baltimore prior to the 1968 riots.
10 These are the issues that Lukes would argue take Crenson beyond Bachrach and Baratz to a three-dimensional view (Lukes, *op. cit.*, Ch. 7).
11 The issue of concept formation is critical to theory building in general and to comparative theory in particular. Here, see Roberts (1972), Chs. 3, 8.
12 While Lukes's position is an interesting one, the directions he drives theory towards are difficult to accomodate and, in spite of his aspirations and protestations, the spectre of 'false consciousness' still looms (cf. Marcuse (1968)).

5.2   M. Brogden

A POLICE AUTHORITY – THE DENIAL OF CONFLICT

From *Sociological Review*, vol. 25 no. 2, pp. 325–49 (1977).

This study is of the relationship between one Police Authority and its senior police officer. In spotlighting the financial relationship, it seeks to illuminate the social and political context of police decision-making and the degree of democratic control over police actions.

Some propositions

The classic study of decision-making in a local authority context is that of Bachrach and Baratz (1971) in Baltimore. Their major theoretical focus was on the process of 'nondecision-making'. This occurs where one of the parties in a situation of potential conflict, 'mobilises bias' to exclude the legitimate consideration of opposing viewpoints. It makes use of the 'rules of the game' which structure the context of the argument in its favour. By this process, the dominant party denies that the particular issue raised by the opposition merits serious consideration. The issue is considered, the conflict recognised but only at a superficial level.

However, Lukes (1974) has argued that this description of the process of the mobilisation of bias process is sociologically unsatisfactory. It assumes that the dominant party in a potential conflict is actually aware of the gravity of the dispute and that, being aware, it deliberately structures the debate in its own favour. According to Lukes (1974), manifest conflict and intentional action are not necessary to the use of nondecision-making power: 'This is to ignore the crucial point that the most effective and insidious use of power is to prevent such conflict arising in the first place. He extends the concept of nondecision-making beyond that of denying entrance of grievances into the political process, claiming that it should also encompass the situation where conflict is latent, neither articulated nor defined but nevertheless real. 'To assume that the absence of grievance equals genuine consensus is simply to rule out the possibility of false or manipulated consensus by definitional *fiat*.'

Westergaard and Resler (1975, p. 146) too have criticised the Bachrach and Baratz formulation:

It does not cover the situation of which the essential feature is the common acceptance of certain basic premises, which nobody directly engaged in dispute, bargaining or advice considers it realistic to challenge and which automatically rule out a wide range of alternative policies. This is a foreclosure of options without manipulation. None is needed here, on or off stage, so long as the unspoken agreement about premises holds. But such agreement cannot be equated with common approval. Nor can it be assumed that the balance of agreement has been struck at a point that somehow favours all interests 'equally', 'impartially' and with neat symmetry.

The relationship between a Police Authority and its Chief Constable is conceived in these terms. Members of the Authority may not believe there to be any potential conflict between local citizens and the police. They may see the relationship between themselves and the local force as being one devoid of critical content. Where conflicts between police and sections of the public do arise, they would not be relevant to the work of the authority but outside the realm of its responsibilities.

Hindess (1971, p. 72) for example, in his study of the changing patterns of local Labour politics in this city has briefly outlined the major features of the decision-making process. He argues that for structural reasons — most noticeably the diminution in working-class membership and influence of the local Labour Party — major decisions by the Party on such topics as housing and employment (those questions most immediately important to the working-class people in the city) have been designated as 'areas for expert decision' and effectively removed from the Party agenda. Their place has been taken by subjects of the more peripheral 'street-lighting' variety which have then provided the substance of political party debate.

If this evidence holds true for the Police Authority then following Lukes, the subsequent propositions are worth considering:

1. The chief concerns of the Police Authority will be essentially peripheral issues. Important matters such as the financing of the police will be delegated to the relevant expert (in this case, the Chief Constable). A process of 'nondecision-making' will therefore characterise the major activities of the committee.
2. The members of the Authority will acknowledge the lack of any actual conflict and will deny the potential for serious disagreement on the committee. They will dismiss as inconceivable any suggestion that the handling of the police accounts may be the cause of conflict between police and public. The police officers will be seen by the members as a body of politically neutral, professional experts. Accounting in this context could be disputed only by a small, deviant minority of the public — the 'criminals'.
3. Bias will be mobilised to exclude potential controversy. This process will occur both through the deliberate acts of committee members in the selection of additional personnel, and through the operation of latent class and economic factors.

...

The subject matter and formal power of a Police Authority

In the last twenty years, local police organisations have altered significantly both in size and in relation to political control. The 1964 Police Act hastened the movement towards large organisations and re-defined the political constraints. It abolished the Watch Committee, which had previously been nominated entirely from the local council, and replaced it with a Police Authority, of which one-third of the membership was to be drawn from the local magistrates' bench, the remainder of the members being elected as before. This new body lost, amongst other rights, the power of appointment of most police ranks – these devolving upon the Chief Constable. Similarly the new Authority was deprived of its previous disciplinary control of police appeals.

Conlin has outlined the functions of the Police Authority as follows:

(a) to provide as its primary duty . n adequate and efficient police force for the area under its jurisdiction;
(b) to appoint the Chief Constable and his immediate officers;
(c) to determine the police establishment and the number of persons of each rank.

Other, and less significant functions, include the provision of police buildings and equipment, and the recognition of instances of meritorious conduct.

The first three functions constitute the core of the power relationship between, on the one side, the Chief Constable and his staff and, on the other, the Police Authority.

1. The agenda of the Police Authority – the 'sick, the lame and the lazy'

The first consideration in developing an overview of the content and character of Police Authority meetings, and particularly of the handling of the financial relationship with the Chief Constable, was to substantiate the common assumption that the finances were actually negotiable. There is a convenient myth that the major factor in police force costs – the size of its establishment – is based on an immutable formula, thus denying the Police Authority any latitude in affecting the expense of the force. Briefly, ... this is not the case. The Police Authority has considerable freedom to alter the size of the force within the authorised establishment figure, and hence to alter the annual costs.

Nevertheless, members of the authority unanimously subscribed to the myth that the establishment was relatively inflexible, being based on objective criteria. A typical viewpoint was, 'it's based on population, that's the basis of it' (Magistrate Granby).

In fact, the variations in establishment size reflect more the idiosyncrasies of successive Chief Constables than any objective criteria. According to one such officer, establishments depend on a multiplicity of factors — each Chief Constable tends to evolve his own criteria — gives particular emphasis to the factors he sees as important in his own area. Establishments are related to the 'feel' one has about the area ... Thus Birmingham has particular ethnic problems with its large black population whereas here in this city, we don't have have such a minority and the crime problem is rather different. (Chief Constable of Steeltown)

Any decision by members on the estimates are therefore pre-empted by the assumption of objectivity in the police officer's requirements. As one member put it (Councillor Dennis), 'The Chief Constable never needs to justify his resources ... all the figures are there ... we're all laymen. We can't quarrel with figures.' Blumberg (1971, p. 60) makes the point this way: 'Like any other bureaucracy the police are under constant pressure to justify their budget. No argument for public funds is more persuasive than a battery of statistics which, valid or not, have a way of offsetting anticipated criticism.' As a former Chairman of the Authority said, 'The first thing that we take into account in considering the request for re- sources is that we are below establishment' (Councillor Alexander).

It was clear from the replies of all members that the authority spent a minimal amount of time in discussion of the police estimates. What then does it actually do during its six-weekly meetings? A magistrate member (Jackson) expressed this succinctly:

Very little! The Watch Committee had considerable power but since the 1964 Act the powers of the committee were very much taken away — our power really is paying the wages and retiring the chaps. Frankly, I've never understood what our powers were — this was one of the early questions that I asked. It seemed rather a waste of time going to a com- mittee where one has no powers of any kind, particularly when you're a senior chap in the law as I am, and I quite frankly don't know what our powers are at all, and I don't think that we do fulfil any great purpose except in an emergency.

As one councillor (Shingles) said, 'What do we talk about? — the sick, the lame and the lazy' — the problems of the police force resulting from the incapacitation of officers either by illness or injury, or the unwilling- ness of ex-policemen to vacate police housing. 'There's nothing meaty about the agenda at all — medical matters, awards to police officers, the closure of police stations, the annual inspections — we never discussed the actual operations of the police.' (Alderman Mint). The agenda — devised in a prior informal meeting by the Chairman and the Chief Constable — is dominated by matters of this type ...

The members of the committee are inundated ('the agenda is two inches thick') with data of a largely insignificant nature. Any disposition to be critical is lost in the morass of such detail. Peripheral issues are magnified as the basis for detailed analysis and discussion. Financial matters are minimised. The detail contributes to an image of the force as a painstaking body of experts. It implies that all issues have already been considered in depth. The nature of the tabulation provides a framework for their analysis which precludes the consideration of alternative factors. The Chief Constable's office effectively controls the issues under discussion and pre-empts the decision-making process.

2. Conflict in decision-making

(i) The extent of actual conflict

According to Lukes's argument, not merely should we expect there to be a lack of controversy over important issues on the Police Authority but also that its members would deny even the potential for conflict. Within their own particular paradigm of the relationship between police officers and local citizens, it would be impossible to envisage areas of substantive conflict.

Not one of the members could remember dissent of any seriousness on the committee. The only example that three members could recall was an earlier disagreement involving the Home Office over the appointment of the Chief Constable. For the vast majority of interviewees, there had been no experience of conflict among themselves or between members and the Chief Constable. There was only one area of even slight disagreement that one typical member (Councillor Prescot) could recall, 'the only thing they ever argue about are the tenders submitted — why some are bigger than others.' Or, alternatively, a total denial 'Conflict on the Police Authority? Never! Always been plenty of debate — we get very worried about officers' illness and whether they should get paid or not. The Police Authority always gives a great deal of thought to the large numbers of police on duty — we give a lot of thought to the families.' (Alderman Thomas).

Similarly a magistrate's point of view (Turner) (he had previously held the local government post of Secretary to the Watch Committee): 'There have been no conflicts on the committee over the last thirty or forty years — some rows but not over police matters irrelevant to its work (and they were in the days of the old Watch Committee). On the Police Authority, we have never had any such rows.'

The local authority members were then asked to compare their experience on the authority with their service on other council committees. Again the responses were unanimous, although their experiences were of several different types of committee. A long-term Chairman of the Fire Brigade Committee (Alderman Wills): 'We would often over-ride what the Chief Fire Officer wanted. We would never do that with the Chief Constable.' Usually, the Education Committee was the reference point;

'members are much more likely to criticise the Director of Education.' (Councillor Pollok) 'There's not the same antipathy on the Police Authority as obtains in the Council Chamber or in a committee of the council. There's far more on the Education Committee. The unanimity's not surprising — it's the conflict on other committees that's surprising.' (Councillor Haggerty) Finally, 'there's lots of political debate on my other committee, Transport. I wanted to get the roads paved in an area of my ward — a Liberal Ward — and of course they didn't want me to get the credit for it so they opposed it.' (Councillor Old).

This consensus is most obvious with regard to the Chief Constable's presentation of the estimates. 'The resources requested by him go through on the nod.' (Councillor Dennis). 'He doesn't have to justify them! He wouldn't ask for more than he needed would he?' In other words, according to a majority of members of this partiuclar police authority it is simply a 'rubber stamp' (Magistrate Gold) for the wishes of the Chief Constable. The peculiar character of this consensus became most apparent when it was breached. The first instance ocurred not in opposition to a high demand for resources by the Chief Constable but because he was not asking for enough. The 1971 minutes of the committee reveal an attempt by a few of its members to persuade the authority and the Chief Constable to raise the demand for new officers beyond that proposed by the police. The second major example of this breach of consensus occurred in the context of plans for the succeeding force establishment following local government reorganisation. The Chief Constable had requested approval from the Home Office for a staff of 5,200 officers. The Home Office would only permit the new force to have a size roughly one-fifth less than requested. This the Chief Constable conceded, and consequently found himself justifying to the authority a smaller force than he had previously estimated as essential. Some members favoured the retention of the original figure but the majority reversed their own original stand and followed the Chief Constable's lead. When dissent did occur, it was directed to more rather than less resources. On both occasions, it was the Chief Constable's lead that was ultimately followed.

In conclusion the political party schisms that were evident on other local government committees were completely absent from the Police Authority. Despite the fact that, during the period of study, three political parties at various times held conflicting positions of interest and ascendancy on the local authority itself, and that this conflict seems to have been reflected extensively in the discussions of other committees, the interviewees were unanimous that 'politics never intruded here' (Councillor Chatburn) ...

(ii) The denial of conflict
In his criticism of Bachrach and Baratz, Lukes (1974) contends that their

argument ignores the extent to which consensus is not merely maintained by the avoidance of overt conflict but by the denial of the potential for such conflict. Conflict is not so much avoided as denied existence. In this context, policing would thus be seen as a form of legitimate social control freely accepted by the vast majority of citizens ...

Perhaps unsurprisingly, the members of this Police Authority entirely denied the possibility of the police being viewed from a conflict perspective. The question was posed to them in terms of possible polarities of Police Authority function – acting on the one hand as a watchdog to oversee the actions of the police on behalf of the public or, on the other hand, helping the police to help themselves by concentrating on the resolution of their administrative requirements. Most members concurred with the following sentiments:

A watchdog on behalf of the public? – Well, no, I think it was both – if you're watching and doing your job correctly you're looking after what the police do – surely then you're looking after the public as well – one covers the other. We're responsible to the public because we're voted in by them and we're looking after the police and therefore we're looking after both. (Alderman Forge)

Two members (both Conservative) markedly dissented from this viewpoint. One summed up his view of the Authority's functions:

the Police Authority should act as a public watchdog to prevent the development of a police state – it should make sure that the law-abiding shouldn't be pushed around by a police state and from the other side to deter the bad boys. (Councillor Baker)

But the rest of the members interviewed agreed with the opinion expressed in Alderman Beale's statement:

It's primary function is to do everything humanly possible to make the police an efficient force ... Having the authority as a kind of watchdog would only get in the way of the police – it would affect their discipline and you can't run a police force without discipline.

Not merely was the potential for opposition stemming from a class or ethnic basis denied, but the very existence of real economic schisms in society were disputed by nearly all members. This is not an unusual reaction from such a group of citizens until one considers them individually. The Chairman, for example, was the son of a pioneer trade unionist of the 1900s. At the other extreme, one of the magistrates, describing himself as a constitutionalist, illustrated his background by reference to his lawyer father and to his own position as High Bailiff of the city. Several of the Labour members had been active in industrial conflict both before and after the 1926 General Strike ...

Nevertheless, there was no obvious distinction between the two extremes in either their perception of the social order or in their perception of the police force itself. For most members, class was a remnant of the Industrial Revolution. Councillor Old represented the typical position: 'People are not class-conscious now – my own youngsters especially – everybody's equal'. It seemed as if long-term service in a position of relative power on the local authority had weaned away the explicit consciousness of class that had drawn many of the Labour councillors into the movement.

Attitudes to the police themselves were also demonstrably outside a class framework. Without exception, all the members interviewed expressed a viewpoint of the police based on a recollected childhood memory of the 'community bobby'. The present-day force was seen by members to be the direct descendant of such 'community police'. As such there could be no basis for legitimate oppositional tendencies.

A more definitive denial of potential conflict occurred in that area in which Hart (1951) claimed that the maximum disagreement between Chief Constable and Police Authority would occur – the response to the former's desire for increased resources. The members did not see it as a prime responsibility in this context to keep down local rates. If the Chief Constable argued, as he invariably did, for an increase in manpower and financial resources, his implicit and sometimes explicit justification in terms of an increased crime rate was accepted as a sufficient rationale. If recorded crime rose, then *ipso facto*, according to the Police Authority, police spending had also to rise.

However, it is possible to demonstrate an empirical refutation of the police financing/crime rate equation. A 1966 study conducted by the Scientific Adviser's Unit of the Home Office during the Chief Constable's own service in the Home Office research branch, concluded that those factors most relevant to decisions on resource allocation – police manpower and expenditure – were not significantly related to the reported crime rate. According to the Taverne Report (1966), 'it is clear that a better equipped police force can give equal or better service with a few men.' Klein (1974) has quoted more recent British and American evidence to support such a conclusion.

In other words, on the issue of the cost of the police, there existed substantial justification for disagreeing with the escalating costs. The members of the Authority unanimously denied the existence of such a potential criticism as a basis for challenging the estimates.

3. The mobilisation of bias to avoid controversy

It was suggested earlier that there are two components of the 'mobilisation of bias'. The phrase covers both the deliberate manipulation of processes in order to create a nondecision-making situation and also the acceptance of certain basic premises which of themselves rule out the basis for legitimate dissent or alternative policies.

The relationship between criminal statistics and police force establishment fits in the latter category. Given the premises on the development of crime – 'while the bobby's away, the criminal will play' (Councillor Bracken) – options in favour of keeping the rates down and the police force smaller were truly foreclosed.

Similarly, the denial of the sort of working-class suspicions of the police mentioned by Bantan (1974) prevented the development in the committee of any awareness of tension between the public and the police.

With regard to the first category of deliberate and conscious manipulation, a significant amount did occur. This involved such practices as the selection of the members for the Police Authority, the socializing of new members, and the influencing of the local press. Council members of the committee were selected on the basis of age and seniority to a far greater extent than on other local government committees. Their average age was in the late sixties and the majority had served on more than four committees.

This was partly for historical reasons – 'it's the major committee of the council – an absolutely premier committee' (Alderman Mint) ... A status prize for local councillors, it was a reward for long service and obedience to the party line.

A deliberate process of selection occurred. 'We made sure that those who were appointed were responsible people' (Councillor Chatburn) ...

The membership of the committee was therefore manipulated. Only more 'responsible' and 'moderate' council members gained easy admittance. Where – due to the changing political structure of the council itself – an assumed 'radical' (Mrs Old) was forced on to an unwilling Police Authority, then over a short period of time, she herself was socialised into a less deviant posture ...

Not only is the membership contrived in a way that deflects possible criticism of the police force accounts, but also the information received on police activity is channelled to members through a process of distortion. Manning (1971) makes this point:

what activity the public does observe is filtered through the media with its special devices for creating a version of reality. The public's meaning of a police action is rarely gathered from first-hand experience, but from the constructed imagery of the media which, in turn, rely upon official police sources for their presentation of the news. The police for their part understandably manipulate public appearances as much as they possibly can in order to gain and maintain public support.

In this research project, a number of such devices were encountered, each of which contributed to an image of the local force as an effective body of law-enforcing experts. The major problem for police officials

is to produce an image of police organisation and efficiency sufficient
to convince the sources of finance — the Police Authorities and the Home
Office — that additional resources will be put to good use.

Several commentators have dealt with the question of the effects of
financial controls on the policies of police administrators. Cain (1973,
p. 239) suggests that,

officials in the Home Office require evidence of output to legitimise their
decisions about expenditure. The Chief Constables need money to police
better in their existing way, but in some cases, the negotiation for money
is self-defeating in their terms, since in order to get it, it may be necessary
to re-define their tasks and start policing in a different way.

... In this study, it was apparent that the action of certain police units
(particularly the activities of the local Task Force) could be construed as
devices for manipulating the image of the police. Two rather different
examples of the 'manipulation of bias' will be outlined here—the handling
of 'complaints against the police' by the Chief Constable and the contribution of local newspapers to the establishment of 'areas of nondecision-
making'.

(i) Complaints against the police
The 1975 study by Box and Russell documents the class bias within the
present system of complaint-handling. They demonstrate several devices
which are utilised by police officers to control processing of such complaints. These complaints are not only potentially damaging to the careers
of individual police officers but they also threaten the image of the local
force itself.

Complaints pose a major problem for any senior officer concerned to
defend and enhance that image. This is particularly true in this city which
in a normal year (1972) had twice the national average number of complaints levied against individual officers. The suggestion that police officers
act on occasion to the detrimental interest of certain members of the public could have unfortunate consequences for a Chief Constable wishing
both to preserve a conception of the force as a model of efficiency and
expertise and also to safeguard the police estimates.

Two techniques are utilised to nullify the effects of such bad publicity on the Police Authority. After the operation of the devices discussed
by Box and Russell, the Chief Constable still has to devise techniques to
deal with the residual group of complainants.

The *first* technique is by manipulative portrayal of the overall situation
in his annual Report. In the 1972 Report, for example, of the recorded
591 complaints, only 43 were upheld after internal police investigation
(this, incidentally, is significantly higher than the national average). This
apparently innocuous piece of accounting was then followed by:

In 96 instances, complaints were voluntarily withdrawn by the complainants when interviewed by the investigating officer. Generally, these complaints were of a trivial nature, more often than not arising from a misunderstanding and, of course, their inclusion gives an impression of a greater rise in recorded complaints than was actually the case ... I would again emphasise that the thorough investigation of complaints ... throws a heavy burden on my senior officers ... Much time is devoted to their enquiries which often results in them being regularly engaged away from their normal duties ... It is becoming evident that many members of the public complain merely to bring their feelings to the attention of the police officer in question ... It is also plain that some complaints are made with a view to delay or even prevent criminal proceedings being taken against the complainant ... I think it is often over-looked that a police officer is an ordinary human being, doing his best to carry out a difficult job in often very trying circumstances. The constant threat of a formal investigation must have an unsettling effect on many officers ... It is perhaps fortunate that the police officer of today has, of necessity, learned to live with the constant sniping at his profession and reluctantly accepts the complaints procedure as an expression of the changing values of our society.

In this statement, the Chief Constable achieves three related objectives. He demonstrates that according to his body of experts, who are presented as neutral and professional, there are very few real complaints. 'We know that 95 per cent of complaints against the police are unjustified.' (Magistrate Jackson). The large number of initial objections is narrowed to a few 'real' ones.

Secondly, many complaints are portrayed as stemming from either naïveté or mischievousness, and the implication is made that the members of the authority should not in general regard them with any gravity. Finally, the Chief Constable reinforces the image of the police officer as a hard-working professional, attempting to cope with the increasing pressures of a changing world.

The *second* device used by the Chief Constable to minimise the harmful effects of complaints is one of juxtaposing the record of complaints with that of the public commendations received. 'The record of police complaints comes to the committee but it is more than counterbalanced by the presentation of the record of public gratitude to the police.' (Magistrate Gold). Immediately after listing the result of the complaints investigation, the Chief Constable reads out to the members of the Authority letters from the public expressing appreciation of the services of the police ...

The members of the authority are not in any case disposed to consider the complaints of the public as being of great significance. None saw it as part of their function as Police Authority members to raise individual complaints with the police. One stark view was 'When the police thump someone, the bloke usually deserves all he gets.' (Alderman Beale). A more detailed outline of members' views came from the former Chairman of the Authority:

If a complaint was made by a member of the public to a councillor on the Police Authority, it wouldn't be brought up at the committee because it would be too lengthy. What I would do in that case would be to ring up the Chief Constable ... and ask for a report ... I am quite happy about the policy carrying out their own investigation because I have always had satisfaction — you're not treated by them as a member of the Authority but as a city councillor. Whether I had any weight because of my position on the Authority I don't know but I have never met a councillor who has not been treated by the police with respect ... as far as the Police Authority is concerned, to try and be judge and jury into police matters wouldn't be effective at all — the police themselves judging their own cases are the most effective ... it is generally satisfying to the Police Federation and all those connected with it is that justice is done. We're laymen — we are not experts — we don't have the knowledge to enquire deeply into police matters. From the police agenda, you see how many people complain against the police and how few are justified. (Councillor Baker).

In conclusion therefore, the police are presented as experts quite capable of handling public complaints with due neutrality. The complaint is not a public concern but an internal police affair. The Chief Constable effectively neutralises the effects of complaints against the police by utilising the formal statement of investigation by the juxta-position device, and by relying on the predisposition of members of the authority both with regard to their own function and also with regard to their view of him and his officers as professional experts. Autonomously derived predispositions are reinforced by procedural and material manipulation.

(ii) The image of the police in the local press
In the city, local newspapers provide the main source of information to the majority of the public on the activities of the police. Like other local inhabitants, Police Authority members are exposed to the particular emphasis and interpretations provided by their media. The newspaper stories contextualised decision-making on police resources and are an important factor in the mobilisation of bias.

The recent substantive research of Chibnall (1975) has illustrated the interpretative influence of newspaper reporting on public perception of the activities of the police. In the present research, the contribution of the press to the decision-making process has been assessed by reference to the treatment given by the two local newspapers to a particular recurrent event — the publication of the annual Chief Constable's Report.

The newspaper stories were seen as having several related functions. They reinforce existing 'common-sense' theories about crime and the police. They emphasise the causal factors on which these theories are based and dismiss other factors as peripheral. In doing so, they map out the area of nondecision-making.

Firstly, the interpretation placed on the Report was that intended by the Chief Constable. The story appearing in the newspapers took its theme directly and without apparent deviation from the major emphasis in the Report. In the three Reports in which the Chief Constable emphasised the relationship between the rise in crime and the size of the force, the newspaper stories followed suit. Conversely, on the other two occasions, when the connection was not made in the Reports, it did not appear in the newspapers. In essence, the Press stories were paraphrases of the Reports.

Secondly, the Reports only merited front-page treatment and major headlines when the connection was made. On the other occasions, the Reports were summarised in a comparatively insignificant context. Typical treatment of the former was the lead story in April 1969 – 'POLICE CHIEF ASKS FOR 625 MORE MEN AS CITY CRIME LEAPS 17%'.

Finally, only when the two factors of crime rate and police shortage were juxtaposed did the Chief Constable's Report justify a follow-up story. The headline story of April 1970 is typical. 'IF THE POLICE HAD THE MANPOWER – 618 BELOW STRENGTH'. This emphasis on the increased manpower needed by the police to cope with a rising crime rate was followed two days later by a full-page interview with the then Chairman of the Police Authority which elaborated exactly the same point.

The implication of this sample of media material is apparent. The connection between the variations in crime and police resources is only made by the Press when the Chief Constable chooses to postulate such a relationship. Secondly, extra emphasis is only given when such a connection is made. Two contributions are consequently made to the image of the force and to the demarcation of decision-making on the Police Authority.

Firstly, crime has increased because insufficient staff have been made available to the police. Secondly, the police are inefficient in crime prevention and solution only because of this understaffing. The specialist on criminal affairs – the Chief Constable – has provided a 'rational' explanation of the increase in crime, an explanation which is readily accepted and which in a circular sense, develops the public view of that officer as an expert and pre-empts criticism of the estimates.

Discussion

The research conducted on this particular Police Authority suggests strongly that it did not provide for an adequate accounting of police expenditure. By implication, its effective power in other areas of the relationship between the Chief Constable and itself would also seem to

have been negligible. The evidence gathered suggests the following conclusions:

1. The Authority conducted a process of nondecision-making with regard
   to the activities and demands of the local police force;
2. Members denied the potential existence of legitimate grounds for
   critically appraising police resources;
3. Various devices were used both to deny and to prevent conflict over
   police demands.

5.3   A. Cawson

PLURALISM, CORPORATISM AND THE ROLE OF THE STATE[1]

From *Government and Opposition*, vol. 13 no. 2, pp. 178–98 (1978).

There has recently been a spate of writing on the concept on corporatism as part of the interpretation of contemporary British politics,[2] and a series of articles by J.T. Winkler (1975, 1976, 1977) has provided a comprehensive and detailed frameword for the analysis of certain features of political practice ...

This literature is primarily concerned with the explanation of the significance of government attempts to establish economic planning.[3] and to regulate the economy through constraints on price and income movements.[4] Such attempts have been justified by an important corporatist trend in the ideologies of both major political parties,[5] so that a convincing case may be made out for the view that corporatism may reflect a significant degree of policy consensus between Conservative and Labour governments, promoted by the objective constraints within which the parties must operate (see Beer, 1969, p. 406).

In its policy prescriptions corporatist thought in both Conservative and Labour Parties appears radical: a strong concern for efficiency and rationality is accompanied by an apparently refreshing insistence on the inappropriateness of earlier ideological conflicts. Thus Tony Benn is able to sidestep the Clause IV debate by his insistence that private industry can be subjected to state control without nationalization, and Peter Walker can criticize the social consequences of market allocation without advocating the overthrow of private capital. A former civil servant sees the extremes of central state control and *laissez-faire* as 'unrealistic' and argues on explicitly non-ideological grounds for 'a concordat between the major political parties and other centres of influence about that area of the national interest concerning economic relations which is not to be continuously subject to the slings and arrows of party politics' (Abraham, 1974, p. 7).

As a shorthand for contemporary political doctrine corporatism appears particularly appropriate for two reasons. First, the insistent emphasis on 'the national interest' reflects a hostilistic social theory in which the interests of society as a whole are argued to transcend narrow sectional interests, and thus dictate specific policy approaches. Society is held to comprise interdependent parts with the health of the whole contingent upon the 'correct' functioning of the parts. Hence the almost inescapable organic analogy and the throwback to medieval doctrines of society as a corporate entity. Second, the emergence of functional groups with real socio-economic and political power has emphasized the reality of inter-dependence in modern industrial society. Whether these groups be trade unions or business corporations, governments have had to adjust to the existence of centres of power outside the state.[6] Thus the corporation — specialized and bureaucratized — has emerged as the organizational form of the corporate society.

There are, however, major problems in attempting to use convenient terms as instruments of political analysis, and Winkler's (1977) claim that corporatism represents an ideal type of economic system requires some investigation. This article will be concerned with the implications of the development of a corporate economy for political theory, and with the analysis of significant trends in corporatist practice outside as well as within the economic sphere ... Here I will argue that contemporary democratic theory, and in particular the emphasis on functional participation in a pluralist democracy, has tended to legitimize important features of corporatist practice. Without a theory which accepts interest groups as a legitimate if not indispensable part of the democratic process, corporatist policies would not find such ready acceptance among political parties and public opinion.

Winkler's insistence that emergent corporatism can be defined by a qualitative change in the role of the state in response to structural changes in the economy seems to neglect an equally important series of develop-ments in politics and administration: in particular the increasing rational-ization of policy-making in central and local government through various forms of planning. Administrative practices such as performance budgeting and corporate management reflect a concern for efficiency in resource allocation which can be seen as part of a deep-rooted transformation in industrial society with profound consequences for the distribution of political power amongst social groups and social classes.[7] In addition a transformation of the way in which interests are represented in the pol-itical process, akin to the corporatization of the industrial economy, forms an important part of the trend towards corporatism. Winkler's concern with the effects of corporatist policy-making neglects the political dimen-sion of the relationship between the state and society. Such considerations require analysis in relation to the constraints of central policy-making posed by the pattern of economic organization, which Winkler has done much to clarify.

Finally attention must be paid to the political consequences of cor-poratism ... In this article I will argue that the political system which corresponds to the advanced capitalist economy embraces both a 'corporate sector' and a 'pluralist sector' of interest representation, and that the growth of the former at the expense of the latter can be seen as leading to the eclipse of liberal democracy. Whether such an eclipse will feature redistributive or conservative corporatism will in large part depend upon the political strategies adopted by the Labour movement and the working class: at the present time the indications are that the brand of corporatist thinking adopted on the left of the Labour Party and in the trade unions will serve to institutionalize rather than to moderate existing inequalities.[8]

Towards a definition of corporatism

Liberal democratic theory rests on the basic assumption that the policy preferences of individuals are transmitted to policy makers through the electoral system, with the assistance of mediation from political parties and interest groups.[9] The political market place is held to be analogous to the competitive economy in that the elector replaces the consumer as the principal determinant of market behaviour. Just as economic theory as adapted to the reality of imperfect competition in the modern economy, contemporary democratic theorists have followed Schumpeter's (1947, p. 269) revision of classical democratic theory, restricting the role of the electorate to a periodic choice between opposing teams of leaders who are then left to make policy independently of direct participation by the mass of electors. Schumpeter's model, however, ignores the increasingly important part in policy formation played by interest groups, and neglects also the equally vital question of the power of elected governments in relation to the permanent bureaucracy (*ibid.*, pp. 256–64).

Both neo-classical theories of imperfect competition and contemporary democratic theories have recently been the subject of growing criticism from Marxist as well as non-Marxist authors.[10] The separation of political power from economic interests which was once held to be the hallmark of liberal democracy is questioned by a revival of interest in political economy ... and the rediscovery of the state as a concept in political analysis.[11]

Political theorists adjusted to the existence and evident power of interest groups by according them a central place in the doctrine of pluralist democracy. It was assumed that government was the arbiter of the competition between groups, and that the outcome of the group process would reflect the public's policy preferences.[12] Thus the student of politics could confine himself to taxonomies which divided interests into promotional or sectional groups,[13] and the basic assumptions of liberal democracy could remain unchallenged. Apart from seminal works by Theodore Lowi (1969) for the United States, and Samuel Beer (1969) for Britain, other political scientists have attempted to detect the changes in democratic practice which accompanied the growth in importance of interest groups. In Britain recently only Robert Benewick (1973; 1974) has heeded the numerous critiques of pluralist democracy by calling for the reclassification of interest groups according to which they are an established (and hence noncompetitive) part of modern government.

If the essential feature of liberal democracy is the relationship between individual electors and sovereign parliament (Birch, 1964), then that of corporatism is the representation of functional interests, whether or not this is institutionalized in parliamentary form ...

It is clear that the relationship between functional interests and the state comprises both interest articulation (the classic pressure group role) and the responsibility for delegated enforcement of government policy. If there is a trend towards corporate representation the former role will increasingly be institutionalized in the form of privileged access to government in exchange for participation in policy implementation. This may be accomplished within the framework of existing groups, or special associations may be created for this purpose.[14] In either case the competitive role of interest groups — which is held to safeguard the democratic nature of pluralism — will be replaced by an orderly co-operative and stable relationship ...

Since the major determinant of the corporatist trend is concentration in the economic structure and in the plurality of political interests, it is clear that corporate representation will become most fully developed in economic issues reflecting the strategic role of the state, and interest groups will be incorporated or established where coordination and planning is recognized as essential to the performance of this role. Thus the development of the corporate economy will require a corporate state to the extent that economic policy is the principal determinant of the global role of the state. Pluralist competition between non-incorporated interests may continue to exist in the interstices of the corporate state, and individual representation through Parliament may continue to coexist with increasingly formalized functional representation. In essence therefore a corporate state may be established without the emergence of society as 'a single vast corporation, with every person an involuntary member or employee', as envisaged by Charles Reich (1971, p. 65) ...

Combining the different concerns of Winkler and Schmitter, the following definition of a corporatist system is suggested:

Corporatism is a politico-economic system in which the state directs the activities of predominantly privately-owned industry in partnership with the representatives of a limited number of singular, compulsory, noncompetitive, hierarchically ordered and functionally differentiated interest groups.

This definition is concerned with practice rather than ideology, and focusses attention on the reciprocal relationships between the state and organized interests in society in respect of the formation and execution of public policy.

Pluralism, elitism and corporatism

A theory of emergent corporatism based on the extent to which interest representation is hierarchically organized into a limited number of functional groups can throw fresh light on a major contemporary debate in the sociology of power in liberal democracies: that between pluralists who maintain that power is widely distributed among competing groups, and those who argue that power is concentrated in the hands of an elite or a number of elites within a ruling class.[15] The most recent aspect of the debate centres around the neo-elitists' contention that an apparent plurality of interests obscures the control by an elite of the agenda for public decision-making, and the argument that the pluralists' obsession with empirically observable power relations obscures the perception of non-decision making and manipulation as aspects of the exercise of power.[16] Thus, it is argued, political routines which cannot be observed by orthodox decisional methods can help to explain why the distribution of rewards in political systems does not reflect the characteristics of observable group competition.[17] According to these theories a sharply pyramidal structure of power, as indicated by persistently inegalitarian distributions of income and wealth,[18] is consistent with observable pluralism insofar as these are maintained by political routines which are not in that part of the agenda malleable through group competition.

The major difficulty in applying such approaches to the analysis of advanced industrial states is that both the pluralists and their neo-elitist critics base their analyses independently of any consideration of the role of the state in relation to the reproduction of the conditions necessary for the maintenance of the social and economic order ...

What appears to be necessary to interpret these contemporary debates is a theory of the extension of the scope and level of state activity in response to economic, social and technological change, in relation to the requirements for an effective system of interest representation.[19] The following is an outline of what might constitute the basic elements of such an approach. The three central developments which require explanation and inter-relating are:

(1) changes in the internal structure, operation, and conditions required for the maintenance of the capitalist economy;
(2) changes in the composition, activities and role of the state, especially as they are contingent upon (1);
(3) changes in the pattern of interest representation which correspond to (1) and (2).

The four factors listed by Winkler (1976, p. 117) as the causes of corporatism can be taken as appropriate starting points: industrial concentration, declining profitability, technological development and increased international competition ...

During the early period of capitalist development the role of the state was restricted to the enforcement of a legal structure necessary for the market to function: the liberal state guaranteed freedom of contract and trade and dismantled the restrictive apparatus of the feudal economy.[20] As industrial capitalism developed on a large scale a disenfranchised urban working class began to threaten the stability of the liberal state. The extension of voting rights to the urban proletariat represented the transformation of the liberal state into liberal democracy, and enabled the state to be more responsive to the requirements of the developing industrial economy. The organization of trade unions and their political incorporation into the Labour Party ensured that working class consciousness would be moulded by acceptance of the legitimacy of the capitalist order, and confined the representation of working-class interests within the party system.[21] British trade unions were 'economist' in that their demands were restricted to economic improvement under capitalism, and there did not develop a class politics dedicated to the overthrow of bourgeois rule.[22] Up to the first world war the liberal-democratic state was *laissez-faire* in its economic policy, and its social concern was largely directed towards removing the worst features of exploitation in capitalist production. The role of the state was thus, in Winkler's useful terminology, facilitative, and the control of the state by the bourgeois class was mediated and moderated by the representation of working class interests through the established political parties.

The crucial period of change for the analysis of emergent corporatism begins with the first world war which precipitated state intervention both in the economy, and increasingly in areas of social policy.[24] The major stimulus towards supportive intervention occurred with the great depression and the acceptance of the Keynesian critique of the self-regulating capitalist economy.[25] At the same time that central government was becoming more involved in economic regulation and the framing of social policy, local government too was expanding the extent and scope of its provision.[26] Among the consequences of increased state activity was a growing emphasis on economic regulation and social policy in the major parties[27] and the emergence of functional interest associations aiming to influence and mediate state activity in various sectors.[28] In the economic field the most influential of these were the cartels through which manufacturers protected themselves against the harmful features of oligopolistic competition.[29]

For the purposes of this analysis the crucial transformation occurs when interest groups change from being private protective associations and move towards the establishment of regular and mutually supportive relationships with government. This 'osmotic process'[30] is determined first of all by the state's role as guarantor of capitalism to perform the integrative and regulatory role which the market can no longer achieve by itself the state requires specialized knowledge and professional capability in addition to the legitimacy conferred by consultation and representation. To the extent that the economic role is the fundamental one, access and mutual support will be granted to the representatives of indispensable economic interests. Thus producer groups will be corporatized as a necessity whilst the expansion and activity of consumer groups will occur largely outside the purview of the state.[31] This important point can help to explain why neither pluralism nor elitism as ideal types can be taken to represent the totality of interests under capitalism, and can permit a better explanation of group politics by distinguishing between groups according to their significance for the activities of the state rather than according to their subjective concerns.

The interpenetration of groups and the state apparatus develops unevenly according to the changing requirements for capitalist reproduction at different stages of development. It is most highly developed and institutionalized where co-operation is most indispensable in the pursuit of collective goals such as stable prices and regulated income growth in the post-war period,[32] and least developed in sectors where market mechanisms can continue to operate, sometimes alongside direct state provision. Thus in the field of housing state intervention to provide council housing was precipitated by working-class demands which seemed likely to pose a threat to the state,[33] whilst at the same time helped to ensure the reproduction of labour power necessary for the survival of capitalist production.[34] Because of the special nature of the housing market as spatially diffused, and of housing as both an investment and consumption good, consumer interests did not need to be specifically organized, but for council housing could be mediated through local government, and for owner-occupied housing could be directed through negotiated agreements with building societies. Since those in most need of housing in the present day tend to be economically inactive, ill-organized and ineffective as an interest group, the state need neither grant housing pressure groups effective access nor attempt to co-opt them into a client relationship. So long as state housing policy copes with the needs and demands of the middle class through owner occupation, and the working class through local authority housing, organizations such as Shelter will remain in Benewick's third world of pressure groups.

If one turns from housing to another area of social provision — health services — the picture is quite different. The foundation of the National Health Service in 1948 followed a prolonged series of negotiations with associations representing the professional interests of doctors and specialists.[35] Their co-operation and expertise was acknowledged to be necessary for the success of government policy, and the price paid by the state in return for this co-operation, apart from concessions for example on private beds within NHS hospitals, was to frame the relevant legislation as an

enabling Act which allowed the details to be completed subsequently
after prolonged bargaining between British Medical Association officials
and civil servants in the Ministry of Health. In part this difference in the
form of interest representation reflects the more urgent commitment of
the Attlee government to the NHS, in part the greater degree of profes-
sionalization in medicine as compared to housing, and in part the greater
potential contribution of socialized medicine to the efficiency of the
labour force.

Clearly the hypotheses advanced here, linking the growth of corporate
forms of interest representation and the role of the state to the needs of
the capitalist economy at particular stages of development, are preliminary and tentative. The implication, however, is that a full understanding
of the significance of pressure group activity and of the distribution of
power in capitalist society needs to be derived not on the basis of abstracted empiricist theories of pluralism or ideologically based assumptions
of class rule, but on a historical and materialist analysis of the changing
political structures which correspond to different stages of capitalist
development. So far I have outlined the uneven process accompanying
the expanding role of the state whereby interests in certain sectors become
corporatized leaving those in other sectors disorganized and pluralistic ...

Conclusion

The imperatives of rationalization and planning which characterize the
advanced capitalist state impose specific requirements for interest representation and legitimacy through institutionalized mechanisms of
participation. Apart from the need to regulate the economy, the trend
towards corporatism can be observed in land-use planning,[36] local government, health administration, water supply, education, and in many other
areas of established public policy. In these areas 'official' ideologies of
public participation have been developed to legitimize state intervention
and mobilize public support.[37] In other areas where the imperative for
state intervention has been less insistent market mechanisms still play
an important part in resource allocation, and interest representation
conforms more nearly to the classic pluralist model. In the economic
sphere small business still lacks corporatist representation on a par with
large industry and organized labour, though even here the ubiquity of
the corporate imperative can be observed.[38] In the non-economic sphere
the progress of corporatist development is more problematic, although
the rationalization of state activity accompanies the increasing scope of
state intervention, and it is unlikely that any policy area can be kept in
isolation from developments within the economic sphere.

As the corporatization of political life proceeds the residual power of
liberal-individualist representational institutions will decrease. The decline

in the power of Parliament is a commonplace observation in textbooks on British politics; almost as frequent are comments upon the accretion of power by technocrats in local government at the expense of that of elected councillors. Less often stressed, but perhaps more significant, is the extent to which rational policy-making methodologies themselves prescribe the form in which information on public preferences should be cast, which itself favours the development of corporate forms of interest representation.[39]

If the fundamental causes of corporatism are long-term changes in economic structure and technological development, then a reversal of the process in the short term seems unlikely. Economic liberalist prescriptions such as those of the Selsdon phase of the Health government in 1970–72 seem destined to be forestalled by objective constraints. Indeed if such policies were intended to reverse rather than merely stem the tide towards corporatism, a *dirigiste* state would be required to enforce anti-monopolistic practices which in the end would be likely to have the opposite effect.

Notes

1   My thanks are due to Robert Benewick for helpful comments on an earlier draft of this article. He is in no way responsible for its deficiencies.
2   For example Pahl and Winkler (1975, 1976). There have also been sceptical and critical views, e.g. Brittan (1975*a*), Joseph (1976) and Drucker (1977).
3   Shonfield's (1965) interpretation of the British experience of indicative planning in the 1960s uses the concept of corporatism.
4   The form of regulation through negotiation between government and the 'peak' associations of industry and organized labour — tripartism — is taken to be an important, though problematic, feature of corporatist administration. See Marsh and Grant (1977).
5   On this point see especially Harris (1972) and Panitch (1976*a*).
6   This is the theme of Ionescu (1975), where the main corporate forces are identified as trade unions, industry and the regions.
7   For preliminary statements of this view in the British context see Benington (1976) and Cockburn (1977).
8   By this I mean the 'revisionist' thesis of socialism as public control without nationalization through the instrument of a quasi-autonomous corporation as advocated by Holland (1975) and adopted with some modifications (or 'watering down') in the Industry Act of 1975.
9   See Dearlove's excellent summary (Dearlove, 1973).
10 Galbraith (1974, 1975); Baran and Sweezey (1968); Miliband (1969); Pateman (1973).
11 Miliband (*op. cit.*); Poulantzas (1975).
12 The arch-exponents of this view were Bentley (1967; first published 1908); Truman (1951) and Latham (1952).

13 This terminology is Potter's (1961), but a similar kind of vertical categorization is made by Birch (1964); Finer (1966); Stewart (1958) and Moodie and Studdert-Kennedy (1970). Kimber and Richardson (1974, p. 3) argue that the classification of groups according to their subjective concerns 'has little analytic value' and that the sectional/ promotional distinction is 'only a guide to classification'. Unfortunately they do not say why it is useful to continue to classify groups according to a theory without much analytic value; perhaps it saves time in producing readers!

14 For example, in Britain the Confederation of British Industry was established in 1965 with government encouragement to facilitate tripartite negotiations on Labour's National Plan. See Marsh and Grant (1977, p. 25).

15 This debate is too well-known to require citation here: a useful bibliography especially of American sources may be found in Bonjean, Clark and Lineberry (1971, pp. 373–83).

16 See especially Bachrach and Baratz (1962, 1963); Bachrach (1969) and Lukes (1973).

17 Parry and Morriss (1974); Dearlove (1973); Saunders (1975).

18 See Urry and Wakeford (1973. Part One) for contributions on this theme.

19 This argument owes a great deal to Schmitter's preliminary and speculative proposition (1974, pp. 106–15).

20 For a concise statement of the connections between the evolution of the capitalist market economy and that of liberal democracy, see Macpherson (1965).

21 Miliband (1973) and Panitch (1976a).

22 Saville (1973) and Nairn (1965).

23 Fraser (1973).

24 Gilbert (1970).

25 Shonfield (1965).

26 Notably with the Local Government Act of 1929 which abolished the Poor Law Guardians and gave most of their functions to the local authorities. Fraser (1973, p. 174).

27 Culminating in the various reports commissioned by the coalition government during the second world war on education, coal, population, a National Health Service, full employment, industrial injuries, family allowances and of course the most famous of them all, that of the Beveridge Committee on social insurance. The social programme of the coalition government proposed 'to maintain the state sector at something like its war-time level, but to shift the bulk of spending from arms to welfare'. Gamble (1974, pp. 29–30).

28 With respect to industrial representation, for example, the precursors of the CBI were the Federation of British Industry (1916) and the National Union of Manufacturers (1916) which developed out of the divergence of interests between bigger industrialists and the smaller manufacturers, traders and professionals represented by the Association of British Chambers of Commerce. Grant and Marsh (1977, pp. 18–21).

29   Channon (1973, p. 27).
30   Schmitter (1974, p. 111).
31   Benewick's (1975, p. 421) study of pressure group politics has con-
     centrated on non-producer interests where he finds that 'the pluralist
     case for group competition and opposition may be exaggerated, but
     not for the civil liberties lobby'. Regulations of such interests by the
     state may become necessary, and thus interest representation more
     nearly approaches the ideal type of corporatism, if non-legitimate
     political activity (direct action) begins to threaten the stability of
     the state. So far this has not been necessary in Britain.
32   In the sense that 'peak' associations have been encouraged by govern-
     ments to attempt to monopolize interest representation, and help to
     'police' prices and incomes policy. The attempts have not, however,
     been a complete success, and a more cautious attitude than Winkler's
     in predicting future corporatist development is wise, as in Grant and
     Marsh (1977). There seems little doubt that the successful regulation
     of prices and incomes is an essential precondition of a fully corpora-
     tist system.
33   Dickens (1977).
34   Clarke and Ginsburg (1975, p. 14).
35   Eckstein (1960) and Foot (1975).
36   For an analysis of land-use planning in the context of corporatist
     development, see Cawson (1977).
37   For land-use planning see Skeffington Committee (1969). Critic of
     the actual practice of public participation in planning have recog-
     nized that for 'public' should be read 'approved middle class interest
     group.' See, for example, Hague and McCourt (1974).
38   Indicative of this might be the relative success of recent efforts to
     organize the self-employed through the National Federation for the
     Self-Employed. If the CBI or Retail Consortium model is followed
     one could predict an ultimate state-encouraged merger between the
     NFSE and other groups representing small business interests, and
     perhaps in future 'quadripartism'. See Grant and Marsh (1974).
39   For an elaboration of this point, see Cawson (1977).

5.4   E. L. Morse

FOREIGN POLICIES IN MODERNIZED SOCIETIES

The effects of *modernization* on the conduct of foreign policy can be analyzed in terms of policy *content*, the *processes* by which policy is formulated, and policy effectiveness, or *outcomes*. My general argument can be summarized as follows:

In terms of policy *content*, the ideal pattern of foreign policy, with its emphasis on high policy functions related to the maintenance of the integrity of the state (security and territorial defense) or to the enhancement of some attribute of the state (population, territory, fulfillment of national ideals), has been widened into — and frequently replaced by — a new pattern. For those states, like the United States and the Soviet Union in particular, with a large territorial and economic base, there is a broadening of the spectrum of policy goals, so that goals of wealth and welfare become as important as those of power and international position associated with high policy. For most other states, these older ideal patterns tend to be almost completely overshadowed by the growth in significance of low policies.[1]

What is apparently distinctive and new about these policies is that they seem to be primarily nonconflictual. At least the general framework of international relations has been reversed to a large degree because of the exigency of international cooperation for the attainment of basic domestic policy goals. If in an earlier period cooperation took place in a primarily conflictual context, now, under the impetus of modernization, conflicts among states tend to take place increasingly in a context that is primarily cooperative. Moreover, like the relations of which they are a part, some of these policies are merely fleeting and casual; others are explicitly cooperative and involve the production and distribution of collective goods at the international level[2] and require compatible efforts on the part of officials and other elite groups in different societies.

An additional distinctive quality in foreign policies of highly modernized societies is that the goods that are produced and that involve cooperative behavior *are seen as* economic goods, even though they may be essentially political. They arise from such phenomena as the growth in international trade and the need to regulate trade imbalances, to produce new liquidity to finance trade, and to maintain the whole set of regulatory devices required to govern economic behavior. Although many such goods are measurable primarily in economic terms, they are largely political and relate to one of the central features of politics under modernized conditions, where the politics of wealth and welfare have overshadowed the politics of power and position. The latter tend to be played out in economic terms, especially though not only among modernized societies. The high costs of the use of force, among other things, have made trade rounds in the General Agreement on Tariffs and Trade (GATT) and reform measures in the International Monetary Fund (IMF) the essence of international politics today for the more highly modernized societies in their relations with one another. Less modernized societies too, especially in their relations with wealthier, more highly industrialized societies, place an emphasis on the distribution of primarily economic goods and sometimes attempt to gain other policy goals by the manipulation of market conditions, as has been the case especially with exporters of resources in recent years.

Before modernization foreign policy goals tended to be transcendental, by which we mean that they were never completely reducible to empirical states of affairs. Goals like 'security', 'grandeur', or 'power' are characteristic transcendental goals of foreign policy.[3] In the case of highly modernized societies an additional spectrum of goals develops, which tend to be predominantly empirical ones, or at least almost completely transferable to empirical ones, and which generally refer to qualities associated with the pursuit of wealth and welfare ...

With respect to the second set of policy conditions, the *processes* by which policy is formulated, it is modernization rather than democratization that seems to have transformed foreign policy decision making. Before modernization reached high levels, cabinet-style, closed-arena decision-making processes prevailed both domestically and in international negotiations. Now, while the locus of decision making has remained fundamentally administrative, the scale of modern administration has changed so greatly that decision making has become far more complex and increasingly open, if only because those involved in the policy process appeal to groups outside the official decision-making structure for support. Moreover, the infusion into foreign policy of ideologies that tend to deal with intersocietal rather than intergovernmental relations, together with enhanced international networks of communication, has made governments appeal increasingly to the populations and not simply the governments of other societies as a means of achieving their foreign policy goals.

Finally, with respect to the third set of foreign policy issues – those dealing with the problems of implementing and controlling foreign policy – conditions have also been transformed under modernization. In one sense, the problem of controlling events external to the state is the major problem of foreign policy regardless of the type of society involved. This is the case because political systems exist in an international arena whose fundamental feature is the absence of any overarching structures of political authority. At one time great powers could be differentiated from others by the degree to which they could control their external environments. But the growth in international interdependence has made the issue of control problematic for all societies, and, as I shall argue ..., all modernized societies have witnessed a loss of control not only over their international environments but also over domestic conditions. As a result of the complexity of the problem of control under conditions of interdependence, no state can be regarded as a great power in the old sense of the term. What is special, then, about foreign policies conducted under modernized conditions is the scale of the problem of control. I shall argue that the loss of control both domestically and in the external environment will prove to be the central problem of international politics in the coming years. This problem has significant implications, including several that concern the future of the nation-state and the nature of functional equivalents to it that can be devised in areas where governments have lost their effectiveness.

We will now investigate each of these components of foreign policy in somewhat greater detail.

The transformation of policy objectives

In recent years scholars concerned with international relations have become increasingly aware of the degree to which economic and other affairs associated with low policies have become central to foreign policy. For a long time, preoccupation with high policies and with traditional foreign policy objectives and instruments drew their attention away from the changes in policy goals that have accompanied modernization, and especially from the increased salience of low policies and the merging of goals of power and of plenty ...

Under modernization, the former identification of power and security with territory and population has been changed to an identification of welfare with economic growth and a just or equitable distribution of resources. As Klaus Knorr (1966, p. 21) has argued, 'Territorial conquest by force of arms has lost the perennial attraction it possessed throughout mankind's violent history.' Unlike the goals of power and prestige, the new goals of growth and the distribution of the fruits of abundance appear to be almost wholly commensurable. It would thus seem that foreign policy goals under modernized conditions are no longer as transcendental as they were under the old regime ...

Two general transformations associated with high levels of modernization appear to be responsible for the change. One has to do with the classical instruments of policy — armaments — and the changes brought about in external goals by the development of nuclear weapons and their delivery systems. The other relates to a more general transformation in domestic society under modernization.

The development of nuclear weapons has had so profound an impact on the conduct of foreign policy that it ought to receive a separate examination. I shall recapitulate here some of the major effects that have been noted as results of these weapons' emergence in global politics.[4] At a minimum, the developments of weapons of massive destruction, of delivery systems capable of launching them on target virtually instanteneously, and of international deterrence have been cross-cutting. On the one hand, these developments have made the territorial state incapable of providing security through defense, not simply because they are based on offensive weapons systems but also because they have created the first truly global system, unified by the possibility of generating unacceptable levels of human destruction that no state can potentially escape. On the other hand, nuclear weapons have paradoxically reaffirmed the viability of the nation-state as a political unit, by making the costs of expansion prohibitive ...

Nuclear weapons, the most massively destructive ones ever created, have helped bring about, not total war, but rather the rebirth of strategy in an era of total war because of the fear of the consequence of their use. They have imposed a rationality on policy and almost forced states — especially the superpowers — to avoid ideological conflict and focus upon mutual interests. They also have provided for stability among nuclear powers. But, given the costs of using them, they have paradoxically enhanced the freedom of action both of less developed societies and of allies of the superpowers. They thus have created a seemingly permanent tension between the major nuclear powers, which have a stake in the international status quo, and the others, which may tend to have a stake in changing the status quo in order to enhance their own autonomy and perhaps lower their dependence on the superpowers.

One key, then, to the obsolescence of territorial goals that accompanied the development of nuclear weapons has been the increased cost of territorial accretion. No modernized society can afford it. It should not be surprising, therefore, that major territorial disputes have virtually disappeared from relations among the highly modernized states. They occur either when there is no danger that nuclear weapons will be used, thus accompanying nation-building efforts in the nonmodernized world, or where little industrial infrastructure has been created that could significantly be destroyed in a territorial dispute (also only in the nonmodernized world). Modernized societies may be involved in major territorial disputes, but generally in cases which also involve some nonmodernized society, as in the border dispute between the Soviet Union and China. The decline in the significance of territoriality has also affected defensive strategies and alliances ...

Domestic economic growth, whose level and rate of change is one of the prime indices of modernization, has a profound effect on the relative priority of domestic and foreign policy goals as well as on their contents. Once economic growth reaches high levels and sets in as a continuous dynamic process increasing the real wealth of most members of society, the value of additions to national territory and population decreases and the 'domestic savings and investment and advancement of education, science, and technology are [seen as] the most profitable means and the most secure avenues to the attainment of wealth and welfare' (Knorr, 1966, p. 22). One consequence of high levels of economic growth, then, is the turning of minds away from those foreign policy goals pursued by the ruling elites of monarchic Europe and toward the further development of domestic wealth through domestic means and under peaceful conditions.[6]

Economic growth and the costs of pursuing activist foreign policy in a nuclear world offer only partial explanations of how foreign policy goals are transformed. The development of transnational structures and a set of interdependences among highly modernized societies also helps to explain the increased significance of low policies and the emergence of cooperative strategies in foreign policy. As will be argued ... the interactions of citizens across boundaries and actions by governments either to foster the interests of their citizens or as responses to private group behavior also help foster the pursuit of low policies. One paradox is that the goals of low policies are themselves undermined by the growing scope of nongovernmental, private interactions across boundaries.

Like that of nuclear weapons, the emergence of low policies both reflects and fosters cross-cutting effects. One aspect of them reflects a motivation of governments to cooperate with others and to build new transnational structures, not simply to foster foreign policy goals but, more importantly, for the achievement of domestic goals ...

The incentives for cooperative behavior and the construction of new international organizations may be seen in the creation of the customs union in Europe (European Economic Community). One of the motivations for the fostering of the Common Market was the increased wealth such as an enlarged market brings to the citizens of each member state as a result of increased levels of trade. The fostering of domestic goals through international behavior creates that principal characteristic of foreign policies under modernized conditions that reflects more the pole of cooperation than the pole of conflict. Conflictual or political activities, therefore, take place within the context of predominantly cooperative arrangements ...

It would be wrong, however, to overestimate the degree to which governments have transcended a world of conflictual behavior. There are in fact several elements of conflict in the economic goals that the industrialized market-based economies have been pursuing and that make the international coordination of policies highly desirable but also extremely difficult. Some of these stem from confusion that has accompanied the rapid shifts in economic power which began to take place after the late 1960s. Others, labeled 'neomercantilism' in recent discussions of foreign economic policy, stem from the various reasons that impel governments to pursue policies aimed at the achievement of a current account surplus in their balance of payments.[7] Such policies are inevitably conflictual, since it is impossible for all to achieve a surplus simultaneously — at least one must be in deficit if the others are to achieve that goal ... And if the advanced industrialized societies manage to minimize economic conflict by successfully and simultaneously maintaining current account surpluses, it will be the less developed countries which will have to accept deficits.

The fostering of economic and other low policies results, then, in both cooperative and conflictual behavior. The common interest of all industrialized societies in domestic gains forces them to cooperate with one another. The very act of cooperation and of fostering international interdependence also sets severe restrictions upon the traditional policy of independence and autonomy. With the emergence of high levels of interdependence reflecting both technological change and policies intentionally fostered by governments, the ideal view of state autonomy has been challenged, and this has greatly affected foreign policy behavior. No amount of political will can recreate a world where independence and autonomy can be obtained, except perhaps at costs that no governments are willing to incur because losses in wealth that would accompany increased autonomy would handicap the legitimacy of those governments in the eyes of their citizens.

Increased domestic demands and the allocation of resources

We have seen that one of the major influences in the transformation of foreign policy goals under modernization has been the replacement of the quest for power by the quest for social and economic wealth. This quest for wealth itself reflects one of the primary domestic consequences of modernization: the politicization of increasingly larger sectors in society, which place increasing demands upon governments to provide an enormous variety of social services. It is also a paradox at the heart of foreign policies in all modernized societies that these increased demands on governments create problems of resource allocation, at least in the short run. One result is that predominantly external goals decrease in priority relative to predominantly domestic goals. This has occurred at the same time that domestic conditions have become increasingly sensitive to international events as a result of the growth in international interdependence as well as of absolute increases in international activities by the citizens of most modernized societies.[8]

It is a distinctive feature of all governments in modernized societies, be they democratic or authoritarian, capitalist or socialist, that they have assumed great multifunctionality. Governments are looked to as creators of — as well as redistributors of — the common wealth. While the modern social-service state has been created by increasing demands put upon governments, these demands themselves have resulted from the increased politicization of individuals and groups. A government is impaled upon 'the dilemma of rising demands and insufficient resources' (Sprout and Sprout, 1963) when domestic demands are greater than available resources and, especially, when it wishes to maintain simultaneously existing levels of commitment abroad. Demands can arise from a variety of sources, including poverty groups desirous of obtaining a greater share of social wealth, military groups wanting new weapons systems, or citizens sensitive to the need for maintaining public order in societies increasingly sensitive to labor or minority group disruption. It is no accident that governmental allocations to education, health services, and other collective social enterprises have increased dramatically in all modernized societies. They reflect demands for a better life by all and increased costs of labor in the social sector, where gains from increased productivity are not great. These costs may be added to the 'rising cost and widening scope of activities required to keep mature urban societies viable' (*ibid.*, p. 685).

One of the inexorable results of governments of increased demands and rising costs is the curtailment of external commitments, or the decreased relative priority of foreign goals in comparison to domestic objectives. These curtailments add to the costs to any government of defense autonomy and independence ... However, as society becomes highly politicized, it also becomes increasingly likely that externally oriented allocations are highly visible, as in the case of British expenditures on maintaining forest east of Suez, or American expenditures on Vietnam. Such expenditures are therefore likely to be viewed as squandering of domestic wealth or as perverted governmental priorities. This is especially the case in democracies where allocations to external expenditures become weapons in the critical hands of political opposition groups.

The dilemma posed for governmental resource allocation by these demands can be met in several ways, but each has its costs to a government's domestic and foreign policies. The Sprouts (*ibid.*, pp. 690–91) summarize them as follows:

First, efforts may be made to *expand the economy* ...
Second, the rulers may prudentially *revise their order of priorities* ...
Third, the rulers may ... *divert public attention* to other values ...
Fourth, the men in power may try to *change the opinions of dissenters* ...
Fifth, ... the rulers may try to *silence dissent and opposition* ...

A sixth means of dealing with the dilemma is the fostering of cooperative and compatible efforts with other governments designed to share costs and increase the economic wealth available to all.

Each of the six ways out of the dilemma has been tried by most governments in modernized societies. Economic growth has been the most central and successful means, since it avoids some of the difficulties of redistributing social income. But it can have disruptive effects on some members of society who prefer the stability of the status quo, especially when some gains might be lost as a consequence of technological advance. One obvious example is the fear of shop owners that construction of large stores, including discount stores, will jeopardize their businesses. It also serves to increase international interdependence, which sacrifices national autonomy. Moreover, growth becomes more difficult to obtain as natural resources become scarce or rise in cost, as the oil crisis of 1973–74 vividly demonstrated.

Revising governmental priorities also helps meet domestic demands, but usually as the cost of international commitments and potentially at the cost of international stability if security is affected detrimentally. Diverting public attention and changing or silencing the views of dissenters also can be relied upon, but only for short-run gains, given the political repercussions of pursuing such policies over long periods of time. Finally, international cooperation, while it serves to create international goods, also increases international interdependence, which further limits the freedom of a modern state to pursue a traditional policy of national autonomy.

In the final analysis, there is no easy way out of this dilemma for a government. A decreased relative priority for external commitments, especially for military purposes, does seem inevitable, although other external commitments of a predominantly economic nature may be created. This relative decline in external priorities is, of course, reinforced by the international stability created by nuclear deterrence. In a world where international tensions rose dramatically from present levels, governments might well be more able to make domestic sacrifices for security purposes than they are today. The decline in national extroversion, it should be emphasized, has taken place paradoxically at a time when international interdependences have sensitized national economies to external events in an unprecedented fashion ...

Changes in the processes of foreign policy making

It would be surprising if the great changes that societies undergo as they become highly modernized did not have a profound effect upon the processes of policy making in domestic as well as foreign affairs. At the turn of the century a number of predictions were made that industrialization would breed democratization and that cabinet-style decision making in closed forums would yield to open diplomacy, more likely to lead to international stability and peace. Cabinet-style decision making is apparently something of the past, but despite the predictions concerning the democratization of foreign policy, policy processes have succumbed to administrative politics and have been bureaucratized. This has resulted from several factors, including the amount of information that must be gathered for effective policy making, especially as the number of states and functional areas that a government must deal with increases. Ironically, one rationale for the growth of administration in the policy process has been the need to increase national control; yet with the administrative revolution in government, great losses of control from the top have occurred. Policy, therefore, has become no more – and perhaps a good deal less – rational than it once was, at the very time when growth in complexity of international life has required rational policy making more than ever for state survival.

It is a paradox, then, that just as modernization has bred administrative professionalism and promises the growth of a rational administrative science, rationality models capable of understanding policy have decreased in importance and models of bureaucratic behavior purporting to explain policy making have become more important.[9] In modern bureaucracies, policy making tends to undermine rather than to enhance the ability of political leadership to pursue rationally a set of explicit external goals. Interest group politics have become more important, and foreign policy has tended to reflect what occurs within the bureaucracies upon which leadership depends for information and position papers, more than it does national policy requirements. One result is a form of policy rigidification that contradicts the needs of foreign policy for flexibility and freedom to maneuver.[10]

In modern bureaucracies, policy making involves two sorts of bargaining 'games'. One is lateral, between members of various administrative units, with overlapping jurisdictions in a particular set of issues (as for example, the overlapping jurisdictions of the Departments of Defense and State, the CIA, and the Arms Control and Disarmament Agency in arms control issues). The other is hierarchical, among members of different strata in a single agency (where one encounters cross-cutting efforts of different people to advance their own positions and power).[11] The emergence of a single spokesman in foreign affairs, frequently prescribed as necessary for security and policy flexibility, is made impossible by the characteristics of modern bureaucracies.[12] Plurality in the number of foreign policy voices inevitably accompanies the increased significance of routine, daily decision making, especially in areas of low policy ... With increases in routine policy making, control at the top is restricted and the autonomy of lower-level officials enhanced.

Several aspects of controlling routine decision making can be summarized in an examination of two problems, which I shall label the organizational problem and the problem of size.

The organizational problem is one that has perplexed specialists in administrative science and eluded most efforts to reform the processes of decision making for foreign affairs. The problem stems from the need to divide the functions of government according to predominantly domestic areas. Thus all modern governments have ministries or departments such as agriculture, labor, education, transportation, and finance. Unlike such departments under nonmodernized conditions, now each domestic area has a significant international bureau, which represents a response to the breakdown in the distinction between foreign and domestic affairs that fit the nineteenth-century model of administration. With the multiplication of international bureaus, the ability of a foreign ministry to control foreign policy or even to coordinate it on a rational basis is severely restricted. In fact, as low policies gain in importance, this problem is further exacerbated. It is made all the more difficult insofar as the representatives of these departments tend to seek total foreign as well as domestic control over issues that appear to be in their own domain. Thus, for example, the Treasury Department in the United States has sought to maintain control over foreign monetary policy, even though in some cases the interests of the Departments of State and Defense are at stake. This has been frequently detrimental to the pursuit of a policy that ought to take into account the manifold foreign policy stakes of the US government, as, for example, during the monetary crisis of 1971, when the decision to change the exchange rate of the dollar was made without consultation of the Secretaries of State and Defense or the President's Adviser for National Security Affairs.

This problem can sometimes be handled by interministerial committees that cross-cut different departments, thus enhancing the coordination of information and decision making. But the manifold attempts within the US and other governments to reorganize foreign policy decision making to counter the debilitating effects of the organizational problem have largely failed. The problem, moreover, is more difficult to handle the larger the size of the governmental organization involved. Thus the problem is more intractable in the United States than in a smaller government like France, and more difficult there than in Denmark. This leads us to the second difficulty in providing rational decision-making structures, that of size. The larger the organizations involved in foreign policy decision making, the greater is the information provided for decision making and the larger the number of individual stakes in decision making. One result is increased 'noise' within the government and a greater propensity for policy rigidification.

In summary, modernization has been associated with the notion that political structures can become increasingly rationalized and thus better able to maintain control over the events within society as well as in the environment of international affairs. Yet modernization also worsens the problem of control by creating roadblocks to efficient and rational policy-making. Modernization has also worsened another problem of control, one that has always been of central concern to foreign policy: the control over events external to the state ...

Problems of control

There is a special problem of control in foreign policy which is not found in domestic affairs and which stems from the inherent nature of international society. The international system is, by definition, composed of a collection of relatively autonomous and legally sovereign political units, with no highly institutionalized and overarching structure of political authority. This creates a perennial problem for foreign policy: how to control and coordinate events which take place outside one's society and which have an immediate impact on one's security and well-being. This problem is compounded when interdependences develop among societies, as they do after modernization begins. This is the case because interdependence erodes the autonomy of governmental action in both domestic and foreign affairs, but it does not necessarily affect the juridical status of the sovereignty of different decision-making units. With the development of interdependence, not only can benefits be gained for all societies, but international catastrophes and costs can also become worldwide, including nuclear war, uncontrolled inflation, or depression.

... For now, we will accept the assumption that interdependence creates losses of control both within and among societies, so long as mechanisms of international coordination and cooperation remain rudimentary, and we will look at some of the consequences of this problem for the conduct of foreign policy in highly modernized societies.

The major problem for foreign policy that stems from interdependence is that of the autonomy of rational decision making. Interdependence, by definition, makes governments increasingly dependent upon actions taken by other governments for the achievement of both domestic and foreign policy goals. Autonomy can usually be reasserted, but only by reducing international interdependence or by accepting some mechanisms of accommodation with foreign governments, including some forms of political integration. But this option is also highly costly, because of the increased domestic demands on governments to increase social wealth and the national need to maintain interdependences to get that wealth. Autonomy could also be reasserted if governments reduced the number of tasks that they have assumed, but that action would seriously jeopardize governmental legitimacy because it would result in a refusal to accept responsibilities expected by a highly politicized populace.

Governments have been aware of the dilemma that is posed for them by interdependence and have by and large been capable of adjusting to the cross-cutting costs and gains from interdependence. As Rosenau (1972, p. 163) has argued, 'the adaptive capacities of the modern nation-state are considerable'. What he calls 'preservative adaption' is the policy response to an environment that has changed rapidly and that is oriented to the conservative preservation of domestic social and political structures. Samuel Huntington goes further, arguing that interdependence and autonomy grow symbiotically.

Related to the problem of national autonomy is a second problem associated with the increased vulnerability of modernized societies to the actions of others under interdependent conditions. Governmental actions, as a consequence, are oriented less to the achievement of positive goals than they are to the more negative attempt to reduce their vulnerability to the actions of others and to increase others' vulnerabilities to their own actions. The result is a more subtle form of foreign policy than hitherto existed, based on the intended as well as unintended consequences of transnational activities. As Pierre Hassner (1971–72, pp. 12–13) has argued.

The essential characteristic of this state [of affairs] is neither force nor cooperation but the constant influence of societies on one another within the framework of a competition whose goals are less and less tangible, whose means are less and less direct, whose consequences are less and less calculable, precisely because they involve activities rather than strategies and because these activities are important as much because of their effects on what societies are as on what they *do* ...

The real race may be less to increase one's comparative power than to decrease one's comparative vulnerability, to manipulate not only an opponent's weaknesses but one's own, to encourage exported erosion or to control contagious explosions, to modify or maintain not so much territorial borders or even diplomatic alignments as what might be called the balance of will and the balance of expectations.

As a result of this exacerbation of the problem of control, a third issue has become significant in foreign policy in highly modernized societies. With increased interdependences and vulnerabilities, governments tend to pursue short-range and conservative foreign policies. Since interdependence brings about possibilities for uncontrolled change, governments fear the adverse consequences of any change that carries with it a large number of unknown factors. They would prefer generally to maintain the status quo, whose costs and benefits are familiar. The fear of uncertainties created by the international situation are, moreover, compounded by domestic uncertainties. The stability of highly modernized societies rests on political traditions and institutions that developed over a centuries-long process of nation building. Yet these structures submit to a fragility engendered by rapid social change. One result is that governance tends to be based on short-term and daily decision making oriented more to the maintenance of the status quo and operating the machinery of public affairs than to steering a course for the future based on grand political designs.

Conclusions

The argument [here] has rested on the hypothesis that under modernization, societies and governments confront a set of common problems and options that result in a convergence of their foreign policies along certain specified dimensions. I argued that governments of highly modernized societies may be characterized by the large scope of the objectives they pursue, the depth of demands placed upon them by constituents, the intermeshing of foreign and domestic concerns, the fragility of the societies that they govern, and the withering of governmental legitimacy that results from their inability to perform effectively. As a result of these changes, along with the growth in international interdependence, transformations have taken place in all three aspects of foreign policies. Their contents have become increasingly centered on low policies associated with the achievement of economic growth ... Policies have also undergone a radical change in administrative process, which has been designed to enhance the rationality and consistency of policy but which also results in a growth of irrationality and losses of control at the top because of the growth of politics within administrations. The control of policy effects has also been severely withered at a time when the stability imposed by nuclear deterrence has fostered a new type of international stability but when interdependence creates a new exigency for increased control.

These changes in foreign policies offer the citizens of all modernized societies opportunities for increased wealth and welfare that were unthinkable before modernization took place. They also, however, increase international instability insofar as interdependence has grown far in advance of either the instruments capable of controlling it or the knowledge social scientists have of its effects. The transformation of foreign policy, moreover, takes place wherever modernized societies exist, regardless of the ideologies and political myths accepted within them or the political institutions they possess.

Notes

1 Some scholars, like Stanley Hoffmann, offer another argument concerning low policies and high policies ... Hoffmann (1966) argues that nuclear deterrence has served to reinforce the attributes of the nation-state by stabilizing the structure of postwar international society. Low policies do not generate the spillover expected of them by prophets of international integration.

2 Definitions of public goods generally place emphasis on one society rather than on a group of societies. The focus is then on nonexclusivity

or the incapacity of a single organization or government to prevent any individual members from receiving its benefits. See Olson (1965). It is also true, however, that incentives exist for cooperation with a group, based on the attraction of greater benefits.

3   For a discussion of the transfer of referents of social action from transcendental to empirical ones, see Levy (1965).

4   See, for example, Brodie (1959) and Osgood and Tucker (1967).

5   For an analysis of the set of cross-cutting effects of nuclear weapons on the state, see Hassner (1968). Also see the two essays by Herz (1957 and 1968).

6   The 'introversive' tendencies of highly industrialized societies are examined in greater detail in Deutsch (1968).

7   This discussion is based on analyses found in Malmgren (1972, Chs. 1 and 2); Preeg (1974, Ch. 10); Robinson (1966); and, especially, Schmitt (1974, pp. 200–205).

8   Where governments try to repress dissent, as in the case of the Soviet Union, significant additional costs result, including costs to governmental legitimacy.

9   See, in particular, Allison (1969).

10 This problem of bureaucracies has been an obsession of Henry Kissinger, both while an academic and in government. See Kissinger (1974).

11 See Hammond (1965).

12 For an evaluation of the ability of Henry Kissinger successfully to wear his many hats in government, see Destler (1971–72).

REFERENCES

ABEL, R. L. (1973) 'A Comparative Theory of Dispute Institutions in Society', *Law and Society Review*, 8, 217.

ABRAHAM, N. (1974) *Big Business and Government*. Macmillan, London.

ACKOFF, R. L. and SASIENI, M. (1968) *Fundamentals of Operations Research*. John Wiley, New York.

AGGER, R., GOLDRICH, D. and SWANSON, B. (1964) *The Rulers and the Ruled*. John Wiley, New York.

ALBERT, J. (1969) *Economic Policy and Planning in the Netherlands*. Yale University Press, New Haven.

ALLARDT, E. *et al.* (1958) 'On the Cumulative Nature of Leisure Time Activities', *Acta Sociologica*, 3, fasc. 4, 165–72.

ALLISON, G. T. (1969) 'Conceptual Models and the Cuban Missile Crisis', *American Political Science Review*, 63, September, 689–718.

ALLISON, G. T. (1971) *Essence of Decision: Explaining the Cuban Missile Crisis*. Little, Brown, Boston.

ALMOND, G. A. and POWELL, G. B. (1966) *Comparative Politics; A Developmental Approach*. Little, Brown, Boston.

ALMOND, G. A. and VERBA, S. (1965) *The Civic Culture*. Little, Brown, Boston.

ALSCHULER, A. W. (1968) 'The Prosecutor's Role in Plea Bargaining', *University of Chicago Law Review*, 36, 50.

ALSCHULER, A. W. (1975) 'The Defense Attorney's Role in Plea Bargaining', *Yale Law Journal*, 84, 1179.

AMBLER, J. (1966) *The French Army in Politics*. Ohio State University Press, Columbus.

ANDERSON, C. W. (1970) *The Political Economy of Modern Spain*. University of Wisconsin Press, Madison.

ANTON, T. J., LINDE, C. and MELBOURN, A. (1973) 'Bureaucrats in Politics: A Profile of the Swedish Administrative Elite', *Canadian Public Administration*, 16, Winter, 626–51.

ARNOLD, D. (1979) *Congress and the Bureaucracy*. Yale University Press, New Haven.

ARROW, K. J. (1954) *Social Choice and Individual Values*, 2nd edition, John Wiley, New York.

AUBERT, V. (1963) 'Competition and Dissensus: Two Types of Conflict and of Conflict Resolution', *Journal of Conflict Resolution*, 7, 26.

BAAR, C. (1973) 'Will Urban Trial Courts Survive the War on Crime?', unpublished paper presented at American Political Science Association, New Orleans.

BACHRACH, P. (1969) *The Theory of Democratic Elitism*. University of London Press, London.

BACHRACH, P. (1969—70) 'A Power Analysis', *Public Policy*, 18, 155—86.

BACHRACH, P. and BARATZ, M.S. (1962) 'The Two Faces of Power', *American Political Science Review*, 56, 947—52.

BACHRACH, P. and BARATZ, M.S. (1963) 'Decision and Non-decisions: An Analytical Framework', *American Political Science Review*, 57, 641—51.

BACHRACH, P. and BARATZ, M.S. (1971) *Power and Poverty: Theory and Practice*. Oxford University Press, London.

(Bains Report) Ministry of Housing and Local Government (1972) *The New Local Authorities: Management and Structure*. HMSO, London.

BANTAN, M. (1974) *The Policemen in the Community*, Tavistock, London.

BARAN, P.A. and SWEEZEY, P.M. (1968) *Monopoly Capital*. Penguin, Harmondsworth.

BAUER, R.A. (1968) 'The Study of Policy Formulation: An Introduction', *in* Bauer, R.A. and Gergen, K.J. (1968).

BAUER, R.A. and GERGEN, K.J. (eds.) (1968) *The Study of Policy Formulation*. Collier-Macmillan Free Press, New York.

BAUER, R., de SOLA POOL, I. and DEXTER, L. (1963) *American Business and Public Policy*. Atherton Press, New York.

BEALEY, E., BLONDEL, J. and McCANN, W. (1965) *Constituency Politics: A Study of Newcastle-Under-Lyme*. Faber, London.

BECKER, S.W. (1952) 'The Career of the Chicago Public School Teacher', *American Journal of Sociology*, 470—77.

BEER, S.H. (1965) *Modern British Politics*. Faber, London.

BEER, S.H. (1969) *Modern British Politics*, 2nd edn. Faber, London.

BEER, S.H. (1976) 'The Adoption of General Revenue Sharing: A Case Study in Public Sector Politics', *Public Policy*, 24, Spring, 157—60.

BEER, S.H. (forthcoming) 'Political Overload and Federalism' *in* Schuck, V. and Milburn, J. (eds.) *New England Politics*. Schenkman, Cambridge, Mass.

BEICHMAN, A. (1967) *The 'Other' State Department: The United States Mission to the United Nations*. Basic Books, New York.

BELL, D. (1973) *The Coming of Post-Industrial Society: A Venture in Social Forecasting*. Basic Books, New York.

BELL, D. (1974) 'The Public Household — on "Fiscal Sociology" and the Liberal Society', *The Public Interest*, 37, 29—68.

BENEWICK, R. (1973) 'Politics without Ideology: The Perimeters of Pluralism', *in* Benewick, R., Berki, R.N. and Parekh, B. (eds.) *Knowledge and Belief in Politics*. Allen and Unwin, London.

BENEWICK, R. (1974) 'British Pressure Group Politics: The National Council for Civil Liberties', *Annals of the American Academy of Political and Social Science*, 413, 145—57.

BENINGTON, J. (1976) *Local Government Becomes Big Business.*
National Community Development Project, London.
BENTLEY, A.F. (1967) *The Process of Government,* ed. Odegard, P.
Belknap Press, Harvard, Mass.
BIRCH, A.H. (1964) *Representative and Responsible Government.* Allen
and Unwin, London.
BIRLEY, D. (1970) *The Education Officer and His World.* Routledge and
Kegan Paul, London.
BLACKIE, J. (1970) *Inspecting and the Inspectorate.* Routledge and
Kegan Paul, London.
BLAU, P. (1963) *The Dynamics of Bureaucracy.* University of Chicago
Press, Chicago.
BLONDEL, J. (1963) *Voters, Parties and Leaders.* Penguin Books,
Harmondsworth.
BLUMBERG, A.S. (1967) *Criminal Justice.* Quadrangle Books, Chicago.
BLUMBERG, A.S. (1971) 'Criminal Justice in America', *in* Douglas, J.
(1971).
BOADEN, N. (1971) *Urban Policy-Making: Influences on County Boroughs
in England and Wales.* Cambridge University Press, Cambridge.
BONJEAN, C.M., CLARK, T.N., and LINEBERRY, R.L. (eds.) (1971)
Community Politics: A Behavioural Approach. Free Press, New York
and Collier-Macmillan, London.
BOOTH, K. (1974) *Navies and Foreign Policy.* Croom Helm, London.
BOOTH, T. (1978) 'Finding Alternatives to Residential Care — The
Problem of Innovation in the Personal Social Services', *Local Govern-
ment Studies,* 9, 3—14.
BORNFRIEND, A.J. (1969) 'Political Parties and Pressure Groups',
Proceedings of the Academy of Political Science, 29 (4), 64—5.
BOWER, J.L. (1968) 'Descriptive Decision Theory from the "Adminis-
trative" Viewpoint', *in* Bauer, R.A. and Gergen, K.J. (1968).
BOX, S. and RUSSELL, K. (1975) 'The Politics of Discredibility', *Socio-
logical Review,* 23, No. 2.
BRADSHAW, A. (1976) 'A Critique of Steven Lukes' "Power: A Radical
View" ', *Sociology,* 10, 121—8.
BRAYBROOKE, D. and LINDBLOM, C.E. (1963) *A Strategy of Decision.*
Free Press, New York.
BRENNAN, T. (1959) *Reshaping a City.* Grant, Glasgow.
BRENT, R.J. (1979) 'Imputing Weights Behind Past Railway Closure
Decisions Within a Cost-Benefit Framework', *Applied Economics,*
11, 157—70.
BRETON, A. (1974) *The Economic Theory of Representative Govern-
ment.* Aldine, Chicago.
BRITTAN, S. (1975a) 'Towards a Corporate State?', *Encounter,* 44,
58—63.
BRITTAN, S. (1975b) 'The Economic Contradictions of Democracy',
British Journal of Political Science, 5, April, 129—59.
BRODIE, B. (1959) *Strategy in the Missile Age.* Princeton University
Press, Princeton.

BROWN, C. V. and JACKSON, P. M. (1978) *Public Sector Economics*, Martin Robertson, London.
BRUCE-GARDYNE, J. (1975) 'Who Speaks for British Business?', *The Director*, September, 269–71.
BRZEZINSKI, Z. and HUNTINGTON, S. P. (1965) *Political Power USA/USSR*. Viking Press, New York.
BULPITT, J. (1976) *Party Politics in English Local Government*. Longman, London.
BURNS, T. and STALKER, G. M. (1961) *The Management of Innovation*. Tavistock, London.
BUTT, R. (1967) *The Power of Parliament*. Constable, London.
BUTT, R. (1972) 'Feasibility Study of PPBS in Gloucestershire', *Local Government Studies*, 2, April.
BYRNE, E. (1974) *Planning and Educational Inequality: A Study of the Rationale of Resource Allocation*. National Foundation for Educational Research, Slough, Bucks.

The Cabinet Office (1970) *The Reorganization of Central Government* (Cmnd. 5406). HMSO, London.
CAIN, M. (1973) *Society and the Policeman's Role*. Routledge and Kegan Paul, London.
CARLSON, B. (1969) *Trade Unions in Sweden*. Tidens, Stockholm.
CASTLE, B. (1973) 'Mandarin Power', *Sunday Times*, June 10.
CASTLES, F. (1973) 'The Political Functions of Organized Groups: the Swedish Case', *Political Studies*, 21 (March).
CASTLES, F. *et al.* (1971) *Decisions, Organizations and Society*. Penguin, Harmondsworth.
CAULCOTT, T. H. (1977) 'The Consultative Council on Local Government Finance', *Telescope*, November.
CAWSON, A. (1977) 'Environmental Planning and the Politics of Corporatism', *Working Papers in Urban and Regional Studies*, No. 7, University of Sussex.
CBI (1972) *Annual Report*. CBI, London.
CBI (1974) *Annual Report*. CBI, London.
CBI (1975) *Annual Report*. CBI, London.
CBI (1976) *The Road to Recovery*. CBI, London.
Central Policy Review Staff (1977) *Relations between Central Government and Local Authorities*. HMSO, London.
CHADWICK, G. (1971) *A Systems View of Planning*. Pergamon, Oxford.
CHANNON, D. F. (1973) *The Strategy and Structure of British Enterprise*. Macmillan, London.
CHAPMAN, B. (1959) *The Profession of Government*. Unwin University Books, London.
CHAPMAN, L. (1978) *Your Disobedient Servant*. Penguin, Harmondsworth.
CHENOT, B. (1967) *Être Ministre*. Plon, Paris.
CHIBNALL, S. (1975) 'The Crime Reporter', *Sociology*, 9, 49–66.
CHILD, J. (1972b) 'Organizational Structure, Environment and Performance: The Role of Strategic Choice. *Sociology*, 6, 1.

CHURCHMAN, C.W. et. al. (1957) Introduction to Operations Research. John Wiley, New York.

CHURCHMAN, C.W. (1968) Challenge to Reason. McGraw-Hill.

CLARKE, S. and GINSBURG, N. (1975) 'The Political Economy of Housing', in Political Economy and the Housing Question, Conference of Socialist Economists, London.

COCKBURN, C. (1977) The Local State. Pluto Press, London.

COHEN, M.D., MARCH, J.G. and OLSEN, J.P. (1972) 'The Garbage Can Model of Organizational Choice', Administrative Science Quarterly, 17, March, 1–25.

COLE, G.F. (1973) Politics and Administration of Justice. Sage Publications, Beverley Hills.

COLEMAN, J.S. (1966) 'Individual Interests and Collective Action'. Papers on Non-Market Decision-Making, 1, 49–62.

COLEMAN, J. (1970) 'Political Money', American Political Science Review, 64, 1074–87.

Committee on the Management of Local Government (1967) Vol 3, The Local Government Elector. HMSO, London.

CONNOLLY, W. (ed.) (1969) The Bias of Pluralism. Atherton Press, New York.

COONS, J.E. (1964) 'Approaches to Court-Imposed Compromise – The Uses of Doubt and Reason', The Northwestern University Law Review, 58, 750.

COX, R. (1969a) 'The Executive Head', International Organization, 23 (Spring)

COX, R. (ed.) (1969b) International Organization: World Politics. London.

COX, W. and JACOBSON, H. (1973) The Anatomy of Influence. Yale University Press, New Haven.

CRENSON, M. (1971) The Unpolitics of Air Pollution. Johns Hopkins Press, Baltimore.

CROSSMAN, R. (1975–79) The Diaries of a Cabinet Minister. Vols. I–III. Hamish Hamilton and Jonathan Cape, London.

CROUCH, C. (1976) 'The Corporate State: Crisis or Compromise?', paper delivered at the Conference of Contemporary British Politics Workshop of the Political Studies Association of the United Kingdom, Sheffield.

CROWTHER-HUNT, Lord and KELLNER, P. (1980) The Civil Servants: An Inquiry into Britain's Ruling Class. Macdonald and Janes, London.

CROZIER, M. (1964) The Bureaucratic Phenomenon. University of Chicago Press, Chicago.

CROZIER, M. (1975) 'Western Europe' in Crozier, M. et al., The Crisis of Democracy. Trilateral Commission, New York.

CULP DAVIS, K. et al. (1976) Discretionary Justice in Europe and America. University of Illinois Press, Urbana, Illinois.

CYERT, R.M. and MARCH, J.G. (1963) A Behavioral Theory of The Firm. Prentice-Hall, Englewood Cliffs, N.J.

CUTT, J. (1975) 'Policy Analysis: A Conceptual Base for a Theory of Improvement', Policy Sciences, 6, 223–98.

DAHL, R. A. (1956) *Preface to Democratic Theory*. University of Chicago Press, Chicago.
DAHL, R. A. (1961) *Who Governs?* Yale University Press, New Haven, Conn.
DAHL, R. A. (1962) 'A critique of the ruling class model', *American Political Science Review*, **56**, iv.
DAHL, R. A. (1967) *Pluralist Democracy in the United States*. Rand McNally, Chicago.
DALTON, M. (1959) *Men Who Manage*. John Wiley, New York.
DAHRENDORF, R. (1972) *in* Hodges, M. (1972)
DARBY, P. (1973) *British Defence Policy East of Suez 1947–68*. Oxford University Press, London.
DAVIES, J. C. (1970) *The Politics of Pollution*. Pegasus, New York.
DEARLOVE, J. (1973) *The Politics of Policy in Local Government*. Cambridge University Press, Cambridge.
DE MEYER, R. F. and PLOTT, C. R. (1970) 'The Probability of a Cyclical Majority', *Econometrica*, **38**, 345–54.
Department of Education and Science (1970*a*) *HMI Today and Tomorrow*. HMSO, London.
Department of Education and Science (1970*b*) *Output Budgeting for the Department of Education and Science: Report of a Feasibility Study* (Education Planning Paper No 1). HMSO, London.
Department of Education and Science (1974) *Management in the Education Service*. HMSO, London.
DESAI, M. (1972) 'Social Science Goes to War', *Survival*, March/April.
DESTLER, I. M. (1971/2) 'Can One Man Do?', *Foreign Policy*, No. 5, Winter, 28–40.
DEUTSCH, K. W. (1968) *The Analysis of International Relations*. Prentice-Hall, Englewood Cliffs, N. J.
DIAMANT, A. A. (1968) 'Tradition and Innovation in French Administration', *Comparative Political Studies*, 1 July, 251–74.
DICKENS, P. (1977) 'Social Change, Housing and the State', Centre for Environmental Studies Conference Paper.
DOGAN, M. (1975) 'The Political Power of Western Mandarins', *in* Dogan, M. (ed.) *The Mandarins of Western Europe*. Halsted, New York.
DOUGLAS, J. (ed.) (1971) *Crime and Justice in American Society*. Bobbs-Merrill, New York.
DOWNS, A. (1957) *An Economic Theory of Democracy*. Harper and Brothers, New York.
DOWNS, A. (1967) *Inside Bureaucracy*. Little, Brown, Boston.
DROR, Y. (1964) ' "Muddling Through" – "Science" or Inertia?', *Public Administration Review*, **24**, 153–7.
DROR, Y. (1968) *Public Policymaking Reexamined*. Chandler, Scranton, Pa.
DRUCKER, J. M. (1977) 'Devolution and Corporatism', *Government and Opposition*, **12**, 178–93.
DUNCAN, R. B. (1972) 'Characteristics of Organizational Environments and Perceived Environmental Uncertainty', *Administrative Science Quarterly*, **17**, 313.

ECKSTEIN, H. (1960) *Pressure Group Politics: The Case of The British Medical Association.* Allen and Unwin, London.

ECONOMIST (1978) 'America's Invigorating Paralysis', **269**, 23 December, 52–5.

EDDISON, T. (1973) *Local Government: Management and Corporate Planning.* Leonard Hill Books, Aylesbury.

EDGETT, J.S. (1972) *How to Manage Your Way to the Top.* Parker Press, New York.

EDINGER, L. (1968) *Politics in Germany.* Little, Brown, Boston.

EDMONDS, E.L. (1962) *The School Inspector.* Routledge and Kegan Paul, London.

EISENSTEIN, J. and JACOB, H. (1977) *Felony Justice: An Organizational Analysis of Criminal Courts.* Little, Brown, Boston.

ELDERSVELD, S., HUBÉE-BOONZAAIJER, S. and KOOIMAN, J. (1975) 'Elite Perceptions of the Political Process in the Netherlands', *in* Dogan, M. (ed.) *The Mandarins of Western Europe.* Halsted, New York.

ELVANDER, N. (1966) *Interesseorganisationerna i dagens Sverige.* C.W.K. Gleerup, Lund.

ETZIONI, A. (1960) 'Two Approaches to Organisation Analysis: A Critique and a Suggestion', *Administrative Science Quarterly*, **5**, 257–78.

ETZIONI, A. (1961) *A Comparative Analysis of Complex Organizations.* Free Press of Glencoe, New York.

ETZIONI, A. (1967) 'Mixed-Scanning: A "Third" Approach to Decision-Making', *Public Administration Review*, **27**.

ETZIONI, A. (1968) *The Active Society: A Theory of Societal and Political Processes.* Collier-Macmillan, London.

FAYOL, H. (1949) *General and Industrial Management.* Isaac Pitman, London.

FEELEY, M.M. (1973) 'Two Models of the Criminal Justice System: An Organizational Perspective', *Law and Society Review*, **7**, 408.

FELDMAN, J. (1963) 'Simulation of Behaviour in the Binary Choice Experiment', *in* Fergenbaum, E.A. and Feldman, J. (eds.) *Computers and Thought.*

FINER, S.E. (1966) *Anonymous Empire.* 2nd edn. Pall Mall Press, London.

FIORINA, M. (1978) *Congress: Keystone of the Washington Establishment.* Yale University Press, New Haven.

FOOT, M. (1975) *Aneurin Bevan, Volume Two. 1945–1960.* Paladin, Frogmore.

FORCESE, D.P. and RICHER, S. (1973) *Social Research Methods.* Prentice Hall, Englewood Cliffs, N.J.

FOWLER, G. (1974) Central Government of Education 1: Policy Formation, Unit 2 of OU.

FOX, A. (1976) 'The Corporate State: Reality or Myth? An Industrial Perspective', *in* papers of the conference The Corporate State — Reality or Myth?, London.

FOYER, L. (1969) 'Former for Kontakt och samverkan mellan staten och organisationera'. *Statens Offentliga Utredningar:* 21.
FRANKEL, J. (1963) *The Making of Foreign Policy*. Oxford University Press, London.
FRASER, D. (1973) *The Evolution of the British Welfare State*. Macmillan, London.
FREEMAN, J. L. (1955) *The Political Process*. Random House, New York.
FRIEND, J. and SPINK, P. S. (1978) 'Networks in Public Administration', *Linkage*, 3, July.
FROHLICH, N., OPPENHEIMER, J. A. and YOUNG, O. R. (1971) *Political Leadership and Collective Goods*. Princeton University Press, Princeton.

GALANTER, M. (1974) 'Why the "Haves" Have Come Out Ahead: Speculations on the Limits of Legal Change', *Law and Society Review*, 7, 408.
GALBRAITH, J. K. (1952) American Capitalism. Houghton Mifflin, Boston.
GALBRAITH, J. K. (1974) *The New Industrial State*. 2nd edn. Penguin, Harmondsworth.
GALBRAITH, J. K. (1975) *Economics and the Public Purpose*. Penguin Harmondsworth.
GAMBLE, A. (1974) *The Conservative Nation*. Routledge and Kegan Paul, London.
GANS, H. (1967) *The Levittowners*. Pantheon.
GARLICHS, D. and HULL, C. (1978) 'Central Control and Information Dependence: Highway Planning in the Federal Republic of Germany', in Hanf, R. and Scharpf, G. W. (1978)
GERSHUNY, J. I. (1978) 'Policy Making Rationality: A Reformulation', *Policy Sciences*, 9, 295–316.
GILBERT, B. B. (1970) *British Social Policy, 1914–1939*. Batsford, London.
GLASER, B. G. (1968) *Organizational Careers*. Aldine, Chicago.
GLASS, V. (ed.) (1954) *Social Mobility in Britain*. Routledge and Kegan Paul, London.
GOODIN, R. E. (1975) 'The Logic of Bureaucratic Backscratching', *Public Choice*, 21, 53–68.
GORDENKER, L. (1969) 'Multilateral Aid and Influence on Government Policies', in Cox (1969*b*).
GORDON, I., LEWIS, J. and YOUNG, K. (1977) 'Perspectives on Policy Analysis', *Public Administration Bulletin*, 25, 26–35.
GOULDNER, A. W. (ed.) (1950) *Studies in Leadership*. Harper, New York.
GOULDNER, A. W. (1974) *The Coming Crisis of Western Sociology*. Heinemann, London.
GRANT, W. (1977) 'Insider Groups, Outsider Groups and Interest Group Strategies in Britain', unpublished paper.
GRANT, W. (1978) 'Industrialists and Farmers: British Interests and the European Community', *West European Politics*, 1, No. 1.
GRANT, W. and MARSH, D. (1974) 'The Representation of Retail Interests in Britain', *Political Studies*, 22, 168–77.

GRANT, W. and MARSH, D. (1975) 'The Politics of the CBI: 1974 and After', *Government and Opposition*, **10**, 90–104.

GRANT, W. and MARSH, D. (1977) *The Confederation of British Industry*. Hodder and Stoughton, London.

GRAVES, J. (1940) 'The use of advisory bodies by the Board of Education', *in* Vernon, R.V. and Mansergh, N. (eds.) *Advisory Bodies*. Allen and Unwin, London.

GREENLAGH, W.F. (1966) *Police Regression Analysis*. Home Office, London.

GREENWOOD, R., NORTON, A.L. and STEWART, J.D. (1969) *Recent Reforms in the Management Arrangements of County Boroughs in England and Wales; Recent Reforms in the Management of Local Authorities – the London Boroughs*; and *Recent Reforms in the Management Structure of Local Authorities – The County Councils* (Occasional Papers Nos. 1, 2 and 3) INLOGOV, Univeristy of Birmingham.

GRETTON, P. (1965) *Maritime Strategy*. Cassell, London.

GRIFFITH, J.A.G. and STREET, H. (1952) *Administrative Law*. Pitman, London.

GROTTIAN, P. (1972) 'Zum Planungsbewusstsein der Bonner Ministerial-bürokratie – Vorläufige Ergebnisse einer empirischen Studie', Politische Vierteljahresschrift, Sonderheft, **4**.

GULICK, L. and URWICK, L. (eds.) (1937) *Papers on the Science of Administration*. Institute of Public Administration, Columbia University, New York.

HAGAN, J. (1974) 'Extra-Legal Attributes and Criminal Sentencing', *Law and Society Review*, **8**, 357.

HAGUE, C. and McCOURT, A. (1974) 'Comprehensive Planning, Public Participation and the Public Interest', *Urban Studies*, **11**, 143–55.

HAHN, H. (ed.) (1972) *People and Politics in Urban Society*. Sage Publications, Beverley Hills.

HAINES, J. (1977) *The Politics of Power*. Coronet, London.

HALL, R.L. and HITCH, C.H. (1939) 'Price Theory and Business Behaviour', *Oxford Economic Papers*, **2**, 12–45.

HAMMOND, P.Y. (1965) 'Foreign Policy-Making and Administrative Politics', *World Politics*, **17**, July, 656–71.

HANF, K. and SCHARPF, F.W. (eds.) (1978) *Interorganizational Policy Making*. Sage Publications, Beverley Hills.

HARRIS, N. (1971) *Beliefs in Society*. Penguin, Harmondsworth.

HARRIS, N. (1972) *Competition and the Corporate Society*. Methuen, London.

HART, J.M. (1951) *The British Police*. Allen and Unwin, London.

HASSNER, P. (1968) 'The Nation-State in the Nuclear Age', *Survey*, **67**, April, 3–27.

HASSNER, P. (1971–72) 'The New Europe: From Cold War to Hot Peace', *International Journal*, **27**, Winter.

HEADEY, B. (1975) *British Cabinet Ministers*. Allen and Unwin, London.

HECLO, H. (1969) 'The Councillor's Job', *Public Administration*, 47, 185–202.
HECLO, H. (1977) *A Government of Strangers: Executive Politics in Washington.* The Brookings Institution, Washington, D.C.
HECLO, H. and WILDAVSKY, A. (1974) *The Private Government of Public Money.* Macmillan, London.
HEISLER, M.O. and KRISTENSEN, O.P. (1979) 'The Mixed Polity in the Welfare State· Corporate Pluralist Politics in Scandinavia in Comparative Perspective', paper presented to 1979 Annual Meeting of the Southern Political Science Association, Gatlinburg, Tennessee.
HEISLER, M.O. and KVAVIK, R. (1974) 'Patterns of European politics: the "European Polity" model', *in* Heisler, M. (ed.) *Politics in Europe.* David McKay, New York.
HENNESSEY, J.M. and PETERS, B.G. (1975) 'Political Paradoxes in Postindustrialism: A Political Economy Perspective', *Policy Studies Journal*, 3, Spring, 233–9.
HERZ, J. (1957) 'The Rise and Demise of the Territorial State', *World Politics*, 9, 473–93.
HERZ, J. (1968) 'The Territorial State Revisited', *Polity*, 1, 12–34.
HEUMANN, M. (1976) 'Adapting to Plea Bargaining: The Experiences of Prosecutors, Judges and Defense Attorneys', Ph.D. dissertation, Department of Political Science, Yale University.
HILL, D. (1970) *Participating in Local Affairs.* Penguin Books, Harmondsworth.
HILL, M.J. (1972) *The Sociology of Public Administration.* Weidenfeld and Nicolson.
HILSMAN, R. (1967) *To Move a Nation.* Dell, New York.
HILSMAN, R. (1971) *The Politics of Policy Making in Defence and Foreign Affairs.* Harper and Row, New York.
HINDESS, B. (1971) *Working Class Politics.* MacGibbon and Kee, London.
HINDESS, B. (1976) 'On Three-Dimensional Power', *Political Studies*, 24, 329–33.
HIRSCHMAN, A.O. and LINDBLOM, C.D. (1962) 'Economic Development, Research and Development, Policy Making: Some Converging Theories', *Behavioral Science*, 7, 211–22.
HIRSCHMAN, A.O. (1965) *Journeys Toward Progress: Studies of Economic Policy-Making in Latin America.* Greenwood, New York.
(HMI) *Select Committee on Education and Science (1968) Her Majesty's Inspectorate (England and Wales)* (Report Part 1, Session 1967–68, HC 182–1) HMSO, London.
HODGES, M. (ed.) (1972) *European Integration.* Penguin, Harmondsworth.
HOFFMAN, S. (1965) *The State of War.* Praeger, New York.
HOFFMAN, S. (1966) 'Obstinate or Obsolete? The Fate of the Nation-State and the Case of Western Europe', *Daedalus*, 95, Summer, 862–915.
HOLDEN, M. (1966) 'Imperialism and Bureaucracy', *American Political Science Review*, 60, December, 943–51.
HOLLAND, S. *The Socialist Challenge.* Quartet, London.

HOOD, C. (1976) *The Limits of Administration*. Wiley, New York.
HOPKINS, P. (1972) *in* Reed, B. and Williams, G. (1972).
HORN, J. D. (1964) *How to Become Head of Your Firm Before Forty*.
  Coleridge Press, New York.
HORTON SMITH, D. (ed.) (1973) *Voluntary Action Research*. D. C.
  Heath, Lexington, Mass.
House of Commons (1976) *Policy making in the Department of Education
  and Science*. House of Commons Expenditure Committee, 10th Report.
  HMSO, London.
HUNTER, F. (1953) *Community Power Structure*. University of North
  Carolina Press.
HUNTINGTON, S. P. (1961) *The Common Defence*. Columbia University
  Press, New York.
HUTCHESON, J. D. and STEGGERT, F. X. (undated) *Organized Citizen
  Participation in Urban Areas*. Center for Research in Social Change,
  Emory University.

IONESCU, G. (1975) *Centripetal Politics*. Hart-Davis, MacGibbon, London.

JAMES, W. (1890) *Principles of Psychology*.
JANSSON, D. S. and TAYLOR, S. H. (1978) 'Search Activity in Social
  Agencies: Institutional Factors that Influence Policy Analysis', *Social
  Services Review*, 52, 189–201.
JENKINS, P. (1970) *The Battle of Downing Street*. Charles Knight,
  London.
JENNINGS, R. E. (1977) *Education and Politics: Policy-Making in Local
  Education Authorities*. Batsford, London.
JOHNSON, J. J. (1962) *The Role of the Military in Underdeveloped
  Countries*. Princeton University Press, Princeton.
JONES, J. C. H. (1975) 'The Bureaucracy and Public Policy: Canadian
  Foreign Policy and the Combines Branch, 1960–1971', *Canadian
  Public Administration*, 18, Summer, 269–96.
JORDAN, R. (1971) *International Administration*. Oxford University
  Press, London.
JOSEPH, Sir K. (1976) 'Corporatism and Liberty do not go together', *The
  Times*, 17 May.

KAISER, K. (1971) 'Transnational Politics: Toward a theory of multi-
  national politics', *International Organization*, 25.
KAISER, K. (1972) 'Transnational Relations as a Threat to the Democratic
  Process, *in* Keohane and Nye (1972).
KAUFMAN, H. (1975) *Are Government Organizations Immortal?* The
  Brookings Institution, Washington D.C.
KELLY, D. (1952) *The Ruling Few*. London.
KEOHANE, R. (1971) 'The Big Influence of Small Allies' *Foreign Policy*,
  No 11.
KEOHANE, R. and NYE, J. (eds.) (1972) *Transnational Relations and
  World Politics*. Harvard University Press, Cambridge, Mass.

KEOHANE, R. and NYE, J. (1974) 'Transgovernmental Relations and International Organizations', *World Politics*, 27, No. 1.
KEY, V.O. (1958) *Parties, Politics and Pressure Groups*, 4th edition. Thomas Y. Crowell, New York.
KIDDER, R.L. (1974) 'Formal Litigation and Professional Insecurity: Legal Entrepreneurship in South India', *Law and Society Review*, 9, 11.
KIMBER, R. and RICHARDSON, J.J. (eds.) (1974) *Pressure Groups in Britain: A Reader*. Dent, London.
KING, A. (1975) 'Overloaded Governments', *Political Studies*, 23, June/September, 284–96.
KISSINGER, H. (1974) 'Domestic Structure and Foreign Policy', in *American Foreign Policy*, Revised edition. Norton, New York.
KLEIN, R. (1974) *Social Policy and Public Expenditure*. Centre for Studies in Social Policy, London.
KNORR, K. (1966) *On the Uses of Military Power in the Nuclear Age*. Princeton University Press, Princeton, N.J.
KOGAN, M. (1971) *The Politics of Education*. Penguin, Harmondsworth.
KOGAN, M. (1973) 'The function of the Central Advisory Council in Educational Change', in Fowler, G. *et al. Decision-Making in British Education*. Heinemann, London.
KOGAN, M. (1975) *Educational Policy-Making*. Allen and Unwin, London.
KOGAN, M. (1978) *The Politics of Educational Change*. Fontana, London.
KOGAN, M. and PACKWOOD, T. (1974) *Advisory Councils and Committees in Education*. Routledge and Kegan Paul, London.
KRASNER, S. (1972) 'Are Bureaucracies Important?', *Foreign Policy*, 7, Summer, 159–79.
KRISTENSEN, O.P. (1979) 'The Logic of Political-Bureaucratic Decision-Making as a Course of Governmental Growth', paper presented to the Sandberg Danish Political Science Association.
KVAVIK, R. (1974) 'Interest groups in a "cooptive" polity: the case of Norway' in Heisler, M. (ed.) *Politics in Europe*. David McKay, New York.

LAKOFF, S.A. (ed.) (1973) *Private Government*. Scott Foreman and Co., Glenview, Illinois.
LaPALOMBARA, J. (1965) *Interest Groups in Italian Politics*. Princeton University Press, Princeton.
LAPORTE, T. (1975) *Organized Social Complexity*. Princeton University Press, Princeton.
LATHAM, E. (1952) *The Group Basis of Politics*. Cornell University Press, Ithaca, N.Y.
LATSIS, S.J. (1972) 'Situational Determinism in Economics', *The British Journal for the Philosophy of Science*, 23, 207–45.
LEHMBRUCH, G. (1976) 'Liberal Corporatism and Party Government', paper delivered to the International Political Science Association Congress, Edinburgh.
LEVINE, J., MUSHENO, M. and PALUMBOM, D. (1975) 'The Limits of Rational Choice in Evaluating Criminal Justice Policy', in Nagel, S.S. (ed.) (1975).

LEVY, M.J. Jr. (1965) 'Rapid Social Change and Some Implications for Modernization', International Conference on the Problems of Modernization in Asia, June 28 – July 7 1965, Seoul, 657–8.

LEWIN, K., DEMBO, T., FESTINGER, L. and SEARS, P.S. (1944) 'Levels of Aspiration', *in* Hunt, J.M. (ed.) *Personality and the Behavior Disorders*, vol. 1, pp. 333–78. Ronald, New York.

LIJPHARDT, A. (1968) *The Politics of Accommodation: Pluralism and Democracy in the Netherlands*. University of California Press, Berkeley and Los Angeles.

LINDBERG, L. and SCHEINGOLD, S. (1970) *Europe's Would-Be Polity*. Prentice-Hill, New Jersey.

LINDBLOM, C.E. (1959) 'The Science of "Muddling Through" ' *Public Administration Review*, 19, 79–99.

LINDBLOM, C.E. (1964) 'Contexts for Change and Strategy: A Reply', *Public Administration Review*, 24, 157–8.

LINDBLOM, C.E. (1965) *The Intelligence of Democracy*. Free Press, New York.

LINDBLOM, C.E. (1968) *The Policy-Making Process*. Prentice-Hall, Englewood Cliffs, New Jersey.

LINDBLOM, C.E. (1977) *Politics and Markets*. Basic Books, New York.

LINDBLOM, C.E. and COHEN, D.K. (1979) *Usable Knowledge*. Yale University Press, New Haven.

LINEBERRY, R.L. (1979) 'Pricing The Welfare State?' Paper presented to symposium on decentralisation and diversity, Policy Studies Institute, London.

LOCKARD, D. (1971) *The Perverted Priorities of American Politics*. Macmillan, London.

LOCKE, M. (1974) *Power and Politics in the School System: A Guidebook*. Routledge and Kegan Paul, London.

LOCKWOOD, D. (1958) *The Blackcoated Worker: A Study in Class Consciousness*. Allen and Unwin, London.

LOWI, T. (1964) 'American Business Public Policy' *World Politics*, July.

LOWI, T. (1967) 'The Public Philosophy: Interest Group Liberalism', *American Political Science Review*, 61, March, 5–24.

LOWI, T. (1969) *The End of Liberalism*. Norton, New York.

LOWI, T. (1970) 'Decision Making vs Public Policy: Toward an Antidote for Technocracy', *Public Administration Review*, 30, 314–25.

LUKES, S. (1974) *Power: a Radical View*. Macmillan, London.

LUND, H.F. (1973) *The Real Official Executive Survival Handbook*. Dial Press, New York.

McCLEERY, M. (1964) 'On Remarks Taken out of Context', *Public Administration Review*, 24, No. 3, 160–2.

McCONNELL, G. (1966) *Private Power and American Democracy*. Knopf, New York.

MACPHERSON, C.B. (1965) *The Real World of Democracy*. Oxford University Press, London.

MAGEE, J. (1970) 'ECA and the Paradox of African Cooperation', *International Conciliation*, No. 580.

MALMGREN, H. (1972) *International Economic Peacekeeping in Phase II.* Revised edition. Quadrangle, New York.

MANNING, P.K. (1971) 'The Police: Mandate, Strategies and Appearances', *in* Douglas, J. (1971).

MARCH, J.G. and SIMON, H.A. (1958) *Organizations,* John Wiley, New York.

MARCUSE, H. (1968) *One-Dimensional Man.* Sphere Books, London.

MARINI, F. (ed.) (1971) *Toward a New Public Administration: The Minnowbrook Perspective.* Chandler, San Francisco.

MARPLES, E. (1969) 'A Dog's Life in the Ministry', *in* Rose, R. (ed.) *Policy-making in Britain.* Macmillan, London.

MARRIS, P. and REIN, M. (1972) *The Dilemmas of Social Reform.* Penguin, Harmondsworth.

MARSH, D. and GRANT, W. (1977) 'Tripartism: Reality or Myth?', *Government and Opposition,* 12, 194–211.

MARSH, D. and SMITH, A. (undated) 'The Trade Unions Rule, OK?' Research Paper No. 4 of the Polytechnic of Central London School of Social Science and Business Studies.

MATHER, L.M. (1974) 'Some Determinants of the Method of Case Disposition: Decision Making by Public Defenders in Los Angeles', *Law and Society Review,* 8, 187.

(Maud Report) *Ministry of Housing and Local Government. Committee on the Management of Local Government* (1967) Volume I: *Report of the Committee.* HMSO, London.

MAY, T. and MORAN, M. (1973) 'Trade Unions as Pressure Groups', *New Society,* 6 September, 570–73.

MAYER, J. and TIMMS, N. (1970) *The Client Speaks.* Routledge and Kegan Paul, London.

MAYNTZ, R. and SCHARPF, F.W. (1975) *Policy-making in the German Federal Bureaucracy.* Elsevier, Amsterdam.

MELTSNER, A.J. (1979) 'Don't Slight Communication: Some Problems of Analytical Practice', *Policy Analysis,* 5, 367–92.

MEYNAUD, J. (1962) *Nouvelles études sur les groupes de pression.* A. Colin, Paris.

MILBRATH, L.W. (1963) *The Washington Lobbyists.* Rand McNally, Chicago.

MILES, E. (1970) 'Transnationalism in Space', *in* Keohane and Nye, (1970).

MILIBAND, R. (1969) *The State in Capitalist Society.* Weidenfeld and Nicolson, London.

MILIBAND, R. (1973) *Parliamentary Socialism.* Merlin, London.

MILLER, G.A. (1956) 'The Magical Number Seven, Plus or Minus Two: Some Limits On Our Capacity for processing information', *Psychological Review,* 63, 81–97.

MINKIN, L. (1974) 'The British Labour Party and the Trade Unions: Crisis and Compact', *Industrial and Labour Relations Review,* October, 7–37.

MOHR, L.B. (1971) 'Organizational Technology and Organizational Structure', *Administrative Science Quarterly,* 16, 444.

MOHR, L. B. (1973) 'The Concept of Organizational Goal', *American Political Science Review*, 67, 140.
MOHR, L. B. (1975) *Administrative Structure, Effectiveness and Efficiency: A Prospectus for Research in Organizational Aspects of Education.* National Institute of Education, Washington.
MOLIN, B. *et al.* (1973) *Burakråti och Politik.* Almqvist and Wiksell, Stockholm.
MOODIE, G. and STUDDERT-KENNEDY, G. (1970) *Opinions, Publics and Pressure Groups.* Allen and Unwin, London.
MOREN, J. (1958) *Organsasjonere og Forvaltiningen.* Norges Handelhoyskole, Bergen.
MOSHER, F. C. (1968) *Democracy and the Public Service.* Oxford University Press, New York.
MOSHER, F. C. (1978) 'Professions in the Public Service', *Public Administration Review*, 38, March/April, 144–50.
MOYNIHAN, D. P. (1969) *Maximum Feasibility Misunderstanding.* Free Press, New York.
MURRAY, D. J. *et al.* (1972) *Patterns of Decision Making.* Open University Press, Milton Keynes.
MYERS, J. L. and FORT, J. G. (1963) 'A Sequential Analysis of Gambling Behavior', *Journal of General Psychology*, 69, 299–309.

NADER, L. (1965) 'Styles of Court Procedure: To Make the Balance' *in* Nader, L. (ed.) *Law and Culture in Society.* Aldine, Chicago.
NAIRN, T. (1965) 'The Nature of the Labour Party' *in* Anderson, P. and Blackburn, R. (eds.) *Towards Socialism.* Fontana, London.
NEUSTADT, R. (1970) *Alliance Politics.* Columbia, New York.
NEWTON, K. (1969*a*) 'A Critique of the Pluralist Model', *Acta Sociologica*, 12, 209–23.
NEWTON, K. (1969*b*) 'City Politics in the US and the UK', *Political Studies*, 17, 208–18.
NEWTON, K. (1972) 'Democracy, Community Power and Non-decision Making', *Political Studies*, 20, 484–7.
NEWTON, K. (1975) 'Community Politics and Decision-Making: The American Experience and the Lessons', *in* Young, K. (ed.) (1975).
NEWTON, K. (1976) *Second City Politics – Democratic Process and Decision Making in Birmingham.* Oxford University Press, London.
NISKANEN, W. A. (1968) 'The peculiar economics of bureaucracy', *American Economic Review Proceedings*, 58, May, 293–305.
NISKANEN, W. A. (1971) *Bureaucracy and Representative Government.* Aldine/Atherton, Chicago.
NISKANEN, W. A. (1973) 'Bureaucracy: Servant or Master?' Hobart Paper No. 5, IEA, London.
NISKANEN, W. A. (1979) 'Competition among Government Agencies', *American Behavioral Scientist*, 22, May/June, 517–24.
NORTON, A. L. and STEWART, J. D. (1973) 'Recommendations to the New Local Authorities 1973', *Local Government Studies*, 6, October.

NYE, J.S. (1967) 'Central American Regional Integration', *International Conciliation*, No. 562.

NYE, J.S. (1973) 'Unctad: Poor Nations' Pressure Group', *in* Cox, W. and Jacobson, H. (1973).

NYE, J.S. (1974) 'Transnational Relation and Interstate Conflict', *International Organization*, 28.

OECD (1975) *Educational Development Strategy in England and Wales.* OECD, Paris.

OLSON, M. Jr. (1965) *The Logic of Collective Action and the Theory of Groups.* Harvard University Press, Cambridge, Mass.

OSGOOD, R.E. and TUCKER, R.W. (1967) *Force, Order and Justice.* Johns Hopkins Press, Baltimore.

OSTRAM, V. (1973) *The Intellectual Crisis in American Public Administration.* University of Alabama Press.

(OU) Open University (1974) *Decision-Making in British Education Systems (E 221, Units 5–7).* Open University Press, Milton Keynes.

PACKER, H.L. (1968) *The Limits of Criminal Sanction.* Stanford University Press, Stanford.

PAHL, R.E. and WINKLER, J.T. (1975) 'The Coming Corporatism', *Challenge*, March/April, 28–35.

PAHL, R.E. and WINKLER, J.T. (1976) 'Corporatism in Britain', *The Times*, 26 March.

PANITCH, L. (1976*a*) *Social Democracy and Industrial Militancy.* Cambridge University Press, Cambridge.

PANITCH, L. (1976*b*) 'The Development of Corporatism in Liberal Democracies', paper presented at the annual meeting of the American Political Science Association, Chicago.

PARENTI, M. (1970) 'Power and Pluralism: The View from the Bottom', *Journal of Politics*, 32, August, 501–30.

PARKINSON, M. (1970) *The Labour Party and the Organisation of Secondary Education, 1918–1965.* Routledge and Kegan Paul, London.

PARRY, G. and MORRISS, P. (1974) 'When is a Decision not a Decision?', *in* Crewe, I. (ed.) *British Political Sociology Yearbook*, Volume One: *Elites in Western Democracy.* Croom Helm, London.

PATEMAN, C. (1973) *Participation and Democratic Theory.* Cambridge University Press, Cambridge.

PATTERSON, G. (1966) *Discrimination in International Trade.* Princeton University Press, Princeton.

PEACOCK, A.T. and WISEMAN, J. (1964) 'Education for Democrats', Hobart Paper 25, IEA, London.

PENNOCK, J.R. (1962) 'Responsible Government, Separated Powers, and Special Interests: Agricultural Subsidies in Britain and America', *American Political Science Review*, 56, 621–33.

PENNOCK, J.R. and CHAPMAN, J.W. (eds.) (1969) *Voluntary Associations.* Atherton Press, New York.

PENTLAND, C. (1973) *International Theory and European Integration.* Faber, London.

PERROW, C. (1967) 'A Framework for the Comparative Analysis of Organizations', *American Sociological Review*, 32, 194.

PETER, L.J. (1970) *The Peter Principle: Why Things Always Go Wrong.* Souvenir Press, London.

PETERS, G.G. (1977) 'Insiders and Outsiders', *Administration and Society*, 9, No. 2, 191–218.

PETERS, B.G. (1978) *The Politics of Bureaucracy.* Longmans, New York.

PETERS, B.G., DOUGHTIE, J. and McCULLOCH, K. (1977) 'Types of democratic systems and types of public policy: an empirical assessment,' *Comparative Politics*, 9, No. 3, 327–55.

PETERS, B.G. and HEISLER, M.O. (1980) 'The Growth of Government: What is Growing, Why, How and How Do We Know?', unpublished paper, Tulane University.

PILE, W. (1979) *The Department of Education and Science.* Allen and Unwin, London.

PIZZORNO, A. (1971) 'Amoral Familialism and Historical Marginality', *in* Rose, R. and Dogan, M. (eds.) *European Politics: A Reader.* Little, Brown, Boston.

POLSBY, N.W. (1963) *Community Power and Political Theory.* Yale University Press, New Haven.

POTTER, A. (1961) *Organized Groups in British National Politics.* Faber, London.

POULANTZAS, N. (1973) *Political Power and Social Classes.* New Left Books.

PREEG, E.H. (1974) *Economic Blocs and US Foreign Policy.* National Planning Association, Washington.

PRESSMAN, J.L. and WILDAVSKY, A. (1973) *Implementation.* University of California Press, Berkeley.

PRESTHUS, R. (1964) *Men at the Top.* Oxford University Press, New York.

PROXY, G. (1969) *How to Get Your Boss's Job.* Funk and Wagnalls, New York.

PUTNAM, R. (1973) 'The Political Attitudes of Senior Civil Servants in Britain, Germany and Italy', *British Journal of Political Science*, 3, July, 257–90.

RACKOFF, S. and SCHAEFER, G.L. (1970) 'Politics, Policy and Political Science', *Politics and Society*, 1, 51–71.

RAO, C.R. (1965) *Linear Statistical Inference and Its Applications.* John Wiley, New York.

RAPAPORT, A. and WALLSTEN, T.S. (1972) 'Individual Decision Behavior', *Annual Review of Psychology*, 23, 131–76.

RAWLS, J. (1972) *A Theory of Justice.* Clarendon Press, Oxford.

REDCLIFFE-MAUD, Lord, and WOOD, B. (1974) *English Local Government Reformed.* Oxford University Press, London.

REED, B. and WILLIAMS, G. (eds.) (1972) *Dennis Healey and the Policies of Power.* Sidgwick and Jackson, London.

REES, S. (1978) *Social Work Face to Face.* Edward Arnold, London.

REICH, C. (1971) *The Greening of America*. Allen Lane, London.
Report of the Committee on Local Authority and Allied Personal Social Services (1968) (*The Seerbohm Report*) Cmnd. 3703, HMSO, London.
RICHARDSON, J.J. and JORDAN, A.G. (1979) *Governing Under Pressure*. Martin Robertson, London.
RIGGS, F. (1964) *Administration in Developing Countries: The Theory of Prismatic Society*. Houghton Mifflin, Boston.
RIKER, W.H. and ORDESHOOK, P.C. (1968) 'A Theory of Calculus of Voting', *American Political Science Review*, 62, 25—42.
RITTEL, H.W.J. and WEBBER, M.M. (1973) 'Dilemmas in a General Theory of Planning', *Policy Sciences*, 4, 155—69.
ROBERTS, G.K. (1972) *What is Comparative Politics?* Macmillan, London.
ROBINSON, A.D. (1961) *Dutch Organised Agriculture in International Politics*. Nijhoff, The Hague.
ROBINSON, J. (1966) *The New Mercantilism*. Cambridge University Press, London.
ROKHAN, S. and CAMPBELL, A. (1960) 'Citizen Participation in Political Life: Norway and the United States of America', *International Social Science Journal*, 12, Part 1, 69—99.
ROSE, R. (1974) *The Problem of Party Government*. Macmillan, London.
ROSE, R. (1975) 'Overloaded Governments', *European Studies Newsletter*, 3.
ROSE, R. and PETERS, B. (1978) *Can Government Go Bankrupt?* Basic Books, New York.
ROSENAU, J.N. (1967) *Domestic Sources of Foreign Policy*. Free Press, New York.
ROSENAU, J.N. (1972) 'Adaptive Politics in an Interdependent World', *Orbis*, 16, Spring.
ROSS, H.L. (1970) *Settled Out of Court: The Social Process of Insurance Claims Adjustment*. Aldine, Chicago.
ROURKE, F.E. (1979) 'Bureaucratic Autonomy and the Public Interest', *American Behavioral Scientist*, 22, May/June, 537—46.
RUGGIE, J.G. (1972) 'The World Weather Watch', unpublished paper.

SAINSBURY, E. (1975) *Social Work with Families*. Routledge and Kegan Paul, London.
SALAMAN, G. and THOMPSON, K. (eds.) (1973) *People and Organisations*. Longmans for The Open University Press, London.
SALISBURY, R.H. (1968) 'The Analysis of Public Policy', *in* Ranney, A. (ed.) *Political Science and Public Policy*. Markham, Chicago.
SALISBURY, R.H. and HEINZ, J. (1970) 'A theory of policy analysis and some preliminary applications', *in* Sharkansky, I. (ed.) *Policy Analysis in Political Science*. Markham, Chicago.
SARAN, R. (1973) *Policy-Making in Secondary Education*. Clarendon Press, Oxford.
SAUNDERS, P. (1975) 'They Make the Rules', *Policy and Politics*, 4, 31—58.

SAVILLE, J. (1973) 'The Ideology of Labourism', *in* Benewick, R. *et al.* (eds.) *Knowledge and Belief in Politics.* Allen and Unwin, London.

SCARROW, H. A. (1971) 'Policy Pressures by British Local Government: The Case of Regulation in the "Public Interest" '. *Comparative Politics,* **4**, October, 1–28.

SCHARPF, F. W. (1977) 'Public Organization and the Waning of the Welfare State', *European Journal of Political Research,* **5**, December, 339–62.

SCHATTSNEIDER, E. (1960) *Semi-Sovereign People: A Realist's View of Democracy in America.* Holt, Rinehart and Winston.

SCHEINMAN, L. (1966) 'Some Preliminary Notes on Bureaucratic Relationships in the EEC', *International Organization,* **20**.

SCHEINMAN, L. (1971) *in* Jordan, R. (1971).

SCHLESINGER, A. Jr. (1960) *The Politics of Upheaval.* Houghton Mifflin, Boston.

SCHMITT, H. O. (1974) 'The International Monetary System: Three Options for Reform', *International Affairs,* **50**: 2, April, 200–205.

SCHMITT, K. (1972) *The Roman Catholic Church in Modern Latin America.* Knopf, New York.

SCHMITTER, P. C. (1974) 'Still the Century of Corporatism?', *Review of Politics,* **36**, 85–131.

SCHUMPETER, J. (1947) *Capitalism, Socialism and Democracy*, 2nd edition. Allen and Unwin, London.

SCOTT, W. G. (1971) 'Decision Concepts' *in* Castles, F. G. *et al.* (eds.), *Decisions, Organizations and Society.* Penguin, Harmondsworth.

SEARS, D. (1968) 'The Structure of Power', *in* Thomas, H. (ed.) *Crisis in the Civil Service.* Anthony Blond, London.

SEIDMAN, H. (1980) *Politics, Position and Power.* 3rd edition. Oxford University Press, New York.

SELF, P. (1973) 'Is Comprehensive Planning Possible and Rational?' University of Birmingham. Conference on the Study of Public Policy.

SELF, P. (1974) 'Is Comprehensive Planning Possible and Rational?' *Policy and Politics.* **2**, 193–203.

SELF, P. and STORING, H. (1962) *The State and the Farmer.* Allen and Unwin, London.

SELF, P. and STORING, H. (1974) 'The Farmer and the State', *in* Kimber, R. and Richardson, J. J. (eds.) *Pressure Groups in Britain.* J. M. Dent, London.

SHARPE, L. J. (1973) 'American Democracy Revisited', *British Journal of Political Science,* **3**, pt I 1–23 and pt II, 1–28.

SHERMAN, A. (1973) 'Fabian Re-think Local Government – Forward from Elitism', *Local Government Review,* **137**.

SHONFIELD, A. (1965) *Modern Capitalism.* Oxford University Press, London.

SHUBIK, M. (1958) 'Studies and Theories of Decision Making', *Administrative Science Quarterly,* **3**, 289–306.

SILKIN, J. (1979) *The Guardian,* 5 December.

SILVERMAN, D. (1970) *The Theory of Organizations.* Heinemann.

SIMMIE, J.M. (1974) *Citizens in Conflict: The Sociology of Town Planning.* Hutchinson, London.
SIMON, H.A. (1947), *Administrative Behavior.* Macmillan, New York.
SIMON, H.A. (1955) 'A Behavioral Model of Rational Choice', *Quarterly Journal of Economics,* **69,** February 1955.
SIMON, H.A. (1957) *Models of Man.* John Wiley, New York.
SIMON, H.A. (1957) *Administrative Behavior,* 2nd edn. Free Press of Glencoe, N.Y.
SIMON, H.A., SMITHBURG, D.W. and THOMPSON, V.A. (1958) *Public Administration,* Knopf, New York.
SIMON, H.A. (1959) 'Theories of Decision Making in Economics and Behavioral Science', *American Economic Review,* **49,** 253–83.
SIMON, H.A. (1960) *The New Science of Management Decision.* Harper and Row, New York.
SKEFFINGTON COMMITTEE (1969) *People and Planning: The Report of the Committee on Public Participation in Planning.* HMSO, London.
SKOLNICK, J. (1966) *Justice Without Trial.* John Wiley, New York.
SKOLNICK, J. (1967) 'Social Control in the Adversary System', *Journal of Conflict Resolution,* **11,** 52.
SKOLNIKOFF, E. (1971) 'Science and Technology: The Implications for International Institutions', *International Organization,* **25.**
SMITH, G. (1972) *Politics in Western Europe.* Methuen, London.
SMITH, B. (1976) *Policy Making in British Government.* Martin Robertson, London.
SOELBERG, P. (1966) 'Unprogrammed Decision Making', Papers and Proceedings, 26th Annual Meeting, Academy of Management, December 27–29.
SPROUT, H. and SPROUT, M. (1963) 'The Dilemma of Rising Demands and Insufficient Resources', *World Politics,* **20:** 4, July, 660–93.
STACEY, M. (1960) *Tradition and Change.* Oxford University Press, Oxford.
STEDMAN, M.S. (1972) *Urban Politics.* Winthrop Publishers, Cambridge, Mass.
STEWART, J.D. (1958) *British Pressure Groups.* Oxford University Press, London.
STEWART, J.D. (1971) *Management in Local Government: A Viewpoint.* Charles Knight, London.
STRAUSS, A. *et al.* (1976) 'The Hospital and its Negotiated Order' (1963) reprinted in Castles, F. *et al.* (1976).
SULEIMAN, E. (1974) *Politics, Power and Bureaucracy in France.* Princeton University Press, Princeton.
SWANSON, R. (1972) 'The United States Canadian Constellation I: Washington D.C.', *International Journal,* **28,** 185–218.

TARSCHYS, D. (1975) *Petita.* Liber, Stockholm.
TAVERNE REPORT (1966) *Police Manpower, Equipment and Efficiency.* Home Office, London.

TAYLOR, G. and AYRES, N. (1969) *Born and Bred Unequal*. Longman, London.
TERKEL, S. (1974) *Working*. Avan Books, New York.
THOMPSON, V. (1961) *Modern Organizations*. Knopf, New York.
TRUMAN, D.B. (1951) *Governmental Process: Political Interest and Public Opinion*, 2nd edition. Knopf, New York.
TULLICK, G. (1967) 'The General Irrelevance of the General Possibility Theorem', *Quarterly Journal of Economics*, 81, 256–70.
TULLOCK, G. (1965) *The Politics of Bureaucracy*. Public Affairs Press, Washington D.C.
TULLOCK, G. (1976) *The Vote Motive*. IEA, London.

URRY, J. and WAKEFORD, J. (eds.) (1973) *Power in Britain*. Heinemann, London.

VAN HASSEL, H. (1973) 'Belgian Ministerial Cabinets', *Res Publica*, 15, 357–69.
VAN HASSEL, H. (1975) 'Belgian Civil Servants and Political Decision Making', in Dogan, M. (ed.) *The Mandarins of Western Europe*. Halsted, New York.
VARLEY, E. (1975) 'The Enactment of the Industry Bill', *Trade and Industry*, 21 November, 474–6.
VERRIER, A. (1963) 'Defence and Politics After Nassau', *Political Quarterly*, July/September.
von MISES, L. (1972) *Bureaucracy*. Yale University Press, New Haven.

WADE, L.L. (unpublished) 'Public Administration, Public Choice and the Pathos of Reform', University of California, Davis, California.
WAGNER, R.E. (1966) 'Pressure Groups and Political Entrepreneurs', A Review Article (1), *Papers on Non-Marker Decision-Making*, 1, 161–70.
WALDO, D. (ed.) (1971) *Public Administration in a Time of Turbulence*. Chandler, San Francisco.
WALKER, A. (1973) 'The Labour Party in Search of a Defence Policy 1959–1967.' University of Wales (M.Sc. Dissertation).
WARWICK, D.P. (1975) *A Theory of Public Bureaucracy*. Harvard University Press.
WATKINSON, Viscount (1976) *Blueprint for Industrial Survival*. Allen and Unwin, London.
WEBB, A. (1972) 'Planning Enquiries and Amenity Policy', *Policy and Politics*, 1, 65–74.
WEBER, M. (1947) *The Theory of Social and Economic Organization*. Macmillan, New York.
WEBER, Y. (1968) *L'administration consultative*. Librarie General du Droit et Jurisprudence, Paris.
WEBSTER, R. (1961) *Christian Democracy in Italy*. Hollins and Cautes, London.
WEISS, C.H. (1977) 'Research for Policy's Sake: The Enlightenment Function of Social Research', *Policy Analysis*, 3, 531–46.

WESTERGAARD, J. and RESLER, H. (1975) *Class in Capitalist Society*. Heinemann, London.

WILDAVSKY, A. (1964) *The Politics of the Budgetary Process*. Little, Brown, Boston.

WILLIAMSON, S.R. (1969) *The Politics of Grand Strategy*. Harvard University Press, Cambridge, Mass.

WILSON, B.R. (ed.) (1970) *Rationality*. Blackwell, Oxford.

WILSON, G.K. (1977) *Special Interests and Policymaking: Agricultural Policies and Politics in Britain and the United States of America 1966–70*. John Wiley, New York.

WILSON, J. (1968) *Varieties of Police Behavior*. Harvard University Press, Cambridge, Mass.

WINKLER, J.T. (1975) 'Law, Society and Economy. The Industry Act 1975 in Context', *British Journal of Law and Society*, 2, 103–28.

WINKLER, J.T. (1976) 'Corporatism', *Archives Européenes de Sociologie*, 17, 100–136.

WINKLER, J.T. (1977) 'The Corporate Economy: Theory and Administration', *in* Scase, R. (ed.) *Industrial Society: Class, Cleavage and Control*. Allen and Unwin, London.

WOLFERS, A. (1962) *Discord and Collaboration*. Johns Hopkins University Press, Baltimore.

WOODWARD, J. (1965) *Industrial Organization: Theory and Practice*. Oxford University Press, London.

WORMS, J.P. (1966) 'Le Préfet et ses notables'. *Sociologie du travail*, 7, July–September: 249–76.

YOUNG, K. (ed.) (1975) *Essays on the Study of Urban Politics*. Macmillan, London.

ZECKHAUSER, R. and SCHAEFER, E. (1968) 'Public Policy and Normative Economic Theory', *in* Bauer, R.A. and Gergen, K.J., (1968).

ZIMMERMAN, D.M. (1971) 'The Practicalities of Rule Use', *in* Douglas, J.D. (ed.) *Understanding Everyday Life*. Routledge and Kegan Paul, London.

ZISK, B.H. (1973) *Local Interest Politics: A One Way Street*. Bobbs-Merrill, Indianapolis.

INDEX

Abel, R.L. 187, 366
Abraham, N. 341, 366
abstract thinking 147–9
access, politics of 272
accommodation in policy process
    279–80
Ackoff, R.L. 47, 366
activities, sequential 60–61
Adamson, C. 280
agenda
    community 20
    policy 329–31
Agger, R. 29, 191, 366
aggregating functions of educational
    policy 192
Agreement to Disagree 279–80
agriculture, groups in 223, 263–5,
    268, 273, 277, 287–8
Agriculture Act (1947) 287
Allardt, E. 244, 366
Allen, D., Sir 280
Allison, G.T. 7, 11, 14–15, 36,
    43–5, 180, 209–10, 213,
    365–6
Almond, G.A. 244, 264, 366
Alschuler, A.W. 185, 366
Ambler, J. 264, 366
analysis, synoptic 126–9, 138,
    210–11
analytic rationality 60–66
Anderson, C.W. 269, 366
anticipated reactions 29
apathy, rational 29, 34
armaments 214–15, 354–5, 358
Armstrong, W., Sir 280
Arrow, K.J. 63, 366
Aubert, V. 187, 366

Austin, J.L. 34
authoritarian regimes 133
authority, police 327–40
avoidance of risks 161–2
Ayres, N. 199, 386

Baar, C. 175–6, 187, 367
Bachrach, P. 6, 11, 18, 20, 23–8,
    138, 321–7, 333, 350, 367
BAM see Behaviour Alternatives
    Model
Bantan, M. 335, 367
Baran, P.A. 349, 367
Baratz, M.S. 6, 11, 18, 20, 23–8,
    138, 321–7, 333, 350, 367
bargaining 180, 238
Barry, B. 30, 50, 97, 110
Bator, F. 226
Bauer, R.A. 47, 217, 225, 367
Bealey, E. 248, 367
Becker, S.W. 155, 367
Beer, S.H. 232, 341, 343, 367
Behaviour Alternatives Model 113
Beichman, A. 222, 367
Bell, D. 44, 367
benefits of voting 98, 100–101, 110
Benewick, R. 343, 349, 351, 367
Benington, J. 349, 368
Bentham, J. 56
Bentley, A.F. 349, 368
Benveniste, G. 9, 140–41, 154
Berlin, I., Sir 21
betting 58
bias
    class 336
    mobilisation of 23, 145, 327,
        334–9

Birch, A.H. 344, 350, 368
Birmingham, voluntary organ-
  isations in 233–45
Blackie, J. 200, 368
Blau, P. 246, 368
Blondel, J. 108, 368
Blumberg, A.S. 175, 177, 185–7,
  330, 368
Boaden, N. 199, 368
Booth, K. 213, 368
Booth, T. 119, 368
Bornfriend, A.J. 245, 368
bounded rationality 51
Bower, J.L. 46–7, 368
Box, S. 336, 368
Boyle, E. 196, 199
Bradshaw, A. 326, 368
Braybrooke, D. 124, 138
Brennan, T. 245, 368
Brent, R.J. 65, 368
Breton, A. 267, 368
Britain
  Concorde project 140, 168–9
  corporatism in 341–51
  defence policy 205, 207–8,
    211–15
  education policy 190–204,
    225, 250–51, 255–60
  foreign affairs 207, 217–18
  groups in 47, 261–90
  local government 246–54,
    281–7, 327–8
  monetary policy 126, 275–6
  pluralism in 227, 231–3
  policy in 26, 275–90
  tripartism 291–302
  unemployment policy 167–8
  in wartime 109, 150–51, 213
Brittan, S. 349, 368
Brodie, B. 365, 368
Brogden, M. 315–16, 327
Brown, C.V. 64, 369
Bruce-Gardyne, J. 302, 369
Brzezinski, Z. 211, 369
Bulpitt, J. 250, 369
bureaucracy 36, 46–7
  and defence policy 205–15
  documented histories of 164–5

economic theory of 167–74
and education 190–204
  passim
grooved thinking in 145–6
of life 133
maximisation of 140–41
and pressure groups 261–74
survival inside 154–66
see also government; policy-
  making
Burns, T. 176–7, 369
business
  policy 92–3
  public 275–8
Business of Politics rule 279
Butt, R. 214, 369
Byrne, E. 199, 369

CAC *see* Central Advisory Council
Cain, M. 336, 369
Cambodia 133
Campbell, A. 244, 383
Canada 218, 220, 226
career paths 154–9
Carley, M. 51, 60
Carlson, B. 263, 369
Castles, F. 263, 325, 369
Caulcott, T.H. 290, 369
Cawson, A. 11, 316–17, 341, 351,
  369
CBI *see* Confederation of British
  Industry
Central Advisory Council 202–3
Central American Common Market
  219
Central Policy Review Staff 281–2,
  369
certainty 54
Chadwick, G. 47, 369
changes in foreign policy 359–62
Channon, D.F. 351, 369
Chapman, J.W. 244, 381
chess-playing 91
Chibnall, S. 338, 369
Chief Constable and police 327–
  40
Child, J. 176, 369
Chile 220, 224

China 133, 226
choice 13, 16–18, 54, 177–8
Churchman, C.W. 47, 57, 370
cities 20, 26, 29
Clark, T.N. 350, 368
Clarke, S. 351, 370
class
    bias 336
    and groups 241
    unity 291–2
clientela relationships 263–8, 273,
    277
closed sector career paths 156–8
coalition building, transgovern-
    mental 217–25
    see also coordination
Cockburn, C. 349, 370
coercion 26, 74
cognitive dimensions of organ-
    izational phenomena 144–
    53
    grooved thinking 140, 142,
        145–7, 153
    theoretical thinking 149–53
    uncommitted thinking 142,
        147–9, 153
    see also Steinbruner
cognitive processes 88
    see also rationality
Cohen, D.K. 138, 378
Cohen, M.D. 177, 180–81, 370
Cole, G.F. 175, 177, 370
Coleman, J. 109, 370
collectivism 97, 101–8, 232
Committee of Permanent
    Representatives 304–6, 308,
    312
community
    agenda 20
    power 19, 30, 46
    sense of 276
compatibility, goal 179, 182–3, 185
competition and free enterprise
    68–73, 98, 172, 267
    imperfect 50, 72–3, 85–6,
        93–4
    perfect 69–70, 73, 85–6, 90
    see also market

comprehensive rationality 50,
    62–3, 113–15
computational efficiency 88–92
computers 91
concept attainment research 88
conceptual models 37–9, 43–7
Conciliation and Arbitration
    Council 295
Concorde project 140, 168–9
Confederation of British Industry
    228, 292–302, 350–51, 369
conflict
    and groups 45, 237–9, 261
    lack of 352
    model of 260
    in police 327–40
    political 21
Connolly, W. 244, 370
consensual model 260
conservatism in politics 22–3
consistency of participants 179,
    183–6
constraints
    in courts 141, 179, 183–8
    on defence policy 205–15
    see also rationality
consultation and pressure groups
    262–3, 275
control
    of education policy 197–201
    in foreign policy 354, 362–4
controversy, avoidance of 334–9
Coons, J.E. 188, 370
coordination (cooperation)
    excessive 163–4
    group 239–40
    international 356–9
    transgovernmental 217–19
    see also coalition
COREPER *see* Committee of
    Permanent Representatives
corporatism 231–2, 291–2,
    341–51
cost
    of bureaucratic inefficiency
        173
    of defence 140, 209, 358
    of education 198–9

of foreign affairs 216
of groups 234—5, 267—8
of police 316, 336
cost—benefit studies 140
courts 175—89
Cox, W. 224—55, 370
Crenson, M.A. 6, 24, 30, 34—5,
 318, 320, 324—5, 370
Crick, B. 34
critical perspective 315—65
 foreign policies 352—65
 non-decisions 318—26
 police authority 327—40
 pluralism, corporatism and role
 of state 341—51
Crosland, A. 196, 198, 202
Crossman, R.H.S. 22, 302, 370
Crowther Report 202
Crowther-Hunt, Lord 196, 370
Croydon 246—7
Cuban missile crisis 14, 25, 36—8,
 43, 213—14
custom and economic organisation
 67—8
Cutt, J. 65, 370
cybernetics 140
 see also Steinbruner, J.
Cyert, R.M. 177—80, 182, 370

Dahl, R.A. 35, 244, 325, 371
 on bargaining 238
 incremental model 42
 on pluralism 19—21, 25, 31,
 233, 236, 320
Dahrendorf, R. 45, 303, 371
Dalton, M. 177, 182, 371
Darby, P. 208, 371
Davies, A.F. 34
Davies, J.C. 325, 371
De Meyer, R.F. 64, 371
Dearlove, J. 277, 319, 349—50,
 371
demand and supply 75—85
decision 4—7
decision making
 critical perspective of 315—65
 organisational 139—226
 politics of 227—313

rational 49—138
 understanding 13—47
decisionless decision 25, 27, 33,
 319
 see also non-decisions
decision-space 51, 61—2, 140, 142
default, decisions by 17
defence
 armaments 354—5, 358
 cost of 140, 209, 358
 policy 205—15, 220, 223
 see also foreign policy
deliberative rationality 62—3
democracy, pluralist 233—45
denial of conflict 332—4
Denmark 361
Department of Education and
 Science 142, 190—204, 228,
 371
Department of the Environment
 281, 284—7
dependent variables in courts 176—
 8, 188
Depoliticisation rule 280
Desai, M. 206, 371
design activity 54
Destler, I.M. 365, 371
Deutsch, K.W. 365, 371
Dexter, L. 225, 367
Dickens, P. 351, 371
disclosure, bureaucratic 172—3
discord *see* conflict
discounted pay-off 103, 110
disjointed incrementalism 27, 126,
 129—30, 139
distortion of information 140,
 168—9
distributional policy 267
documented histories 164—5
domestic demands and foreign
 policy 357—9
domination 181—2
Doughtie, J. 264, 382
Downs, A. 29, 34, 50, 97—100,
 105, 261, 371
downward-sloping demand, law of
 77—8
drift 25, 27

Dror, Y. 47, 119–21, 124, 129,
    138, 371
Drucker, J.M. 349, 371
Duncan, R.B. 176, 371
duty, sense of 105

Eckstein, H. 351, 372
economic approach and explanation
    44–6, 87, 94–5, 97–101,
    105–10, 257, 259
economic growth 354–9
economic organization, problems of
    67–86
economic rationality 56–7, 92–6,
    107–10
economic theory of bureaucracy
    167–74
economising models 44–6
Edgett, J.S. 158, 372
Edmonds, E.L. 200, 372
Education Act (1944) 193, 197
educational policy 142, 190–204,
    225, 250–51, 255–60
EEC *see* European Economic
    Community
efficiency, computational 88–92
Eisenstein, J. 175, 177–8, 187,
    189, 372
elitism
    and corporatism 231–2, 345–8
    and pluralism 231–2, 316,
        320–23, 345–8
    political 13, 28, 32, 246–54
empires, bureaucratic 167–8
Employment Protection Act (1975)
    295, 299
ends and means 16–17, 57
environment, negotiated 278–9
equality, political 231
equilibrium, economic 79–83, 98
essence of decision 36–40
established groups 228
Etzioni, A. 42, 47, 117, 120,
    122–3, 129, 138, 372
European Economic Community
    228–9, 303–13, 356
    and agriculture 288
    and cooperation 219, 222–3

as intergovernmental framework
    303–7
policy-making context 309–12
as transnational framework
    307–9
evaluation 155–61
event matching 90
expectations and uncertainty 94–6

false consciousness 28–30, 33, 326
false risks 163
feasibility studies 140
Feather, V. 280
Feeley, M.M. 175, 186–7, 372
Feldman, J. 90, 372
Figgures, F., Sir 280
finances *see* costs
Finer, S.E. 350, 372
firm, model 45, 92, 177–80,
    186–9
Foot, M. 351, 372
force 26, 74
Forcese, D.P. 61, 372
foreign policy
    in Britain 207, 217–18
    control problems 354, 362–4
    cost of 216
    changes in 359–62
    and domestic demands and
        resource allocations 357–9
    and modernisation 352–65
    and rational actor model 14
    transformation of policy
        objectives 354–7
    in USA 14, 20, 25, 36–9, 207,
        216, 218–26
    see also defence policy
formality 26
Fort, J.G. 58, 380
Fowler, G. 192, 372
Fox, A. 297, 372
Foyer, L. 264, 373
France 261, 265, 269, 271, 306,
    361
Frankel, J. 207, 373
Fraser, D. 350, 373
free enterprise and competition
    68–73

Frey, F.W. 20, 24, 29, 33–4
Friend, J. 290, 373
Frohlich, N. 261, 373
Fromm, E. 134

Galanter, M. 188, 373
Galbraith, J.K. 238, 349, 373
Gamble, A. 350, 373
game-playing models 45–6
game theory 60, 141, 154, 360
Gans, H. 248, 373
garbage-can submodel 177–81,
    184
Garnett, J.C. 9, 140, 143, 205
General Agreement on Tariffs and
    Trade 222, 353
general-equilibrium system 70–71
Gershuny, J.I. 62, 65, 373
Gilbert, B.B. 350, 373
Ginsburg, N. 351, 370
Gitlin, T. 33
Gittins Report (1967) 202
Glaser, B.G. 154, 373
Glass, V. 245, 373
goal
    compatibility 179, 182–3,
        185–6
    maximisation of 178–80
    see also rationality
goal-directed behaviour 58
Gordenker, L. 224, 373
Gouldner, A.W. 16, 244, 373
government 14, 162, 195
    and corporatism 341–51
    economic role of 68, 73–4
    in EEC 303, 313
    and elitism 345–8
    local 246–54, 281–7, 327–
        8
    and pluralism 341–51
    and policy process 190–204,
        275–90
    and pressure groups 261–74
    Right to Govern rule 280
    sub-units in 220–23
    transgovernmental politics 143,
        216–26, 229, 307–9
    tripartite 291–302

    see also bureaucracy; policy-
        making; politics
governmental politics model 38–9,
    43–4
Grant, W. 228–9, 277, 289–91,
    302, 349–51, 373–4, 379
Graves, J. 202, 374
Gretton, P., Admiral 213, 374
Griffith, J.A.G. 174, 374
grooved thinking 140, 142, 145–7,
    153
group
    and class 241
    competition 267
    and conflict 45, 237–9, 261
    and consultation 262–3, 275
    coordination 239–40
    decision making 46–7
    and education policy 191
    finances 234–5, 267–8
    implementation 263–5
    interaction 263, 270–73, 277
    membership of 103
    and pluralism 231–2, 343–7,
        351
    and policy process 275–90
    politics 52, 107, 110, 228–9,
        242–4
    pressure and bureaucracy
        261–74
    reclassification of 344
    relationships 265–70
    voluntary 233–45
Gulick, L. 176, 374

Hague, C. 351, 374
Hahn, H. 245, 374
Hall, P. 14–15, 41
Hall, R.L. 92, 374
Hammond, P.Y. 365, 374
Harris, N. 250, 349, 374
Hart, J.M. 334, 374
Hassner, P. 363, 365, 374
Healey, D. 168
health services 295, 347–8, 350
Heath, E. 295
Heclo, H. 251, 276, 278, 375
Heinz, J. 265, 268, 383

Heisler, M. 264, 375
Her Majesty's Inspectorate 200–
    201, 375
Herz, J. 365, 375
Heumann, M. 175, 177, 180,
    185–6, 189, 375
hierarchical coordination 164
high-level officials 56–9, 147–9,
    162
    and collective action 106–7
    and defence 214
    and education policy 196–7
    and foreign affairs 217
    in groups 242–4
    in police 327–40 *passim*
    see also management
Hill, D. 245, 375
Hill, M.J. 325, 375
Hilsman, R. 209, 211, 375
Hindess, B. 326, 328, 375
Hirschman, A.O. 58, 224, 375
histories, documented 164–5
Hitch, C.H. 92, 206, 374
Hoffman, S. 207, 303, 305, 364,
    375
Holland, S. 349, 375
Hopkins, F., Sir 212
Horton Smith, D. 244, 376
Hunter, F. 320, 325, 376
Huntington, S. 205, 211, 369, 376
Hutcheson, J.D. 244, 376

identification of problem 54
illegitimate group interaction 263,
    270–73, 277
ILO *see* International Labor
    Organization
image of police in press 338–9
imperfect competition 50, 72–3,
    85–6, 93–4
implementation by pressure groups
    263–5
implications of policy process
    288–9
implicit conceptual models 37
incentives 103–9, 172
incrementalism (muddling through)
    42, 51, 62, 113–15, 310, 321

in defence policy 208, 211
disjointed 27, 126, 129–30,
    139
models 113–15
in policy analysis 125–38
and politics 125, 131–4
and rationalism 116–38
simple 126, 130, 134–5
indecision 17
    see also non-decisions
individual career paths 154–9
individual decision making 17, 42,
    53–9
individual group membership 108
Industrial Relations Act (1971)
    294–5, 299
Industry Acts (1972, 1975) 294,
    299–300
inefficiency 172–3
information and bureaucracy 140,
    168–70
insider groups 277
institutional groups 264
interaction 46–7, 262–73, 277
interdependence 362–4
intergovernmental framework of
    EEC 303–7
internal relations in local govern-
    ment 240–54
internalisation of problem processes
    289
international organisation and
    transgovernmental politics
    143, 216–26
international coordination 356–9
International Labor Organization
    225
International Monetary Fund 222,
    224, 310, 313, 353
    see also monetary policy
interorganisational analysis 187
Invisible Hand 69–70
Ionescu, G. 349, 376
irrationality 49
Ireland 32–3
iron triangle 268
Israel 226
issues, group 242–4

Italy 266, 268

Jabes, J. 50–53
Jacob, H. 175, 177–8, 187, 189,
    372
Jacobson, H. 224–5, 370
James, W. 88, 376
Jannson, D.S. 118, 376
Japan 220
JCP *see* Job Creation Programme
Jenkins, P. 11, 302, 376
Jenkins, W.E. 315, 318
Jennings, R.E. 191, 376
Job Creation Programme 167–8
Johnson, J.J. 264, 376
Jordan, A.G. 10, 50, 52, 111, 229,
    275, 383
Joseph, K., Sir 349, 376

Kaiser, K. 226, 376
Kellner, P. 196, 370
Kennedy, G. 168
Keohane, R. 9, 142–3, 216, 226,
    307, 309, 376–7
Kelly, D., Sir 205, 376
Key, V.O. 242, 377
key decisions 19, 33
key issues 322
Kidder, R.L. 181, 377
Kimber, R. 350, 377
King, G, 83
Kissinger, H. 365, 377
Klein, R. 334, 377
Knorr, K. 354, 356, 377
Kogan, M. 191, 193–4, 196, 199,
    202–3, 277, 377
Korea 36
Krasner, S. 217, 377
Kvavik, R. 263–4, 375, 377

Lakoff, S.A. 245, 377
LaPalombara, J. 265–6, 268, 270,
    377
Laporte, T. 138, 377
latent groups 106
lateral coordination 163–4
Latham, E. 349, 377
Latin America 271

LEA *see* local education authority
leadership *see* high-level officials;
    management
learning research 88
legal commands 74
legal system 175–89
legislation, continuity of 22
legitimate interaction 225, 262–5,
    272, 277
legitimation of state power 201–4
Levine, J. 60, 377
Levy, M.J., Jr 365, 378
Lijphart, A. 279–80, 378
Lindblom, C.E. 34, 111, 124, 368,
    375, 378
  on Dror 121
  on goal redefinition 58
  on incrementalism 42, 113–15,
    122, 125, 143, 310, 321
  on means and ends 118
  on policy agreement 232
  on rationality 50, 62, 112
  on routines, analysis of 27
  on strategic analysis 51
  on synoptic approach 210–11
Lindberg, L. 219, 378
Lineberry, R.L. 350, 368, 378
local education authority 198–9
local government 240–54, 181–7,
    327–8
Local Government Planning and
    Land Act (1980) 199
Lockard, D. 319, 378
Locke, J. 35
Locke, M. 197, 378
Lockwood, D. 104, 378
logic of collectivism 97, 101–7
log-rolling 64
Lowi, T. 240, 266–7, 277, 343,
    378
Lukes, S. 6, 11, 34, 322–7, 333,
    350, 378
Lund, H.F. 157, 378

McCleery, M. 117, 122, 378
McConnell, G. 110, 245, 266–7,
    378
McCourt, A. 351, 374

McCulloch, K. 264, 382
Mackenzie, W.J.M. 13, 16, 34
McNamara, R. 206
Macpherson, C.B. 350, 378
Magee, J. 226, 378
majority voting paradox 62–4
Malmgren, H. 365, 379
management 54, 170–71, 176,
    275–8
see also high-level officials
Manning, P.K. 335, 379
Manpower Services Commission
    167–8, 295
March, J.G. 59, 177–82, 370, 379
Marcuse, H. 326, 379
market
    and politics 131–2, 137–8
    and prices 71–5
    see also competition
Marsh, D. 228–9, 289, 291, 302,
    373–4, 349–51, 379
mathematics 88–92
Mather, L.M. 175, 178, 187, 189,
    379
Marxism 103
Maud Report (1967) 379
maximisation
    of bureaucracy 140–41
    of goals 178–80
May, D. 50–51, 116, 299
Mayer, J. 124, 379
means and ends 16–17, 57
Meynaud, J. 261, 379
Milbrath, L.W. 238, 379
Miles, E. 220, 379
Miliband, R. 134, 349–50, 379
Mill, J.S. 56
Miller, G.A. 55, 379
Mills, C.W. 25, 320
Mills Committee (1968) 169
Ministry of Agriculture, Fisheries
    and Food 287–8
Minkin, L. 302, 379
mixed economy 73, 86
mixed-scanning 42, 120–21
    see also Etzioni
mobilisation of bias 23, 145, 327,
    334–9

model
    of analytic rationality 62–6
    conceptual 37–9, 43–7
    of conflict 260
    of courts 175–89
    criticised 315–16
    defined 61
    economising 44–6
    of game-playing 111–24
    political 10–11, 179, 181–2,
        184, 187–9
    rational 7–8, 14, 37–8, 40,
        43–4, 50, 111–24
    sociologising 44–6
modernised societies, foreign policy
    in 3, 316, 352–65
Mohr, L.B. 141, 175–6, 379–80
monetary policy 126, 275–6, 361
    see also International Monetary
    Fund
monopoly elements 72–3
Moodie, G. 350, 380
moral motives 108
Moran, M. 299, 379
Morriss, P. 6, 9, 13–14, 19, 315–
    16, 350, 381
Morse, E.L. 316–17, 352
MSC *see* Manpower Services
    Commission
muddling through 125–38
    see also incrementalism
Myers, J.L. 58, 380

Nader, L. 187, 380
Nairn, T. 350, 380
national interest 109, 341, 363
neomercantilism 357
negotiated order and environment
    278–9
Netherlands 263, 279
Neustadt, R. 218, 380
neutrality 231, 253
Newton, K. 10, 47, 227–8, 233,
    252, 325, 380
Niskanen, W.A. 140, 169–70, 261,
    267–8, 380
Nixon, R. 164
non-cooperation 283–7

non-decisions 19–35, 315, 318–26
non-economical rationalism 57–9
non-enforcement 319
non-events 24
non-issue 28, 325
non-programmed decisions 55–7
non-rationality 49, 64
normative analysis 41–2
normative-optimum model 120–21
norms against redistribution 179, 183–6
Norway 263
nuclear weapons 214–15, 355
Nye, J. 9, 142–3, 216, 219, 224, 226, 307, 309, 376–7, 381

objective decisions 50
OECD report on education 197, 201, 381
officials *see* high-level officials
oligopoly 94
Olsen, J.P. 177, 180–82, 261, 370
Olson, M., Jr 44–5, 97, 101–7, 110, 365, 381
open-sector career paths 158–9
operationalisation 255
Oppenheimer, J.A. 261, 373
opposition to groups 237–8
optimal solution 91
order, negotiated 278–9
Ordeshook, P.C. 98, 383
Organisation for European Economic Cooperation 303–4, 312
organisational decision making 55–9, 139–226
    bureaucracy, economic theory of 167–74
    bureaucracy, survival inside 154–66
    cognitive dimensions 144–53
    and courts 175–89
    defence policy 205–15
    models 8–10, 14, 38–9, 43–4
    policy making and State 190–204

politics, transgovernmental 216–26
organisational problem 360–61
organisations 104, 154–5, 175–8
organised anarchy 177
Osgood, R.E. 365, 381
outcome 40, 352
output measures 159–60
outsider groups 277
overlap 241

Packer, H.L. 175, 381
Packwood, T. 202, 377
Pahl, R.E. 291–2, 302, 349
Panitch, L. 349–50, 381
PAR *see* Programme Analysis and Review
parantela relationships 263, 268–70
Parenti, M. 34–5, 244, 381
Pareto optimality 44
Parkinson, M. 192, 381
Parkinson's Law 252
Parry, G. 6, 9, 13–14, 19, 315–16, 350, 381
Parsons, T. 16, 18, 45
participants, consistency of 179, 183–5
partisan mutual adjustment 135–8, 232
party politics
    and defence 214–15
    and local government 252–4, 328
    and tripartism 294–5, 299–301
Pateman, C. 349, 381
Patterson, G. 218, 381
pay-off, discounted 103, 110
Peacock, A.T. 173, 381
Pearl Harbor 36
Pennock, J.R. 244, 273, 381
Pentland, C. 310, 381
perfect competition 69–70, 73, 85–6, 93
Perlman, M. 9, 140–41, 167
Perrow, C. 176, 178, 382
PESC *see* Public Expenditure Survey

Peter, L.J. 154, 382
Peters, B.G. 228, 261, 264, 375, 382–3
Peters, G.G. 289, 382
Pile, W., Sir 194, 203, 382
Pizzorno, A. 266, 382
planning *see* policy
pleasure principle 56–7
Plott, C.R. 64, 371
Plowden Report (1967) 202
pluralism 135–8
  beyond 320–21
  and corporatism 231–2, 341–51
  and democracy 233–45
  and elitism 316, 320–23, 345–8
  and partisan mutual adjustment 135–8, 232
  and politics 227, 231–2
  and power 13, 19, 27, 31, 33
  and voluntary organisations 233–45
police 142, 327–40, 385
Police Act (1964) 329–30
policy analysis 64, 125–38
policy making
  accommodation in 279–80
  and business 92–3
  controls 197–201
  defence 205–15, 220, 223
  educational 142, 190–204, 225, 250–51, 255–60
  in EEC 303–13
  foreign 352–65
  and groups 275–90
  legitimation of 201–4
  local government 246–54
  maintence 319
  models 111–24
  and non-decisions 318–19
  and rationality 61–2, 65–6
  and state apparatus 190–204
  studies of 191–2
  transgovernmental coordination 217–19
  see also bureaucracy; government

politics
  and conflict 21
  decisions in 21–40 *passim*, 46
  of decision making 227–313
  and education 196, 255, 258–9
  elite in 13, 28, 32, 246–54
  incremental 125, 131–4
  interaction in 262–72
  models and submodels 10–11, 179, 181–2, 184, 187–9
  organisational 177–8
  party 214–15, 252–4, 294–5, 299–301, 328
  and pluralism 227, 231–2
  transgovernmental 216–26
  and unions 107
  in USA 19–24, 31, 37–8, 47, 99, 131–2, 149, 267
  and voting 97–110
  see also government
pollution 318–19, 324
Polsby, N.W. 24, 245, 382
polyarchy 19
  see also pluralism
POSDCORB 176
positive analysis 41–2, 46–7
potential coalitions and international organisations 222–5
Potter, A. 350, 382
Poulantzas, N. 253, 349, 382
Powell, G.B. 264, 366
power 13, 17, 19, 27, 31–3, 46
  see also elite; pluralism; politics
Preeg, E.H. 365, 382
press image of police 338–9
pressure groups
  see group pressure; pluralism
Presthus, R. 245, 382
price system 70–72, 92–3
priorities, perverted 318–19
private management of public business 275–8
problem identification 53
problem-solving research 88, 91–5
procedural rationality 50, 88–96
Programme Analysis and Review 195–6

programmed decisions 14, 52, 55–7, 140
Proportionality rule 280
Proxy, G. 157, 382
psychology 87–91
public
  business 275–8
  good 102, 364
  interest 266–7
  opinion 192, 209, 300
  services 74
Public Expenditure Survey 195

race relations 29, 322–3
Rackoff, S. 318, 382
Rapaport, A. 90, 382
Raphael, D.D. 34
rational actor model 14, 37–8, 40, 43–4
rational apathy 29, 34
rationality 49–138
  analytic 60–61
  bounded 51
  in courts 179–80, 188
  criticised 62–6
  and defence 211
  defined 49, 60–61
  economic 56–7, 92–6, 107–10
  and economic organisation, problems of 67–86
  and incrementalism 116–38
  individual 53–9
  local authority 246
  models 7–8, 14, 37–8, 40, 43–4, 50, 111–24
  policy-making 61–2, 65–6, 111–15, 211
  and positivism 41–2, 46–7
  procedural 50, 88–96
  substantive 50, 87
  thinking 144–53
  and voting 50, 97–110
Rawls, J. 62, 134, 382
Redcliffe-Maud, Lord 290, 382
redistribution
  and groups 264
  norms against 179, 184–6
Rees, S. 124, 382

regulation 264, 266, 270
Reich, C. 344, 383
renunciation 27
required consultation in groups 262–3
Resler, H. 327, 387
resource
  constraints 179, 183–8
  distribution 233, 236
rewards *see* benefits
Rex, J. 45
Richardson, J.J. 10, 50, 52, 111, 229, 275, 350, 377, 383
Richer, S. 61, 372
relationships
  in local government 240–54
  in pressure groups 265–70
resource
  allocation 357–9
  constraints 184–6
Riggs, F. 269, 383
Riker, W.H. 98–9, 383
risk 54–5, 161–4
Rittel, H.W.J. 47, 383
Robbins Report 202, 255
Roberts, G.K. 326, 383
Robinson, A.D. 279, 383
Robinson, J. 365, 383
Rokhan, S. 244, 383
Roosevelt, F.D. 149
Rosenau, J.N. 311, 363, 383
Ross, H.L. 188, 383
Rousseau, J.J. 134
Ruggie, J.G. 224, 383
rules
  as evaluation insurance 160–61
  of game, accommodation as 279–80
ruling, politics as 22–3, 31
Russell, K. 336, 368
Ryder, Lord 300

Sainsbury, E. 124, 383
Salaman, G. 124, 383
Salisbury, R.H. 264–5, 268, 289, 383
Salter, B. 9, 142, 190

Samuelson, P. 50, 67
sanctions against reformer 26
Sandys, D. 208
Saran, R. 191, 383
Sasieni, M. 47, 366
satisficing 51, 57–8, 62, 129, 188
Saunders, P. 228, 246, 350, 383
Saville, J. 350, 384
Scarrow, H. A. 264, 384
Schaefer, E. 47, 387
Schaefer, G. L. 318, 382
Schattsneider, E. 23, 321, 384
Scheingold, S. 219, 378
Scheinman, L. 305, 384
scientific analysis *see* synoptic
    analysis
Schlesinger, A., Jr 149, 384
Schmitt, H. O. 365, 384
Schmitt, K. 264, 384
Schmitter, P. C. 269, 291, 344,
    350–51, 384
Schumpeter, J. 343, 384
Scott, W. G. 116, 384
Secrecy rule 280
Seidman, H. 268, 384
selective incentives to vote 103,
    105–6, 108–9
Self, P. 232, 287, 290, 384
sequential activities 60–61
SEU *see* subjective expected utility
Sharkansky, I. 22–3, 27, 32, 34–5
Sharpe, L. J. 264, 266, 384
Sheinman, L. 219, 384
Sherman, A. 249, 384
shift in supply and demand 83–4
Shonfield, A. 134, 349–50, 384
Shubik, M. 57, 384
Silverman, D. 246, 385
Simmie, J. M. 47, 385
Simon, H. A. 50–62 *passim*, 87,
    111–14, 129, 138, 379, 385
simple incrementalism 126, 130,
    134–5
size, problem of 360–61
Skeffington Committee (1969)
    385
Skolnick, J. 175, 182, 385
Skolnikoff, E. 225, 385

SLC *see* successive limited com-
    parison
Smith, A. 302, 379
Smith, Adam 68–9, 141
Smith, B. 10, 60, 227–8, 231, 385
Smith, G. 50–51, 116, 302, 385
Social Welfare Function 52, 63–6
sociologists' explanations of models
    44–6
Soelberg, P. 58, 385
Sola Pool, I. de 225, 367
Soviet Union 133, 207, 210, 218,
    223, 352
space research 218
Spain 220, 226, 269
Spink, S. 290, 373
Sprout, H. and M. 358, 385
stability of society 363
Stacey, M. 245, 385
Stalker, G. M. 176–7, 369
state *see* government policy;
    politics
Stedman, M. S. 233, 385
Steggert, F. X. 244, 376
Steinbruner, J. 140, 142, 144
Stewart, J. D. 47, 350, 374, 380,
    385
Storing, H. 287, 290, 384
strategic: agglomeration 180–81
    analysis 51, 126
Strauss, A. 278, 385
Street, H. 174, 374
strike, local government 283–7
Studdert-Kennedy, G. 350, 380
sub-groups 46
subjective expected utility 90
sub-models 178–83, 186–9
substantive rationality 50, 87
sub-units in government 220–23
successive limited comparison
    113–15, 232
Suleiman, E. 265, 271, 385
Summit Diplomacy rule 280
supply and demand 75–85
survival inside bureaucracy 154–
    66
Swanson, R. 226, 385
Sweden 261, 263–4

Sweezey, P.M. 349, 367
SWF *see* Social Welfare Functions
symbiosis 265
synoptic analysis 126–9, 138, 210–11
systems analysis 60

Tapper, T. 9, 142, 190
Taverne Report (1966) 334, 385
Taylor, G. 199, 386
Taylor, S.H. 118, 376
taxes 74
technocratic model 255–7
Terkel, S. 156, 159, 386
Thatcher, M. 199
theoretical thinking 149–53
thinking 140, 142, 144–53
Thompson, K. 124, 383
threshold in voting 107
Timms, N. 124, 379
trade discrimination 218–19, 222, 225
trade unions 47, 104, 228, 237, 277
and collectivism 107–8
and Labour Party 295, 299
in tripartite system 292–302
Trade Union and Labour Relations Acts (1974, 1976) 295, 299
traditional behaviour 67–8
transformation of foreign policy objectives 354–7
transgovernmental politics 143, 216–26, 229
and EEC 307–9
tripartism 291–302
Truman, D.B. 104, 245, 349, 386
TUC *see* trade unions
Tucher, R.W. 365, 381
Tullock, G. 64, 140, 173, 261, 267, 386
Turkey 219–20

uncertainty 50, 55, 94–6, 141, 150, 238
uncommitted thinking 142, 147–9, 153
understanding decision making 13–47

approaching problem 41–7
choice and decision 16–18
essence of decision 36–40
non-decision 19–35
unemployment 167–8
unions *see* trade unions
United Nations 224
United States
business in 93
community power in 19, 30
courts in 187
Cuban crisis 14, 25, 36–8, 43, 213–14
defence policy 206, 210, 212–13, 220, 223
elite in 320
foreign policy 14, 20, 25, 36–9, 207, 216, 218–26
groups in 104, 267–8, 271, 343
incrementalism in 131–2
monetary policy 126, 361
non-decisions in 318–19
pluralism in 233, 236
policy in 319–19, 326, 352
politics of 19–24, 31, 37–8, 47, 99, 131–2, 149, 267
pollution in 318–19, 324
race relations in 29, 322–3
urban problems 20, 26, 29
and Vietnam 20, 206, 271, 358
urban problems 20, 26, 29
Urry, J. 350, 386
utility function 51

variables, contextual 182–5
Varley, E. 300, 386
Verba, S. 244, 366
Verrier, A. 215, 386
veto 131, 238
Vietnam war 20, 206, 271, 358
vindication by rationality 66
violence 270
voluntary organisations 47, 233–45
voting 17, 29, 34, 50, 97–110, 231
vulnerability 363

Wagner, R.E. 107, 386
Wakeford, J. 350, 386
Walker, A. 214, 386
Wallsten, T.S. 90, 382
wartime policies 109, 150–51, 213
  see also Vietnam
Warwick, D.P. 163, 386
Water Act (1973) 283, 286
water problems 283–9
Watkinson, Viscount 294, 298,
  300, 302, 386
weapons 214–15, 354–5, 358
Weaver, T. 196
Webb, A. 319, 386
Webb, C. 303
Webber, M.M. 47, 383
Weber, M. 22, 177, 251, 386
Weber, Y. 261, 386
Webster, R. 264, 386
welfare minima 73
Westergaard, J. 327, 387
WHO *see* World Health Organisation
Wildavsky, A. 111, 180, 276, 278,
  375, 387

Williams, G. 228, 255, 382
Williamson, S.R. 153, 387
Wilson, B.R. 124, 387
Wilson, G.K. 287, 290, 387
Wilson, H., Brig. Gen. 150, 153
Wilson, Harold 215
Winkler, J.T. 291–2, 302, 341–5,
  349, 381, 387
Winner, L. 130
Wiseman, J. 173, 381
Wolfers, A. 206, 387
Wolfinger, R. 20, 24, 27–9, 33–4
Wood, B. 290, 382
Woodward, J. 176–7, 387
World Health Organization 224–5
World Weather Watch 220, 224
Worms, J.P. 264, 387

Young, O.R. 261, 373

Zeckhauser, R. 47, 387
Zimmerman, D.M. 124, 387
Zisk, B.H. 245, 387